TRADITIONS OF THE SEVEN ṚṢIS

Frontispiece

Rāma, Lakṣmaṇa and Sītā in the hermitage of Bharadvāja

Traditions of the Seven Ṛṣis

JOHN E. MITCHINER

MOTILAL BANARSIDASS PUBLISHERS
PRIVATE LIMITED • DELHI

First Edition: Delhi, 1982
Corrected Edition : Delhi, 2000

ISBN: 81-208-1324-3 (Cloth)
ISBN: 81-208-1762-1 (Paper)

Also available at:
MOTILAL BANARSIDASS
236, 9th Main III Block, Jayanagar, Bangalore 560 011
41 U.A. Bungalow Road, Jawahar Nagar, Delhi 110 007
8 Mahalaxmi Chamber, Warden Road, Mumbai 400 026
120 Royapettah High Road, Mylapore, Chennai 600 004
Sanas Plaza, 1302 Baji Rao Road, Pune 411 002
8 Camac Street, Calcutta 700 017
Ashok Rajpath, Patna 800 004
Chowk, Varanasi 221 001

Printed in India
BY JAINENDRA PRAKASH JAIN AT SHRI JAINENDRA PRESS,
A-45 NARAINA, PHASE-I, NEW DELHI 110 028
AND PUBLISHED BY NARENDRA PRAKASH JAIN FOR
MOTILAL BANARSIDASS PUBLISHERS PRIVATE LIMITED,
BUNGALOW ROAD, DELHI 110 007

for

Wendy O'Flaherty

and

John de Casparis

CONTENTS

LIST OF TABLES

MAP

GUIDE TO PRONUNCIATION

Most Sanskrit consonants and vowels may for practical purposes be pronounced in the same way as their English counterparts; but the following points should be observed.

1. The short *a* is pronounced like the English *u* in "but"; the long *ā* is like the *a* in "father". The short *i* is like the *i* in "him"; the long *ī* is like the *ee* in "been". The short *u* is like the *u* in "pull"; the long *ū* is like the *u* in "rule". As for the other vowels, *e* is pronounced as the French é; *ai* as the second *i* in "divine"; *o* as in the German "geboten": and *au* as the *ow* in "power".
2. *ṛ* is also a vowel, and is pronounced midway between the *ri* in "river" and the *er* in "father".
3. All aspirated consonants—*kh, th, ph* and so forth—should be pronounced distinctly : as in "block-head", "hot-house" and "top-heavy".
4. *c* is pronounced like the *ch* in "church"; *j* is pronounced as in "join".
5. The cerebrals *ṭ, ṭh, ḍ, ḍh* and *ṇ* are pronounced with the tongue turned back against the roof of the mouth.
6. *ṅ* is pronounced like the *ng* in "king"; *ñ* is pronounced midway between *n* and *ny*.
7. The cerebral *ṣ* is pronounced as the other cerebrals, and sounds like *sh*; *s* is pronounced as in "sun"; while *ś* is midway between *s* and *ṣ*, and is pronounced like the *sh* in "shun".
8. *ḥ* is pronounced with an exhalation of breath, and a short echo of the preceding vowel; *ṃ* is nasalised, and sounds like the *n* in the French bon".

INTRODUCTION

The Ṛṣis (pronounced "Rishis") occupy a uniquely important place in Indian literature and thought. Particularly in the Epics and Purāṇas, the Ṛṣi-traditions receive more attention than those of the gods themselves—indeed, the Ṛṣis are the progenitors of the gods, as also of men, demons, and all other orders of creation. The Ṛṣis may be classified as both ascetics and mystics. They are prominent performers of *tapas* or asceticism in various forms—as also performers of sacrifice and visionary seers of hymns; they also attain heaven through these various means, where they commune with the gods and merge with *brahman* or the Absolute. Yet more than this : the Ṛṣis are also stars in the sky, a position which they attain through their ascetic practices; they are the breaths of life in the body, resulting again from their asceticism and from their merging with *brahman*; and they are also the progenitors of all creation, the founders of mankind. All of these various roles are interconnected and interact with each other, and these are some of the traditions which we shall be examining in this book.

Two main approaches have been adopted to the study of the Ṛṣi-traditions, and the book is accordingly divided into two main parts. The approach in Part One is text-historical : it examines the formulation of different traditions, analysing the processes as well as the various causes and influences which have brought about changes in the traditions. The first part also constitutes the ground-work for Part Two of the book, which aims at understanding the nature of Ṛṣi-hood through examining the various activities and concepts associated with the Ṛṣis—thereby illustrating the place of the Ṛṣis within the religious and philosophical framework of Hinduism.

The amount of material concerning Ṛṣis in general is vast; no study could ever hope to encompass all of their traditions in a single volume—or indeed in many volumes—and a number of limitations have therefore had to be imposed in the present work. Especially in later texts, a bewildering variety of Ṛṣis is mentioned : *brahma*-Ṛṣis, *deva*-Ṛṣis, *vipra*-Ṛṣis, *parama*-Ṛṣis and *mahā*-Ṛṣis; *rāja*-Ṛṣis and śruta-Ṛṣis, *jana*-Ṛṣis, *tapa*-Ṛṣis, *satya*-Ṛṣis and *kāṇḍa* Ṛṣis; Ṛṣi-*kas*, Ṛṣi-*putras*, Ṛṣi-*pautras*—the list becomes almost endless.[1] Many of these categories are somewhat artificially fabricated; others refer to particular categories of sages or ascetics—such as the *rāja*-Ṛṣis or royal Ṛṣis, a term which is used especially of kings who attained the status of Ṛṣis through their ascetic practices or wisdom in sacred matters. In this book, we shall be dealing exclusively with the Seven Ṛṣis—the most important of all the Ṛṣis, as indeed the ancestors and progenitors of all other Ṛṣis; the traditions of the Seven Ṛṣis are the most voluminous of all, and themselves encompass virtually all the themes which are met with in the individual traditions of other Ṛṣis. The Seven Ṛṣis are themselves referred to as *brahma*-Ṛṣis/*brahmarṣis* ("Brahmin-Ṛṣis"), *deva*-Ṛṣis/*devarṣis* ("godly Ṛṣis"), *vipra*-Ṛṣis/*viprarṣis* ("inspired" or "Brahmin Ṛṣis"), *parama*-Ṛṣis/*paramarṣis* ("supreme Ṛṣis"), and *mahā*-Ṛṣis/*maharṣis* ("great Ṛṣis") in various contexts; and like the *Mahābhārata*, one might even say that whatever is worth knowing about other Ṛṣis is contained within the traditions of the Seven Ṛṣis. Nonetheless, the present work does not claim to be a *Mahābhārata* of the Seven Ṛṣis; but it does attempt to cover all the main themes which are met with in the traditions related of them. The identities of the Ṛṣis who are included in the group of Seven Ṛṣis are discussed in the first chapter.

The term *ṛṣi* has sometimes been translated as "Seer" or "Sage": but, as will become clear during the course of our investigations, these translations are somewhat inadequate. The form "Ṛṣi" has therefore been retained throughout the book.

---

1. Such lists may be found in *Baudhāyana Dharma Sūtra* 2.5.9.13; *Matsya Purāṇa* 145.81-118, and elsewhere.

The sources used are primarily those of the Sanskrit tradition, encompassing especially Vedic, Epic and Purāṇic literature; reference is also made where appropriate to Tamil texts and to Indian tribal material, as well as to prominent parallels in extra-Indian sources and contexts. In the case of cited passages, these are usually translated *verbatim* from the Sanskrit; but where the original account is either excessively lengthy or not relevant in its entirety (as is the case in a number of instances in Part Two of the book), the form cited is a summary of the original.

As far as the chronology of the texts is concerned, the dating of Sanskrit texts is a notoriously difficult problem. This is especially so in the case of the Epics and Purāṇas, many of which may be relatively late in their overall or final composition yet contain passages of considerable antiquity alongside much later additions. Only very approximate dates can in many cases be given, and the following *approximate* chronology has been followed :[1]

Ṛgveda 1400—1100 B.C. (Books 1 and 10 are the latest)

Sāmaveda and *Yajurveda* 1200—1000 B.C.

Atharvaveda 1300—900 B.C.

Brāhmaṇas 900—600 B.C. (*Taittirīya* and *Aitareya* probably earliest: then *Kauṣitaki*, *Jaiminīya* and *Pañcaviṃśa*; *Śatapatha* later; *Gopatha* among the latest)

Āraṇyakas 700—500 B.C.

Upaniṣads 600—400 B.C. (*Bṛhadāraṇyaka*, *Chāndogya*, *Aitareya* and *Kauṣitaki* earliest: then *Kena*, *Taittirīya* and *Īśa*; then

---

1. Reference may be made to J. N. Farquhar, *An Outline of the Religious Literature of India* : J. Gonda, *Die Religionen Indiens*, vols. 1-2 : R. C. Hazra, *Studies in the Upapurāṇas* and *Studies in the Purāṇic Records on Hindu Rites and Customs* : P. V. Kane, *History of the Dharmaśāstra* : A. B. Keith, *A History of Sanskrit Literature* : W. Kirfel, *Das Purāṇa Pañcalakṣaṇa* and *Das Purāṇa vom Weltgebäude* : F. E. Pargiter, *Ancient Indian Historical Tradition*, and *The Purāṇa Text of the Dynasties of the Kali Age* : L. Renou, *L'Inde Classique* : M. Winternitz, *A History of Indian Literature*.

	Kaṭha, *Śvetāśvatara*, *Praśna* and *Muṇḍaka*; the rest probably after this date)
Kalpa Sūtras 600—200 B.C.	(Śrauta, Gṛhya and Dharma Sūtras in chronological succession)
Nirukta 500 B.C.	(of Yāska)
Bṛhaddevatā 400 B.C.	(of Śaunaka)
Vedāṅga-jyotiṣa 200 B.C.	
Yuga-Purāṇa 25 B.C.	(contained in the *Gārgiya-Jyotiṣa*)
Dharma Śāstras 200 B.C.—A.D. 500	(*Mānava* probably oldest, 200 B.C.–A.D. 200 : *Viṣṇu* and *Yājñavalkya* next, then *Nārada*, then *Bṛhaspati*)
Rāmāyaṇa 250 B.C.—A.D. 200	(Books 1 and 7 are the latest)
Mahābhārata 350 B.C.—A.D. 350	(Books 1, 3, 12 and 13 contain the latest material)
Harivaṃśa A.D. 100—300	
Early Purāṇas A.D. 200–500	(notably *Brahmāṇḍa*, *Matsya*, *Mārkaṇḍeya*, *Vāyu* and *Viṣṇu*)
Bhāsa A.D. 200	
Śūdraka A.D. 300	
Sūrya-siddhānta A.D. 250—500	
Parāśara A.D. 300	
Kālidāsa A.D. 400	
Āryabhaṭa A.D. 500	
Varāhamihira A.D. 550	
Middle Purāṇas A.D. 500–1000	(notably *Agni*, *Bhāgavata*, *Brahma*, *Brahmavaivarta*, *Garuḍa*, *Kūrma*, *Liṅga*, *Nārada*, *Padma*, *Sāmba*, *Saura*, *Śiva*, *Skanda*, *Vāmana*, and *Varāha*: also, additions to many Early Purāṇas)
Rājataraṅgiṇī A.D. 1100	(of Kalhaṇa)
Kathāsaritsāgara A.D. 1100	(of Somadeva)
Late Purāṇas A.D. 1000—1500	(notably *Bhaviṣya*, *Bṛhaddharma*, *Devībhāgavata*, *Kālikā*, *Mahābhāgavata* and others: also additions

	to many Middle Purāṇas during this period; additions to Late Purāṇas continue to c. A.D. 1850)
Rāmacaritamānasa A.D. 1600	(of Tulasīdāsa)
Tamil Purāṇas A.D. 1500—1800	(but some earlier: old *Tiruviḷaiyāṭar* A.D. 1100)
Folk and Tribal material A.D. 1800 to present day	

Further indications of both relative and absolute textual chronology will be noted during the course of the book, especially in Chapters 1, 2 and 4.

A note must be added on the writing of Sanskrit words and names in the book. Technical terms are generally italicised, particularly where there is no single English word which adequately translates them. Names of individual works are also italicised, and written with an initial capital letter; such names are generally written according to conventional usage—thus for example with Sanskrit Purāṇas the class of literature is written separately from the particular text (for example *Skanda Purāṇa*), whereas with Tamil Purāṇas these two are written conjointly (for example *Kandapurāṇam*). Where the class of literature is referred to rather than an individual text, the name of the class is written with an initial capital letter, but is not italicised (for example Brāhmaṇas, Purāṇas). The names of the various time and space divisions (Yuga, Loka, *etc.*) are similarly written with an initial capital letter but not italicised, as is also the case with the names of individuals and of classes or categories of individuals (divine, human and demonic). The meanings of the main technical terms—as also of further important names referred to throughout the book—are listed in the Glossary.

This work has gradually evolved out of a doctoral thesis at the School of Oriental and African Studies, London University, which dealt—in a somewhat different form—with much of the material in Chapters 1 to 4 and 7 to 8. Without the successive guidance of Professors Wendy O'Flaherty and John de Casparis (who have since moved to Chicago and Leiden respectively), the work would never have got under way; I am also indebted for help and guidance to Professor Kenneth Ballhatchet, Dr. Alexander Piatigorski and Mr. John Gray. I would further express my gratitude to Professors Thomas Burrow and Christoph von Fürer-Haimendorf for having gone so painstakingly through the work at that stage, pointing out a number of deficiencies and making numerous suggestions for further improvements. A Studentship from the Social Science Research Council during this period made it possible to work not only in London but also in Banaras (1974-75); and I would thank especially His Highness Dr. Vibhuti Narain Singh, Sri Anand Svarup Gupta and Dr. Ganga Sagar Rai of the Kashirāj Trust for having helped to make my stay in Banaras an enjoyable and profitable one. The material in chapters 5, 6 and 9—together with most of the Purāṇic material throughout the book—was largely added during 1977-78, while attached to Viśva-Bhāratī, Śāntiniketan, under the Commonwealth Scholarship and Fellowship Plan; and the book was completed during a further stay in Śāntiniketan through the winter of 1978. My particular thanks—for both guidance and hospitality during my stays there—go to Professors Santosh Sengupta and Viśvanath Banerjee, and to Drs. A. Ramamurty, Sushanta Sen and G. Subbiah; I would also thank Peter and Ferelith Davies and other members of the British Council in Calcutta for extending hospitality and help throughout my stay in West Bengal. I am indebted also to Dr. David Shulman for several translations of Tamil material; while my silent thanks go to the many others who have contributed in one way or another to the evolution of this book. I would finally thank Mr. J. P. Jain and the staff of Motilal Banarsidass for guiding the work into print.

—J.E.M.

PART ONE

TEXT—HISTORICAL TRADITIONS

1

THE FORMULATION OF THE GROUP

A. Introduction

In this part of the book, we shall be concerned especially with examining the historical evolution of several major traditions associated with the Seven Ṛṣis, and with tracing such evolution through the different texts in which these traditions appear. One of the most basic topics which we shall be considering first of all is the question of the identity of the Seven Ṛṣis—that is to say, the question of which Ṛṣis are actually included within the group of seven, and of how consistent such groupings remain between different texts. There are two main lists of the Seven Ṛṣis, only one of which appears in Vedic literature. In addition to these two main lists, there are also a number of lists in the Epics and Purāṇas which include most or all of the Ṛṣis in the two main lists: especially the various lists of Prajāpatis and Mind-born Sons of Brahmā. A further development is to be found in the Purāṇas, many of which contain lists of Seven Ṛṣis for each of the fourteen Manvantaras or time-divisions within the present Kalpa. We shall examine each of these various lists in this and the following chapter, seeing how the identity of the Seven Ṛṣis alters and develops between different texts: and in Chapter 3 we shall look at the causes which have given rise to the most important of these changes.

B. Vedic Literature

Complete lists of the Seven Ṛṣis—giving both their names and their identity as the Seven Ṛṣis—are only to be found from the Sūtras onwards: although references to the group appear already in the *Ṛgveda.* In this section we shall, therefore, examine the Sūtras first of all, and then trace references to the group and its members back through the Brāhmaṇas and Upaniṣads to the Vedic *saṃhitās.*

(*a*) *The Sūtras*

In the Sūtras, the members of the group of Seven Ṛṣis constitute a well-defined and ordered list: consisting of the Ṛṣis Viśvāmitra, Jamadagni, Bharadvāja, Gotama, Atri, Vasiṣṭha, and Kaśyapa—usually listed in that same order. Such lists are particularly to be found in the context of the *gotra* organisation of family lineages (see Chapter 3): thus, for example, several of the Śrauta Sūtras, in their sections on *gotra* and *pravara*, relate that:

> Viśvāmitra, Jamadagni, Bharadvāja and Gotama, Atri, Vasiṣṭha and Kaśyapa—these are the Seven Ṛṣis; it is seen that where there are descendants of the Seven Ṛṣis and of Agastya as the eighth, there indeed is a *gotra.*[1]

The appearance in such lists of Agastya as the eighth Ṛṣi—"added on," as it were, to the group of seven—occurs in several further contexts. One passage in the *Hiraṇyakeśin Gṛhya Sūtra*, for example, gives the same list of Seven Ṛṣis, and gives instructions for setting up seats (in the ritual) for these seven together with Arundhatī (the wife of Vasiṣṭha), and also for Agastya:

> Viśvāmitra, Jamadagni, Bharadvāja and Gotama, Atri, Vasiṣṭha and Kaśyapa—these are the Seven Ṛṣis. They prepare seats (for them) facing east, in a place inclined to the north, with north-pointing *darbha*-grass; in the space between Vasiṣṭha and Kaśyapa they prepare (a seat) for Arundhatī: and (a seat) for Agastya in the south, in a place inclined to the south.[2]

1. For example the *pariśiṣṭabhāga* to *Āśvalāyana Śrauta Sūtra* 12.15 : the *pravarapraśna* line 54 of the *Baudhāyana Śrauta Sūtra* : *et.al.*
2. *Hiraṇyakeśin Gṛhya Sūtra* 2.8.19.2-7.

The regional association of the Ṛṣis which is suggested in this passage is a topic which we shall be discussing in detail in Chapter 3. In the present context we may simply note that in listing the members of the group—and actually calling them the Seven Ṛṣis—such Sūtras list the Seven Ṛṣis as Viśvāmitra, Jamadagni, Bharadvāja, Gotama, Atri, Vasiṣṭha, and Kaśyapa: with the addition of Agastya as the eighth Ṛṣi.

It is necessary at this point to make one important qualification in respect of the lists which are found in the Śrauta Sūtras in connection with the *gotra* and *pravara* organisations of family lineages. The passage cited above—which is to be found in several Śrauta Sūtras—is unequivocal in stating the identities of the Seven Ṛṣis to be as listed therein. In practice, however, when dealing with each of the individual *gotras* and *pravaras*, these same Śrauta Sūtras invariably subordinate the Jāmadagnyas (descendants of Jamadagni) to the Bhṛgus or Bhārgavas (descendants of Bhṛgu): and subordinate to the Gautamas and Bhāradvājas (descendants of Gotama and Bharadvāja) to the Aṅgirases or Āṅgirases (descendants of Aṅgiras). Thus the Bhṛgus are always subdivided into the Jāmadagnya-Bhṛgus and the Kevala-Bhṛgus ("just Bhṛgus," "Bhṛgus by themselves"): while similarly the Āṅgirases are subdivided into Gautama-Āṅgirases, Bhāradvāja-Āṅgirases, and Kevala-Āṅgirases. Hence the resulting list of Ṛṣi-*gotras* and -*pravaras* is indeed seven in number: but the Ṛṣis who are regarded as their founders are now listed as Bhṛgu, Aṅgiras, Atri, Viśvāmitra, Vasiṣṭha, Kaśyapa, and Agastya.[1] It should, however, be noted that these seven are never referred to in the Sūtras as the Seven Ṛṣis: and indeed, both these and also later texts—such as the medieval *Gotrapravaramañjari*—explicitly state the identities of the Seven Ṛṣis to be as in the passage cited above; the latter text also states explicitly that Bhṛgu and Aṅgiras do not belong to the Seven Ṛṣis.[2] We shall be examining in detail this variant list of Ṛṣis given in the *gotra*

---

1. For example *Āśvalāyana Śrauta Sūtra* 12.1-15 : *Āpastamba Śrauta Sūtra* 24.5-10 : *Mānava Śrauta Sūtra* 11.8.1-9; for further details, see Chapter 3 section B (b).

2. *Gotrapravaramañjarī* 1.11-12, 10.131-132.

and *pravara* sections of the Śrauta Sūtras in Chapter 3: but it is useful to note here that the subordination of the Ṛṣis Jamadagni, Bharadvāja and Gotama to the Ṛṣis Bhṛgu and Aṅgiras represents an incipient trend to bring Bhṛgu and Aṅgiras—as also Agastya—into closer connection with the group of Seven Ṛṣis; for as we shall be seeing below, this trend is greatly developed in the Epics and Purāṇas. For present purposes, we can see that the Sūtras recognise one main list of Ṛṣis who are called the Seven Ṛṣis, which consists of the Ṛṣis Viśvāmitra, Jamadagni, Bharadvāja, Gotama, Atri, Vasiṣṭha, and Kaśyapa: while they also append Agastya to the group, terming him the eighth Ṛṣi and thus giving him the status of an outsider to this group of Seven Ṛṣis.

(*b*) *The Brāhmaṇas and Upaniṣads*

While the Sūtras make explicit the dual statements both that there are Seven Ṛṣis and also as to who are those Seven Ṛṣis, earlier Vedic texts frequently refer either to the Seven Ṛṣis as a group, or to the members of that group, without explicitly connecting the two.

The *Jaiminīya Brāhmaṇa*, for example, at one point gives a list of Ṛṣis who strove to attain Svargaloka ("the heavenly world"). The Ṛṣis listed in turn in this context are Vasiṣṭha, Bharadvāja, Jamadagni, Gotama, Atri, and Viśvāmitra: and then, in addition to these six, also Agastya—who went last of all to Svargaloka after uttering a hymn.[1] We may note that, in this passage, Kaśyapa is omitted from what is otherwise the standard list of the Seven Ṛṣis found in the Sūtras: while Agastya appears to be included within the group of seven, yet only just—for the passage makes it plain that he went last of all behind the other Ṛṣis, and uses this as a justification for adding that his descendants are for this very reason considered as "outsiders":

> Therefore, indeed, the Agastis are excluded from the Kuru-Pañcālas.

The *Gopatha Brāhmaṇa*—a relatively late Brāhmaṇa text—gives a list of Ṛṣis who performed *tapas* or ascetic practices:

1. *Jaiminīya Brāhmaṇa* 2.218-221.

these Ṛṣis being listed as Vasiṣṭha, Viśvāmitra, Jamadagni, Gotama, Bharadvāja, Guṅgu, Agastya, and Kaśyapa.[1] The "Guṅgu" mentioned in this context appears once also in the *Ṛgveda* in plural form, denoting the name of a certain tribe of people.[2] Yet in this Brāhmaṇa passage it would seem more likely that "Guṅgu" may be taken as an alternative designation or as a replacement of the Ṛṣi Atri: since the list would then read as yet another list of what was then becoming the standard group of Seven Ṛṣis, together with Agastya as the eighth.

One further passage is of considerable interest inasmuch as it contains a list of the Seven Ṛṣis in a form which suggests that the individual members of this group had not yet been finally constituted in the period of composition of the Brāhmaṇas and Upaniṣads. The passage occurs in the final section of the *Śatapatha Brāhmaṇa*, which constitutes the *Bṛhadāraṇyaka Upaniṣad*. It commences by quoting a verse from the *Atharvaveda*, with minor alterations:

> There is a cup with its opening at the side and its bottom turned upwards, in which is placed the glory of all forms [*yaśo viśvarūpam*]: there the Seven Ṛṣis are seated together, they have become the keepers of that great one.[3]

The *Bṛhadāraṇyaka* passage makes an explicit connection and identification of the Seven Ṛṣis with the seven *prāṇas* or vital airs in the head (see Chapter 8), as also of the cup with the head: while it also adds *vāc* or voice as the eighth *prāṇa*, a situation which immediately calls to mind the addition of Agastya as the eighth Ṛṣi in other Brāhmaṇa and Sūtra contexts. Yet this Upaniṣadic passage continues by listing each of these Ṛṣis in a manner which can only be described as self-contradictory and confused. The passage is in the form of a visual and tactual exposition of the identity of the Seven Ṛṣis as the *prāṇas* (in this context, the ears, eyes, nostrils,

---

1. *Gopatha Brāhmaṇa* 1.2.8.
2. *Ṛgveda* 10.48.8.
3. *Atharvaveda* 10.8.9.

and mouth: for further discussion of this passage and of the *prāṇas*, see Chapter 8), as demonstrated by the teacher to his pupil:

> These two (ears) are Gotama and Bharadvāja . . . these two (eyes) are Viśvāmitra and Jamadagni . . . these two (nostrils) are Vasiṣṭha and Kaśyapa . . . the mouth [*vāc*: literally, voice] is Atri, for food is eaten by the mouth [*adyate*], and the word "eater" [*atti*] is the same as Atri.[1]

Although the passage commences by saying that there are Seven Ṛṣis, and that *vāc* (the mouth or voice) is the eighth, we can nonetheless see that in practice *vāc* is here viewed as the seventh—while the eighth appears to be missing. We may presume that the text has been emended and reworked by some later commentator, so that the list of Ṛṣis now includes Atri (as *vāc*) among the seven: thus bringing this list of Seven Ṛṣis in line with the standard list found in the Sūtras and elsewhere. We may perhaps also infer that this has taken place at the expense of Agastya, who by the Sūtras has come to be termed the eighth Ṛṣi—and who, as in the passage cited earlier from the *Jaiminīya Brāhmaṇa*, is occasionally included alongside the other Ṛṣis, but nonetheless regarded as somewhat of an outsider to the Ṛṣis who come to constitute the group of Seven Ṛṣis.

We can thus observe at this stage that the individual identities of the Ṛṣis who were to be included within the group of Seven Ṛṣis were still being formulated during the period covered by the Brāhmaṇas and Upaniṣads: and that the list of these Ṛṣis reached a more or less standardised form only during the period of the Sūtras.

(*c*) *The Vedic saṃhitās*

While the Seven Ṛṣis were coming to be listed in a formalised manner in the Brāhmaṇas, it would seem that the individual identities of the members of the group remained largely unformulated—and was certainly largely unexpressed—by the

1. *Śatapatha Brāhmaṇa* 14.5.2.6=*Bṛhadāraṇyaka Upaniṣad* 2.2.3-4. The passage is cited and discussed at greater length in Chapter 8, Section C.

composers of the Vedic hymns and texts. That is not to say that the group itself was unknown during this early period: on the contrary, there occur many references to the group of Seven Ṛṣis throughout the Vedic *saṃhitās* which will be examined in this and subsequent chapters. But it is to say that the individual members of the group were neither fully specified nor fully listed in the Vedic *saṃhitās*.

The Vedic hymns do, however, on occasions provide a prototype which is then expanded upon in later texts to give a list of the Seven Ṛṣis. One example of this has already been seen in the case of a passage in the *Atharvaveda*, which speaks of the Seven Ṛṣis as sitting on the edges of a bowl: a passage which is subsequently quoted in the *Bṛhadāraṇyaka Upaniṣad*, together this time with a list of each of the Seven Ṛṣis.[1]

One passage in a *Ṛgveda* hymn—which appears also with minor variations in the *Atharvaveda*—may similarly be seen to act as a prototype for several traditions associated with the Seven Ṛṣis: even though it does not mention any of the Ṛṣis by name. The passage states that:

> Of those Ṛṣis born together, they say that the seventh is born by himself [*saptatham ekajam*] while six are twins, God-born Ṛṣis [*ṣaḷ idyamā ṛṣayo devajāḥ*].[2]

Furthermore, in another *Ṛgveda* hymn, Viśvāmitra is similarly referred to as being "God-born" (*devaja*).[3] Hence within the *Ṛgveda* itself it is said that, of the Seven Ṛṣis who were born together, six are "God-born" twins—and one of them is Viśvāmitra. In this respect it would appear that the inclusion of Viśvāmitra among the Seven Ṛṣis is already implied in this *Ṛgveda* passage.

The idea of six Ṛṣis as twins and one as born alone applies to the group of Seven Ṛṣis in two separate ways. On the one hand, the idea is expressed through the concept of the Seven Ṛṣis as the *prāṇas* in the body. As we have seen above, the

---

1. *Atharvaveda* 10.8.9: *Bṛhadāraṇyaka Upaniṣad* 2.2.3-4.
2. *Ṛgveda* 1.164.15: *Atharvaveda* 9.9.16, 10.8.5.
3. *Ṛgveda* 3.53.9.

list of the Seven Ṛṣis as the *prāṇas* which appears in the *Bṛhadāraṇyaka Upaniṣad* speaks in terms of six Ṛṣis who are paired together : namely Gotama and Bharadvāja, Viśvāmitra and Jamadagni, Vasiṣṭha and Kaśyapa; and it then speaks of one Ṛṣi as being a "loner," identifying this Ṛṣi with the Voice and with Atri. Thus, as applied to the concept of the Seven Ṛṣis as the *prāṇas*, "six twins and one loner" may be interpreted as the two ears, two eyes, and two nostrils, together with the mouth or voice.

On the other hand, the idea is expressed through the concept of the Seven Ṛṣis as stars in the sky, namely as the constellation Ursa Major (the Plough or Dipper—see further in Chapter 7). The stars of Ursa Major are divided latitudinally into three pair-groups : namely Dubhe and Megrez (α and δ), Merak and Phedka (β and γ), Mizar and Alkaid (ζ and η); thus leaving Alioth (ϵ) as a lone or unpaired star. Since the passage just cited from the *Ṛgveda* continues by saying that "he who has eyes can see this, not he who is blind" (*paśyad akṣaṇvān na vi cetad andhaḥ*), it is likely that some visual observation is primarily intended by this passage : hence that the reference is primarily directed towards the Seven Ṛṣis in the sky. It may be noted that the star ϵ Ursa Major—the unpaired star—is the fifth of these seven stars : while the *Ṛgveda* passage speaks of the seventh as being the unpaired Ṛṣi. But on the other hand the term *saptatham* may be taken as referring not to the seventh in order of listing, but rather to the seventh in the sense of the one which is "beyond" or set apart from the six paired ones. Thus the expression "six are twins, the seventh is born alone" overcomes the ambiguity inherent in saying "six are twins, the fifth is born alone" : while it also conveys the information that there is a total of seven Ṛṣis to which reference is being made. We may observe that the variant form of this verse in the *Atharvaveda* omits the term *saptatham*, saying merely that six are twins and one born alone (*ṣaḍ yamā eka ekajaḥ*) : and it would seem that this has been done once again in order to overcome a possible misunderstanding or misinterpretation of the term *saptatham* as denoting the seventh in order of listing, rather than the seventh in the sense of being beyond or set apart from the other six "twins."

While the lone or unpaired star ε Ursa Major is the fifth in order of listing of the stars of that group, so too this might be expected to correspond to the fifth Ṛṣi in order of listing of the Seven Ṛṣis. As was seen in the case of the Sūtra lists of the Seven Ṛṣis, the standard lists of the group in such contexts place the Ṛṣi Atri as the fifth in order of listing. Hence the *saptatham ekajam* or *eka ekajaḥ* may here be taken as the Ṛṣi Atri, both in respect of the Seven Ṛṣis in the body and also in respect of the Seven Ṛṣis in the sky. Once again, then, such passages in the *Ṛg* and *Atharvavedas* may be seen to provide a model or prototype for the group of Seven Ṛṣis, while not yet providing individual identifications of each of the Ṛṣis who compose that group : while the Brāhmaṇas and Sūtras provide such individual identifications, which are fully and consistently in accord with the Vedic passages referring to the group as a whole. Thus while the Vedic texts refer to one of the Seven Ṛṣis as being a "loner" or "born alone", such references apply to the mouth (in the body) and to the fifth star of Ursa Major (in the sky), and accordingly apply in later texts to the Ṛṣi Atri who is listed as the fifth Ṛṣi in the group of seven.

In the cases of all of these passages, we may infer that while the group of Seven Ṛṣis was well-known during Vedic times—as stars in the sky, as the *prāṇas* in the body, as speakers of *ṛks* and as the founders of the Aryan *gotras*—nevertheless the individual identities of the members of that group were not yet fully formulated in the Vedic *saṃhitās*, and became expressed and firmly established only from the Brāhmaṇas onwards.

C. The Vedic-Epic Transition

(a) *The Lists of the Group*

An abrupt change in listing the members of the group of Seven Ṛṣis is evident between the Vedic and Epic texts. As we saw in the last section, the Vedic texts—particularly the Sūtras—come to formulate the members of the group as Viśvāmitra, Jamadagni, Bharadvāja, Gotama, Atri, Vasiṣṭha, and Kaśyapa. The Epics also know of and refer to this group of Seven Ṛṣis, frequently listing them in this same order: although it is to be noted that the earlier form 'Gotama' is consistently superseded by the form 'Gautama,' denoting literally "son" or "descendant" of Gotama. However, the Epics also refer to another group of Seven Ṛṣis, four of whom are unknown to—or at least unmentioned by—the authors of the Vedic texts: and this second list of the group assumes for the Epic writers—as also for the subsequent Purāṇic authors—an importance far greater than that of the first list of the group. The second list consists of the Ṛṣis Marīci, Atri, Aṅgiras, Pulastya, Pulaha, Kratu, and Vasiṣṭha: hence Atri and Vasiṣṭha are the only Ṛṣis who appear in both lists of the group. Once again, the Ṛṣis of the second list are most frequently enumerated in the same order as that just given. We shall hereafter refer to the earlier or Vedic list as the first main list, and the later Epic and post-Epic list as the second main list of the group of Seven Ṛṣis. During the remaining sections of this chapter, and also in the next chapter, we shall be examining in particular the process of change between these two main lists: while in Chapter 3 we shall investigate the reasons underlying the emergence, formulation and eventual predominance of the second main list.

(*b*) *Further Designations of the Group*

The Epics and Purāṇas in places use different appellations or designations for the same group of Ṛṣis who are otherwise called the Seven Ṛṣis. The two most important appellations are the Prajāpatis and the Mind-born Sons of Brahmā.

The Prajāpatis are usually six or seven in number, and occasionally also nine or ten: and they then invariably consist of the same group of Ṛṣis as the Mind-born Sons of Brahmā. There additionally appear further groups of seventeen and twenty-one Prajāpatis, which include the six or seven just mentioned.

The Mind-born Sons of Brahmā (*brahmaṇo mānasāḥ sutāḥ*, *manasā jātāḥ*, *brahmaṇaḥ putrā mānasāḥ*, *sapta mānasāḥ*, and similar) are sometimes six but more often seven in number: while, particularly in the Purāṇas, this number is frequently increased to eight, nine and ten. The group invariably consists of most or all of the Ṛṣis who appear in the second main list of the Seven Ṛṣis—namely Marīci, Atri, Aṅgiras, Pulastya, Pulaha, Kratu, and Vasiṣṭha—together on several occasions with one or more further Ṛṣis.

The three appellations "Seven Ṛṣis," "Seven Prajāpatis," and "Seven Mind-born Sons of Brahmā" most frequently denote in the Epics and Purāṇas the same group of Ṛṣis—namely the Ṛṣis of the second main list. The latter two of these appellations—which are not used of the Seven Ṛṣis in Vedic literature—are scarcely ever used in the Epics and Purāṇas to denote the Ṛṣis of the first main list (namely that commencing with Viśvāmitra).

It should be noted that all three appellations are on many occasions used interchangeably to designate the Ṛṣis of the second main list. It is nonetheless useful to keep in mind a certain distinction between them, in analysing the evolution and growth of the Ṛṣi-lists: particularly since this helps to highlight both the process of formulation of the second main list of the Seven Ṛṣis, and also the influences operative in that formulation—as we shall see in this and in the next two chapters.

(*c*) *Variant and Alternative Names of Ṛṣis*

We may here take brief note of the variant and alternative names by which individual Ṛṣis are on occasions known. Kaśyapa is in places said to be known also as Ariṣṭanemi[1] : although in most contexts Ariṣṭanemi appears as a son of Kaśyapa.[2] Kaśyapa is also frequently referred to simply as Mārīca or son of Marīci : similarly Viśvāmitra is often termed simply Gādhija (son of Gādhi) or Kauśika (son or descendant of Kuśika), Jamadagni is often termed simply Ṛcīkaputra (son of Ṛcīka) or Bhārgava (descendant of Bhṛgu), and Bharadvāja is sometimes termed simply Āṅgirasa (descendant of Aṅgiras—a designation more frequently used of Bṛhaspati). Vasiṣṭha is in places said to be known also as Āpava[3] : and the form Vaśiṣṭha sometimes appears, which in one passage is derived from an etymology from *vaśin* ("one who has mastery over his passions")[4] —although the form Vasiṣṭha is clearly primary. Both he and

1. *Mahābhārata* 12.201.8.

2. For example *Mahābhārata* 1.59.39: see also *Rāmāyaṇa* 3.13.6-32, *Brahmāṇḍa Purāṇa* 2.3.1.53-54.

3. *Mahābhārata* 1.93.5: *Brahma Purāṇa* 13.194: *Brahmāṇḍa Purāṇa* 2.3.69.44: *Vāyu Purāṇa* 2.32.43-44.

4. *Brahmāṇḍa Purāṇa* 2.3.1.46: *Vāyu Purāṇa* 2.4.46-47.

Agastya are also frequently termed simply Maitrāvaruṇa, Kumbhayoni or Kumbhaja, referring to their births from the pot into which the seed of Mitra-Varuṇa fell : and Agastya is also sometimes termed Agasti (especially in certain Vedic texts). Bharadvāja is sometimes termed Vidathin or Vitatha : although in other contexts Vitatha appears as a son of Bharadvāja.[1] Most complex of all is, however, Gotama. As we have noted, "Gotama" is consistently referred to in post-Vedic literature as Gautama (son or descendant of Gotama). The *Mahābhārata* complicates matters by speaking of Medhātithi—who in the *Ṛg-veda* and subsequent contexts is referred to as a son of Kaṇva, quite unconnected with Gotama—as identical with Gautama, the husband of Ahalyā;[2] and adds a still further complication by relating in one passage that Dīrghatamas begot Gautama, and then journeyed down the Gaṅgā to the realm of king Bali and begot Kakṣīvat and other sons[3]—but relating in another passage that it was Gautama who begot Kakṣīvat and others.[4] To compound matters, a number of texts relate that Dīrghatamas "became" and assumed the name of Gautama on being cured of his blindness[5] : while several Purāṇas in their Manvantara lists have Autathya Gautama Śaradvat as the member of the group of Seven Ṛṣis—where the term Autathya refers to the birth of Dīrghatamas from the union of Bṛhaspati and Mamatā, the wife of Utathya.[6]

In all of these instances, therefore, the additional names by which these various Ṛṣis are sometimes known will be taken into account when examining their traditions : although we shall consider alternative names in detail only when they appear on a large number of occasions synonymous with or in place of the Ṛṣis concerned—as most notably in the case of Gautama and Dīrghatamas.

1. *Bṛhaddevatā* 5.102-103: *Matsya Purāṇa* 49-32-35; *Harivaṃśa* 23.49-53.
2. *Mahābhārata* 12.258.1-59.
3. Ibid., 1.98.6-33.
4. Ibid., 2.19.5.
5. For example *Mahābhārata* 12.328.50: *Brahmāṇḍa Purāṇa* 2.3.74.94: *Matsya Purāṇa* 48.84: *Vāyu Purāṇa* 2.37.92.
6. For example *Brahmāṇḍa Purāṇa* 1.2.38.28: *Vāyu Purāṇa* 2.3.24-28; see also *Bṛhaddevatā* 3.142-150: *Mahābhārata* 1.98.6-16.

D. The Epics

(*a*) *The Rāmāyaṇa*

The authors of the *Rāmāyaṇa*, in giving lists of the Ṛṣis, draw a clear distinction between the Seven Ṛṣis on the one hand—a title which it reserves for the group of Ṛṣis commencing with Viśvāmitra, who constitute the first main list of the group—and the Prajāpatis and Mind-born Sons of Brahmā on the other hand. The latter groups consist of the Ṛṣis of the second main list, commencing with Marīci : and these Ṛṣis are not referred to in the *Rāmāyaṇa* as the Seven Ṛṣis. Thus, for example, a passage in the *Uttara Kāṇḍa* (seventh book—a relatively late part of the work) gives a list of those *munis* or sages who come to honour Rāma after he has defeated the Rākṣasas and regained his kingdom—among whom are the Ṛṣis of the first main list, referred to as the Seven Ṛṣis :

> Vasiṣṭha, Kaśyapa and Atri, Viśvāmitra and Gautama, Jamadagni, Bharadvāja : these indeed are the Seven Ṛṣis.[1]

The *Rāmāyaṇa* does not contain a complete enumeration of the Ṛṣis of the second main list. It does, however, in places mention each of them by name: and one passage in the *Araṇya Kāṇḍa* gives a list of seventeen Prajāpatis, among whom are (in order of appearance) Marīci, Atri, Kratu, Pulastya, Aṅgiras, and Pulaha—namely the Ṛṣis of the second main list, with the exception of Vasiṣṭha :

> In a former age, O powerful one, these Prajāpatis came into being; listen, son of Raghu, as I recite them all from the beginning. Kardama was the first of them, then Vikṛta after him; Śeṣa and Saṃśraya, and powerful Bahuputra; Sthāṇu, Marīci and Atri, and strong Kratu; Pulastya and Aṅgiras, Pracetas and Pulaha; Dakṣa, unrivalled Vivasvat, and Ariṣṭanemi, O son of Raghu; and splendorous Kaśyapa was the last of them.[2]

1. *Rāmāyaṇa* 7.1.5.
2. Ibid., 3.13.6-9.

A further passage in the *Sundara Kāṇḍa* mentions a definitive group of six Prajāpatis, the fourth of whom is Pulastya—who is also called a Mind-born Son of Brahmā :

> This one is the fourth of the six Prajāpatis—well-known Pulastya, a Mind-born Son of Brahmā.[1]

It is evident here that even in the *Rāmāyaṇa* the six Prajāpatis are already being associated with and identified as the six Mind-born Sons of Brahmā. This passage also suggests that the order in which the six Prajāpatis were listed had already been formalised in a fairly definitive manner, with Pulastya as the fourth in the group of six : thus according with the form in which the Ṛṣis of the second main list are usually enumerated, namely as Marīci, Atri, Aṅgiras, Pulastya, Pulaha, and Kratu, together with Vasiṣṭha as the seventh in the *Mahābhārata* and the Purāṇas. It might indeed be inferred from this passage that since Pulastya—who is here referred to as being a Mind-born Son—appears only in the second main list of the Seven Ṛṣis, therefore the Mind-born Sons as a whole might similarly be primarily those of the second main list : and such an inference does indeed turn out to be the case, as we shall see in examining the lists in the *Mahābhārata* and the Purāṇas. The *Rāmāyaṇa* does not list together all of the Mind-born Sons : but it does on occasions refer to other individual Ṛṣis as being Sons of Brahmā, notably Marīci[2] and Vasiṣṭha,[3] in addition to Pulastya.

It may, therefore, be concluded that the *Rāmāyaṇa*, when speaking of the Seven Ṛṣis, refers only to the Ṛṣis of the first main list (commencing with Viśvāmitra) : while it also knows of a definitive group of six Prajāpatis and Mind-born Sons, which—although not listed in full—would appear to consist of the Ṛṣis who subsequently appear in the second main list of the Seven Ṛṣis.

(*b*) *The Mahābhārata*

The Ṛṣis of the first main list of the Seven Ṛṣis—namely those commencing with Viśvāmitra, as in the Vedic texts—are

---

1. *Rāmāyaṇa* 5.21.6.
2. Ibid., 1.69.17ff, 2.102.3ff, *etc.*
3. Ibid., 1.53.7, 1.55.13, *etc.*

well-known to the authors of the *Mahābhārata.* A passage in the *Ādi Parvan* relates that, at the birth of Arjuna, the Seven great Ṛṣis assembled to pay homage to him—namely the seven of the first main list. The passage continues by listing certain other Ṛṣis who also came to pay homage, including Marīci, Aṅgiras, Pulastya, Pulaha, and Kratu : thus in effect listing all twelve of the Ṛṣis who appear in one or the other of the two main lists, but reserving the title of Seven Ṛṣis for those of the first main list :

> There came all the Prajāpatis, and also the Seven great Ṛṣis : Bharadvāja, Kaśyapa and Gautama, Viśvāmitra, Jamadagni, Vasiṣṭha, as also lord Atri who rose up (to the sky) when the sun was destroyed; also Marīci and Aṅgiras, Pulastya, Pulaha, Kratu, and Dakṣa Prajāpati, with Gandharvas and Apsarases [celestial musicians and maidens].[1]

Similarly in the *Droṇa Parvan* it is related that, when Droṇa was on the point of committing an *adharmika* action (contrary to *dharma* or right action) by exterminating all the Kṣatriyas, the Ṛṣis Viśvāmitra, Jamadagni, Bharadvāja, Gautama, Vasiṣṭha, Kaśyapa, and Atri come to discourse with him and to take him to Brahmaloka—accompanied by the Bhṛgus, the Āṅgirases, the Vālakhilyas, and other groups.[2] Thus here again the group of Seven Ṛṣis commencing with Viśvāmitra is distinguished from any other group of Ṛṣis.

One passage in the *Anuśāsana Parvan* contains a myth concerning Vṛṣādarbhi and the Seven Ṛṣis : wherein the Seven Ṛṣis are once again those of the first main list, and in order of appearance are Kaśyapa, Atri, Vasiṣṭha, Bharadvāja, Gautama, Viśvāmitra, and Jamadagni.[3] Another passage, this time in the *Āśvamedhika Parvan,* relates that a certain group of Ṛṣis went to the abode of Brahmā in order to question him : these Ṛṣis being, in order of listing, Bṛhaspati, Bharadvāja, Gautama, Bhārgava, Vasiṣṭha, Kaśyapa, Viśvāmitra, and Atri.[4] In this

1. *Mahābhārata* 1.114.40-42.
2. Ibid., 7.164.86-89.
3. Ibid., 13.94.2ff.
4. Ibid., 14.35.15ff.

context, the term "Bhārgava" may almost certainly be taken to denote Jamadagni Bhārgava : a usage of the *gotra* name which is frequently employed in further passages.[1] Thus the list of Ṛṣis is here once again that which constitutes the first main list of the Seven Ṛṣis, together with Bṛhaspati who is said to act as a spokesman for the others. We can, therefore, see that in certain parts of the *Mahābhārata*, the Seven Ṛṣis are recognised to be those of the first main list.

Elsewhere in the *Mahābhārata*—particularly in the *Śānti Parvan*, as also in the *Ādi* and *Vana Parvans*, all three of which are generally acknowledged to be relatively late books—greater prominence is given to the Ṛṣis of the second main list, who themselves come to be termed the Seven Ṛṣis. This is particularly evident in one passage in the *Śānti Parvan*, which lists both groups—but applies the term "the Seven Ṛṣis" only to the Ṛṣis of the second main list, whom it also terms Prajāpatis and Mind-born Sons:

> These are the Seven Sons of Brahmā Svayambhū, the great-souled ones: Marīci, Atri, Aṅgiras, Pulastya, Pulaha, Kratu, and illustrious Vasiṣṭha, resembling Svayambhū; these are called the Seven Brahmās in the Purāṇa [or, in ancient tradition], and have attained certainty [*sapta brahmāṇa ity ete purāṇe niścayaṃ gatāḥ*]. Next I shall describe all these Prajāpatis . . . .they are the creators of the three worlds, the Seven Ṛṣis in the east . . . . Ātreya and Vasiṣṭha, and Kaśyapa the great Ṛṣi, Gautama and Bharadvāja, and Viśvāmitra Kauśika, and Jamadagni the illustrious son of great-souled Ṛcīka—these seven dwell in the northern region.[2]

---

1. For example *Mahābhārata* 3.115.9-30, 12.49.1ff., 13.4.1ff., *etc.*; note also the very large number of references to Paraśurāma as Jāmadagnya or simply Bhārgava.

2. *Mahābhārata* 12.201.2ff. It is to be noted that in the first half of *śloka* 5, the form *sapta brahmāṇa ity ete purāṇe niścayaṃ gatāḥ* is given in a total of 31 mss. out of a total of 36 mss. used for the B.O.R.I. Critical Edition. The remaining 5 mss. contain the variant reading *eṣa* in place of *ete* (=Śāradā+3 Kashmiri +1 Devanāgarī) : while 4 of these also contain the further variant *niścayo gataḥ* in place of *niścayaṃ gatāḥ* (=Śāradā+3 Kashmiri). The editors of the B.O.R.I. Critical Edition nevertheless give the readings *eṣa* and *niścayo gataḥ* in their main text: yet the alternative forms would seem to be very much better attested, and are accordingly adopted in the above passage. See also the discussion in the next section on parallel passages in the Purāṇas.

The regional association of the various groups of Ṛṣis is a topic which will be discussed in Chapter 3. It is evident from the above passage that the author, while speaking of the Ṛṣis of the first main list who are here said to live in the north, does not wish to ascribe the term Seven Ṛṣis to them : and instead he ascribes this term to the Ṛṣis of the second main list, who are here said to live in the east. This passage is particularly noteworthy also for a further reason : since the first part of it—listing the Mind-born Sons of the second main list—is copied in many Purāṇas, but the number of Ṛṣis is expanded from seven to nine; hence the line now following the list of Ṛṣis is altered to read *nava brahmāṇa ity ete purāṇe niścayaṃ gatāḥ*. This development of the list will be further discussed and examined in the next section in the context of the Purāṇas.

A similar clear distinction between the two groups of Ṛṣis is drawn within the *Vana Parvan*, in the version given there of the myth in which the Seven Ṛṣis reject their wives after suspecting them of having been seduced by Agni. In the myth, Svāhā impersonates in turn each of the six wives of the Ṛṣis—excluding Arundhatī, the chaste wife of Vasiṣṭha—and in that guise makes love to Agni : and the first wife whom she impersonates is Śivā, the wife of Aṅgiras.[1] By implication, therefore, the Seven Ṛṣis whose wives are impersonated by Svāhā must include as one of their members the Ṛṣi Aṅgiras : hence the Seven Ṛṣis who are involved in this myth must be those of the second main list—namely Marīci, Atri, Aṅgiras, Pulastya, Pulaha, Kratu, and Vasiṣṭha—as opposed to the Ṛṣis of the first main list, commencing with Viśvāmitra. This is indeed confirmed within the myth itself : for it is subsequently related that Viśvāmitra had witnessed the various impersonations of Svāhā, and so knew that the wives of the Seven Ṛṣis were innocent ; this he attempted to tell to the Seven Ṛṣis, but the Seven Ṛṣis nevertheless abandoned their wives.[2] Thus Viśvāmitra in this passage acts as an outsider to the Seven Ṛṣis who abandon their wives : and there is clearly no question of the wife of Viśvāmitra being one of those who is abandoned, since

1. *Mahābhārata* 3.214.1ff.
2. Ibid., 3.215.5-12.

it is Viśvāmitra himself who protests the innocence of the wives to the Seven Ṛṣis. Consequently, the Seven Ṛṣis who are referred to in this myth must be those of the second main list, rather than those of the first main list of the group.

It would seem reasonably certain that the second main list of the Seven Ṛṣis was developed from the list of six Ṛṣis—the Prajāpatis and Mind-born Sons—which was noted in the last sub-section to appear first in the *Rāmāyaṇa*. Comparable to that list, the *Ādi Parvan* contains two separate lists of the six Ṛṣis who are known as Mind-born Sons of Brahmā. The first of these relates that :

> The six great Ṛṣis are celebrated as the Mind-born Sons of Brahmā : Marīci, Atri, Aṅgiras, Pulastya, Pulaha, and Kratu.[1]

The second is closely similar : merely changing the order in which Atri and Aṅgiras appear in the list.[2] The second passage thereafter proceeds to relate that Dakṣa was born from the right toe of Brahmā, and that Manu was another son of Brahmā. Such references are particularly noteworthy insofar as both Dakṣa and Manu subsequently appear in certain contexts within the group of Mind-born Sons of Brahmā. Thus a further passage in the *Vana Parvan* similarly speaks of the six Mind-born Sons of Brahmā—without however listing them by name—and adds that Dakṣa is the seventh member of this group :

> They call these the Mind-born Sons of Brahmā, who have Dakṣa as their seventh; great Meru is their auspicious and sound abode. There too the Seven godly Ṛṣis, with Vasiṣṭha at their head, constantly rise and set.[3]

The passage, in drawing an apparent distinction between the Mind-born Sons of Brahmā on the one hand—who have now become seven in number through the addition of Dakṣa—and the group of Seven Ṛṣis headed by Vasiṣṭha on the other

1. *Mahābhārata* 1.59.10.
2. Ibid., 1.60.4.
3. Ibid., 3.160.14-15.

hand, provides evidence that at the time of the composition of this text the two groups of Mind-born Sons and Seven Ṛṣis had not yet come to be identified with one another. Nevertheless there is evidently an attempt being made in the passage to increase the number of Mind-born Sons from six to seven: and thereby to bring the group in line with the group of Seven Ṛṣis—which is effected in this passage through the addition of Dakṣa, but in other passages, as will be seen below, through the addition of Vasiṣṭha.

One further passage in this same *Vana Parvan* refers to the Ṛṣis Aṅgiras as the third Son of Brahmā[1]—just as the *Rāmāyaṇa* referred to Pulastya as the fourth Son of Brahmā. This once again suggests that, by the time of the composition of this book, the members of this group of Mind-born Sons of Brahmā constituted a definitively formulated and ordered list: namely in the order Marīci, Atri, Aṅgiras, Pulastya, Pulaha, and Kratu.

A passage in the *Anuśāsana Parvan* again draws a distinction between this same group of six Ṛṣis on the one hand, and further Ṛṣis—including Vasiṣṭha, Bhṛgu and Dakṣa—on the other hand; relating that, standing before Mahādeva, Viṣṇu observed the Ṛṣis:

> Marīci, Aṅgiras, Atri, Pulastya, Pulaha, Kratu; the seven Manus and Soma, Atharvan and Bṛhaspati; Bhṛgu, Dakṣa and Kaśyapa, Vasiṣṭha and Kāśya.[2]

Thus in this passage the same six Ṛṣis are again grouped together—with this time a change in the order of listing of Atri and Aṅgiras—and are associated with, but nonetheless separated from, certain other Ṛṣis, most notably Bhṛgu, Dakṣa, Kaśyapa and Vasiṣṭha.

One passage in the *Bhagavad-Gītā* section of the *Bhīṣma Parvan* is noteworthy inasmuch as it speaks of the Seven Ṛṣis—as also of the four Manus—as being Mind-born Sons, without actually listing them:

1. *Mahābhārata* 3.208.1.
2. Ibid., 13.15.20-21.

> The Seven great Ṛṣis of old, and the four Manus, were born of my being and my mind [*madbhāvā mānasā jātāḥ*]: from them have come these creatures in the world.[1]

Thus, by the time of the composition of this passage, the Mind-born Sons had come to be identified with the Seven Ṛṣis.

It is above all in the *Śānti Parvan* that the Seven Ṛṣis come to be explicitly equated with the (now) seven Mind-born Sons of Brahmā. One passage, recalling that quoted above from the *Vana Parvan*, relates the birth of six Mind-born Sons together with Dakṣa as the seventh:

> Brahmā created Mind-born Sons, with Dakṣa as the seventh: Marīci, Atri, Aṅgiras, Pulastya, Pulaha, and Kratu.[2]

Yet it then continues by relating the birth of Dakṣa from the toe of Brahmā:

> Brahmā created from his toe the first-born son of Marīci: he became, O best of the Bharatas, the Prajāpati called Dakṣa.[3]

There would thus seem to be some confusion here as to whether Dakṣa is born from the mind or the toe of Brahmā. However, the very next chapter of this *parvan* gives a list of Seven Ṛṣis—who are called both Prajāpatis and Mind-born Sons of Brahmā—which excludes Dakṣa and replaces him with Vasiṣṭha:

> These are the Seven Sons of Brahmā Svayambhū, the great-souled ones: Marīci, Atri, Aṅgiras, Pulastya, Pulaha, Kratu, and illustrious Vasiṣṭha, resembling Svayambhū; these are called the Seven Brahmās in the Purāṇa, and have attained certainty. Next I shall describe all these Prajāpatis.[4]

Thus in this context the number of Mind-born Sons of Brahmā has been increased from six to seven: and Vasiṣṭha now appears as the seventh member of the group.

---

1. *Mahābhārata* 6.32.6 (*Bhagavad-Gītā* 10.6).
2. Ibid., 12.200.17.
3. Ibid., 12.200.19.
4. Ibid., 12.201.3-5.

A further passage in this *parvan* refers to the seven Mind-born Sons who were created to be knowers and teachers of the Veda:

> Marīci, Aṅgiras and Atri, Pulastya, Pulaha, Kratu, and Vasiṣṭha—these are the seven Mind-created ones; they are the foremost knowers of the Veda, and were created as teachers of the Veda.[1]

Here again the order of Atri and Aṅgiras has been reversed from that in which they more usually appear: yet the identity of the seven is clearly established in a form which subsequently remains constant throughout the Purāṇas.

Two further passages from the *Śānti Parvan* are of interest for two separate reasons: firstly because they implicitly accept Vasiṣṭha as a member of the group of Seven; and secondly because they already demonstrate a tendency to increase the number of the group from seven to eight, through including Manu Svāyaṃbhuva as the eighth member. The first of these passages further implies that this group of Seven Ṛṣis—who are called here the *prakṛti* elements (the sources of the material world)—are also to be identified as the Seven Ṛṣis:

> These *munis* [Ṛṣis] are called the Seven Bright-Crested ones [*citraśikhaṇḍinaḥ*]: by their unanimous opinion there came into being what is called the supreme *śāstra*; Marīci, Atri, Aṅgiras, Pulastya, Pulaha, Kratu, and illustrious Vasiṣṭha—these are the Bright-Crested ones: they are the seven *prakṛti* elements, and Svāyaṃbhuva is the eighth.[2]

The second passage again reverses the order of Atri and Aṅgiras, but otherwise retains the same implications and contains the same information as that in the passage just cited.[3]

Before drawing conclusions on the lists in the *Mahābhārata*, we shall refer to one further passage—again in the *Śānti Parvan*—which contains a list of twenty-one Prajāpatis, including the

1. *Mahābhārata* 12.327.61-62.
2. Ibid., 12.322.26-28.
3. Ibid., 12.327.29.

seven who elsewhere constitute the second main list of the Seven Ṛṣis:

> Brahmā, Sthāṇu, Manu, Dakṣa, Bhṛgu, Dharma, Tapas, Dama: Marīci, Aṅgiras and Atri, Pulastya, Pulaha, Kratu, Vasiṣṭha and Parameṣṭhin, Vivasvat and Soma: Kardama, and he who is called Krodha, and Vikrīta: these twenty-one were born, who are known as Prajāpatis.[1]

It can be seen that there are a great many differences between this lengthened list of Prajāpatis and that cited in the last section from the *Rāmāyaṇa*: but it is nonetheless of interest, since it groups together both the Seven Ṛṣis and also other Ṛṣis who in Purāṇic contexts come to be assimilated among the lists of Mind-born Sons of Brahmā.

It may be concluded that the *Mahābhārata* itself bears witness to an amalgamation of various traditions in respect of the lists of Ṛṣis. In particular, the group of Seven Ṛṣis of the Vedic texts—namely those of the first main list, commencing with Viśvāmitra—is acknowledged as the group of Seven Ṛṣis especially in the (chronologically) earlier *parvans* of the *Mahābhārata*: but in the later *parvans*—and especially in the *Śānti Parvan*—that group of Seven Ṛṣis comes gradually to be superseded by a different group of Ṛṣis. This latter group of Ṛṣis is at first termed the six Prajāpatis and the six Mind-born Sons of Brahmā, and is first met with in the *Rāmāyaṇa* as a definitive group: the number of Ṛṣis in the group is subsequently expanded to seven, and as such these Ṛṣis come to be identified as the Seven Ṛṣis, and to take the place of that group of Ṛṣis who are termed the Seven Ṛṣis throughout Vedic literature. The later *parvans* of the *Mahābhārata*—especially the *Śānti Parvan*—also demonstrate a tendency to expand this group still further, through the addition of an eighth Ṛṣi: and this is a tendency which is more fully to be seen in the Purāṇas, as we shall see in the next section.

1. *Mahābhārata* 12.321.33-35.

(*c*) *The Harivaṃśa*

The *Harivaṃśa* may be classified either under the Epics—since it claims to be a supplement to the *Mahābhārata*—or under the Purāṇas—as it is often referred to as the *Harivaṃśa-Purāṇa*. In this respect, it forms a bridge between the Epic and Purāṇic literatures, sharing features in common with both. For present purposes we shall consider it alongside the Epics: but it should nonetheless be kept in mind that it does not fall wholly within this category—as will be seen especially in the next chapter, where it will be observed that Manvantara lists of the Seven Ṛṣis appear only in the *Harivaṃśa* and in the Purāṇas, and not in either of the two main Epics.

In several contexts in the *Harivaṃśa*, the Mind-born Sons of Brahmā are explicitly equated with the Seven Ṛṣis. One passage thus relates that:

> Formerly the Grandsire himself [i.e. Brahmā] established as his sons the Seven Mind-born ones, who were born as *brahma*-Ṛṣis.[1]

Lists of these Seven Mind-born Ṛṣis are to be found in a number of different passages; and they are generally in the same order as found elsewhere, as, for example, in the following:

> He [Brahmā]created the Seven Mind-born ones—Marīci, Atri, Aṅgiras, Pulastya, Pulaha, Kratu, and Vasiṣṭha: these are called the Seven Brahmās in the Purāṇa, and have attained certainty [*sapta brahmāṇa ity ete purāṇe niścayaṃ gatāḥ*].[2]

It will be noted that the final line of this passage is identical with that discussed in the last section from *Mahābhārata* 12.201.5. This is indeed one noteworthy correspondence linking the *Harivaṃśa* with the *Mahābhārata* rather than with the Purāṇas, most of which expand the group of Ṛṣis to nine members and read the line accordingly—as will be seen in the next section.

A further passage again emphasises the identity of the (seven) Mind-born Sons with the Seven Ṛṣis: locating this group of

1. *Harivaṃśa* 3.96.
2. Ibid., 1.29-30.

Ṛṣis in the northern region (the implications of which will be discussed in Chapter 3), and also placing the Ṛṣis in a different order—with Pulastya placed sixth rather than fourth:

> Marīci, lord Atri, Aṅgiras, Pulaha, Kratu, Pulastya and Vasiṣṭha—these are the Seven Sons of Brahmā: they are established, O king, in the northern region as the Seven Ṛṣis.[1]

A different variant ordering occurs in another passage, in which Sanatkumāra is speaking to Mārkaṇḍeya and tells him that :

> Those other Sons of Brahmā who are younger than me, they are the Seven unassailable brothers whose *vaṃśas* [lines of descendents] are celebrated: Kratu, Vasiṣṭha, Pulaha, Pulastya, Atri, and Aṅgiras; they sustain these three worlds, and are honoured by gods and demons.[2]

The passage as it is translated here follows the form given in the reconstituted text of the Critical Edition (B.O.R.I.). Yet it would seem to be clearly defective: for the passage itself speaks explicitly of the Seven Sons of Brahmā, while the version presented in the text of the Critical Edition lists only six Ṛṣis. The Critical Edition does, however, list two textual variants for this passage. The first of these replaces the section of the passage commencing "Kratu, . . ." with the following:

> Marīci, lord Atri, Pulastya, Pulaha, Kratu, Aṅgiras and Vasiṣṭha: these are the Seven Sons of Brahmā.[3]

This variant appears, however, only in three Southern Grantha recensions, all undated, and in one Southern Telugu version dated 1839; and it is not, therefore, well-attested. The second variant replaces the section of the passage commencing "they sustain . . ." with the following:

1. *Harivaṃśa* 7.7-8.
2. Ibid., 12.13-14.
3. *239 to *Harivaṃśa* 12.13-14.

> And the learned Marīci; they are worshipped by gods and Gandharvas.[1]

This variant is considerably better attested: it appears in the only extant Śāradā version ("seems to be at least 500 years old"): in two allied Devanāgarī versions, one dated 1625, the other undated: in the Devanāgarī versions of Nīlakaṇṭha, dated 1753 and 1757: and in three further Devanāgarī versions, two of which are undated, while the third is dated 1550. There are two earlier manuscripts referred to by the compilers of the Critical Edition (and presumably followed by them in the above passage): one dated 1445 (Ñ3), the other dated 1446 (D1). Yet if one accepts their own assessment of the Śāradā version as being at least 500 years old (c.1450?), then it would seem that the evidence for both readings is equally well-attested. Yet since the text itself demands that seven—rather than six—Ṛṣis should be listed, then it would appear that the "variant" passage *240 should be accepted as an integral part of the original text, rather than be relegated to a variant footnote as has been done in the Critical Edition. Thus the passage as a whole should preferably read:

> Those other Sons of Brahmā who are younger than me, they are the Seven unassailable brothers whose *vaṃśas* are celebrated: Kratu, Vasiṣṭha, Pulaha, Pulastya, Atri, Aṅgiras, and learned Marīci; they are worshipped by gods and Gandharvas.

Accordingly these seven Ṛṣis are once again the six who are listed in other Epic contexts as the six Mind-born Sons of Brahmā, together with Vasiṣṭha as the seventh.

The *Harivaṃśa* may consequently be said to follow in many respects the pattern set in the *Mahābhārata* for listing the Seven Ṛṣis and the Mind-born Sons of Brahmā. In particular, it reflects the stage reached in the *Mahābhārata* wherein the Mind-born Sons are said to be seven in number (rather than six, as in the *Rāmāyaṇa*), and are explicitly equated with and identified as the Seven Ṛṣis—thereby constituting the second main list of the Seven Ṛṣis. On the other hand, it does not reflect the

1. *240 to *Harivaṃśa* 12.13-14.

stage reached in several passages in the *Śānti Parvan* of the *Mahābhārata* wherein the number of Mind-born Sons is increased from seven to eight or more: and this is a development which is next to be seen only in the Purāṇas.

E. The Purāṇas

The Purāṇas are, generally speaking, quite notoriously difficult to date. Much of the material contained in them is probably of considerable antiquity, going back at least to the start of the Christian era: while in most Purāṇas, such material is placed alongside further material of considerably more recent date—thereby making it impossible in many cases to ascribe a date to any Purāṇa as a whole, but only to particular passages or sections contained in them. Sometimes only a relative chronology between similar Purāṇic passages can be established: but in other cases, a more definite date of composition is apparent. At the latest end of the time-scale, for example, we have such semi-historical works as the *Mahārāṣṭra Purāṇa*, which describes the 18th century Maratha invasions of Bengal[1] : and also the *Pratisarga Parvan* of the *Bhaviṣya Purāṇa* (probably added to the rest of the work in the late 19th century), which relates stories about Adam and Noah, about Nānak, Kabīr, Caitanya and other teachers, about Nadīr Shāh and Śivājī, and about early British rule in India.[2] Even the distinction between the eighteen main Mahā-Purāṇas and the (supposedly later) Upa-Purāṇas cannot be taken as a firm guide: since certain passages in the former are of manifestly late date (as with the *Pratisarga Parvan* of the *Bhaviṣya Purāṇa*), while conversely many passages in the latter often preserve

1. Published as the *Maharashtra Purāṇa*, translated, annotated, and with an introduction by Edward C. Dimock, Jr., and Pratul Chandra Gupta.

2. *Bhaviṣya Purāṇa* 3.1.4.1-46, 3.4.17.1ff. : see also chapters 3.4.8, 3.4.10, 3.4.12, 3.4.14 *et.al.* The British—called "Guruṇḍas"—are said to have come for trade, to have established the city of Kalikātā after 1800 years of the Vikrama era had passed (namely in c. A.D. 1743), and to have set up a kingdom with its *aṣṭakauśalya* (the popular name for the Indian Council or Parliament) : the tenth ruler, called "Larḍla," is mentioned as having ruled over all India; chs. 3.4.22ff.

material deriving from the earliest levels of Purāṇic composition.

Rather than attempt to impose a historical sequence upon the various Purāṇic passages, we shall in this section seek to trace in the texts themselves a development wherein the number of Ṛṣis who are called either the Seven Ṛṣis or the Mind-born Sons is gradually increased from the original seven (or, still earlier, six) to ten or more: a process which we have seen to be already evident in the Epics. In doing so, a pattern will be seen to emerge which itself helps to establish a relative chronology between these various passages in different Purāṇas.

On a few very rare occasions, the Ṛṣis of the first main list of the Seven Ṛṣis appear—as a group—in the Purāṇas. The *Skanda Purāṇa* repeats the *Mahābhārata* myth of the Seven Ṛṣis and Vṛṣādarbhi, noted in the last section : listing the Ṛṣis in the order Atri, Vasiṣṭha, Kaśyapa, Bharadvāja, Gautama, Kauśika (Viśvāmitra) and Jamadagni.[1] The *Padma Purāṇa* recounts a conversation between these same Seven Ṛṣis and a certain king during a drought[2] : while the *Vāmana Purāṇa* contains the myth of the Seven Ṛṣis' obtaining Pārvatī to be the wife of Śiva—but omits Jamadagni from the list of Ṛṣis, replacing him with Aṅgiras.[3] Further lists of this group of Ṛṣis are to be found in other contexts in the *Skanda* and *Vāmana Purāṇas.*[4]

The Ṛṣis of the second main list appear—as a group—on a number of occasions. The *Viṣṇu* and *Skanda Purāṇas* recount versions of the myth of Dhruva who, after he has left the city to pursue a life of asceticism, meets and questions the Seven Ṛṣis in the forest—the Seven Ṛṣis being in this context Marīci, Atri, Aṅgiras, Pulastya, Pulaha, Kratu, and Vasiṣṭha.[5] The *Skanda Purāṇa* also repeats the *Mahābhārata* myth wherein the Seven Ṛṣis reject their wives for suspected infidelity, despite

1. *Skanda Purāṇa* 6.32.1-100.
2. *Padma Purāṇa* 5.19.209-391.
3. *Vāmana Purāṇa* 26.1-71.
4. *Skanda Purāṇa* 7.2.14.60: *Vāmana Purāṇa, saromāhātmya* 15.7-13.
5. *Viṣṇu Purāṇa* 1.11.29-56: *Skanda Purāṇa* 4.1.19.101ff.

the protestations of Viśvāmitra to the contrary—as noted in the last section;[1] while the *Padma Purāṇa* relates a myth wherein the Seven Ṛṣis perform *tapas* and bathe at a *tīrtha* in order to obtain offspring.[2] The *Varāha Purāṇa* tells the story of how Gautama was tricked by some Brahmins into believing that he had killed a cow—until he was informed of the deception by the Seven Ṛṣis : a story which is to be found with altered details in several Purāṇas.[3] In all of these contexts, the Seven Ṛṣis who appear in the myths are those of the second main list of the Seven Ṛṣis.

In a number of Purāṇas there appears a list of those Ṛṣis who occupy the chariot of Sūrya or the Sun during each of the twelve months of the year.[4] The *Viṣṇu*, *Bhāgavata* and *Garuḍa Purāṇas* list each of the Ṛṣis and months individually: while the *Vāyu*, *Brahmāṇḍa*, *Matsya*, *Bhaviṣya* and *Liṅga Purāṇas* list both the Ṛṣis and the months in pairs. These twelve Ṛṣis are usually found listed in the order : Pulastya and Pulaha, Atri and Vasiṣṭha, Aṅgiras and Bhṛgu, Bharadvāja and Gautama, Kaśyapa and Kratu, Jamadagni and Viśvāmitra; although minor variations occur between these various texts—thus, for example, in the first three texts the ordering of Bharadvāja and Gautama is reversed, and in the *Bhāgavata Purāṇa* Kratu is conjoined with Gautama and Bharadvāja while Ariṣṭanemi is introduced as the pair of Kaśyapa. It can be seen that, with one exception, this list includes all twelve of the Ṛṣis who otherwise appear in one or the other of the two main lists of the Seven Ṛṣis. The one exception is in the case of the Ṛṣi Marīci, who does not appear in this list : and it is particularly noteworthy that his place has been taken by Bhṛgu, since—as will be seen shortly—one of the most important and frequent changes which occurs with the lists of Ṛṣis in the Purāṇas is that wherein Bhṛgu comes to be listed alongside the other Ṛṣis.

---

1. *Skanda Purāṇa* 1.2.29.89-123.
2. *Padma Purāṇa* 6.218.57-65.
3. *Varāha Purāṇa* 71.1-62.
4. *Viṣṇu Purāṇa* 2.10.1-22: *Bhāgavata Purāṇa* 12.11.33-34: *Garuḍa Purāṇa* 58.1ff.: *Vāyu Purāṇa* 1.52.2-20: *Brahmāṇḍa Purāṇa* 1.2.23.2-20 : *Matsya Purāṇa* 126.3-4: *Bhaviṣya Purāṇa* 1.52.29-50 : *Liṅga Purāṇa* 1.55.25-69.

Turning attention once again to the Ṛṣis of the second main list, the *Skanda Purāṇa* repeats the same list of six Ṛṣis—excluding Vasiṣṭha—which was noted in the Epics as being the forerunner of the second main list of the Seven Ṛṣis :

> Marīci, Atri, Aṅgiras, Pulastya, Pulaha, Kratu : these are the Mind-born Sons of Brahmā, the six great Ṛṣis.[1]

The *Vāyu* and *Brahmāṇḍa Purāṇas* similarly give a list of six Mind-born Ṛṣis: but they include Vasiṣṭha and exclude Aṅgiras, prefacing the list with an account of the births of Bhṛgu, Śukra and Aṅgiras from the sacrificial fire of Brahmā.[2] Both of these lists of six Mind-born Sons may therefore be seen as variants of the second main list of the Seven Ṛṣis—which includes both Aṅgiras and Vasiṣṭha in order to make the total of seven Ṛṣis. The list in the *Vāyu* and *Brahmāṇḍa Purāṇas* implicitly accepts Vasiṣṭha as one of the Mind-born Sons: at the same time attempting to harmonise this with certain further traditions, deriving especially from the Brāhmaṇas, which relate the births of particular Ṛṣis—including Aṅgiras—from the fire into which the seed of Prajāpati-Brahmā is poured : rather than from the mind of Brāhmā. Thus certain Brāhmaṇas relate the birth of Aṅgiras in this way[3] : others relate that of Bhṛgu[4] : and others relate the births of both of these Ṛṣis, with on occasions the addition of a third Ṛṣi—sometimes Atri,[5] sometimes Bṛhaspati,[6] or sometimes Atharvan.[7] Similarly a passage in the *Anuśāsana Parvan* of the *Mahābhārata* relates firstly the births of Bhṛgu, Aṅgiras, and Kavi-Śukra from the sacrificial fire :

> Formerly Bhṛgu arose from the flames, and Aṅgiras from the coals: then Kavi arose from the charcoal.[8]

1. *Skanda Purāṇa* 3.2.8.40.
2. *Vāyu Purāṇa* 2.4.34-48 : *Brahmāṇḍa Purāṇa* 2.3.1.34-48.
3. E.g. *Jaiminīya Brāhmaṇa* 3.263: *Śatapatha Brāhmaṇa* 4.5.1.8.
4. E.g. *Pañcaviṃśa Brāhmaṇa* 18.9.1-2.
5. E.g. *Śatapatha Brāhmaṇa* 1.4.5.13: *Bṛhaddevatā* 5.97-101: *Nirukta* 3.17.
6. E.g. *Aitareya Brāhmaṇa* 3.34.
7. E.g. *Gopatha Brāhmaṇa* 1.1.1-9.
8. *Mahābhārata* 13.85.15-34.

The passage then continues by relating the births of subsequent Ṛṣis—namely Marīci, the Vālakhilyas, and Atri. Thus the list in the *Vāyu* and *Brahmāṇḍa Purāṇas* continues this same tradition—found from the Brāhmaṇas onwards—of recounting the exalted births of the Ṛṣis Aṅgiras, Bhṛgu, and also Śukra-Kavi from the sacrificial fire : while it also attempts to combine this with a further tradition—found from the *Rāmāyaṇa* onwards—of recounting the births of the six Mind-born Sons of Brahmā. Moreover, since the Ṛṣi Aṅgiras—who is usually termed one of the six Mind-born Sons—has already been listed in the passage as one of the three Ṛṣis born from the sacrificial fire, his place in the list of Mind-born Sons is therefore given to Vasiṣṭha—who, as was seen in the last section, gradually comes to join the group as its seventh member.

A passage which appears in both the *Vāyu* and *Brahmāṇḍa Purāṇas* gives a list of what at first sight seems a group of eight Ṛṣis—namely the seven of the second main list, together with Bhṛgu; but the passage uses the compound *bhṛgvaṅgirāḥ* to denote a single Ṛṣi, thereby retaining the number of Ṛṣis as seven :

> Bhṛgvaṅgiras and Marīci, Pulastya, Pulaha, Kratu, Atri, and Vasiṣṭha are the Seven (Ṛṣis) in the Svāyaṃbhuva age.[1]

The device of the compound form is, to say the least, somewhat artificial : and indeed, a further passage in the *Brahmāṇḍa Purāṇa* uses the same compound *bhṛgvaṅgirāḥ*, but this time distinguishes between Bhṛgu and Aṅgiras by stating that the Ṛṣis are eight in number :

> Bhṛgu, Aṅgiras and Marīci, Pulastya, Pulaha, Kratu, Atri, and Vasiṣṭha, those are the eight Sons of Brahmā.[2]

Passages such as these seem to indicate an attempt to incorporate Bhṛgu within the group of Seven Ṛṣis: which results in the latter of these passages with the acknowledgement that eight separate Ṛṣis are listed—and thus with the expansion

1. *Vāyu Purāṇa* 1.31.16-17 : *Brahmāṇḍa Purāṇa* 1.2.13.103.
2. *Brahmāṇḍa Purāṇa* 2.3.1.21.

of the group of Ṛṣis from seven to eight members. It should further be noted that the latter passage has in fact been speaking in preceding verses of the Seven Ṛṣis, and of the seven Mind-born Sons of Brahmā: hence the passage, when read as a whole, demonstrates an explicitly ambiguous and self-contradictory nature which may be taken as an indication that Bhṛgu has in effect been added to the group of Seven Ṛṣis, probably at a stage subsequent to the composition of the first part of the passage:

> Formerly in the Svāyaṃbhuva age these were the Seven great Ṛṣis; when the age of Cākṣuṣa had passed and the Vaivasvata was again reached, . . . the Seven Ṛṣis were again born as the seven Mind-born. (The question is asked : How were the Seven Ṛṣis formerly born as the seven Mind-born ? and the answer is given :) After a long period, the Ṛṣis were born a second time—so we have heard. Bhṛgu, Aṅgiras, and Marīci, Pulastya, Pulaha, Kratu, Atri, and Vasiṣṭha, those are the eight Sons of Brahmā.[1]

Several editions of the *Vāyu Purāṇa* give in this passage the form *bhṛguraṅgirāḥ* in place of *bhṛgvaṅgirāḥ*: thereby clearly demonstrating that, although the passage has been speaking of the Seven Ṛṣis and seven Mind-born Sons, in the actual list it gives eight Ṛṣis—this time acknowledging the fact that it has listed eight, and thereby formulating a new group of eight Mind-born Sons of Brahmā with the addition of Bhṛgu to the other seven. A corresponding passage is also found in the *Skanda Purāṇa*, again giving the total number of Ṛṣis as eight rather than seven.[2]

In several contexts in the *Vāyu*, *Brahmāṇḍa* and *Matsya Purāṇas*, Bhṛgu is included within the group of Ṛṣis of the second main list. One passage in the *Vāyu Purāṇa*, for example, gives a quite variant list of the seven Mind-born Sons:

> He [Brahmā], the brilliant one, created the seven Mind-born ones: Bhṛgu, Aṅgiras, Dakṣa, Pulastya, Pulaha, Kratu, and Vasiṣṭha.[3]

1. *Vāyu Purāṇa* 2.4.8-22 : *Brahmāṇḍa Purāṇa* 2.3.1.1-21.
2. *Skanda Purāṇa* 7.1.19.63ff.
3. *Vāyu Purāṇa* 1.25.80.

In this context, therefore, both Marīci and Atri have been omitted from the list, while Bhṛgu and Dakṣa have been included—even though, as was noted in the last section, Dakṣa is often said to have been born from the toe rather than from the mind of Brahmā. We shall shortly see that Bhṛgu and Dakṣa subsequently appear very frequently added to the other Seven Ṛṣis, thereby formulating a new group of nine Mind-born Sons: consequently this relatively isolated passage in the *Vāyu Purāṇa* probably represents an intermediate stage of the tradition, prior to the commonly extended listing of nine rather than seven Ṛṣis. A further passage in both the *Vāyu* and *Brahmāṇḍa Purāṇas* gives a list of the *gaṇas* or groups of descendants of various Ṛṣis—such Ṛṣis being Marīci, Bhṛgu, Aṅgiras, Pulastya, Pulaha, Vasiṣṭha, and Atri.[1] In this context in would again appear that Bhṛgu has been assimilated within the group of seven: and that, in doing so, he has taken the place of Kratu who is omitted from the list. A plausible mythological explanation for why the *gaṇa* of Kratu should be omitted from this list is given in many further contexts, which relate that his offspring—namely the sixty thousand Vālakhilyas—had no wives but remained *ūrdhvaretas* or ascetic.[2] A passage in the *Matsya Purāṇa*, in speaking of the birth of Seven Ṛṣis from Brahmā, similarly omits Kratu from the list and inserts Bhṛgu in his place[3]: thus the Ṛṣis are listed in the order Bhṛgu, Aṅgiras, Atri, Marīci, Pulastya, Pulaha, and Vasiṣṭha—and Bhṛgu has once again come to usurp a place within the group of Seven Ṛṣis.

A great many Purāṇas contain, at considerable length, lists of the wives and descendants of the Ṛṣis who are created by Brahmā.[4] These lists are of a fairly standardised form, and

1. *Vāyu Purāṇa* 2.4.49-50 : *Brahmāṇḍa Purāṇa* 2.3.1.49-51.

2. E.g. *Brahmāṇḍa Purāṇa* 1.2.11.36-37 : *Vāyu Purāṇa* 1.28 30 : *Mahābhārata* 1.60.9 : *etc.*

3. *Matsya Purāṇa* 195.8-11.

4. *Agni Purāṇa* 20.8-17 : *Bhāgavata Purāṇa* 3.24.9-25, 4.1.8-45: *Brahmāṇḍa Purāṇa* 1.2.11.1-39 : *Garuḍa Purāṇa* 5.1ff. : *Kūrma Purāṇa* 1.8.16-19 : *Liṅga Purāṇa* 1.5.37-50 : *Mārkaṇḍeya Purāṇa* 50.22-25, 52.14-26 : *Padma Purāṇa* 5.3.175-179 : *Śiva Purāṇa* 7.1.17.9-35 : *Skanda Purāṇa* 2.9.27.63-66 : *Saura Purāṇa* 26.1ff. : *Vāyu Purāṇa* 1.10.27-31, 1.28.1-35 : *Viṣṇu Purāṇa* 1.7.23-25, 1.10.6-14 : *Kandapurāṇam* 6.3.1-66 : *Agastyaparva* 347.6ff. See further in Chapter 6.

show little variation between different Purāṇas: it is not necessary to study them in detail here, since the relevant point to note in the present context is that these Ṛṣis are listed as being eight in number—namely the seven of the second main list, together with Bhṛgu. Thus Bhṛgu has once again come to be added to the list of Ṛṣis who elsewhere appear as the Seven Ṛṣis and seven Mind-born Sons of Brahmā.

In a comparable manner, the same group of eight Ṛṣis is listed in several further contexts, with Bhṛgu added to the other Seven Ṛṣis of the second main list. A passage in the *Vāyu, Brahmāṇḍa* and *Brahma Purāṇas* gives Dakṣa's not very enthusiastic reply to his daughter Satī when she requests to be allowed to marry Śiva :

> Vasiṣṭha, Atri, Pulastya and Aṅgiras, Pulaha, Kratu, Bhṛgu and Marīci—these are the best sons-in-law for me.[1]

The *Bhāgavata Purāṇa* gives at one point the same list of eight Ṛṣis as being *brahmacārins* and *brahmavādins*[2] : while the *Liṅga Purāṇa* contains a stylised list of Ṛṣis and their wives as incarnations of Śiva and Śivā, wherein Bhṛgu is once again added to the other Seven Ṛṣis.[3] Thus in all of these passages Bhṛgu appears alongside the Seven Ṛṣis of the second main list : and this in effect formulates a new group of eight Ṛṣis, who are however only on rare occasions referred to as being Mind-born Sons.

We shall now turn our attention to a passage which appears in a large number of Purāṇas : and which affords perhaps the clearest evidence of development within the tradition of listing the Ṛṣis or Mind-born Sons. The passage in question has already been seen in the last section to appear in both the *Mahābhārata* and the *Harivaṃśa*; and it also appears in three Purāṇas, namely the *Brahma, Śiva* and *Skanda* :

> Brahmā created Mind-born Sons: Marīci, Atri, Aṅgiras, Pulastya, Pulaha, Kratu, and Vasiṣṭha; these are called the

1. *Vāyu Purāṇa* 1.30.47-48 : *Brahmāṇḍa Purāṇa* 1.2.13.52-54 : *Brahma Purāṇa* 34.17-18.
2. *Bhāgavata Purāṇa* 4.29,42-44.
3. *Liṅga Purāṇa* 2.11.14-18.

seven Brahmās in the Purāṇa, and have attained certainty [*sapta brahmāṇa ity ete purāṇe niścayaṃ gatāḥ*].[1]

In these contexts, therefore, the Mind-born Sons are declared to be seven in number—and are identical with the Seven Ṛṣis of the second main list. Further passages in the *Agni* and *Devī bhāgavata Purāṇas* also give the same account and list of the birth of seven Mind-born Sons, but without quoting the final line.[2] However, in a great many other Purāṇas, a similar account of the birth of Mind-born Sons is given: but in addition to the seven, Bhṛgu and Dakṣa are added to the list—which thus now contains nine members :

> Brahmā created Mind-born Sons: Marīci, Bhṛgu, Aṅgiras, Pulastya, Pulaha, Kratu, Dakṣa, Atri, and Vasiṣṭha; these are called the nine Brahmās in the Purāṇa, and have attained certainty [*nava brahmāṇa ity ete purāṇe niścayaṃ gatāḥ*].

This account, together with the final line, is found in the *Brahmāṇḍa*, *Kūrma*, *Liṅga*, *Mārkaṇḍeya*, *Padma*, *Vāyu*, and *Viṣṇu Purāṇas*.[3] The account of the creation of the nine sons, without the final line, is also found in further passages in the *Bhaviṣya*, *Kūrma* (twice more), *Liṅga*, *Śiva*, and *Saura Purāṇas*[4] : and it may be noted that while the latter passage in the *Bhaviṣya Purāṇa* (without the line) adds that Kaśyapa is the tenth Mind-born Son, a further passage in this same work includes the final line, but this time replaces Dakṣa with Nārada.[5] It can thus be seen that this account of the creation of nine Sons is clearly developed from the earlier (especially Epic) tradition of the creation of seven Sons: and that once again Bhṛgu—

1. *Mahābhārata* 12.201.2-5 : *Harivaṃśa* 1.29-30 : *Brahma Purāṇa* 1.43-44 : *Śiva Purāṇa* 5.29.16-17 : *Skanda Purāṇa* 4.1.18.7-8.

2. *Agni Purāṇa* 17.11-16 : *Devībhāgavata Purāṇa* 7.1.10ff.

3. *Brahmāṇḍa Purāṇa* 1.1.5.69-71, 1.2.9.18-19 : *Kūrma Purāṇa* 1.10.86-87 : *Liṅga Purāṇa* 1.70.178-190 : *Mārkaṇḍeya Purāṇa* 50.1-7 : *Padma Purāṇa* 5.3.159-160 : *Vāyu Purāṇa* 1.9.61-63 : *Viṣṇu Purāṇa* 1.7.3-6.

4. *Bhaviṣya Purāṇa* 1.78.5-10 : *Kūrma Purāṇa* 1.2.22-23, 1.7.33-37 : *Liṅga Purāṇa* 1.5.9-11 : *Śiva Purāṇa* 7.1.12.49-51 : *Saura Purāṇa* 26.1ff.

5. *Bhaviṣya Purāṇa* 4.2.21-22. This passage gives the variant form *nava brahmāṇa ity eṣa purāṇe niścayaḥ smṛtaḥ* : on this, see the comment for note 2 on p. 18.

together now with Dakṣa—has been given a place within this group of Mind-born Sons. The isolated appearance of Nārada is one of these lists will be further commented upon below, in the context of his appearance in several lists of ten Mind-born Sons.

Several Purāṇas additionally give more detailed accounts of the births of Ṛṣis from different parts of the body of Brahmā. Such accounts are found especially in the *Brahmāṇḍa*, *Kūrma*, *Liṅga*, *Śiva*, and *Vāyu Purāṇas*[1] : and they once again list the Ṛṣis as being nine in number—namely the seven of the second main list, together with Bhṛgu and Dakṣa

We have so far seen how the number of Mind-born Sons is gradually increased in the Purāṇas from seven to nine : through the addition firstly of Bhṛgu, and secondly of both Bhṛgu and Dakṣa. There are additionally a number of variant and more isolated lists which are to be found in these texts. The *Devībhāgavata Purāṇa*, for example, gives one list of the eight Mind-born Sons which excludes Aṅgiras from the second main list of the Seven Ṛṣis, and adds Nārada and Dakṣa to the group.[2] As will be seen below, both Nārada and Dakṣa—together with Bhṛgu, who is on this one occasion omitted from the list—come to be included in lists of the ten Mind-born Sons. In further passages, other Ṛṣis are omitted from the second main list of the Seven Ṛṣis, to give place to relative newcomers. A passage in the *Padma Purāṇa* omits Vasiṣṭha, and inserts instead Bhṛgu, Dakṣa, and Kardama in a list of nine Prajāpatis;[3] while passages in the *Vāyu* and *Brahmāṇḍa Purāṇas* omit Atri, and insert Bhṛgu, Dakṣa, and Kaśyapa as the nine Mind-born Sons of Brahmā.[4] It will be observed that in each of the latter two instances, both Bhṛgu and Dakṣa appear once again within these lists. In other contexts, further Ṛṣis are added to the seven members of the group of Seven Ṛṣis. Thus the *Śiva Purāṇa*, in giving a stylised list of Ṛṣis and

1. *Brahmāṇḍa Purāṇa* 1.1.5.74-79, 1.2.9.22-29 : *Kūrma Purāṇa* 1.7.33-37 : *Liṅga Purāṇa* 1.70.178-190 : *Śiva Purāṇa* 2.1.16.4-7 : *Vāyu Purāṇa* 1.9.92-98.
2. *Devībhāgavata Purāṇa* 3.13.12.
3. *Padma Purāṇa* 6.258.6-7.
4. *Vāyu Purāṇa* 2.39.34-36, .49-58 : *Brahmāṇḍa Purāṇa* 3.4.2.32-34, 47-55.

their wives as incarnations of Śiva and Śivā (comparable to that noted above in the *Liṅga Purāṇa*), refers to nine Ṛṣis—namely the seven, together this time with Bhṛgu and Kaśyapa;[1] while the *Vāmana Purāṇa* contains at one point a list of nine Ṛṣis which adds Bhṛgu and Mārkaṇḍeya to the other seven.[2] Once again it can be seen that the inclusion of Bhṛgu in these lists is a phenomenon of very frequent occurrence.

In addition to these lists of between seven and nine Mind-born Sons, there occur a number of lists of ten Sons. A passage in the *Bhāgavata Purāṇa* relates :

> Brahmā performed severe *tapas*, and produced ten Sons who multiplied the creation : Marīci, Atri, Aṅgiras, Pulastya, Pulaha, Kratu, Bhṛgu, Vasiṣṭha, Dakṣa, and Nārada.[3]

The *Śiva Purāṇa* presents a similar list : adding Bhṛgu, Dakṣa and Nārada to the Seven Ṛṣis of the second main list.[4] The *Vāyu* and *Brahmāṇḍa Purāṇas*, on the other hand, give an alternative account :

> Brahmā created ten Mind-born Sons : Bhṛgu, Marīci, Atri, Aṅgiras, Pulaha, Kratu, Manu, Dakṣa, Vasiṣṭha, and Pulastya.[5]

In this context, therefore, the Seven Ṛṣis have been joined by Bhṛgu, Dakṣa, and Manu—the addition of Manu to the group having been seen to be already foreshadowed in the *Mahābhārata* list of eight *prakṛti* elements.[6] The *Matsya Purāṇa* gives in one passage the same list of ten Ṛṣis[7] : while in another passage it further adds Gautama, to make a total of eleven Ṛṣis.[8] The addition of Gautama also occurs in one passage in the

1. *Śiva Purāṇa* 7.2.4.49-54.
2. *Vāmana Purāṇa* 32.18.
3. *Bhāgavata Purāṇa* 3.12.21-23.
4. *Śiva Purāṇa* 2.2.2.18-22.
5. *Vāyu Purāṇa* 1.59.88 : *Brahmāṇḍa Purāṇa* 1.2.32.96.
6. *Mahābhārata* 12.322.26-28, 12.327.29 : see p. 23.
7. *Matsya Purāṇa* 145.81-118.
8. Ibid., 171.24-33.

Padma Purāṇa : but here the Sons are once again ten in number —namely the Seven of the second main list, together with Bhṛgu, Dakṣa, and Gautama.[1] Thus the addition of Gautama to such lists is a relatively rare occurrence—unlike the additions of both Bhṛgu and Dakṣa. A number of further Purāṇas give yet again a slightly different list of Ṛṣis :

> Brahmā created ten Mind-born Sons: Marīci, Atri, Aṅgiras, Pulastya, Pulaha, Kratu, Pracetas, Vasiṣṭha, Bhṛgu, and Nārada.

This account of their creation is to be found in the *Matsya*, *Bhaviṣya*, *Narasiṃha*, and *Varāha Purāṇas*, as also in the *Mānava Dharma Śāstra*[2] : while the same list of ten Ṛṣis—adding Bhṛgu, Nārada and Pracetas to the Seven Ṛṣis of the second main list—is again given in further passages in the *Matsya*, *Bhaviṣya*, *Garuḍa*, and *Padma Purāṇas*.[3] Thus it may be said that both Pracetas and Manu are on several occasions included in the lists of ten Mind-born Sons; Nārada is on many occasions included in those lists, as is also Dakṣa; and Bhṛgu is in every case considered to be a member of the group of ten Mind-born Sons of Brahmā.

Notice should also be taken of longer—generally isolated—lists of Ṛṣis, Prajāpatis or Mind-born Sons, which again include most or all of the Seven Ṛṣis of the second main list. A passage in the *Vāyu Purāṇa* gives an extended list of Prajāpatis :

> Make obeisance to the Prajāpatis . . . . Bhṛgu, Marīci, Parameṣṭhin, Manu, Rajas, Tamas, Dharma, and Kaśyapa; Vasiṣṭha, Dakṣa, Atri, Pulastya, Kardama, Ruci, Vivasvat, and Kratu; also Aṅgiras and Pulaha.[4]

Although the passage is more in the manner of a collection of names rather than a definitively ordered list, it can be seen

1. *Padma Purāṇa* 5.37.71-74.
2. *Matsya Purāṇa* 3.2-12 : *Bhaviṣya Purāṇa* 1.2.60-62 : *Narasiṃha Purāṇa* 4.2-4: *Varāha Purāṇa* 2.43-44 : *Mānava Dharma Śāstra* (*Manu*) 1.34-35.
3. Ibid., 102.19: *Bhaviṣya Purāṇa* 4.123.20-21: *Garuḍa Purāṇa* 135.1ff.: *Padma Purāṇa* 5.20.164-165.
4. *Vāyu Purāṇa* 1.3.2-3.

that it includes both the Seven Ṛṣis of the second main list and also further figures—notably Bhṛgu, Dakṣa, Manu, Kaśyapa, and Kardama—who have been noted to appear in certain lists of the Mind-born Sons. A list in the *Śiva Purāṇa* includes another of these figures—namely Ruci—in a list of eleven Prajāpatis :

> These are the famous Prajāpatis : Dakṣa, Ruci, Bhṛgu, Marīci, Aṅgiras, Pulastya, Pulaha, Kratu, Atri, Kaśyapa, and Vasiṣṭha.[1]

This list may be considered as a still further development of the lists of nine Mind-born Sons, which include the Seven together with Bhṛgu and Dakṣa—and one of which, in the *Bhaviṣya Purāṇa*, adds that Kaśyapa is the tenth.[2] It is also comparable with the lists noted earlier of nine Mind-born Sons, which omit Atri from the Seven Ṛṣis and add Bhṛgu, Dakṣa and Kaśyapa. A list in the *Garuḍa Purāṇa* gives a number of further names :

> After creating the world, Brahmā created Mind-born Sons to multiply the creation: Dharma, Rudra, Manu, Sanaka, Sanātana, Bhṛgu, Sanatkumāra, Ruci, Śuddha, Marīci, Atri, Aṅgiras, Pulastya, Pulaha, Kratu, Nārada, and the Barhiṣad *pitṛs*.[3]

Here Vasiṣṭha has been omitted from the Seven : while Bhṛgu, Nārada, Manu, Ruci and others have been added. Several passages in the *Brahmavaivarta Purāṇa* similarly give extended lists of Ṛṣis. One of these relates Brahmā's complaint to Nārada :

> My sons Sanaka, Sananda, Sanātana, Sanatkumāra, Yati, Haṃsi, Aruṇi, and Pañcaśikha have become devotees of Hari due to their indifference to the world, only Marīci,

1. *Śiva Purāṇa* 7.2.30.43-46.
2. *Bhaviṣya Purāṇa* 1.78.5-10.
3. *Garuḍa Purāṇa* 5.1ff.

> Aṅgiras, Bhṛgu, Ruci, Atri, Kardama, Pracetas, Kratu, Manu, and Vasiṣṭha are obedient to me.[1]

In this list, Pulastya and Pulaha are omitted from the Seven : while Bhṛgu, Ruci, Kardama, Pracetas and Manu are included. Further passages in this work relate the births of Ṛṣis from different parts of the body of Brahmā, as also the etymologies of Ṛṣi-names : where such Ṛṣis are the Seven of the second main list, together with Bhṛgu, Dakṣa, Nārada, Pracetas, Kardama—and also Aruṇi, Pañcaśikha, Boḍhu, Haṃsi, Yati, and either Ira or Apāntartamas or Ruci.[2] One further list in this same work is of sixteen Sons created by Brahmā :

> Brahmā created Sons . . . . Atri, Pulastya, Pulaha, Marīci, Bhṛgu, Aṅgiras, Kratu, Vasiṣṭha, Voḍhu, Kapila, Āsuri, Kavi, Śaṅku, Śaṅkha, Pañcaśikha, and Pracetas.[3]

The list once again contains several relatively isolated names : but it is nonetheless noteworthy, particularly since it includes both the Seven Ṛṣis of the second main list and also further Ṛṣis—notably Bhṛgu and Pracetas—who elsewhere appear in lists of the Mind-born Sons of Brahmā.

Having now surveyed the various lists of Ṛṣis which appear in the Purāṇas, we are in a position to summarise the main pattern of development which is evident between such lists, and to draw certain further conclusions. In the first place, it has been seen that—with only a very few exceptions—the Purāṇas in general recognise as the Seven Ṛṣis those of the second main list of the group—namely Marīci, Atri, Aṅgiras, Pulastya, Pulaha, Kratu, and Vasiṣṭha; and they pay relatively little attention to the first main list of the group (as distinct from the individual members of that group). In the second place, the Purāṇas demonstrate a marked tendency—evident already in the later parts of the *Mahābhārata*—to increase the number of members of the group: especially through the addition of Bhṛgu, as also to a slightly lesser extent of

1. *Brahmavaivarta Purāṇa* 1.24.1-5.
2. Ibid., 1.8.25-28, 1.22.1-20.
3. Ibid., 4.30.30-35.

Dakṣa, to the group. This is occasionally achieved by excluding one or more of the Ṛṣis usually included in the list of Seven Ṛṣis, and inserting Bhṛgu and/or Dakṣa: but it is most commonly achieved by simply adding Bhṛgu and Dakṣa to the other Seven Ṛṣis of the second main list—thereby formulating a new list of eight or nine Ṛṣis, who are generally referred to as the Mind-born Sons of Brahmā. Moreover, in a number of instances a third Ṛṣi is also added to the group, which thus comes to be called the ten Mind-born Sons: and on a few occasions, still more Ṛṣis are added, expanding the group further.

Some of the possible reasons for the expansion of the group—and in particular for the prominent addition of Bhṛgu to the group—will be discussed in Chapter 3. In the concluding section of this chapter, we shall attempt to discern the main period of development of these lists, particularly that wherein the first main list came to be superseded and virtually replaced by the second: but before doing so, we must examine one further category of texts whose dating is fortunately more easily ascertained than that of the Purāṇas, and which can, therefore, help to throw light upon the precise period in which the development of these lists occurred.

F. Astronomical and Literary Works

Although neither the *Sūrya-siddhānta* nor the works of Āryabhaṭa contain any lists of the group of Seven Ṛṣis, such a list is given in the *Bṛhat-saṃhitā* of Varāhamihira: and as would be expected, Varāhamihira deals with the Seven Ṛṣis as being identified with the seven stars of Ursa Major (on this concept, see subsequent chapters below). In one passage he speaks both of the group as a whole and also of the positions of the Seven Ṛṣis relative to one another—the latter part of which we are here concerned with:

> At the eastern end is lord Marīci, next to him is Vasiṣṭha: then comes Aṅgiras, then Atri, and then Pulastya: then Pulaha, and then lord Kratu—each in order, beginning at the

east; chaste Arundhatī has resorted to the excellent *muni* Vasiṣṭha.[1]

It may be seen that this list of the Seven Ṛṣis is the same as that already noted in the Epics and Purāṇas which constitutes the second main list of the group.

In astronomical terms, Arundhatī—the wife of the Ṛṣi Vasiṣṭha—is identified with Alcor, the small (almost invisible to the naked eye) close beside ζ Ursa Major. A passage in the *Ādi Parvan* of the *Mahābhārata* offers an explanation for her being sometimes visible and sometimes invisible, saying that this is because she once doubted her husband Vasiṣṭha.[2] Just as she here appears in a list alongside the Seven Ṛṣis, so too it was noted in section B of this chapter that a passage in the *Hiraṇyakeśin Gṛhya Sūtra*—which gives a list of the Seven Ṛṣis of the first main list—places Arundhatī between Vasiṣṭha and Kaśyapa[3] : thus corresponding to a position between Vasiṣṭha and Marīci in the above list of Varāhamihira. This is on the one hand an indication that Marīci in the second list has in a sense taken over the position formerly occupied by Kaśyapa in the first list—the latter of whom is termed the son of Marīci throughout the Epics and Purāṇas (see further discussion of this topic in Chapter 3). It may also be noted that, in astronomical terms, Vasiṣṭha as the husband of Arundhatī must necessarily be identified with the star ζ Ursa Major adjoining the star Alcor: and he must, therefore, appear in a penultimate position within the group of Seven Ṛṣis. In the first main list of the Seven Ṛṣis, Vasiṣṭha does indeed appear in such a penultimate position : the standard list of that group being, as was seen in section B, in the order Viśvāmitra, Jamadagni, Bharadvāja, Gotama, Atri, Vasiṣṭha, and Kaśyapa. Yet it has been seen that, in the Epic formulation of the second main list of the Seven Ṛṣis, Vasiṣṭha is a relative late-comer : he does not appear in the earlier group of six Ṛṣis, and when he is added to the group as the seventh Ṛṣi he usually appears as the final member of that group. Thus the standard form of the second main list is usually in the order Marīci, Atri, Aṅgiras,

1. *Bṛhat-saṃhitā* 13.1-6.
2. *Mahābhārata* 1.224.27-31.
3. *Hiraṇyakeśin Gṛhya Sūtra* 2.8.19.1-6.

Pulastya, Pulaha, Kratu, and Vasiṣṭha. Hence Varāhamihira has in the above passage been obliged to alter the usual order of this list, in order to accord with the astronomical significance of the Ṛṣis—and to place Vasiṣṭha in a penultimate, rather than in a final position within the group. It would consequently appear that the origins of the second main list of the Seven Ṛṣis do not arise from any astronomical basis, identifying the Ṛṣis with the seven stars of Ursa Major : and this conclusion is in any case implied by the fact that this particular group of Ṛṣis would seem to have been originally only six in number (namely the six Mind-born Sons of the *Rāmāyaṇa* and *Mahābhārata*), and to have been expanded to seven only at a later stage of development (namely from the *Śānti Parvan* of the *Mahābhārata*, and subsequently). Thus Varāhamihira—writing around the first half of the 6th century A.D. (he bases all his calculations on the year Śaka 427 or A.D. 505 throughout his works)—refers to only one list of the Seven Ṛṣis : namely the second main list of the group.

Several of the literary figures around the same period mention the Seven Ṛṣis as a group, but do not speak of the individual members of that group in a way to indicate whether they are referring to the first or the second main list of the group. Kālidāsa, however, recounts in the *Kumārasaṃbhava* the story of how Śiva obtained Pārvatī as his wife through the mediation of the Seven Ṛṣis[1] : and relates that the Ṛṣis, after debating amongst themselves, decided that it should be Aṅgiras who would speak in this connection with Himālaya.[2] Since the Ṛṣi Aṅgiras appears only in the second main list of the Seven Ṛṣis, it would seem that Kālidāsa here implicitly refers to this second main list as constituting the group of Seven Ṛṣis, at a period probably around A.D. 400 or thereabouts.[3]

G. Conclusion

We shall here bring together the various observations as to the development of lists of the Seven Ṛṣis which have been

1. *Kumārasaṃbhava* 6.3-95.
2. Ibid., 6.65.
3. The chronology outlined and discussed by A.B. Keith in *A History of Sanskrit Literature* is accepted in the present context.

made during the course of this chapter: and then draw certain further conclusions as to the likely period during which major changes occur between the lists—leaving to a later context (Chapter 3) the discussion of why such changes should have occurred.

We have seen that the Vedic tradition—from the *saṃhitās* to the Sūtras—comes to formulate a list of the Seven Ṛṣis which is most commonly given in the order : Viśvāmitra, Jamadagni, Bharadvāja, Gotama, Atri, Vasiṣṭha, and Kaśyapa; together, in some contexts, with Agastya as the eighth Ṛṣi. This group is also to be found in a number of Epic contexts: and in a far fewer number of Purāṇic contexts, where its importance as a group has been very greatly diminished.

In the *Rāmāyaṇa*, a new group of Mind-born Sons appears, consisting primarily of Ṛṣis who are unknown to the Vedic tradition. They are there six in number: but in the *Mahābhārata* their number is increased to seven—particularly in the later *Śānti Parvan*—and as such they are referred to as the Seven Ṛṣis, thereby constituting the second main list of the group. These Ṛṣis are usually listed in the order Marīci, Atri, Aṅgiras, Pulastya, Pulaha, Kratu, and Vasiṣṭha.

This same second list of the Seven Ṛṣis is generally followed throughout the Purāṇas. A further development is, however, evident therein: whereby further Ṛṣis—especially Bhṛgu, and also Dakṣa—are added to the group. Consequently the group comes to be known more commonly not as the Seven Ṛṣis but as the Mind-born Sons: and their number is increased on many occasions to eight, nine, or ten members—and on a few occasions still further.

In literary terms, the change between the two main lists of the Seven Ṛṣis occurs later than the *Hiraṇyakeśin Gṛhya Sūtra*, and later than the *Rāmāyaṇa*—the latter of which, while mentioning the six Mind-born Sons, nonetheless recognises only the Ṛṣis of the first main list as constituting the group of Seven Ṛṣis. On the other hand, the change is evidently in process in different *parvans* of the *Mahābhārata* : it is fully accepted in the *Śānti Parvan*, and is similarly accepted both in the *Harivaṃśa* and also throughout the Purāṇas. It is furthermore implicitly accepted by such 5th/6th century A.D. writers as Kālidāsa and Varāhamihira. As was mentioned earlier in this chapter, the traditions presented in these various texts most probably overlapped in many instances, with different traditions being presented contemporaneously in different texts. Nonetheless a reasonably unitary developmental pattern would seem to emerge from this study, which is itself suggestive of a chronological development of the traditions. In this respect the *Mahābhārata* affords a bridge between the two main traditions of listing the Seven Ṛṣis: inasmuch as it accepts the Ṛṣis of both of the main lists, in different contexts, as representing the Seven Ṛṣis,—although in especially the later *Śānti Parvan* only the second main list is generally accepted as constituting the Seven Ṛṣis. Thus in attempting to establish a relative textual chronology for the change between these two main lists, it may be said that the origins of the change are evident in the *Rāmāyaṇa*: that the change is already under way in the *Mahābhārata*: and that the change has been fully effected in the *Harivaṃśa* and in the Purāṇas.

Turning to the question of establishing an absolute chronology for the period of this change between the two main lists of the Seven Ṛṣis, we have already noted that there are many difficulties involved in the precise dating of these texts. A terminal point for the effecting of the change is provided through the references in the works of Kālidāsa and Varāhamihira: and since these may, as indicated earlier, be assigned to the 5th/6th centuries A.D., it would seem likely that the change itself had already occurred and been accepted prior to these works—and had therefore most probably been effected by perhaps A.D. 300. This latter date is necessarily approximate: but it does also coincide with the date usually ascribed to the final composition of the *Mahābhārata*, which is generally considered to have been composed during the period between c. 300 B.C. and A.D. 300. Moreover, certain sections of the Purāṇas—as for example the lists of kings in the *Matsya Purāṇa*[1]—were almost certainly composed prior to the establishment of the Gupta dynasty in A.D. 320: and some parts—as

1. *Matsya Purāṇa* 273.1-45, where the lists of kings do not include or reach as far as the Guptas.

for example the accounts of the Era of the Seven Ṛṣis—were probably composed close to A.D. 250 (see Chapter 4 below). Consequently, since such Purāṇas implicitly accept and recognise only the second main list of Seven Ṛṣis as constituting the group, the change between the lists may probably be ascribed to a still earlier period, prior to A.D. 200. At the other end of the time-scale, the change may be said to have occurred subsequent to the composition of the *Hiraṇyakeśin Gṛhya Sūtra* (?c. 300 B.C.): as also subsequent to the composition of the main *kāṇḍas* of the *Rāmāyaṇa* (usually ascribed to the approximate period between c. 250 B.C. and A.D. 200): while yet contemporary with many of the *parvans* of the *Mahābhārata*. Consequently, the period of change between the two main lists of the Seven Ṛṣis may be said to be post-Maurya and pre-Gupta: the likelihood being that the change was effected during the period between approximalely 100 B.C. and A.D. 200.

2

THE MANVANTARA TRADITIONS OF THE SEVEN ṚṢIS

A. Introduction to the Manvantara Theory

In Hindu cosmogony, the Manvantara (literally "the interval of a Manu") is the period of time which is presided over by one Manu and his sons, one Indra, one group of gods, and one group of Seven Ṛṣis. The Manvantara theory itself is of relatively late appearance in the literary sources : it is scarcely dealt with in any detail in the Epics, and is more fully elaborated only in the Harivaṃśa and in certain Purāṇas. It is furthermore only in these latter post-Epic works that lists are to be found of the Seven Ṛṣis in each of the different Manvantaras. Before examining in detail the lists and traditions of these various groups of Seven Ṛṣis, we shall first take a brief look at the underlying Purāṇic theory of Manvantaras.

One of the main components of time-division in both the Epics and the Purāṇas is the succession of four Yugas ("Ages") —namely Kṛta or Satya, Tretā, Dvāpara, and Kali. Each of these Yugas contains a descending degree of *dharma* or virtue : and at the end of each Kali Yuga there occurs a period of dissolution, which is then followed by the commencement of a new Kṛta Yuga—thereby giving a continual cyclical succession of the four Yugas. One complete succession of the four Yugas is termed a Mahāyuga ("great Yuga"): and in each new Mahāyuga it is the task of Manu and the Seven Ṛṣis to instruct men in the Vedas and to renew *dharma*. Each Mahāyuga lasts for a total of 1200 Divine Years, or 4,320,000 years of men. The Manvantara is said to consist of a total of just over 71 Mahāyugas (slightly different totals being given in different texts): hence one group of Seven Ṛṣis reappears on the earth to instruct men in *dharma* during 71 consecutive series of the four Yugas, or during 71 Mahāyugas. There is a total of 14 Manvantaras, and thus a total of 14 different groups of Seven Ṛṣis: and this total of 14 Manvantaras is equal to a total of 1,000 Mahāyugas, or 4,320,000,000 years of men—which is the measure of a Kalpa or Day of Brahmā. At the end of each Kalpa there occurs a dissolution of the worlds (*naimittika pralaya*); the three lower worlds are burnt to ashes by the seven suns, then flooded until they become but a single ocean. Thereafter follows the night of Brahmā—of equal duration to one day of Brahmā—which is in turn followed by a further new day of Brahmā, consisting once again of 14 Manvantaras, having 14 different groups of Seven Ṛṣis, a further 1,000 Mahāyugas, and so forth. As elaborated especially in later Purāṇas, this cosmogonic scheme continues virtually without end. The life of a Brahmā extends over a period of 100 such years whereof the measure of a single day is equal to the period of 14 Manvantaras: and at the end of the life of a Brahmā, there arises a further Brahmā to take his place. Yet even this length of time is considered miniscular within the compass of Divine Time: for each passing of a Brahmā occupies a time which is but a flicker of the eyelids of Viṣṇu . . . . and so continues the cosmogony of the endless cycle of existence.

In addition to this time-dimension, there is additionally a space-dimension which may be briefly mentioned here. While Vedic cosmogony generally refers to three Lokas or worlds—namely Bhūr (the earth), Bhuvar (the atmosphere), and Svar (the sky, heaven)—Purāṇic cosmogony usually refers to seven Lokas—namely these three, together with Mahar, Jana, Tapas, and Brahma or Satya Lokas, the latter of which is the highest or supreme world and the abode of Brahmā. In passages relating to the Manvantara theory, the Seven Ṛṣis are generally said to reside in Maharloka, the fourth of these worlds;[1] then at the end of each Kalpa, when the three worlds (Bhūr,

1. For example *Brahmāṇḍa Purāṇa* 3.4.2.3-4: *Vāyu Purāṇa* 2.39.3-5: *etc.*

Bhuvar and Svar Lokas) are burnt to ashes and flooded, the Seven Ṛṣis move to the next or Jana Loka to escape from the heat,[1] from where they observe Brahmā in the form of Kāla or Time asleep in Maharloka.[2] It should be noted that alternative traditions are also to be found in places: thus for example certain passages relate that the Seven Ṛṣis went directly from the earth to Janaloka;[3] while another passage relates that each group of Seven Ṛṣis is created in each Manvantara, and passes again to destruction at the end of that Manvantara.[4] It would seem likely that such alternative traditions are partly due to the fact that the role of the Seven Ṛṣis within the Manvantara theory—as indeed the Manvantara theory itself—was still in the process of formulation within these texts: a point which we shall further be examining below. Nonetheless, the most frequently-appearing conception in the Purāṇas is that in each Manvantara a group of Seven Ṛṣis appears on the earth to instruct men in the Vedas and in *dharma* (which they have heard from the Ṛṣis of the preceding Manvantara[5]), whereafter they depart to their abode in Maharloka: this process being repeated in every Mahāyuga of the Manvantara, until at the end of the Kalpa of 14 Manvantaras they move to Janaloka while the three lower worlds are successively burnt to ashes and then flooded during the night of Brahmā.[6]

1. For example *Mārkaṇḍeya Purāṇa* 46.39-40: *Viṣṇu Purāṇa* 1.3.20-21.
2. For example *Brahmāṇḍa Purāṇa* 1.2.6.68-69, 3.4.1.184-188: *Mārkaṇḍeya Purāṇa* 46.40-41: *Vāyu Purāṇa* 2.38.186-193: *Viṣṇu Purāṇa* 1.3.22-23.
3. *Brahmāṇḍa Purāṇa* 3.4.2.47-49 : *Vāyu Purāṇa* 2.39.49-51.
4. *Mārkaṇḍeya Purāṇa* 46 33.
5. For example *Matsya Purāṇa* 9.30-31, 145.31-40: *Padma Purāṇa* 5.7.105-106: *Viṣṇu Purāṇa* 3.2.44.
6. Further passages on the Manvantara theory—in addition to those cited in preceding notes—are also to be found in the context of the lists of Seven Ṛṣis in Manvantaras (see below), and at *Agni Purāṇa* 349.4-13: *Brahma Purāṇa* 231.1-232.49: *Garuḍa Purāṇa* 233.1ff.: *Kūrma Purāṇa* 2.43.11ff.: *Saura Purāṇa* 33.9ff.: *Viṣṇu Purāṇa* 6.1.1ff. For further discussion and interpretation, see especially C. D. Church, 'The Purāṇic Myth of the Four Yugas' and 'The Myth of the Four Yugas in the Sanskrit Purāṇas': J. E. Mitchiner, 'The Evolution of the Manvantara Theory': W. D. O'Flaherty, *The Origins of Evil in Hindu Mythology*, pp. 14-45: D. Pocock, 'The Anthropology of Time-Reckoning': H. Zimmer, *Myths and Symbols in Indian Art and Civilisation*.

B. The Lists of the Seven Ṛṣis

As has already been mentioned in the last section, the Epics contain few references to the Manvantara theory, and no lists of the different groups of Seven Ṛṣis in each Manvantara. It would nonetheless appear from certain references that the underlying idea of different groups appearing in each Manvantara was already becoming current: thus for example a passage in the *Anuśāsana Parvan* of the *Mahābhārata* relates that Kṛṣṇa will be reckoned among the Seven Ṛṣis in the Sāvarṇi Manvantara :

> From the fruition of that (spiritual act of) uniting with me, Kṛṣṇa will be born: and he will be one of the Seven Ṛṣis [*saptarṣiś ca bhaviṣyati*] in the creation of Manu Sāvarṇa.[1]

It is at the same time clear that this passage indicates the lack of any definitive Epic formulation of the groups of Seven Ṛṣis in Manvantaras : for as will shortly be seen in examining the Manvantara lists, Kṛṣṇa is nowhere listed as one of the Seven Ṛṣis in the Sāvarṇi—nor indeed in any—Manvantara. Hence, such passages in the *Mahābhārata* witness to an awareness of—but lack of definitive formulation of—the tradition of the appearance of different groups of Seven Ṛṣis in different Manvantaras.

The *Harivaṃśa* is the first text to contain lists of the Seven Ṛṣis in different Manvantaras. Here, however, it would seem that the latter part of the lists—for Manvantaras 9 to 14—was composed and added subsequent to the composition of the main text: for such lists appear in only a relatively few manuscripts and editions of the work—thus for example the B.O.R.I. Critical Edition refers to only 7 manuscripts which contain lists for all 14 Manvantaras,[2] but to a further 28 manuscripts which contain lists for only the first 8 Manvantaras.[3]

1. *Mahābhārata* 12.18.29.

2. Mss. as follows: 1 Śāradā, 2 (of 4) Devanāgarī versions allied to the Śāradā, Devanāgarī versions of Nīlakaṇṭha and Śivadāsa, and 2 (of 6) further Devanāgarī versions.

3. Mss. as follows : 3 Newārī, 3 Maithilī, 3 Bengali, 4 Telugu, 4 Malayālam, 5 Grantha, 2 (of 4) Devanāgarī versions allied to the Śāradā, 4 (of 6) further Devanāgarī versions.

Furthermore, the Ṛṣis who are listed in this work for Manvantaras 9-14 appear with family or *gotra* names (Āṅgirasa, Bhārgava, etc.)—a phenomenon which does not occur with the Ṛṣis listed for Manvantaras 1-8. The addition of *gotra* names is only to be found in the *Vāyu* and *Brahmāṇḍa Purāṇas* for all 14 Manvantaras, and in the *Harivaṃśa* and the *Śiva Purāṇa* for Manvantaras 9 to 14 : and it would seem logical to conclude that such an addition is likely to denote a subsequent development from the mere listing of personal names.

Aside from the *Harivaṃśa* (as just discussed), the *Matsya, Brahma* and *Padma Purāṇas*.contain lists for only the first eight Manvantaras : while the *Kūrma* and *Saura Purāṇas* give lists for only Manvantaras 1 to 7. The *Śiva Purāṇa* lists the Ṛṣis in Manvantaras 1 to 5 singly, omits Manvantaras 6 and 7, and lists the Ṛṣis in Manvantaras 8 to 14 with *gotra* names : while the *Agni* and *Bhāgavata Purāṇas* give only one or two names of Ṛṣis in each Manvantara, for all 14 Manvantaras. Full lists for all fourteen Manvantaras are thus to be found in the *Harivaṃśa* (but only in certain manuscripts of this work), and in the *Mārkaṇḍeya, Viṣṇu, Brahmāṇḍa, Vāyu, Garuḍa,* and *Śiva Purāṇas.*

One noteworthy point with all of these lists is that the Seven Ṛṣis of the second main list of the group (as discussed in Chapter 1) invariably appear as the Ṛṣis of the first or Svāyaṃbhuva Manvantara : and they are frequently not explicitly listed in such contexts, since they have previously been discussed in these texts at great length in connection with their being the Sons of Brahmā or Svayambhū. On the other hand, the Seven Ṛṣis of the first main list invariably appear as the Ṛṣis of the seventh or Vaivasvata Manvantara, the present age.[1] The implications of these appearances will be further examined in section C.

We shall next set out in detail a full list of each of the Seven Ṛṣis in each of the 14 Manvantaras, incorporating all the names and variants as given in the various texts. The relevant passages—and the textual abbreviations used below—

---

1. E.g. *Brahmāṇḍa Purāṇa* 1.2.38.30: *Vāyu Purāṇa* 2.3.24-28.

are as follows :

Agni Purāṇa (*A*) 144.1-22 : *Bhāgavata Purāṇa* (*Bh*) 8.1.20-28, 8.5.3-8, 8.13.5-34 : *Brahma Purāṇa* (*B*) 5.7-45 : *Brahmāṇḍa Purāṇa* (*Bḍ*) 1.2.13.103, 1.2.36.17-78, 1.2.38.26-30, 3.4.1.9-12, 3.4.1.69-114 : *Garuḍa Purāṇa* (*G*) 88.1ff. : *Harivaṃśa* (*H*) 7.7-44, Appendix 1.1 : *Kūrma Purāṇa* (*K*) 1.49.8-33 : *Mārkaṇḍeya Purāṇa* (*Mk*) 67.4, 73.13, 74.59, 75.73-74, 76.54, 79.9-10, 80.4, 94.8-30, 100.31 : *Matsya Purāṇa* (*Mt*) 9.4-36 : *Padma Purāṇa* (*P*) 5.7.83-108 : *Saura Purāṇa* (*S*) 32.1-9, 33.1-8 : *Śiva Purāṇa* (*Ś*) 5.34.9-65 : *Vāyu Purāṇa* (*Vā*) 1.31.15-17, 2.1.15-66, 2.3.24-28, 2.38.9-12, 2.38.66-116: *Viṣṇu Purāṇa* (*Vṣ*) 3.1.11-32, 3.2.17-42.

TABLE 1

The Manvantara Lists of the Seven Ṛṣis

Svāyaṃbhuva Manvantara (1*st*)

Marīci, Atri, Aṅgiras, Pulastya, Pulaha, Kratu, Vasiṣṭha (all).

n.b. also order Marīci, Atri, Aṅgiras, Pulaha, Kratu, Pulastya, Vasiṣṭha (*B*, *Mt*, *Ś*).

note : *Bḍ* and *Vā* have Bhṛgvaṅgiras in place of Aṅgiras (see Chapter 1).

Svārociṣa Manvantara (2*nd*)

1. Ūrja (*A*, *Bh*, *Bḍ*, *G*, *K*, *Mk*, *S*, *Ś*, *Vā*, *Vṣ*) : Aurva (*H*, *B*, *Mt*) : Arvā (*P*).
2. Stamba (all except *Mt*) : Vanastamba (*Mt*).
3. Prāṇa (all except *Vā* and *Ś*) : Droṇa (*Vā*).
4. Dattoli (*Mk*, *Vṣ*) : Dattotri (*B*, *Bḍ*, *H*, *P*) : Dattātri (*Vā*) : Dambholi (*G*) : Datta (*Mt*) : Dānta (*K*, *S*).
5. Ṛṣabha (*Bḍ*, *G*, *Mk*, *S*, *Ś*, *Vā*, *Vṣ*) : Vṛṣabha (*K*) : Bṛhaspati (*B*, *H*, *Mt*, *P*).
6. Niścala (*Bḍ*, *G*, *Vā*) : Niścara (*Mk*, *Vṣ*) : Niścaya (*Mt*): Cyavana (*B*, *H*, *P*) : Timira (*K*, *S*).
7. Arvarīvat (*Bḍ*, *K*, *S*) : Arvavīrat (*G*, *Mk*) : Urvarīvat (*Vṣ*) : Dhāvat (*Vā*) : Kaśyapa (*B*, *H*, *Mt*, *P*).

note : Ś lists Ūrja, Stamba, Parastamba, Ṛṣabha, Vasumat, Jyotiṣmat, Dyutimat, and the 7th (*sic*) Rociṣmat.

Auttami Manvantara (3*rd*)

7 sons of Vasiṣṭha (*A, Bh, Bḍ, Vṣ*) : 7 sons of Vasiṣṭha, the *ūrjāḥ* (*B, H, Mt, Ś*) :

7 sons of that Manu (*Mk*).

These 7 sons of Vasiṣṭha are also named—in the *K, S, G* tradition—in further non-Manvantara contexts in *A* (20.15), *Bḍ* (1.2.11.39-42), *G* (5.1ff.), *L* (1.5.37-50), *Mk* (52.14-26), *Ś* (7.1.17.33-34), *Vā* (1.28.33-35), and *Vṣ* (1.10.13-14) as follows :

Rajas (all except *Bḍ*)/Rakṣa (*Bḍ*); Gātra (*G, Mk, Ś, Vṣ*)/ Gotra (*A*)/Putra (*Vā*)/Gartta (*Bḍ*)/Suhotra (*L*); Ūrdhvabāhu (all except *L*)/Bahu (*L*); Savana (all except *G* and *Mk*)/Sabala (*Mk*)/Śarana (*G*); Anagha (*G, L, Mk, Vṣ*)/Alaghu (*A*)/Anaya (*Ś*)/Adhana (*Vā*)/Pavana (*Bḍ*); Sutapas (all); and Śukra (*A, G, L, Ś, Vṣ*)/Śukla (*Mk, Vā*)/ Śaṃku (*Bḍ*).

A further non-Manvantara list in *Bh* (4.1.40-41) names them as : Citraketu, Suroci, Virajas, Mitra, Ulbaṇa, Vasubhṛdyāna, and Dyumān.

Vā omits altogether : lists in *Mt, P, G, K, S* as follows :

1.	Kaukuruṇḍi (*Mt*) : Kaukibhiṇḍi (*P*).	: 1.	Raja (*K, S*): Rathaujas (G).
2.	Dālbhya (*Mt, P*).	: 2.	Ūrdhvabāhu (*G, K, S*).
3.	Śaṅga (*Mt*) : Śaṅkha (*P*).	: 3.	Ūrdhva (*K*) : Muni (*G*) : Gotra (*S*).
4.	Pravahaṇa (*Mt*) : Pravāhina (*P*).	: 4.	Śarana (*G*) : Sabala (*K*) : Savana (*S*).
5.	Śiva (*Mt*) : Katuṇḍa (*P*).	: 5.	Anagha (*G, S*) : Anaya (*K*).
6.	Sita (*Mt*) : Mita (*P*).	: 6.	Sutapas (*G, K, S*).
7.	Sasmita (*Mt*) : Sammati (*P*).	: 7.	Śaṅku (*G*) : Śukra (*K, S*).

Tāmasa Manvantara (4*th*)

1. Kāvya (*B, Bḍ, H, K, Mk, Vā, Vṣ*) : Kavi (*Mt, P*) : Kalpa (*S*) : Dṛṣṭakavya (*G*) : Gārgya (*Ś*).

2. Pṛthu (all).
3. Agni (all except *Ś*) : Vāgmin (*Ś*).
4. Caitra (*Bḍ*, *G*, *K*, *Mk*, *S*, *Vā*, *Vṣ*) : Jahnu (*B*, *H*) : Jalpa (*Mt*) : Janya (*P*, *Ś*).
5. Jyotirdhāman (*A*, *Bh*, *Bḍ*, *G*, *K*, *Mk*, *S*, *Vā*, *Vṣ*) : Dhātṛ (*B*, *H*, *Ś*) : Dhīmān (*Mt*) : Dhāmān (*P*).
6. Kapīvān (*B*, *H*, *Ś*) : Kapi (*Mt*, *P*) : Valaka (*Mk*) : Vanaka (*K*, *Vṣ*) : Vanapītha (*Vā*) : Caraka (*Bḍ*) : Savana (*S*) : Hemaka (*G*).
7. Pīvara (*Bḍ*, *K*, *Mk*, *S*, *Vṣ*) : Akapīvān (*B*, *H*) : Akapi (*Mt*, *P*) : Kapīnaka (*Ś*) : Gotra (*Vā*).

note : *G* omits 2 Ṛṣis (nos. 2 and 7).

Raivata Manvantara (5*th*)

1. Hiraṇyaroma (all except *H* and *Mk*) : Hiraṇyaloma (*H*, *Mk*).
2. Vedaśrī (*Bḍ*, *K*, *Mk*, *Vā*, *Vṣ*) : Vedaśiras (*B*, *Bh*, *H*, *Ś*) : Devaśrī (*G*) : Viśvaśrī (*S*) : Saptāśva (*Mt*, *P*).
3. Ūrdhvabāhu (all except *Mt* and *P*) : Subāhu (*Mt*, *P*).
4. Vedabāhu (*H*, *K*, *Mk*, *Vā*, *Vṣ*) : Devabāhu (*B*, *Bḍ*, *Mt*, *Ś*) : Vadavāda (*P*) : Aindrabāhu (*S*).
5. Sudhāman (*Bḍ*, *K*, *Mk*, *Vṣ*) : Yadudhra (*B*, *H*) : Yajurnāman (*Vā*) : Somapa (*Mt*, *P*, *Ś*) : Satyanama (*G*) : Subāhu (*S*).
6. Parjanya (all).
7. Satyanetra (*B*, *Bḍ*, *H*, *Vā*) : Mahāmuni (*K*, *S*, *Vṣ*) : Muni (*Mt*, *P*) : Vaśiṣṭha (*Mk*) : Jaya (*Ś*) : Svadharma (*G*).

note : *Mk* no. 6 = Parjanya mahāmuni; *B* no. 2 = muni Vedaśiras; *G* nos. 3-4 = Vedaurdhabāhu.

Cākṣuṣa Manvantara (6*th*)

1. Sudhāman (*B*, *Bḍ*, *H*, *Mt*, *P*, *Vā*) : Sumedhas (*A*, *K*, *Mk*, *S*, *Vṣ*) : Sudyumna+Sadharma (*G*).
2. Virajas (all).
3. Haviṣmat (*Bh*, *Bḍ*, *G*, *K*, *Mk*, *S*, *Vā*, *Vṣ*) : Vivasvat (*B*, *H*, *Mt*, *P*).
4. Uttama (*Bḍ*, *K*, *S*, *Vṣ*) : Unnata (*Mk*, *Vā*) : Bhṛgu (*B*, *H*, *Mt*, *P*) : Sutanu+Śrīmān (*G*).

5. Madhu (*Bḍ*, *K*, *Mk*, *Vā*, *Vṣ*) : Nabha (*B*, *H*) : Nāda (*Mt*) : Budha (*S*) : Nārada (*P*) : Madhuśrī+Nara (*G*).
6. Atināman (*B*, *Bḍ*, *H*, *K*, *Mk*, *Mt*, *Vṣ*) : Atimāna (*Vā*) : Abhimāna (*P*) : Atri (*S*) : Atirartra+Abhimana (*G*).
7. Sahiṣṇu (all except *P*) : Viṣṇu (*P*) : also Agniṣṇu (*G*).

note : *G* gives 12 names; *Ś* omits this Manvantara.

Vaivasvata Manvantara (7*th*)

Viśvāmitra, Jamadagni, Bharadvāja, Gautama, Atri, Vasiṣṭha, Kaśyapa (all except *Ś*, which omits this Manvantara).

n.b. also orders : Atri, Vasiṣṭha, Kaśyapa, Gautama, Bharadvāja, Viśvāmitra, Jamadagni (*B*, *Mk*, *Mt*, *P*, *H*); Atri, Vas, Jam, Kaś, Gaut, Bhar, Viś (*G*); Vas, Kaś, Atri, Jam, Gaut, Viś, Bhar (*Ą*, *K*, *S*, *Vṣ*); Kaś, Atri, Vas, Viś, Gaut, Jam, Bhar (*Bh*).

note : *K* and *S* end their lists with this Manvantara.

Sāvarṇi Manvantara (8*th*)

1. Rāma (all except *Bḍ* and *Vā*) : Jāmadagnya (*Bḍ*, *Vā*).
2. Vyāsa (*B*, *G*, *H*, *Mk*, *Ś*, *Vṣ*) : Dvaipāyaṇa (*Bḍ*, *Vā*) : Kauśika (*Mt*, *P*) : Bādarāyaṇa (*Bh*).
3. Dīptimat (all except *Mt* and *P*) : Śatānanda (*Mt*, *P*).
4. Drauṇiraśvatthāman (*B*, *Bḍ*, *H*, *Ś*, *Vā*) : Aśvatthāman (*G*, *Mt*, *P*) : Droṇi (*Bh*, *Mk*, *Vṣ*).
5. Śaradvat (*B*, *H*, *Mt*, *Ś*) : Kṛpa (*Bh*, *G*, *Mk*, *Vṣ*) : Kṛpa Śaradvat (*Bḍ*, *Vā*).
6. Gālava (all).
7. Ṛṣyaśṛṅga (*Bh*, *Bḍ*, *G*, *Mk*, *P*, *Vā*, *Vṣ*) : Ruru (*H*, *Ś*) : Kāśyapa (*Mt*, *P*) : Aurva Kāśyapa (*B*).
   note : *H* no. 7 = Ruru Kāśyapa; *Mt* and *P* list Gālava and Kauśika separately (as nos. 2 and 6), while rest list singly as Gālava Kauśika.

B, *H*, *Mt* and *P* end their lists with this Manvantara.

Dakṣa-sāvarṇi Manvantara (9*th*)

1. Medhātithi (all except *Vṣ*) : Medhādhṛti (*Vṣ*).
2. Vasu (all).
3. Satya (*Mk*, *Vṣ*) : Sutapas (*Bḍ*, *Vā*) : Paulaha (*H*, *Ś*).

4. Jyotiṣmat (all).
5. Dyutimat (all except *Ś*) : Dhṛtimat (*Ś*).
6. Savana (*A*, *H*, *Ś*) : Sabala (*Mk*) : Śabala (*Vṣ*) : Vasita (*Vā*) : Vasinas (*Bḍ*).
7. Havyavāhana (*Bḍ*, *H*, *Mk*, *Vā*) : Havya (*Ś*) : Bhavya (*Vṣ*).

note : *G* omits this Manvantara; *H* and *Ś* give only the *gotra* name for no. 3.

Brahma-sāvarṇi Manvantara* (10*th*)

1. Haviṣmat (all).
2. Sukṛti (*Bh*, *G*, *Mk*, *Vṣ*) : Sukīrti (*Bḍ*, *Vā*) : Sukriti (*H*) : Prakṛti (*Ś*).
3. Apomūrti (*Bḍ*, *H*, *Mk*, *Vā*, *Vṣ*) : Ayomūrti (*G*) : Ayamukti (*Ś*) : Jayamūrti (*Bh*).
4. Āpava (*Bḍ*) : *api yaḥ* (*Vā*) : Avyaya (*G*) : Aśvatthāman (*H*) : Satyaketu (*Vṣ*) : Vāsiṣṭha (*Mk*, *Ś*).
5. Apratima (*Bḍ*, *G*, *Mk*) : Pratipa (*Vā*) : Pramati (*H*) : Prayati (*Ś*) : Apratimaujas (*Vṣ*).
6. Nābhāga (*Bḍ*, *H*, *Mk*, *Vā*, *Vṣ*) : Lābhāga (*G*) : Bhāmāra (*Ś*).
7. Abhimanyu (*Bḍ*, *Vā*) : Surabha (*G*) : Satya (*Bh*, *Mk*, *Ś*, *Vṣ*) : Nadhas+Satya (*H*) : Ananasa (Ś).

note : *H* and *Ś* list two Ṛṣis for no. 7.

**Bḍ*, *G* and *Vā* call this Manvantara the Dharma-sāvarṇi.

Dharma-sāvarṇi Manvantara* (11*th*)

1. Niścara (*A*, *Bḍ*, *H*, *Mk*, *Vā*, *Vṣ*) : Niḥsvara (*Ś*) : Vistara (*G*).
2. Agnitejas (*Bḍ*, *G*, *H*, *Ś*, *Vā*, *Vṣ*) : Agnideva (*Mk*) : Atitejas (*Bḍ*).
3. Vapuṣmat (*Bḍ*, *Ś*, *Vā*, *Vṣ*): Haviṣmat (*H*): Haviṣya (*G*): Variṣṭa (*Mk*).
4. Viṣṇu (*G*, *Vṣ*): Viṣṭi (*Mk*) : Puṣṭi (*Bḍ*, *Vā*) : Urudhiṣṇu (*H*) : Cārudhṛṣya (*Ś*).

5. Aruṇi (*Bḍ, Mk, Vṣ*): Vāruṇi (*Vā*) : Varuṇa (*G*) : Vāruṇa (*Ś*) : Aruṇa (*Bh*) : Taruṇa (*H*).
6. Haviṣmat (all).
7. Anagha (*Mk, Vṣ*): Anaya (*Ś*): Naga (*Bḍ*) : Bhaga (*Vā*): Viśva (G) : Taruṇa (*H*).

note : **Bḍ* and *Vā* call this Manvantara the Brahma-sāvarṇi; *G* calls it that of Rudra-putra.

Rudra-sāvarṇi Manvantara (12*th*)

1. Dyuti (all except *Vā*) : Kṛti (*Vā*).
2. Tapasvin (all).
3. Sutapas (all).
4. Tapomūrtti (all).
5. Taponidhi (*Mk*): Tapodhana (*Bḍ, Vṣ*) : Tapoṣana (*H*) : Tapo'śayāna (*Vā*): "another" (no name : *G*).
6. Taporati (all).
7. Tapodhṛti (*Bḍ, G, Mk, Ś, Vṣ*) : Tapovriti (*H*): Tapomati (*Vā*).

note : *H* lists only 5 Ṛṣis.

Raucya Manvantara (13*th*)

1. Dhṛtimat (all).
2. Avyaya (*Bḍ, G, Mk, Vṣ*) : Havyaya (*H*) : Havyavat (*Ś*): Pathyavat (*Vā*).
3. Tattvadarśin (all).
4. Nirutsuka (all except *Ś*) : Nirutsava (*Ś*).
5. Nirmoha (all except *Ś*) : Nirdeha (*Ś*).
6. Sutapas (all except *Vā*) : Svarūpa (*Vā*).
7. Niṣprakampa (*H, Mk, Vā, Vṣ*) : Niṣprakampya (*Bḍ*) : Niṣprapañca (*Ś*) : Niśarūpa (*G*).

note : *G* omits no. 6.

Bhautya Manvantara (14*th*)

1. Agnīdhra (all).
2. Agnibāhu (all except *H* and *Ś*) : Ativahu (*H*): Atibāhya (*Ś*).
3. Śuci (all).
4. Mukta (*Bḍ, G, Mk*) : Yukta (*H, Ś, Vṣ*).

5. Māgadha (all except *Mk*) : Mādhava (*Mk*).
6. Śukra (*Bḍ*, *G*, *Mk*, *Vṣ*) : Asukra (*H*) : Śuddha (*Bh*).
7. Ajita (all except *Bḍ*) : Svājita (*Bḍ*).

note : *Vā* omits 3 Ṛṣis (nos. 4, 6, 7); *H* omits no. 5; *Ś* omits no. 6.

From examining the lists in this Table, certain conclusions can be drawn as to which texts draw upon a common tradition, and which follow one tradition as opposed to another.

It is evident throu ghout these lists that the *Harivaṃśa* and the *Brahma*, *Matsya*, and *Padma Purāṇas* are all closely interrelated: very frequently giving names which do not appear in any of the other texts. Furthermore, all four of these texts contain lists for only the first 8 Manvantaras—as has been noted above, the lists in the *Harivaṃśa* for Manvantaras 9-14 have evidently been added subsequent to the main composition of the work. Hence all four of these texts may be said to draw upon a common tradition: and since the *Harivaṃśa* is generally acknowledged to have been composed prior to or contemporary with the earliest Purāṇas, it may be deemed that the *Brahma*, *Matsya* and *Padma Purāṇas* derive their Manvantara lists from the *Harivaṃśa*.

It is also evident that, for Manvantaras 9 to 14, the *Harivaṃśa* and the *Śiva Purāṇa* similarly contain many readings in common which are distinct from those in the other texts: hence they would appear to draw upon a further common tradition for this portion of the lists.

The *Brahmāṇḍa* and *Vāyu Purāṇas* are closely allied throughout their lists: and they additionally contain *gotra* names for each of the Ṛṣis in each Manvantara—in distinction from all of the other texts apart from the lists for Manvantaras 9 to 14 in the *Harivaṃśa* and the *Śiva Purāṇa*. It would consequently seem quite likely that the *Brahmāṇḍa* and *Vāyu Purāṇas* both follow a common tradition: and that the *Harivaṃśa* and the *Śiva Purāṇa* have derived from them their portions of the lists for Manvantaras 9 to 14.

The *Mārkaṇḍeya* and *Viṣṇu Purāṇas* again contain many names in common, in distinction to the other texts, suggestive once again of their drawing upon a common source. The *Agni* and *Bhāgavata Purāṇas*, though they contain only one or two names for each Manvantara, would appear to derive these names from the same source, or from one or both of these texts: while the *Kūrma* and *Saura Purāṇas*, both closely allied to each other (and both containing lists for only the first seven Manvantaras), also appear to follow most closely the lists in the *Mārkaṇḍeya* and *Viṣṇu Purāṇas* (more especially those in the *Viṣṇu*—see Manvantaras 4.6, 5.7, 6.4 and the order in 7). The *Garuḍa Purāṇa* is more independent in its lists: but it too is more closely linked to the *Kūrma-Saura* tradition (see especially Manvantara 3) and to that of the *Viṣṇu Purāṇa* (see for example Manvantaras 8.5, 10.2, 11.4, 12.7, 13.2, 14.6) as opposed to that deriving from the *Harivaṃśa*—while it also has certain features in common with the lists in the *Brahmāṇḍa Purāṇa* (for example Manvantara 2.6 and the name of the 10th Manvantara). The fact that the *Garuḍa Purāṇa* thus draws from several different sources suggests that its lists were probably composed somewhat later than those in many of the other texts.

Three main sources may thus be discerned for the Manvantara lists of the Seven Ṛṣis. The first—and almost certainly the earliest—source is that in the *Harivaṃśa*, listing the Ṛṣis for Manvantaras 1 to 8: which has been followed also in the *Brahma*, *Matsya* and *Padma Purāṇas*. The *Śiva Purāṇa*, in its lists for Manvantaras 1 to 5, is also allied to this source, while also introducing a number of independent names. The second source is that in the *Brahmāṇḍa* and *Vāyu Purāṇas*, characterised both by the inclusion of different names and also by the addition of *gotra* names: and this source has also been followed by the *Harivaṃśa* and the *Śiva Purāṇa* in their lists for Manvantaras 9 to 14. The third source is that in the *Mārkaṇḍeya* and *Viṣṇu Purāṇas*: this has been followed on the one hand by the *Agni* and *Bhāgavata Purāṇas* (listing only one or two Ṛṣis for each Manvantara), and on the other hand by the *Kūrma* and *Saura Purāṇas* (listing the Ṛṣis for only Manvantaras 1 to 7); while it has also been generally followed by the *Garuḍa Purāṇa*, which however also draws upon the *Brahmāṇḍa* source. The relationships between these various texts may thus be set out as follows:

TABLE 2

Sources of the Manvantara Lists

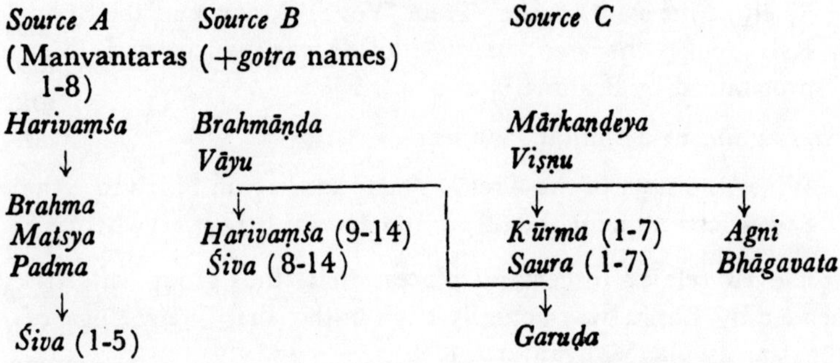

C. The Seven Ṛṣis in Manvantaras and Yugas

Different views are expressed within the Purāṇas as to the precise time at which the Seven Ṛṣis appear on the earth in order to promulgate Vedic knowledge among men. As was noted in section A, in Purāṇic cosmogony each succession of the four Yugas—namely Kṛta or Satya, Tretā, Dvāpara and Kali—is considered to form a part of a constant cyclical succession of Mahāyugas within a Manvantara: thus the end of each Kali Yuga is followed by the commencement of a new Kṛta Yuga, and this process continues throughout the 71 Mahāyugas which constitute a Manvantara. It is variously related that the Seven Ṛṣis appear on earth in either the Kṛta, Tretā or Dvāpara Yugas: although never in the Kali Yuga, which is invariably depicted as being the Yuga during which there occurs the destruction of Vedic knowledge. Certain passages thus relate that the Seven Ṛṣis appear in the Kṛta Yuga in order to establish *dharma*:

> Once the *dharma* of those things established on *śruti* and *smṛti* has been expounded by the Seven Ṛṣis, those ones are present here in the Kṛta Yuga for the sake of establishing *dharma*.[1]

1. *Matsya Purāṇa* 144.97: *Brahmāṇḍa Purāṇa* 1.2.31.108: *etc.*

Other passages relate that the Seven Ṛṣis appear on earth at the start of the Tretā Yuga, in order to promulgate their teachings:

> Then at the start of the Tretā Yuga, Manu and the Seven Ṛṣis spoke the *śruti*, *smṛti* and *dharma* which had been proclaimed by Brahmā.[1]

And again, in a similar manner:

> When the start of the Tretā Yuga has again arrived, the Seven Ṛṣis appoint the *varṇas* and *āśramas* here everywhere.[2]

It is even related in certain places that the group of Ṛṣis headed by Bhṛgu was actually born in the first Tretā Yuga of the Vaivasvata Manvantara:

> Bhṛgu and the others, these Seven great Ṛṣis, were born formerly in the first Tretā Yuga of Manu Vaivasvata.[3]

In further passages, however, the Seven Ṛṣis are said to have been born or to have appeared on earth in the Dvāpara Yuga—as for example in the following:

> The Seven Ṛṣis, desiring offspring, were born here in the Dvāpara: they desired to protect their lineage, and consequently death was conquered by them.[4]

Thus various passages in the Purāṇas ascribe the birth or appearance on earth of the Seven Ṛṣis to either the Kṛta, Tretā, or Dvāpara Yugas.

The tradition of the appearance of Seven Ṛṣis in the Dvāpara Yuga may be in some measure derived from an association between certain of the Ṛṣis in the Sāvarṇi Manvantara—notably Aśvatthāman, son of Droṇa, and Kṛpa—and their well-known appearance as warriors in the Mahābhārata war, which is consistently said to have taken place at the end of the Dvāpara Yuga and shortly before the start of the Kali

1. *Brahmāṇḍa Purāṇa* 1.2.29.43: *Vāyu Purāṇa* 1.57.39.
2. *Brahmāṇḍa Purāṇa* 1.2.35.108: *Vāyu Purāṇa* 1.61.98: *Matsya Purāṇa* 142.47-48.
3. *Brahmāṇḍa Purāṇa* 1.2.13.83: *Vāyu Purāṇa* 1.30.76.
4. *Matsya Purāṇa* 124.106.

Yuga. Thus the Kali Yuga is said to have commenced in the 36th year after the Mahābhārata war, at the moment of Kṛṣṇa's death :

> When the portion of Lord Viṣṇu, he who was born in the family of Vasudeva, had gone to heaven, O Twice-born, then indeed did the Kali arrive.[1]

> When the 36th year (after the war) had been reached, Yudhiṣṭhira, the son of the Kurus, observed inauspicious omens (heralding the death of Kṛṣṇa and the start of the Kali Yuga).[2]

It may also be recalled in this connection that one passage in the *Anuśāsana Parvan* of the *Mahābhārata* relates that Kṛṣṇa will be included as one of the Seven Ṛṣis in the Sāvarṇi Manvantara[3] : an association which again suggests some kind of connection between the Ṛṣis of the Sāvarṇi Manvantara and the period of the Mahābhārata war in the Dvāpara Yuga. Hence the fact that such individuals are said in the *Mahābhārata* and elsewhere to have been born shortly before that war implies that, according to this Yuga scheme, such individuals were born in the Dvāpara Yuga. From this, the necessity would have arisen of stating that certain of the groups of Seven Ṛṣis—notably those of the Sāvarṇi Manvantara, in which the above individuals are listed—are also at times born in the Dvāpara Yuga, rather than in the Kṛta or Tretā Yugas. An alternative explanation might have been to suggest that these same individuals became members of the group of Seven Ṛṣis long afterwards, in a different birth and in a different Manvantara : yet such an explanation is never in fact offered in these texts. Indeed, were this so, then it might be expected that in a later birth they would be known by different names : just as the Ṛṣis of the Svāyaṃbhuva Manvantara are said to have been born for a second time under different names (see below), and just as Agastya is said to have been born as Dattoli (in the

1. *Viṣṇu Purāṇa* 4.24.34-38.
2. *Mahābhārata* 16.1.1, 16.2.2, 16.3.18.
3. Ibid., 12.18.29.

Svārociṣa Manvantara—see Manvantara 2.4), having been known as Agastya only in the Svāyaṃbhuva Manvantara :

> Dattoli became his son on Prīti, the wife of Pulastya : in a former birth in the Svāyaṃbhuva-age he was known as Agastya.[1]

But no such explanation or change of name is given in the case of the above individuals.

Several of the individuals who are listed as the Seven Ṛṣis of the Sāvarṇi Manvantara are said in the Epics and Purāṇas to have been literally fathered by individuals who are listed as the Seven Ṛṣis of the Vaivasvata Manvantara, the present seventh age : as for example Rāma by Jamadagni[2], Droṇa and Aśvatthāman by Bharadvāja[3], Kṛpa by Gautama[4], and Gālava by Viśvāmitra[5]. Similarly, the Seven Ṛṣis of the Vaivasvata Manvantara are themselves said to have been fathered by individuals who are listed as the Seven Ṛṣis of the Svāyaṃbhuva Manvantara : as for example Jamadagni (and Viśvāmitra[6]) by Bhṛgu,[7] Bharadvāja and Gautama by Aṅgiras,[8]

1. *Mārkaṇḍeya Purāṇa* 52.22-23: *Brahmāṇḍa Purāṇa* 1.2.11.26: *Vāyu Purāṇa* 1.28.21: *Viṣṇu Purāṇa* 1.10.9.

2. E.g. *Rāmāyaṇa* 1.74.10ff.: *Mahābhārata* 1.60.39-48, 1.98.1-5, 1.121.12-33, 3.83.14-40, 3.85.9-12, 3.115.9ff., 3.286.8, 12.49.1ff., *etc.*

3. E.g. *Mahābhārata* 1.57.88-90, 1.61.63, 1.121.3-9, 3.42.19, 5.54.47-48, 7.159.2, 7.167.37ff., *etc.*

4. E.g. *Mahābhārata* 1.57.88-90, 1.120.2-21, 5.54.37-48, 5.163.20-21, 15.30.6. *etc.*

5. E.g. *Mahābhārata* 5.104.1-5.117.23: *Harivaṃśa* 9.88-100: *Vāyu Purāṇa* 2.29.64-99: *Brahmāṇḍa Purāṇa* 2.3.63.85ff., 2.3.66.35-77: *etc.*

6. E.g. *Mahābhārata* 13.56.1-19: *etc.*

7. E.g. *Mahābhārata* 3.115.9-13, 12.49.1ff., 13.4.1ff., 13.56.1ff.: *Harivaṃśa* 23.82-94: *Brahmāṇḍa Purāṇa* 2.3.66.35-77: *Vāyu Purāṇa* 2.29.64-99: *Viṣṇu Purāṇa* 4.7.1ff.: *etc.* On the inclusion of Bhṛgu among the Seven Ṛṣis. see Chapter 1 and also below. Cf. also Śrauta Sūtras on the descent of Jamadagni from Bhṛgu (next note).

8. E.g. *Mahābhārata* 1.121.12-18, 3.209.1-9, 13.31.22ff.: *Harivaṃśa* 23.49-53: *Matsya Purāṇa* 49.14-35: *Viṣṇu Purāṇa* 4.19,1ff.:*Bṛhaddevatā* 5.102-103: *etc.* See also Bharadvāja and Gautama as Āṅgirases, in *Āśvalāyana Śrauta Sūtra* 12.1-15: *Āpastamba Śrauta Sūtra* 24.5.10: *Hiraṇyakeśin Śrauta Sūtra* 8.714ff. (ASS ed.) : *Baudhāyana Śrauta Sūtra, pariśiṣṭa*: *Mānava Śrauta Sūtra* 11.8.1-10: *Vaikhānasa Sūtra, pravara-praśna.*

and Kaśyapa by Marīci.[1] As we saw in chapter 1, these two lists of Seven Ṛṣis of the Svāyambhuva and Vaivasvata Manvantaras are the only two which are termed the Seven Ṛṣis in the Epics and Purāṇas, apart from within the Purāṇic Manvantara traditions. Consequently, the three groups of Ṛṣis—of the Svāyambhuva, Vaivasvata and Sāvarṇi Manvantaras—are thus linked with one another in a way which does not occur with the other groups of Seven Ṛṣis in other Manvantaras. One passage in the *Brahmāṇḍa* and *Vāyu Purāṇas* goes so far as to state that the Seven Ṛṣis of the Svāyambhuva Manvantara were born again for a second time "after a long period" in the Vaivasvata Manvantara : thereby linking the Ṛṣis of these two Manvantaras yet again, to the exclusion of any Ṛṣi in the five intermediate Manvantaras (since their Vaivasvata rebirth, with new names, is said to be only their second rebirth :

> In the first Manvantara these were the past producers of creation : in the Svāyambhuva Manvantara these were formerly the Seven great Ṛṣis. When the period of Cākṣuṣa had passed and that of Vaivasvata had been reached....They had been the Seven Ṛṣis, born as the Seven Mind-born ones; and having been adopted into sonship by Svayambhū himself, the Ṛṣis were born for a second time after a long period—so we have heard. Bhṛgu, Aṅgiras and Marīci, Pulastya, Pulaha, Kratu, Atri and Vasiṣṭha : these are the eight Sons of Brahmā.[2]

This passage has already been commented upon in Chapter 1, in respect of the addition of Bhṛgu to the group of Ṛṣis. As was seen there, it raises the question as to whether the form *bhṛgvaṅgiras* used in this passage represents one or two (Bhṛgu,

1. E.g. *Rāmāyana* 1.69.17, 2.102.3ff., 1.45.1ff.: *Mahābhārata* 1.59.9ff., 1.60.33-35, 12.200.1-46, 12.201.8, 13.47.61, 13.85.15ff., 13.151.12: *Harivaṃśa* 3.45-49, 31.100-109: *Brahmāṇḍa Purāṇa* 1.2.13.78-80, 1.2.38.1, 2.3.1.113ff., 2.3.3.84-118, 2.3.4.34, 2.3.5.35, 2.3.7.463ff., 3.4.2.32-34: *Vāyu Purāṇa* 1.30.72-73 2.3.1, 2.4.109ff., 2.5.101, 2.6.43-44, 2.6.76, 2.8.334ff., *Mārkaṇḍeya Purāṇa* 104.1-9: *etc.*

2. *Brahmāṇḍa Purāṇa* 2.3.1.7-21: *Vāyu Purāṇa* 2.4.7-21: *Brahma Purāṇa* 34.27-49: *Skanda Purāṇa* 7.1.19.63-67.

Aṅgiras) Ṛṣis; and while the above pa sage speaks first of Seven Ṛṣis and Mind-born Sons but then lists eight Sons of Brahmā, a further parallel passage retains the number seven by envisaging *bhṛgvaṅgiras* in its grammatically correct sense as a single Ṛṣi :

> Bhṛgvaṅgiras and Marīci, Pulastya, Pulaha, Kratu, Atri, and Vasiṣṭha were the Seven in the Svāyambhuva age.[1]

A discussion of this phenomenon of the increasing size of lists of the Seven Ṛṣis may be found in Chapter 1.

The fact that the Ṛṣis of the Svāyambhuva, Vaivasvata and Sāvarṇi Manvantaras are often said to be paternally and filially related to one another—in a way which does not occur with the other Ṛṣis in the Manvantara lists—suggests the possibility that the Manvantara tradition of listing different groups of Seven Ṛṣis evolved in some measure from an earlier pre-Purāṇic idea about the traditional chronological succession of Ṛṣiṣ : wherein these Ṛṣis were separated from one another by a period of relatively short duration, rather than—as in the Purāṇic Manvantara theory—by a period of some $71 \times 4{,}320{,}000$ years of men. In this connection one may note that the Ṛṣis who are listed for both the Vaivasvata and the Sāvarṇi Manvantaras—and to a lesser extent, those listed also for the Svāyambhuva Manvantara—are frequently associated throughout the Epics and Purāṇas with Kings and Kṣatriyas descended from Manu Vaivasvata : hence in one sense all of these Ṛṣis are on one level considered to have lived during the present Vaivasvata Manvantara. It would therefore seem that, prior to the formulation of the Purāṇic Manvantara theory, the period of time separating these three groups of Ṛṣis was thought to be relatively small. In order to find out more precisely what this period of time might have been, we shall next examine the evolution of ideas in the Epics and Purāṇas about the three time-divisions of Yugas, Manvantaras and Kalpas.

We have elsewhere discussed at length the nature of the *Yuga-Purāṇa* chapter cotained in the *Gārgiya-jyotiṣa* : which may be

1. *Brahmāṇḍa Purāṇa* 1.2.13.103: *Vāyu Purāṇa* 1.31.16-17.

considered as an early prototype of the classical Mahā-Purāṇas, and was probably composed in approximately 25 B.C. (i.e. contemporary wth the Epics).[1] This work refers to the two time-divisions of the Yuga and the Kalpa, but it makes no mention whatever of the Manvantara; thus for example it states in one passage (which appears also in the *Brahma Purāṇa*) that a Kalpa is made up of 1,000 (Mahā-) Yugas :

> At the aforesaid end of 1,000 Yugas, the Kalpa is said to be finished.[2]

The omission of the Manvantara from this time-divisional scheme in the *Yuga-Purāṇa* might be interpreted as an indication that the time-division of the Manvantara was a relatively late addition to the earlier scheme of Yugas and Kalpas. A further such indication is evident in the fact that, while the Kalpa is divided into exactly 1,000 Mahāyugas, no such exact division is evident in the number of Mahāyugas which constitute a Manvantara—on the contrary, the texts themselves disagree as to the precise number. Thus different Purāṇas and astronomical texts give the total as either 71, 71 and a fraction, or 72 Mahāyugas : and in exact mathematical terms, a complete Manvantara (given a total of 14 Manvantaras in a Kalpa) will last for $1{,}000 \div 14 = 71.42$ Mahāyugas. Such a mathematical discrepancy in the number of Mahāyugas in a Manvantara is noted for example in the *Mārkaṇḍeya Purāṇa*, which acknowledges the necessity of adding an additional fraction of a Yuga :

> 71 and an excess number of the four Yugas is a Manvantara: hear from me the reckoning of that in years of men.[3]

Moreover, such a scheme logically demands that a Manvantara will end after .42 of a Mahāyuga—or in other words, towards the end of a Tretā Yuga, at which point the next Manvantara will commence. Yet such an idea is not in fact put forward in any

1. See J. E. Mitchiner, 'The Yuga Purāṇa', pp. 923-24; also *ibid.*, *The Yuga-Purāṇa, passim.*
2. *Yuga-Purāṇa* ślokas 115; *Brahma Purāṇa* 5.60.
3. *Mārkaṇḍeya Purāṇa* 46.34.

of the Purāṇas, which envisage the Manvantara—as also the Kalpa—as commencing with a Kṛta Yuga and ending with a Kali Yuga. It is unlikely that such inaccuracies and discrepancies in the theory would have arisen if the three units of Yuga, Kalpa and Manvantara had been formulated at the same time, since they would otherwise have been combined in a more harmonious system (for example of 10 Manvantaras in a Kalpa, each consisting of 100 Mahāyugas), and the various texts would not then have disagreed upon the exact number (71, 71+or 72) of Mahāyugas in a Manvantara. This consequently again implies that the unit of the Manvantara—as also the various groups of Seven Ṛṣis who appear in each Manvantara—was devised subsequent to the formulation of the units of Yugas and Kalpas.

A divergence of views on these various units of time—division is apparent between the Epics on the one hand and the Purāṇas on the other hand. Firstly virtually the only passage in the *Rāmāyaṇa* which refers in any detail to the Yugas appears in the later *Uttara Kāṇḍa*; it speaks only in terms of a single succession of the four Yugas (namely Kṛta, Tretā, Dvāpara, and Kali), and envisages the universal conflagration as occurring at the end of each of these individual Yugas—followed by a reabsorption of All into Brahmā, prior to the commencement of the next Yuga (rather than of the next Kalpa, as in the Purāṇas).[1] Secondly, one of the relatively few passages in the *Mahābhārata* which makes any detailed reference to the Yugas—and which appears in the *Vana Parvan*—once again implies a scheme wherein the four Yugas occupy the total length of the Kalpa; like both the *Rāmāyaṇa* and the *Yuga-Purāṇa* passages, it makes no mention of the Manvantara as a unit of time. The passage speaks of the different colours assumed by the supreme being in the Kṛta, Tretā, Dvāpara, and Kali Yugas—and then relates that at the end of these he will destroy the three worlds (as occurs, in the Purāṇas, at the end of each Kalpa), thereafter sleeping for a period equal to 1,000 times the length of these four Yugas:

> My colour is white in the Kṛta Yuga, yellow in the Tretā Yuga; having reached the Dvāpara Yuga, it is red, and black

1. *Rāmāyaṇa* 7.65.8-26.

> in the Kali Yuga. In that time [namely in the Kali Yuga] there are three portions of *adharma* [unrighteousness]; and when the time of the end has been reached, I alone—having become fearful Time—shall entirely destroy the three worlds both stationary and mobile. As long as are 1,000 revolutions of the Yugas, O foremost of Ṛṣis, for so long do I sleep, the soul of the universe, the grandsire of all the worlds.[1]

The description of events in this passage continues with the start of a new Kṛta Yuga; yet it would appear that this is not conceived as occurring within the same Kalpa, since the passage relates that when this new Kṛta Yuga arrives, it is heralded by the birth of a Brahmin called Kalki who destroys all things as he brings the former Yuga to an end:

> When the Moon and the Sun, and Tiṣya and Bṛhaspati, move together into the same *rāśi*, then will the Kṛta approach. . . .Kalki, called Viṣṇuyaśas [the glory of Viṣṇu], will be born as a Twice-born under the impulsion of Time—of great energy, and of great intellect and power. . . .Born a brilliant and highly intelligent Brahmin, he will cause the destruction of the whole Yuga, bringing it to an end.[2]

In this passage, the reign of Kalki—which occurs at the end of the Kali Yuga and at the approach of a new Kṛta Yuga—seems to herald the start not merely of a new Yuga but also of a new creation; or in other words, the end of the Kali Yuga seems to herald the end of what in Purāṇic terms is called the Kalpa, when all beings are destroyed through the agency of Kalki. We shall further discuss this interpretation of the passage in a moment.

One further passage in the *Mahābhārata* provides a clear indication that the idea of a single succession of the four Yugas constituting the total extent of a Kalpa or day of Brahmā was

---

1. *Mahābhārata* 3.187.31-39.

2. Ibid., 3.188.87-92; compare for example *Viṣṇu Purāṇa* 4.24.25-31. Corresponding passages in other texts do not always include mention of Kalki: for example *Brahmāṇḍa Purāṇa* omits Kalki at 2.3.74.223, and only contains a brief mention at 2.3.74.206.

at one stage accepted within the theory of Yugas and Kalpas. The passage occurs in the *Śānti Parvan*; as in the passage from the *Vana Parvan*, it makes no mention of the Manvantara as a unit of time—even though it does speak of certain Manus as living within each lifetime of Brahmā (unlike the Purāṇic scheme, which speaks of all 14 Manus as living within a single day of Brahmā). The passage gives an account of the different births of Brahmā—a concept which differs markedly from the expanded time-scheme in the Purāṇas. It first relates that in one of his births, Brahmā instructed Manu Svārociṣa in the Vedas during the Kṛta Yuga, who passed on the knowledge to his son; but when the Kṛta Yuga ended and the Tretā Yuga began, that knowledge was lost. Brahmā then passed through successive births, until in his present seventh birth he instructed Dakṣa, who passed on the knowledge to Āditya his eldest son, from whom Vivasvat obtained it—and at the start of the Tretā Yuga, Vivasvat gave the knowledge to Manu, who in turn passed it on to his son Ikṣvāku:

> Then the god, the bestower of boons, the grandsire of Brahmaloka, created all the worlds, mobile and immobile. At the start he set in motion the auspicious Kṛta Yuga; then indeed *sātvata dharma* [the rule of true righteousness] pervaded and was established in the worlds. Through that first *dharma* Brahmā, the creator of the worlds, paid homage to lord Hari Nārāyaṇa [Viṣṇu], the supreme lord of the gods. Then, for the preservation of *dharma*, he instructed Manu Svārociṣa through desire for the welfare of the worlds; and Svārociṣa, the intent and mighty lord of all the worlds, of old instructed his own son Śaṅkhapāda, O prince. . . .Then that [teaching] became lost, once the Tretā Yuga had arrived. . . .At the start of the Kṛta, O tiger of the Kurus, having studied this *dharma*, Vīraṇas gave it to Raucya Manu. . . .This is the seventh birth of Brahmā, from a lotus, O prince; here, this *dharma* was spoken by Nārāyaṇa himself to the pure grandsire, he who upholds the worlds, at the start of the Yuga. The grandsire formerly gave this *dharma* to Dakṣa: then Dakṣa gave it to the eldest son of his eldest daughter, O best of princes—to Āditya, the eldest of Savitṛ; Vivasvat then

took it. At the start of the Tretā Yuga, once again, Vivasvat gave it to Manu; and Manu, for the well-being of the worlds, gave it to his son Ikṣvāku.[1]

The passage speaks of no further births of Brahmā after his present seventh birth. It clearly indicates that only one Manu is here thought to live during each lifetime of Brahmā, prior to his continual rebirth; it also indicates that such a period of time—of each Manu and each lifetime of Brahmā—is thought to consist of only a single Mahāyuga or succession of the four Yugas—with *dharma* being taught in the Kṛta Yuga, passed on through the Tretā Yuga, and then lost until it is subsequently retaught in the next Kṛta Yuga which follows after a new rebirth of Brahmā. Wide divergences are thus evident between this view and that presented in the Purāṇas. Furthermore, the passage mentions Raucya Manu, placing him after Svārociṣa Manu and before Vaivasvata Manu—in marked contrast to the Purāṇic Manvantara tradition, wherein Raucya or Ruci appears as the 13th Manu; while it also mentions that the second birth of Brahmā was the *cākṣuṣa* birth, wherein he was born from the eyes of Nārāyaṇa.

This was the *cākṣuṣa* birth, the second (birth) of Brahmā, O prince.[2] The term *cākṣuṣa* which is used here is the same as the name of the sixth or Cākṣuṣa Manvantara in the Purāṇic scheme; although there is once again a contrast with that scheme, since the *cākṣuṣa* birth is here termed the second birth, while the Cākṣuṣa Manvantara is the sixth Manvantara which immediately precedes the Vaivasvata Manvantara in the Purāṇic scheme. This passage from the *Śānti Parvan*—as also the passage cited earlier from the *Vana Parvan*—may accordingly be taken to indicate that the *Mahābhārata* follows a different theory of Yugas from that which is followed in the Purāṇas—a theory wherein a single succession of the four Yugas constitutes the total extent of a Kalpa or day of Brahmā (or lifetime of Brahmā, in the case of the *Śānti Parvan* passage), and wherein such a Kalpa of four Yugas is the period of time which is presided

1. *Mahābhārata* 12.336.30-47.
2. Ibid., 12.336.15.

over by one Manu (although the term Manvantara does not appear in these Epic contexts). This theory of a Kalpa as consisting of four Yugas would itself seem to be developed from the earlier-noted *Rāmāyaṇa* idea of a Kalpa—or period between cosmic dissolutions—as consisting of but a single Yuga; wherein each Yuga is followed by a period of destruction, which in the *Mahābhārata* occurs at the end of each Mahāyuga, and in the Purāṇas occurs at the end of each Kalpa (*naimittika pralaya*, destroying the three worlds). Thus a clear evolutionary pattern emerges in respect of the development of this theory, wherein the time-periods are steadily increased between the *Rāmāyaṇa*, the *Mahābhārata*, and the Purāṇas.

A further discrepancy is evident in many of the Flood accounts in these texts. According to the Purāṇic Manvantara scheme, the great flood of the three worlds is said to occur at the end of each Kalpa of 14 Manvantaras; yet the flood-legend in the *Mahābhārata* relates that Manu Vaivasvata—together with the Seven Ṛṣis—survived the flood, and was thereafter the creator of the next age.[1] In other words, the flood-legend in the *Mahābhārata* presupposes that the great flood and period of dissolution occurs at the end of each Kalpa or period of time presided over by a Manu; while in the Purāṇas, the flood is still thought to occur at the end of each Kalpa, but not (since the Kalpa is there divided into 14 Manvantaras) at the end of each period of a Manu. Certain Purāṇas which recount the flood-legend nonetheless adopt the *Mahābhārata* account, and relate that the *pralaya*—the burning and flooding of the three worlds—occurred at the end of the last Yuga, Kalpa or Cākṣuṣa period, when Manu and the Seven Ṛṣis spent the night of Brahmā on the waters before acting as the creators of the new Kalpa or Kṛta Yuga.[2] It is thus clear that certain Purāṇas have incorporated the flood-legend without making an adequate attempt to harmonise it with their further accounts of the Manvantara traditions—wherein the flood occurs not at the end of the Manvantara but at the end of the Kalpa. We can

1. *Mahābhārata*, 3.185.1-54.

2. For example *Agni Purāṇa* 2.3ff,: *Bhāgavata Purāṇa* 8.24.1ff.; *Matsya Purāṇa* 1.11ff.

consequently see here once again a still unfinalised stage in the formulation of the Manvantara tradition in the early Purāṇas.

Since the Manvantara unit is not referred to in any of the above-noted Epic passages which deal with the different time-divisions, it is evident that the Manvantara was not considered by the Epic writers to be a constituent part of the units of Yuga and Kalpa—a conclusion which has already been suggested by the omission of the Manvantara from the time-divisional scheme in the *Yuga Purāṇa*. It is further noteworthy that neither the *Rāmāyaṇa* nor the *Mahābhārata*, nor indeed the *Yuga Purāṇa* speaks of either *dharma* or the Vedas as being taught by the Seven Ṛṣis (as appears in the Purāṇic Manvantara tradition); the *Mahābhārata* on the contrary relates that *dharma* was taught by Brahmā himself. This further indicates that both the Manus and the Seven Ṛṣis were assimilated to the scheme of Yugas and Kalpas only at a relatively late and essentially post-Epic stage in the formulation of these traditions; conversely such Epic passages as those just discussed may be seen as precursors of the Manvantara theory as it is to be found developed in the Purāṇas.

According to the scheme in the *Śānti Parvan* of the *Mahābhārata* the seventh birth of Brahmā—which is also said to be the period of Manu Vaivasvata—is considered as the present age within which there live the kings descended from that Manu, commencing with Ikṣvāku. According to this passage, therefore, there should have occurred within this period the births of the Seven Ṛṣis headed by Viśvāmitra (of the Vaivasvata Manvantara, in the Purāṇic scheme), who are consistently associated throughout Vedic, Epic and Purāṇic texts with Ikṣvāku and the Aikṣvākus, hence also with the Tretā Yuga of this period within which Ikṣvāku is said in the above passage to have lived. There should also have occurred within this period the births of the Ṛṣis who appear in the Purāṇic lists as the Seven Ṛṣis of the Sāvarṇi Manvantara, and who took part in the Mahābhārata war in the Dvāpara Yuga of this seventh or Vaivasvata period (as was discussed earlier in this section). Moreover, the Ṛṣis who appear in the Purāṇic lists as the Seven Ṛṣis of the Svāyambhuva Manvantara (namely Marīci, *etc.*) are consistently said to be the sons first created by Brahmā before all other gods, demons and men.[1] they are consequently implicitly associated with the start of a new creation, and thus with the first or Kṛta Yuga of such a creation. It is, therefore, likely that at one stage in the formulation of these traditions—prior to the multiplication of groups of Seven Ṛṣis in the Purāṇic Manvantara lists—each of these three groups of Seven Ṛṣis was thought to have appeared or been born on the earth at different periods within the same Kalpa or day of Brahmā (or lifetime of Brahmā, in terms of the *Śānti Parvan* conception); just as the members of all three groups are in places associated with kings who are said to have lived during the present age of Manu Vaivasvata, and are each said to be directly related, paternally and filially, to each other (as discussed earlier in this section). Hence, given the varying Purāṇic traditions noted at the start of this section as to the appearance or birth of the Seven Ṛṣis on earth during either the Kṛta, Tretā or Dvāpara Yugas, it would seem that at an early pre-Purāṇic stage in the formulation of these traditions, each of these three groups was thought to have lived on earth during the different Yugas of a single Kalpa—such a Kalpa being made up of only a single succession of the four Yugas (as in the *Mahābhārata* scheme). Only at a subsequent stage—with the division of the Kalpa into 14 separate periods or Manvantaras, each containing 71.42 Mahāyugas—was the number of these groups expanded; and different groups of Seven Ṛṣis were formulated, and thought to appear within different Manvantaras.

One reason for the formulation of such a tradition—wherein different groups of Seven Ṛṣis are thought to appear on earth at different times—may be traced in the first instance to the acknowledgement, from the Epics onwards, of two separate lists of the Seven Ṛṣis (see Chapter 1): whence in order to explain this, it was said that each group lived or appeared on the earth at a different period of time. Consequently, once the

1. See most Epic and Purāṇic accounts of creation; e.g. *Mahābhārata* 12.201.1ff., 12.327.29 ff. : *Harivaṃśa* 1.28-30 : *Brahmāṇḍa Purāṇa* 1.1.5.69-84, 1.2.8.1 ff., 1.2.9.18 ff *Vāyu Purāṇa* 1.9.61 ff. : *Matsya Purāṇa* 3.2-46, 4.26-27; *Mārkaṇḍeya Purāṇa* 50.1-25 : *Viṣṇu Purāṇa* 1.7.3 ff. : *etc.*

existence of two separate groups of Seven Ṛṣis was accepted, the way was open for the multiplication of the number of groups of Seven Ṛṣis—as occurs in the Purāṇic Manvantara theory. In theory, any number of groups of Seven Ṛṣis might then have been formulated; and the choice of a number such as 10 would have been a logical step, since a Manvantara would then have been divided into an exact number of 100 Mahāyugas—given a total of 1,000 Mahāyugas in a Kalpa. However, the choice of the number 14 would appear to have been influenced by the particular significance of the number 7. The peculiar importance of the number 7 in both Indian and many other cultures is well-acknowledged, and scarcely needs further comment in the present context; in Indian culture, for example, one may refer to the seven Ṛṣis, seven Mothers, seven Worlds and seven Hells, seven Continents, seven Footsteps, seven Tongues and seven Rays of Agni, seven Horses of the Sun, seven *cakras* and seven *prāṇas* and innumerable further instances of the importance and symbolic significance attached to this number. In the passage cited previously from the *Śānti Parvan* of the *Mahābhārata*, the present age of Manu Vaivasvata is said to be the period of the seventh birth of Brahmā; it is also considered to be the final age, and no further births of Brahmā are referred to in the passage. Hence, given that the present age is the seventh age, it may be seen that the Purāṇic Manvantara theory—in accepting the present age as the seventh, and in speaking of a total of 14 ages in a Kalpa—propounds that an equal length of time as has passed in the Kalpa is also to come about in the future. There is thus a fundamental difference in outlook between such passages in the Epics on the one hand and the Purāṇas on the other hand. The *Mahābhārata* sees the present seventh age as being at the end of time, and it may be said to envisage the reign of Kalki as ushering a universal destruction, as at the end of the Kalpa. The Purāṇic Manvantara theory, on the other hand, takes a different perspective; it places the present seventh age not at the end but at the centre of time—adopting the Epic view that the present age is the seventh, but now holding additionally that a further seven ages are yet to come. Thus a quite different time-perspective is adopted between the Epics and the Purāṇas.

In respect of the views put forward in these texts on the role of Kalki, it would seem likely that the Kalki-concept owes its origin in some measure to similar Jewish, Christian, Zoroastrian and other concepts, wherein a messianic figure appears at the end of time to destroy the present evil world-order and to usher in a new golden age quite different from the present order.[1] The passage cited earlier from the *Vana Parvan* of the *Mahābhārata* agrees with such a view in certain respects—inasmuch as it envisages the appearance of Kalki as heralding the destruction of all beings at the end of the present age, while yet also accommodating this to the further view of a continuation into a new Kṛta Yuga or golden age which is seen in a sense as a re-creation of the former world-order. This is comparable with the conception in the *Yuga-Purāṇa*—which in one place corresponds word for word with the *Vana Parvan* passage[2]—wherein the total destruction at the end of the Kali Yuga is followed by the commencement of a new Kṛta Yuga, which is again a re-creation of the type of world-order which had previously existed. However, the scheme in the *Yuga Purāṇa* would seem to be far more historically-aligned-constructed especially around the post-Maurya/pre-Sātavāhana period of Indo-Greek and Śaka incursions[3]—than those in either the *Mahābhārata* or the Purāṇas; it furthermore makes no reference either to Kalki or to any Manu or group of Seven Ṛṣis, which implies once again that the Yuga-Kalpa divisions were at one time quite independent both of the Manvantara unit and also of the messianic Kalki-concept.

Referring once more to the divergence of views between the Epics and Purāṇas, it is evident that the Manvantara lists deriving from Source A (Section B, Table 2 above)—namely those in the *Harivaṃśa* and in the *Brahma*, *Matsya*, *Padma*, and.

1. See especially the discussions in A. L. Basham, *The Wonder that was India*, p. 309 : E. Abegg, *Der Messiasglaube in Indien und Iran*, pp. 39-144 and 241-244 : W. D. O'Flaherty, *The Origins of Evil in Hindu Mythology*, pp. 83 and 200-204.

2. *Yuga-Purāṇa Śloka* 55 a-b=*Mahābhārata* 3.186.33; discussed in J. E. Mitchiner, 'The Paris Manuscript of the Yuga Purāṇa', and *The Yuga-Purāṇa*.

3. See the discussions in J. E. Mitchiner, 'The Yuga Purāṇa'.

Śiva (for Manvantaras 1-5) *Purāṇas*—represent in one sense an intermediate stage between the two views. For as was seen in the last section, they list a total of 8 groups of Seven Ṛṣis in Manvantaras : namely the 7 groups down to the present age, together with one further group whose members—although they took part in the Mahābhārata war of the present age—are now considered as the Seven Ṛṣis of a future age. In the Purāṇas deriving their Manvantara lists from Sources B and C, the total of 2×7 groups of Seven Ṛṣis in Manvantaras has been formulated, and the embryonic theory of the Epics has reached a considerably fuller stage of development.

We shall conclude this section by indicating the five main stages of development whereby the Seven Ṛṣis were assimilated to the various units of Yugas, Kalpas and Manvantaras.

(1) The first stage—evident from the Epics onwards—recognises the existence of not one but two main lists of the Seven Ṛṣis (as was discussed in detail in Chapter 1). This stage is particularly apparent in the *Mahābhārata*.

(2) The second stage ascribes the appearance of each of these two groups on the earth to a different period of time, and to a different Yuga within a single Kalpa (in accordance with the pre-Manvantara Epic scheme of a Kalpa of four Yugas) : namely the Seven Ṛṣis of the second main list to the Kṛta Yuga, and those of the first main list to the Tretā Yuga.

(3) The third stage formulates a further group of Seven Ṛṣis—consisting of Kṛpa, Aśvatthāman and others—and ascribes their appearance on earth to the Dvāpara Yuga of the same Kalpa.

All three of these stages still presuppose the type of outlook which is present in the *Śānti Parvan* passage of the *Mahābhārata*, wherein a single succession of the four Yugas constitutes the total extent of a Kalpa.

(4) The fourth stage appears in the Manvantara lists deriving from Source A : wherein these three groups are assimilated to the developing post-Epic scheme of Manvantaras, being ascribed respectively to Manvantaras 1, 7 and 8—and five new groups of Seven Ṛṣis are formulated for the intervening Manvantaras 2 to 6.

(5) The fifth stage appears in the Manvantara lists deriving from Sources B and C : wherein six further groups of Seven Ṛṣis are formulated for the remaining Manvantaras 9 to 14—thus completing the tradition of the appearance of different groups of Seven Ṛṣis in each of the 14 Manvantaras.

It is evident that, while the first stage appears in the *Mahābhārata* and the fourth and fifth stages appear in different Purāṇas, the second and third stages are essentially intermediate—being both post-Epic and pre-Purāṇic. Nonetheless, the fourth stage presupposes both the second and the third stages : traces of which may still be seen in the different Purāṇic traditions which ascribe the birth or appearance of the Seven Ṛṣis on earth to either the Kṛta, Tretā or Dvāpara Yugas.

3

FACTORS AFFECTING THE FORMULATION OF THE GROUP

A. Introduction

In this chapter we shall primarily attempt to discern some of the main factors which influenced the formulation of the second main list of the Seven Ṛṣis (as examined in Chapter 1), and which brought about the change between the two main lists of the group. This will be done by examining two sets of factors which appear in the traditions of the Seven Ṛṣis. The first of these factors is that of *gotra* influence : that is to say, influences arising from and reflecting the interests and influence of a particular Brahmin group claiming lineal descent from one or another of the Ṛṣis. Such influences are especially apparent in the formulation of the *gotra* organisation and in the traditionally-outlined kinships or family relationships which are said to exist between individual members of the Seven Ṛṣis : both of which will accordingly be investigated. The second of these factors is that of regional association and influences : that is to say, influences arising from the association of the Seven Ṛṣis—both as a group and also individually—with particular places or regions. By examining these two sets of factors, we shall be able to highlight some of the main reasons underlying the change between the two main lists of the Seven Ṛṣis, and hence also to trace the process of development of the traditions of the Seven Ṛṣis.

B. Gotra Factors

(*a*) *Outline of the Gotra Organisation*

General studies of the *gotra* organisation have been undertaken by a number of previous writers, notably by Brough.[1] While it is not our purpose here to enter upon a detailed examination of that organisation, it is nonetheless instructive to summarise certain of the general characteristics which are relevant to the present context.

One of the main roles of the Seven Ṛṣis within the context of Indian social organisation is that wherein they are regarded as being the founders of the seven main *gotras* or ancestral lineages of the Aryan peoples; in theory, therefore, all true Aryans should be able to trace their own descent from one or another of the Seven Ṛṣis. The origins of the *gotra* organisation have been discerned by Brough and others as being already present in embryonic form in the *Ṛgveda*, where the "hymn-families" to whom composition of the Vedic hymns is attributed are not so much families as clans, and are the direct ancestors of the main *gotras* which are subsequently listed in detail in especially the Sūtras.[2] The *gotra* organisation itself—as presented particularly in the Śrauta Sūtras—is based upon the principle of tracing patrilineal descent back to a common Ṛṣi-ancestor; marriage is generally prohibited within *gotras*, and the organization

---

1. J. Brough, *Early Brahmanical System of Gotra and Pravara*; *ibid*., 'Early History of the Gotras', pp. 41 ff.

2. See Brough, *Early Brahmanical System of Gotra and Pravara*, p. xiii. Both Brough and Benveniste have also suggested that the original meaning of the term *ari* denotes not so much 'enemy' as 'that part of the tribe into which a man can marry : whence the term *ārya* would denote offspring of *aris*, or 'descendants of legitimate marriage unions. According to this suggestion, therefore, the tetm *ārya* would be seen as being closely related to the idea of purity of descent : the form of such descent being formally regulated, by the period of the Sūtras, through the tracing of descent from one of the Seven Ṛṣis. Accordingly, the concept of being an *ārya* would have come to be synonymous with the idea of tracing descent from one of the Seven Ṛṣis. On individual Ṛṣis as being the fathers of the race, see for example *Ṛgveda* 1.139.9; see also Brough, *op. cit.* p. xiv : E. Benveniste, 'The Study of the Indo-European Vocabulary'.

is further consolidated through the largely complementary *pravara* organisation which sets out lists of many additional Ṛṣis who are also said to be the remote ancestors of families. The principal aim of both *gotra* and *pravara* lists is to limit the choice of marriage partners; with the exception of a few cases—notably those of the Bhṛgus and Aṅgirases—it is laid down that a wife must come not only from a different *gotra* to that of her husband, but that she must also have a *pravara* which contains a minimal number of Ṛṣi-names coinciding with those of her husband's *pravara*.

Although the *gotra*-organisation was intended to regulate all marriage alliances, from the period of the Sūtras onwards it is laid down in many places that Kṣatriyas and Vaiśyas should take the *gotra* and *pravara* of their Purohita or family priest[1] : thus suggesting that at this stage the organisation was operated and directed primarily by Brahmins. Since almost all information concerning the *gotra*-organisation—particularly during its early period of formulation—is to be found in works which were composed by—or whose composition was greatly influenced by—Brahmins, these works naturally view the organisation from the standpoint of Brahmins; it is consequently impossible to say with any certainty whether Kṣatriyas or Vaiśyas in reality also claimed descent from particular family *gotras* rather than from the *gotras* of their family priests—or indeed whether they were generally concerned to trace such descent at all. In the case of such medieval accounts as Vasiṣṭha's creation of the four Agnikula clans of Rājpūt Kṣatriyas (namely Paramāra or Pramāra, Pratihāra or Parihāra, Cālukya or Solaṅki, and Cāhamāna or Cauhan) from a sacrificial fire-pit on Mount Abu,[2] it is reasonably clear that such accounts were originated or manipulated by Kṣatriyas, in order to enhance their social status by directly connecting them with an illustrious Brahmin

1. For example *Vaikhānasa Sūtra, pravarapraśna* v. 8 : *Mānava Śrauta Sūtra* 11.8.10.12-15 : *Āpastamba Śrauta Sūtra* 24.10.13 ff.

2. The association of Vasiṣṭha with Mount Abu (Arbudācala) is evident for example in *Skanda Purāṇa* 7.3.1.1-35; for the fire-pit myth, see especially J. Tod, *Annals and Antiquities of Rajasthan*, Vol. 1 pp. 84-94.

or Ṛṣi as their ancestor. Consequently, this is quite likely to have been the case also in earlier periods, particularly in respect of Kṣatriyas and Vaiśyas claiming descent from a Ṛṣi as a means to further their status. It is noteworthy in this connection that the descendants of Jamadagni are said to be Kṣatriyas rather than Brahmins (see below)—thus suggesting that in at least some cases certain Kṣatriya-groups claimed direct descent from a Ṛṣi, rather than simply adopting the claims of their priests to such descent.

The *gotra* organisation may justifiably be termed one of the defining characteristics of Indian—and especially Brahmin—society, inasmuch as all who regarded themselves as full members of that society would seek to justify their claims by tracing their descent and ancestry from one of the "original" seven main families—each of which was thought to have been founded by and to be descended from one of the Seven Ṛṣis. It should be noted here that many (especially Indian) scholars regard these Ṛṣi-founders as fundamentally historical individuals, who lived at a definite time in the past; while many other (especially Western) scholars generally take the opposite view, regarding them as solely fictional or mythological figures. From the standpoint of the present study, it is essentially immaterial—as Brough has also concluded[1]—whether the Ṛṣis in the *gotra* and *pravara* lists are historical or fictional figures, or whether the Seven Ṛṣis were really the ancestors of the families who claimed descent from them. The important point in the present context is that, from at least the period of the Sūtras, these Ṛṣis were *thought of as being* the ancestors of such families, particularly by those who claimed to be descendants from one or another of the Seven "original" Ṛṣis. What we are, therefore, studying—in this as in other chapters—is not the historicity of the Ṛṣis themselves, but the historical development of ideas and beliefs held by others about the Ṛṣis.

(*b*) *The Seven Ṛṣis as Founders of Lineages*

(*i*) *The Sūtras* : The earliest—and indeed the principal—expositions of the *gotra* and *pravara* organisations are to be found

1. See Brough, *Early Brahmanical System of Gotra and Pravara*, pp. 20 f.

in the Sūtras : more specifically in the *Āpastamba*, *Āśvalāyana*, *Baudhāyana*, *Hiraṇyakeśin*, *Mānava* and *Vaikhānasa Śrauta Sūtras*.[1] An account is also to be found in the *pravara pariśiṣṭa* of the White *Yajurveda*;[2] but Brough has characterised this as being a fairly recent plagiarism of the *Mānava* text with extensive interpolations,[3] and its value in the present context is, therefore, somewhat limited. It is not here necessary to consider these lists in every detail, since our present concern rests primarily not with the Ṛṣi-descendants in each *gotra* and *pravara* lists, but rather with the Seven Ṛṣis who are regarded as being the founders of each of the seven main *gotras*. This is a point on which all of these texts concur. In setting out lists for the different *gotras*, each of these texts agrees in listing seven main *gotras* : namely the Bhārgava, Āṅgirasa, Ātreya, Vaiśvāmitra or Kauśika, Kāśyapa, Vāsiṣṭha, and Āgastya *gotras*. The only difference between these texts lies in the slightly different order in which each of these main *gotras* is listed.

The first two of these seven main *gotras* both contain major subdivisions. The Bhārgavas are subdivided into the Jāmadagnya-Bhārgavas and the Kevala-Bhārgavas ("just Bhārgavas", "Bhārgavas alone") ; while the Āṅgirases are subdivided into the Gautama-Āṅgirases, the Bhāradvāja-Āṅgirases, and the Kevala-Āṅgirases. Thus, in the context of social organisation, the seven main *gotras* are said to have been founded by Seven Ṛṣis : but these Ṛṣis are Bhṛgu, Aṅgiras, Atri, Viśvāmitra, Kaśyapa, Vasiṣṭha, and Agastya. The *gotra* lists, therefore, constitute a variant list of the Seven Ṛṣis, wherein Bhṛgu and Agastya are included within the group, while Jamadagni, Gautama and Bharadvāja—while still being represented in the group—are excluded from the list of Seven Ṛṣis through being said to be descended from the Ṛṣis Bhṛgu or Aṅgiras. This latter idea of their descent appears as a somewhat artificial

1. See *Āpastamba Śrauta Sūtra* 24.5-10 : *Āśvalāyana Śrauta Sūtra* 12.1.15 : *Baudhāyana Śrauta Sūtra, pariśiṣṭa* : *Hiraṇyakeśin Śrauta Sūtra* 8:714 ff. (ASS edition) : *Mānava Śrauta Sūtra* 11.8.1-10 : *Vaikhānasa Sūtra, pravarapraśna*.

2. See A. Weber, *Die Handschriften und Verzeichnisse der Koniglichen Bibliothek zu Berlin* Vol. 1, no. 271 (Weber 13.8).

3. See Brough, *Early Brahmanical System of Gotra and Pravara*, p. 50.

arrangement, indicating either that the (Kevala-) Bhārgavas and Āṅgirases were subdivided into further clans at a time following that of the initial commencement of this organisation, or else that it is merely a reclassification of the organisation, designed to include both these groups and also the Āgastyas—an inclusion achieved by rearranging the Seven Ṛṣis of the first main list so as to effectively "swallow-up" three of the perhaps smaller clans, namely the Jāmadagnyas, Gautamas and Bhāradvājas, by subordinating them to the further groups of Bhārgavas and Āṅgirases. It is noteworthy in this respect that in the Vedas and Brāhmaṇas the Jāmadagnyas are not said to be descended from Bhṛgu; nor are the Gautamas or Bhāradvājas said to be descended from Aṅgiras. The idea of their descent from these Ṛṣis is, therefore, one which arises only from the Sūtras onwards. One reason for its appearance is quite likely to be traced to what the Brahmin authors of the Śrauta Sūtras regarded as the increasing importance of the Bhārgavas and Āṅgirases, and the relatively decreasing importance of the Jāmadagnyas, Gautamas and Bhāradvājas—importances which are reflected in their ordering of these clans in the *gotra* and *pravara* sections of these texts. Furthermore, it can be seen that the second main list of the Seven Ṛṣis omits Jamadagni, Gautama and Bharadvāja, while it includes Aṅgiras together with three Ṛṣis said in places to be descended from Agastya (namely Pulastya, Pulaha and Kratu : see below), and also demonstrates a tendency to assimilate Bhṛgu within the group (as discussed in Chapter 1). Thus the list of Seven Ṛṣis who are regarded as the founders of the *gotras* in the Śrauta Sūtras represents an intermediate form between the first and second main lists of the Seven Ṛṣis : just as indeed the Śrauta Sūtras themselves are generally accepted as being chronologically intermediate between the Veda on the one hand and the Epics and Purāṇas on the other hand. Consequently, since this intermediate list occurs in the context of the *gotra* organisation, it may be inferred that the change between the two main lists of the Seven Ṛṣis—the one in the Vedic texts, the other in the Epics and Purāṇas is at least partly due to considerations arising from the sphere of inter-clan marriage and Brahmin lineages, which is the principal concern of the *gotra* organisation.

A curious inconsistency occurs within the *gotra* lists in the Śrauta Sūtras. On the one hand, the seven main *gotras* are listed as above—namely as having been founded by the Ṛṣis Bhṛgu, Aṅgiras, Atri, Viśvāmitra, Kaśyapa, Vasiṣṭha, and Agastya. On the other hand, however, these same *gotra*-sections of the Śrauta Sūtras frequently contain the statement that the Seven Ṛṣis are those of the first main list, together with Agastya as the eighth :

> Viśvāmitra, Jamadagni, Bharadvāja and Gotama, Atri, Vasiṣṭha and Kaśyapa : these are the Seven Ṛṣis. It is said that where there are descendants of the Seven Ṛṣis and of Agastya as the eighth, there indeed is a *gotra.*[1]

This inconsistency is never adequately explained within these texts. Yet it would seem clear that the texts attempt to retain that list of the Seven Ṛṣis which had gained general currency by the period of their composition (namely the first main list of the group, as in the above passage), while at the same time relating it to the relative importance ascribed to each clan or *gotra* at that period by the Brahmin authors of the texts and promoters of the *gotra* organisation—whence the importance of the Bhārgava, Āṅgiras and Āgastya gotras was emphasised in the *gotra* lists at the expense of the Jāmadagnya, Gautama and Bhāradvāja *gotras.* In other words, the Brahmin authors of the Śrauta Sūtras sought to bring the first main list of the Seven Ṛṣis more into line with what they regarded—and sought to establish—as the relative importance of each of the clans claiming descent from one or another of the Ṛṣis. The changes thus introduced in the Śrauta Sūtra lists are subsequently in turn reflected in the formulation, in the Epics and Purāṇas, of the second main list of the Seven Ṛṣis : such changes being at least partly due to the Brahmin-members of different *gotras* who traced their own descent from a particular Ṛṣi, and who desired—and were in a position to demand—greater recognition for their Ṛṣi-ancestor, thereby indirectly

1. For example the *pariśiṣṭas* to *Baudhāyana Śrauta Sūtra,* to *Āśvalāyana Śrauta Sūtra* 12.15, *et. al.*

gaining greater recognition for their own social standing. We shall be examining examples of such Brahmin influence over the Ṛṣi traditions in sub-section (d) below.

(ii) *The Epics and Purāṇas* : In his study of the *gotra* organisation, Brough took into account the *gotra* lists in the *Matsya Purāṇa*; but he did not deal with a more general phenomenon evident in many Purāṇas, namely the listing of *vaṃśas* or lineages of the principal Ṛṣis. Before coming to these, however, two passages in the *Mahābhārata* may first be noted, which seek to emphasise the importance of certain *gotras* at the expense of others. The first of these passages speaks of the *gotras* of Aṅgiras, Kaśyapa, Vasiṣṭha, and Bhṛgu as the four earliest or original clans :

> Four original *gotras* [*mūlagotrāṇi*] came into being, O king—Aṅgiras, Kaśyapa, Vasiṣṭha and Bhṛgu; the other *gotras* came into being due to *karma*.[1]

The second passage highlights the *gotras* of Bhṛgu, Aṅgiras and Kavi-Śukra as those which have filled the entire creation :

> Bhṛgu is called the son of Varuṇa and a creator of offspring; celebrated Aṅgiras is the son of Agni, and famous Kavi is the son of Brahmā. Bhārgavas and Āṅgirases are both appellations of lineages in the world; these three lords of creation are all without ancestors [*vipravarāḥ*], and all this world is said to be the offspring of these ones.[2]

Both of these passages may be viewed as attempts to emphasise and reinforce the importance of these particular Ṛṣis and their *gotra*-descendants : such attempts being at least partly due to the influence of the Brahmin members of those particular *gotras* over the formulation of such passages and traditions. It should constantly be kept in mind that the authors of these various texts would themselves have traced their own descent from one of the Seven Ṛṣis; hence any such emphasis within these texts upon the importance of a particular *gotra* or Ṛṣi is likely to be

1. *Mahābhārata* 12.285.17-18.
2. Ibid., 13.85.34-36.

due in some measure to the authors' desires to emphasise the status of the *gotra* represented by that Ṛṣi—whence also their own status as descendants of the same Ṛṣi. Explicit examples of this process will be examined in sub-section (d). A similar emphasis is evident again in a passage in the *Vāyu* and *Brahmāṇḍa Purāṇas*, which singles out the *gotras* of Kaśyapa, Vasiṣṭha Bhṛgu, Aṅgiras and Atri :

> Among these five *gotras* of Kaśyapa, Vasiṣṭha, Bhṛgu, Aṅgiras and Atri are born *brahmavādins*; because they stir *brahman*, therefore they are called *brahma*-Ṛṣis. The sons of Dharma, Pulastya, Kratu, Pulaha, Pratyūṣas, Prabhāsa, and again Kaśyapa are known as *deva*-Ṛṣis.[1]

Once again, therefore, the same motives may be discerned in this passage.

Many of the Purāṇas contain extremely lengthy and detailed accounts of the descendants of the main Ṛṣis. As in the case of the lists in the Śrauta Sūtras,. it is not necessary in the present context to examine the identities of every Ṛṣi who is said to be descended from one of the main Ṛṣis, since our concern here is rather with the identities of those who are said to be the main or founder Ṛṣis. In these contexts of the Ṛṣi-*vaṃśas*, the *Viṣṇu* and *Bhāgavata Purāṇas* list the descendants of Marīci, Aṅgiras, Atri, Pulastya (one of whose sons is said to be Agastya), Pulaha, Kratu, and Vasiṣṭha[2] : namely the Seven Ṛṣis who constitute the second main list of the group. Parallel accounts are to be found in many further Purāṇas, where the descendants of Bhṛgu are also listed along with those of the other Seven Ṛṣis[3]—the resulting list of eight Ṛṣis being parallel to the straightforward lists of eight Mind-born Sons of Brahmā (noted in Chapter 1) which add Bhṛgu to the Seven

1. *Vāyu Purāṇa* 1.61 81-83 : *Brahmāṇḍa Purāṇa* 1.2.35.90-93.

2. *Viṣṇu Purāṇa* 1.10.6-14 : *Bhāgavata Purāṇa* 4.1.8-41.

3. For example *Agni Purāṇa* 20.8-17 : *Brahmāṇḍa Purāṇa* 1.2.11.1-42 : *Garuḍa Purāṇa* 5.1 ff. : *Kūrma Purāṇa* 1.2.1-13, 1.17.1—1.18.27 : *Liṅga Purāṇa* 1.5.37-50 : *Mārkaṇḍeya Purāṇa* 52.14-26 : *Śiva Purāṇa* 7.1.17 22-35 : *Vāyu Purāṇa* 1.28.1-35. For general *gotra* rules, see for example *Agni Purāṇa* 153.8, 158.27-35 : *Skanda Purāṇa* 3.2.21.1-19, 3.2.31.1ff.

Ṛṣis of the second main list. Another passage in the *Vāyu* and *Brahmāṇḍa Purāṇas* again refers to the *gaṇas* or groups of descendants of Seven Ṛṣis; but these Ṛṣis are Marīci, Bhṛgu, Aṅgiras Pulastya, Pulaha, Vasiṣṭha, and Atri[1]—thus in this context Bhṛgu has been assimilated within the group of Seven Ṛṣis, while Kratu has been excluded from the group. A further passage in these same two works lists the descendants of Seven Ṛṣis : the Ṛṣis being Bhṛgu, Aṅgiras, Kaśyapa, Atri, Vasiṣṭha Viśvāmitra, and Agastya.[2] These Seven Ṛṣis are thus the seven who are listed also in the Śrauta Sūtras as the founders of the seven main *gotras*. This same list of seven is again given in two separate passages in the *Matsya Purāṇa*[3]; the second of these passages also explains that the Ṛṣis Pulastya, Pulaha and Kratu are known as Āgastyas—since they adopted sons of Agastya, whence their descendants came to be called Āgastyas (see below).[4] Further, as was noted in Chapter 1 and 2, the Manvantara lists of Seven Ṛṣis in the *Vāyu* and *Brahmāṇḍa Purāṇas*—as also those for Manvantaras 8 to 14 in the *Harivaṃśa* and the *Śiva Purāṇa*—include *gotra* names for each of the Seven Ṛṣis in each Manvantara : the *gotras* being those of Bhṛgu, Aṅgiras, Kaśyapa, Atri, Vasiṣṭha, Pulastya, and Pulaha.[5]

An approximate pattern of development may be seen in these Purāṇic lists of Ṛṣi-*vaṃśas*. In the first place the, *Matsya*, *Vāyu* and *Brahmāṇḍa Purāṇas* list the *vaṃśas* of those same Seven Ṛṣis who also appear in the Śrauta Sūtra lists as the founders of the seven main *gotras* : namely Bhṛgu, Aṅgiras, Kaśyapa, Atri, Vasiṣṭha, Viśvāmitra, and Agastya. The *Vāyu* and *Brahmāṇḍa Purāṇas*—followed in part by the *Harivaṃśa* and the *Śiva Purāṇa* further replace Viśvāmitra and Agastya in this list with Pulastya and Pulaha, in the Manvantara lists of Seven Ṛṣis. These two

---

1. *Vāyu Purāṇa* 2.4.47-83 (+to 2.9.93) : *Brahmāṇḍa Purāṇa* 2.3.1.47-83 (+to 2.3.8.100).

2. Ibid., 1.59.92-116 : *Brahmāṇḍa Purāṇa* 1.2.32.100-120.

3. *Matsya Purāṇa* 145.81-118, 195.1—202.14.

4. Ibid., 202.7-14.

5. *Vāyu Purāṇa* 2.1.15-66, 2.38.9-116 : *Brahmāṇḍa Purāṇa* 1.2.36.17-78, 3.4.1.9-114 : *Harivaṃśa* appendix 1.1 : *Śiva Purāṇa* 5.34.34-65. See also Chapter 2.

Purāṇas also list the *vaṃśas* of the Seven Ṛṣis who constitute the second main list of the group, as do also many other Purāṇas : sometimes without Bhṛgu (as in the *Viṣṇu* and *Bhāgavata Purāṇas*), but most frequently with the addition of Bhṛgu to the Seven Ṛṣis of the second main list. This pattern of development thus again illustrates the process by which the list of the Seven Ṛṣis becomes radically altered, changing initially from the first main list to the list found in the Śrauta Sūtras and in certain Purāṇas, and thence by stages to the second main list. Since this process of development is evident primarily within the context of the listing of Ṛṣi-*vaṃśas* and Ṛṣi-*gotras*, it would seem clear that at least one major reason for the change between the two main lists of the Seven Ṛṣis may be traced to influences from within the *gotra* organisation itself—namely, as already indicated, to the influence of members of a particular *gotra* seeking to emphasise the importance or status of a Ṛṣi or Ṛṣi-*gotra* at the expense of others.

Before looking at explicit examples of *gotra* influence within the Ṛṣi traditions, we shall examine this process of change and development between the two main lists at a slightly different level : namely through an investigation of the kinships and family relationships which are said to exist between individual Ṛṣis who appear in one or the other of the two main lists of the Seven Ṛṣis. For as will now be seen, this will help to throw further light upon why individual Ṛṣis may be included in the one list but excluded from the other.

(c) *Relationships between the main Ṛṣis*

(i) *Atri and Vasiṣṭha* : Atri and Vasiṣṭha are the only Ṛṣis who appear in both of the main lists of the Seven Ṛṣis. Their *gotras* are also listed independently of all others.

In a similar manner, both Atri and Vasiṣṭha are quite independent of—and are not said to be related in any way to—any of the other Ṛṣis in either of the two main lists of the Seven Ṛṣis. A slight qualification of this statement may be made in the case of Vasiṣṭha, who is said in many places to share a common birth with Agastya when the seed of Mitra-Varuṇa fell into a pot;[1] for as has been seen already, Agastya is closely connected with the group of Seven Ṛṣis, although not actually included within it. However, no instance is given in which either Atri or Vasiṣṭha is said to be born from, or to give birth to, any of the other Ṛṣis in either of the two main lists.

(ii) *Bhṛgu, Jamadagni and Viśvāmitra* : As was noted above, in the Śrauta Sūtras the Jāmadagnya *gotra* is listed as a sub-division of the Bhārgava gotra, while the Vaiśvāmitra or Kauśika *gotra* is listed independently of all others. Also, Viśvāmitra and Jamadagni appear only in the first main list of the Seven Ṛṣis, while Bhṛgu is associated and at times included within only the second main list of the group.

In a number of Epic and Purāṇic contexts there is related a myth which connects the births of both Viśvāmitra and Jamadagni with Bhṛgu. The myth may be summarised as follows :

> Ṛcīka Bhārgava obtained Satyavatī the daughter of Gādhi Kauśika as his wife. Bhṛgu told Satyavatī that, in order to obtain a son, both she and her mother should take baths, embrace respectively an *udumbara* and an *aśvattha* tree, and drink *camas*-vessels containing respectively rice and milk. In this way they would obtain the desired types of son : namely a Brahmin for Satyavatī, and a Kṣatriya for her mother. Satyavatī and her mother performed these rites prescribed by her father-in-law Bhṛgu; but each embraced the wrong tree, and drank from the wrong *camas*-vessel. When Bhṛgu returned, he told Satyavatī that she would give birth to a son who, though born a Brahmin, would be fit to be a Kṣatriya; while her mother would give birth to a son who, though born a Kṣatriya, would be fit to be a Brahmin. Upon entreaty, Satyavatī obtained the boon from Bhṛgu that this should occur to her grandson, rather than to her son;

1. For example *Ṛgveda* 7.33.10-13 : *Nirukta* 5.13-14 : *Bṛhaddevatā* 5.143-160 : *Mahābhārata* 12.291.7ff., 13.143.18 : *Bhāgavata Purāṇa* 6.18.5-6, 9.13.1-11 : *Matsya Purāṇa* 61.18-53, 201.1-39 : *Padma Purāṇa* 5.22.19-40 : *Śiva Purāṇa* 5.4.23-26 : *Viṣṇu Purāṇa* 4.5.1 ff. : *Devībhāgavata Purāṇa* 1.19.20-27, 6.14.10—6.15.63 : *Narasiṃha Purāṇa* 6.1 ff. : *Viṣṇudharmottara Purāṇa* 1.117.1ff.

> accordingly she gave birth to Jamadagni, whose son was the warrior Paraśurāma, while her mother gave birth to Viśvāmitra, who renounced his Kṣatriyahood and became a Brahmin.[1]

This myth accordingly makes explicit the descent of Jamadagni, from Bhṛgu : a descent also referred to by the appellation *Bhārgava* very frequently given to Paraśurāma Jāmadagnya. The myth also implies a close connection between Viśvāmitra and Bhṛgu, and certain versions actually state that the myth has been related in order to explain the connection between the Bhārgavas and the Kauśikas :

> I have related all this in its entirety to you, O prince, with reference to the origin of the relationship between the Bhṛgus and the Kauśikas.[2]

Similarly in some accounts of the adoption of Śunaḥśepa (a Bhārgava) by Viśvāmitra, the interconnection between the Bhārgava and Kauśika *gotras* is again made explicit (for example *bhārgavaḥ kauśikatvaṃ prāptaḥ* . . . "When the Bhārgava had become a Kauśika".[3]

It is thus clear that the descent of Jamadagni from Bhṛgu, although not mentioned in Vedic texts prior to the Sūtras, had become well-accepted in the Epics and Purāṇas : whence the status of Jamadagni came to be regarded as in a sense subordinate to that of Bhṛgu. It is also evident that a close connection was thought to exist between the Bhārgava and Vaiśvāmitra *gotras*, giving rise to the above mythical explanations of this connection : even though, once again, no such connection is mentioned in the earlier literature. It would consequently seem that one of the reasons why neither Jamadagni nor Viśvāmitra appears in the second main list of the Seven Ṛṣis is in part linked with the appearance therein of Bhṛgu, and is in some

1. See *Mahābhārata* 3.115.9-13, 12.49.1ff., 13.4.1ff., 13.56.1ff. : *Harivaṃśa* 23.82-94, appendix 1.6 : *Brahma Purāṇa* 10.28-56 : *Bahmāṇḍa Purāṇa* 2.3.66.35-77 : *Skanda Purāṇa* 6.165.1—6.166.48 : *Vāyu Purāṇa* 2.29.64-99 : *Viṣṇu Purāṇa* 4.7.1 ff.
2. For example *Mahābhārata* 13.56.19.
3. *Brahma Purāṇa* 10.64.

measure connected with the decreasing importance of the Jāmadagnya and Kauśika *gotras* in comparison with that of the Bhārgava *gotra*. In other words, those claiming to be descendants of Viśvāmitra and Jamadagni did not hold sufficient influence over the formulation of these traditions to have their Ṛṣis included in the group of Seven Ṛṣis; while the influence formerly held by the members of these *gotras* had been partly appropriated by members of the Bhārgava *gotra*, who were consequently able to have their Ṛṣi-ancestor included in the group.

(iii) *Aṅgiras, Gautama and Bharadvāja* : In the Śrauta Sūtras both the Gautamas and the Bhāradvājas are listed as subdivisions of the Āṅgirasa *gotra*. Also, while Gautama and Bharadvāja appear only in the first main list of the Seven Ṛṣis Aṅgiras appears only in the second main list of the group.

In several Epic and Purāṇic contexts it is related that Bharadvāja was the son of Bṛhaspati, who was in turn the son of Aṅgiras.[1] Similarly Gautama is in places said to be the son of Bṛhaspati and Mamatā : whence Bharadvāja is said to be the half-brother of Gautama.[2] Thus the subordination of both of these Ṛṣis to Aṅgiras in the context of the *gotra* organisation was evidently well-accepted by the period of the Epics, as reflected in such mythical accounts. In this instance it would again seem that the exclusion of Gautama and Bharadvāja from the second main list of the Seven Ṛṣis is directly related to the inclusion therein of Aṅgiras—this being due in part to the subordinate role of the first two *gotras* in comparison with the increasingly important and influential role of members of the Āṅgirasa *gotra*.

(iv) *Marīci and Kaśyapa* : In the Śrauta Sūtras the Kāśyapa *gotra* is listed independently of any other, while Marīci is not mentioned in the *gotra* lists. Also, while Kaśyapa appears in

---

1. For example *Mahābhārata* 1.121.12-18, 3.209.1-9, 13.31.22 ff. : *Harivaṃśa* 23.49-53 : *Agni Purāṇa* 278.8-10 : *Bhāgavata Purāṇa* 9.20.34-39 : *Brahma Purāṇa* 13.58-61 : *Matsya Purāṇa* 49. 14-35 : *Śiva Purāṇa* 5.4.38 : *Viṣṇu Purāṇa* 4.19.1ff. : *Bṛhaddevatā* 5.102-103.

2. For example *Mahābhārata* 12.328.44 ff. : *Brahmāṇḍa Purāṇa* 2.3.7. 33-94 : *Matsya Purāṇa* 48.32-88 : *Vāyu Purāṇa* 2.37.33-97 : *Viṣṇu Purāṇa* 4.19.1ff.

only the first main list of the Seven Ṛṣis, Marīci appears only in the second main list of the group. Throughout the Epics and Purāṇas, Kaśyapa is on innumerable occasions termed the son of Marīci;[1] as in the preceding instances, therefore, it would appear that the exclusion of Kaśyapa from the second main list of the Seven Ṛṣis may be linked in some measure to the inclusion therein of Marīci. It will be noted that, in the most frequently-encountered ordering of the lists, both Marīci and Kaśyapa are placed in an ultimate position in each of the lists : Kaśyapa usually being listed last in the first main list, Marīci usually being listed first in the second main list. This again suggests that the role of the one Ṛṣi in the one list has in some measure been replaced by the role of the other Ṛṣi in the other list; and as in preceding instances, this is likely to be indicative of a decrease in influence of the descendants of Kaśyapa, in comparison with the growing influence of those regarding themselves as descendants of Marīci.

This in turn raises a further point : since, unlike the Bhārgavas and Āṅgirases—both of whom are encountered already in the *Ṛgveda* and in subsequent texts—the Mārīcas appear only from the *Rāmāyaṇa* onwards. It must, therefore, be asked, who were the Mārīcas, whose importance was such that their ancestor Marīci came to be termed the father of Kaśyapa? For Kaśyapa himself is famed throughout the Epics and Purāṇas with the exalted status of father of all gods, demons and men; this status might otherwise have been thought sufficient to establish him as one of the foremost—if not indeed as the foremost—of the Ṛṣis. It is therefore somewhat surprising to find that his place in the first main list of the Seven Ṛṣis is apparently usurped by a Ṛṣi who is virtually unknown to the authors of the Vedic literature—resulting in the exclusion of Kaśyapa and the inclusion of Marīci in the second main list of the Seven Ṛṣis.

1. For example *Rāmāyaṇa* 1.45.1ff., 1.69.17, 2.102.3ff. : *Mahābhārata* 1.59.9ff , 1.60.33-35, 12.200.1-46, 12.201.8, 13.47.61, 13.85.15 ff., 13.151.12 : *Harivaṃśa* 3.45-49, 31.100-109 : *Brahmāṇḍa Purāṇa* 1.2.13.78-80, 1.2.38.1, 2.3.1.113ff., 2.3.3.84-118, 2.3.4.34, 2.3.5.35, 2.3.7. 463ff., 3.4.2.32-34 : *Mārkaṇḍeya Purāṇa* 104.1-9 : *Vāyu Purāṇa* 1.30.72-73, 2.3.1, 2.4.109ff., 2.5.101 2.6.43-44, 2.6.76, 2.8.334 ff.: *etc.*

Both an individual Mārīca and also the Mārīcas as a group are referred to in several manuscript versions of the *Kiṣkindhā Kāṇḍa* of the *Rāmāyaṇa* as "the sons of the great Ṛṣi", and are said to act as the helpers of Rāma and Sugrīva.[1] An individual Mārīca is also famed throughout the *Rāmāyaṇa* (and in subsequent contexts) as a demon-figure : namely as a companion and helper of Rāvaṇa, who transforms himself into a deer in order to assist Rāvaṇa in the abduction of Sītā, and who is slain by Rāma.[2] This Mārīca is most frequently referred to as being a Rākṣasa; but one passage in the *Bāla Kāṇḍa* relates that he was originally born as a Yakṣa, and was only subsequently transformed into a Rākṣasa by the curse of Agastya :

> After some time, the Yakṣī (Tāṭakā) gave birth to a son called Mārīca, a fearful one who became a Rākṣasa by a curse. When Sunda had been killed, O Rāma, Tāṭakā with her son sought to injure the most excellent Ṛṣi Agastya; Agastya, filled with anger, addressed Mārīca saying "become a Rākṣasa", and he also cursed Tāṭakā.[3]

This Mārīca is therefore by implication associated not only with Agastya but also with Pulastya (who is himself referred to on occasions as the father of Agastya), since both the Yakṣas and the Rākṣasas are usually said to be descended from Pulastya[4]—although a few passages also term them the sons of Kaśyapa.[5] Thus the identity of Mārīca—as indeed of Marīci and of all his Mārīca descendants—may be further considered in connection with Pulastya.

(v) *Agastya, Pulastya, Pulaha, Kratu and Marīci* : In the Śrauta Sūtras the Āgastya *gotra* is listed independently of all others,

1. *Rāmāyaṇa* 4.41.1 *845, 4.41.3 *850.
2. Especially in the *Araṇya Kāṇḍa* of the *Rāmāyaṇa*.
3. *Rāmāyaṇa* 1.24.8-12.
4. For example, *Rāmāyaṇa* 1.4.6, 1.19.15 ff., 5.21.4-7, 6.49.9ff., 6.68.12, 7.4.4 ff. : *Mahābhārata* 1.60.1 ff., 2.28.50, 3.175.2, 3.258.11-16, 3.259.1-8, 5.107.12, 9.30.10, 12.326.87 : *Brahmāṇḍa Purāṇa* 2.3.7.162ff., 2.3.8.38ff. : *Kūrma Purāṇa* 1.18.7-14 : *Padma Purāṇa* 5.9.35 : *Saura Purāṇa* 30.14-20 : *Vāyu Purāṇa* 2.8.189ff., 2.9.31 ff.
5. See *Harivaṃśa* 3.92 : *Mārkaṇḍeya Purāṇa* 104.1-9 : *Viṣṇu Purāṇa* 1.21.24.

while none of the other Ṛṣis mentioned above appear in the *gotra* lists. Also, Agastya is associated with the first main list of the Seven Ṛṣis by being termed the eighth Ṛṣi, listed alongside but rarely included within that group; he is again excluded from the second main list, while all of the other four Ṛṣis are included in that list.

It may be pointed out here that, in astronomical terms, Agastya is identified with the star Canopus in the southern sky, as opposed to the Seven Ṛṣis who are identified with the constellation Ursa Major in the northern sky (see section C below). Thus various astronomical works give the position of Agastya relative to other constellations : the *Sūrya-siddhānta* for example states that Agastya is 80° south from the end of Gemini.[1] Consequently it would be unlikely that Agastya should be included within the group of Seven Ṛṣis, once his astronomical association and identity had become established.

A passage in the *Matsya Purāṇa* listed the Āgastyas as one of the seven main *gotras*; it then adds that those born in the families of Pulastya, Pulaha and Kratu are also known as Āgastyas :

> I shall next describe the Brahmins who are born in the *vaṃśa* of Agastya...these are the Paulastyas, the Paulahas, and those who are of the *vaṃśa* of Kratu.[2]

At this point in the passage, the inevitable question is asked : why are these three Ṛṣis included in the Āgastya *gotra* ? And the passage continues by giving an explanation of this, to the effect that each of the three Ṛṣis became dissatisfied with their own sons and adopted instead a son of Agastya—whence the Paulastyas, Paulahas and Kratus became known as Āgastyas.[3] In this context, therefore, the three Ṛṣis Pulastya, Pulaha and Kratu are regarded as being of subordinate importance to Agastya and to the Agastya *gotra*. In many other contexts,

1. *Sūrya Siddhānta* 8.10 : see also 9.12-15, 13.8.9 : *Bṛhat-saṃhitā* 12.1-21 : *Mahā-siddhānta* 10.8 : *Pañcasiddhāntikā* 14.40-41 : *etc.*

2. *Matsya Purāṇa* 202.1-2.

3. Ibid., 202.7-13.

however, the importance of Agastya is in some measure replaced by that of the other Ṛṣis, particularly of Pulastya; for Agastya is said to have been born as Dattoli, a son of Pulastya, having been known as Agastya in an earlier birth :

> Dattoli was the son of that one [namely Pulastya] by Prītī, the wife of Pulastya; in an earlier birth in the Svāyambhuva age he was known as Agastya.[1]

This again suggests a developmental process within the tradition of listing the Ṛṣis, whereby a Ṛṣi who is virtually unknown in Vedic literature comes to usurp the role of another Ṛṣi who is prominent in that literature. It will be noted that in all such cases examined above, this process invariably occurs by one Ṛṣi being termed the father of another Ṛṣi—even though no such relationship is mentioned in Vedic literature. Once this paternal-filial relatinship becomes established, the Ṛṣi termed "father is invariably accredited with a greater status than that of his "son" (which includes being listed in the sacond main list of the Seven Ṛṣis) ; his reputation is thereby consolidated—as it also, implicitly, the reputation and status of those claiming descent from that Ṛṣi.

One further reference to a relationship between these Ṛṣis occurs in the *Viṣṇu Purāṇa*, where one passage relates that Pulastya is the brother of Pulaha.[2] Alongside this reference, it should be recalled that all the Ṛṣis of the second main list—as also Bhṛgu—are frequently termed in the Epics and Purāṇas the Mind-born Sons of Brahmā, created together by Brahmā; hence they are all viewed as being in a sense brothers, as also the fathers of creation. Consequently, all of these Ṛṣis—sons of Brahmā and fathers of other Ṛṣis—are accorded a greater status in the Epics and Purāṇas than that of any others : most notably greater than that of the Ṛṣis of the first main list.

In discussing the four Ṛṣis Pulastya, Pulaha, Kratu and Marīca, it is to be noted that a markedly mythical element pervades the

---

1. *Bhāgavata Purāṇa* 4.1.35.7 : *Brahmāṇḍa Purāṇa* 1.2.11.26 : *Kūrma Purāṇa* 1.12.1-13 : *Mārkaṇḍeya Purāṇa* 52.22-23 : *Śiva Purāṇa* 7.1.17.25 : *Saura Purāṇa* 26.22-23 : *Vāyu Purāṇa* 1.28.21 : *Viṣṇu Purāṇa* 1.10.9.
2. *Viṣṇu Purāṇa* 1.1.26-27.

accounts of their descendants. The descendants of Pulaha are usually listed as including the Prajāpati Kardama, and also deer, tigers, ghosts, serpents, demons, elephants, monkeys, wolves and similar : in other words, primarily animals and demons of various kinds.[1] Kratu is generally renowned as being the father of the Vālakhilyas who had neither wives nor children but remained *ūrdhvaretas* or ascetic, although in some places Kratu himself is said to have had neither a wife nor children[2]. As has already been mentioned, Marīci is famed as the father of Kaśyapa, progenitor of gods, demons and men; while Pulastya is said to be father of both Yakṣas and Rākṣasas (in addition to other sons, such as Agastya), the most notably of whom are the Yakṣas Viśravas and Kuvera, and the Rākṣasas Rāvaṇa, Vibhīṣaṇa, Kumbhakarṇa, together with all of the other Rākṣasa opponents of Rāma who appear both in the *Rāmāyaṇa* itself and also in subsequent contexts. It is clearly not within our present scope to consider in detail the degree of historicity of the *Rāmāyaṇa* story and of the various peoples therein, or to analyse the question of whether the Rākṣasa-opponents of Rāma —as also his monkey-helpers—should be taken to represent, in mythological form, the early inhabitants of southern India and Śrī Laṅkā as viewed by the northerners who composed the *Rāmāyaṇa*. Such considerations should, however, be borne in mind, particularly in attempting to assess the degree to which any kind of social or *gotra* influences may have been operative in formulating the traditions of these Ṛṣis: that is to say, in attempting to decide whether the inclusion of these Ṛṣis in the second main list of the

---

1. For example *Mahābhārata* 1.60.1-15 : *Harivaṃśa* 13.58-59 : *Brahmāṇḍa Purāṇa* 1.2.11.23, 1.2.35.94ff., 2.3.7.171ff., 2.3.8.70-71 2.3.10.75-93 : *Kūrma Purāṇa* 1.18.15-16 : *Mārkaṇḍeya Purāṇa* 52.14ff.,: *Matsya Purāṇa* 15.20 ff. : *Skanda Purāṇa* 7.1.20.37 : *Vāyu Purāṇa* 1.28.18, 1.61.84 ff., 2.8.198 ff., 2.9.64 ff., 2.11.68-69 : *Viṣṇu Purāṇa* 1.10.6ff. : *Viṣṇudharmottara Purāṇa* 1.248.1 ff., 1.252.1ff.

2. For example *Mahābhārata* 1.60.1-15 : *Bhāgavata Purāṇa* 4.1.38-39 : *Brahmāṇḍa Purāṇa* 1.2.11.36, 1.2.35.24 ff.' 1.2,36.12, 2.3.8.72, 2.3.10.52-53 : *Kūrma Purāṇa* 1.18.15-16 : *Liṅga Purāṇa* 1.63.68-79 : *Mārkaṇḍeya Purāṇa* 52.14 ff. : *Saura Purāṇa* 26.2 ff., 30.24 : *Śiva Purāṇa* 7.1.17.28-29 : *Skanda Purāṇa* 7.1.20.38 : *Vāyu Purāṇa* 1.28.30, 1.61.84 ff., 2.1.8-12, 2.9.66, 2.11.50-51: *Viṣṇu Purāṇa* 1.10.6 ff.

Seven Ṛṣis is due partly to the influence of those who traced their own descent from one or another of these Ṛṣis. In the present context we shall simply conclude that the inclusion of Pulastya, Pulaha and Kratu (as also, to a lesser extent, Marīci) in the second main list of the Seven Ṛṣis is in some degree connected with the role and status of Agastya : who is himself closely connected with the first main list of the group, whose descendants are listed independently as one of the seven main *gotras* in the Śrauta Sūtras (and include these three Ṛṣis in the *gotra* list in the *Matsya* Purāṇa), and who comes to be accorded a subordinate status as a son of Pulastya in the Purāṇas. We shall note further connections between these Ṛṣis, and draw further conclusions, in the subsequent sections of this chapter.

(*d*) *Gotra influences in the Ṛṣi traditions*

So far in this section we have concluded that the changes which occur between the two main lists of the Seven Ṛṣis are due in some measure to the influence of the Brahmin members of particular *gotras* over the development of these traditions. We shall now further illustrate the presence of this type of influence within the literary texts by citing a select number of passages which make explicit the fact of some form of *gotra*-influence operative in the formulation of these traditions. It will be seen that such passages demonstrate the attempts of members of a Ṛṣi-*gotra* either to improve—directly or indirectly—the status of a Ṛṣi or Ṛṣi-gotra, or to account for such status, or else to undermine the status of another Ṛṣi or Ṛṣi-*gotra*.

A number of versions of the adoption of Śunaḥśepa by Viśvāmitra are to be found throughout Vedic, Epic and Purāṇic literature. These frequently mention that the fifty eldest sons of Viśvāmitra did not agree to the adoption, for which reason they were cursed by Viśvāmitra. A version in the *Aitareya Brāhmaṇa* adds that they became such Dasyus or demon-peoples as the Āndhras, Puṇḍras and others:

> Those became these many ones on the borders: Āndhras, Puṇḍras, Śabaras, Pulindas, and Mūtibas; the Vaiśvāmitras who are the most numerous of the Dasyus.[1]

1. *Aitareya Brāhmaṇa* 7.18.

A version in the *Rāmāyaṇa* adds that they were cursed to become *śvamāṃsa-bhojins* or eaters of dogs' flesh[1]; while the *Mahābhārata* relates that they were cursed to become *śvapacas* or those who cook dogs[2]—in other words, Caṇḍālas or outcastes. Another version in the *Bhāgavata Purāṇa* adds that they were cursed to be Mlecchas, after which there arose the divisions within the Kauśika *gotra.*[3] Such passages are evidently in one sense attempts to account for the fact that such "outcaste" groups as Dasyus, Caṇḍālas and Mlecchas claimed to be—or were thought to be—descended from Viśvāmitra and members of the Vaiśvāmitra or Kauśika *gotra.* A comparable situation is evident in the case of certain descendants of Gautama. A passage in the *Jaiminīya Brāhmaṇa* relates that, after the death of Yavakrīta who, according to the Epics, was a son of Bharadvāja[4], his father cursed the descendants of Mauṇḍibha —at which point the text adds that these are lowly descendants of Gautama:

> He then cursed: "May the princely kinsmen perish this day, may these Mauṇḍibhas be removed afar"; those are these ones who act contemptibly, and are declared to be Gotamas.[5]

A somewhat curious passage occurs in the *Vāyu* and *Brahmāṇḍa Purāṇas,* which refers to certain Vaiśvāmitras, Āgastyas and Paulastyas as Rākṣasas:

> The Paulastya Aiḍaviḍa (Kuvera), the golden one of the south, is the king of all the Paulastya Yakṣas and Rākṣasas, and of the cruel Brahmin-Rakṣa (*brahmarakṣas*) Āgastyas and Vaiśvāmitras; these others, who take delight in sacrifices, are the three *gaṇas* of demons (*rakṣogaṇās trayaḥ*)... The Yātudhānas, Brahmadhānas, Vārttas who move by day,

1. *Rāmāyaṇa* 1.61.14-16.
2. *Mahābhārata* 13.3.8.
3. *Bhāgavata Purāṇa* 9.16.28-37.
4. For example, *Mahābhārata* 3.135.7—3.139.24.
5. *Jaiminīya Brāhmaṇa* 2.272.

> Paulastyas, Nairṛtas, Āgastyas, and Kauśikas—these are the seven which are known as Rākṣasa lineages.[1]

Here once again the passage indicates that the *gotra*-descendants of these Ṛṣis were thought to include those regarded as "demons" or outcastes. Further passages relate how individual Ṛṣis or their descendants came to dwell or be present among such outcaste groups. Viśvāmitra, for example, is said to have entered a Caṇḍāla village during a drought and famine and stolen a piece of dog's flesh in order to feed his wife and son[2]; while a certain Gautama is said to have departed from Madhyadeśa to travel northwards and settle in the land of the Mlecchas, eventually becoming himself like a Mleccha—much to the disgust of his Brahmin friends.[3] By explaining in these cases how an individual Ṛṣi came to be present among such peoples, it can be seen that the myth in effect offers an explanation of how such peoples came to be connected with—and to be descended from—that Ṛṣi.

A passage in the *Harivaṃśa*—found also in a different form in the *Śiva Purāṇa*—relates of certain Brahmin sons of Bharadvāja that they became degraded, and were reborn as kinsmen of Kauśika (namely as Vaiśvāmitras)—whence they will again be able to become Brahmins:

> In a former Yuga, O child, there were Brahmins born of Bharadvāja; having attained the *dharma* of *yoga*, they however became depraved through evil conduct... Then, when their *yoga* had decayed, after a long time they dwelt among the gods, and were born as kinsmen of Kauśika in Kurukṣetra ... they will regain their Brahmin-hood by their own deeds.[4]

The passage thus attempts both to account for the degraded status of certain descendants of Bharadvāja, and also to suggest

1. *Brahmāṇḍa Purāṇa* 2.3.8.58-69 : *Vāyu Purāṇa* 2.9.52-63.
2. For example, *Mahābhārata* 12.139.12ff. : *Brahma Purāṇa* 93.1-27 : *Skanda Purāṇa* 6.90.1-82.
3. For example, *Mahābhārata* 12.162.1ff.
4. *Harivaṃśa* 14.1-7 : see also *Śiva Purāṇa* 5.41.10-52.

some connection between the descendants of Bharadvāja and those of Viśvāmitra. As we saw earlier, other passages similarly attempt to account for a connection between the descendants of Viśvāmitra and those of other Ṛṣis: most notably between the Vaiśvāmitras or Kauśikas and the Bhārgavas.[1]

We noted in Chapter I a myth in the *Jaiminiya Brāhmaṇa* wherein Agastya followed the other Ṛṣis to Svargaloka or heaven; because he was the last to go, it is said that for this reason the Āgastyas are similarly excluded or set apart from the Kuru-Pañcālas.[2] Such passages suggest that in at least some instances the very format of a myth has been in some measure directed by an attempt to connect what is said therein not just with the Ṛṣi himself but also with the descendants of that Ṛṣi. Such attempts are made still more explicit in certain contexts. Thus for example, a passage which appears in different forms in several works relates that Vasiṣṭha was privileged in having revealed to him a certain *brāhmaṇa*—for which reason it is said that in former times only those who were Vāsiṣṭhas might become Brahmins :

> The Ṛṣis could not see Indra face to face, but Vasiṣṭha did so and Indra told him: "I will relate to you a *brāhmaṇa*, so that people may flourish with you as their Purohita—but do not tell it to the other Ṛṣis". Therefore he spoke these hymns, and the people flourished with Vasiṣṭha as their Purohita. Because of that, a Vāsiṣṭha should be made the Brahmin.[3]

> Formerly only the Vasiṣṭhas knew the sacred words (*vyāhṛtis*) ; because of that, only Vāsiṣṭhas formerly became Brahmins. But since there is now sin at the present time, anyone can study, and so at present anyone can become a Brahmin.[4]

---

1. See *Mahābhārata* 13.56.19 : *Brahma Purāṇa* 10.64. For a detailed analysis of influences in the cases of Bhṛgu and his descendants, see R. Goldman, *Myth and Metamyth : The Bhārgava Cycle of the Mahābhārata.*

2. *Jaiminīya Brāhmaṇa* 2.221.

3. *Taittirīya Saṃhitā* 3.5.2.1 : see also *Gopatha Brāhmaṇa* 2.2.13 : *Ṣaḍviṃśa Brāhmaṇa* 1.5.1-3 : *Jaiminīya Upaniṣad Brāhmaṇa* 3.5.1-3 : *Bṛhaddevatā* 5.143-160.

4. *Śatapatha Brāhmaṇa* 12.6.1.38 ff.

It is similarly related that the Bharatas prospered—and the Ikṣvākus gained mastery of the earth—because they had Vasiṣṭha as their Purohita or priest.[1] Just as Vasiṣṭha appears in both main lists of the Seven Ṛṣis, and the Vāsiṣṭha *gotra* remains independent of all others, so too the pre-eminence of Vasiṣṭha in relation to the other Ṛṣis is maintained in various forms throughout the literature. We shall here simply note a few instances of this, in order t- demonstrate the point. The entire *Ārṣeya Upaniṣad* is structured to relate how Vasiṣṭha brought enlightenment to the Ṛṣis Viśvāmitra, Jamadagni, Bharadvāja and Gautama, who thereafter became his pupils. Here the pre-eminent status of Vasiṣṭha is quite clearly being demonstrated, in order .to establish him as somehow superior to the other Ṛṣis. Throughout the *Mahābhārata*—as also in the Purāṇas—Vasiṣṭha is frequently described by such terms as the leader of Brahmins, the equal of Brahmā, the foremost of the Seven Ṛṣis, and the incarnation of Indra and Dharma[2]; and since this kind of appellation is not generally given to the other Ṛṣis (particularly not to such a marked degree), it is apparent that such epithets are again designed to emphasise the status of Vasiṣṭha in relation to the other Ṛṣis. In the earlier texts—particularly in the Brāhmaṇas—it is related on several occasions that Jamadagni attained success through sacrifice, on account of which his descendants flourished and became so numerous that no two descendants knew each other :

> Jamadagni desired : "May I generate many offspring and cattle"; he saw this four-night sacrifice, took it and sacrificed with it. Then indeed many offspring and cattle were generated for him—and any two Aurvas among his offspring do not recognise each other.[3]

A passage in the *Taittirīya Saṃhitā* further relates that on one occasion both Viśvāmitra and Jamadagni were quarreling with

1. *Pañcaviṃśa Brāhmaṇa* 15.5.24 : *Mahābhārata* 1.164.10 : *Brahmāṇḍa Purāṇa* 2.3.48.29-30 : *Viṣṇu Purāṇa* 4.2.1 ff.

2. For example *Mahābhārata* 5.104.1-26, 7.5.26, 9.47.1 ff., 12.122.31, 12.201.1 ff., 12.337.47, 14.27.19 : *etc.*

3. *Jaiminīya Brāhmaṇa* 2.285 : see also *Taittirīya Saṃhitā* 7.1.9 : *Pañcaviṃśa Brāhmaṇa* 21.10.5-6.

Vasiṣṭha and that Jamadagni saw the *vihavya* hymn, thereby gaining the power and strength of Vasiṣṭha :

> Viśvāmitra and Jamadagni were vying with Vasiṣṭha; Jamadagni saw this *vihavya* hymn, and by means of it he seized the power and strength of Vasiṣṭha.[1]

The passage may be interpreted on one level as an indication of the relative importance—in the earlier literature—of Jamadagni and his descendants in relation to Vasiṣṭha; it is noteworthy in this respect that similar types of myths—according a greater status to Jamadagni than to Vasiṣṭha—are not met with in the Epics or Purāṇas. Such an interpretation, involving the *gotra*-descendants as well as the Ṛṣi himself, is in a further context made explicit by Śaunaka. In one passage in the *Bṛhaddevatā*, Śaunaka relates that Viśvāmitra was once rendered unconscious by Śakti the son of Vasiṣṭha during a quarrel, but that he was received by the Jāmadagnis. For this reason, adds Śaunaka, certain verses in the *Ṛgveda* (3.53.21-24) are traditionally held to be hostile to the Vāsiṣṭha—and any Vāsiṣṭha who listens to them acquires great guilt thereby :

> The next four verses here are known as being hostile to Vasiṣṭha; they were spoken as a curse by Viśvāmitra, and they are known as magical incantations which are harmful to an enemy. Vāsiṣṭhas should not listen to them—this is the opinion of the Ācāryas; great guilt arises by reciting or listening to them.[2]

Thus here once again a myth or tradition related of an individual Ṛṣi (in this case Vasiṣṭha) is explicitly and directly connected with the descendants of that Ṛṣi.

Similar traditions are also related of other Ṛṣis : as for example of Atri. Several passages relate that, because Atri repelled the darkness of Svarbhānu and restored light to the worlds, therefore Ātreyas should be chosen to officiate at the sacrifice—and they should receive the first *dakṣiṇā*, before members of other *gotras* :

1. *Taittirīya Saṃhitā* 3.1.7.3, see also 5.4.11.
2. *Bṛhaddevatā* 4.105-119.

> The Asura Svarbhānu covered the sun with darkness; the gods could not perceive it, so they ran to Atri, and Atri destroyed its darkness through his utterance . . . . because of this, they choose an Ātreya under the moon, for Atri is indeed the light of that moon.[1]
>
> Darkness seized the sun, but Atri dispersed it . . . . he said to Atri : "Choose a boon", and Atri replied : "Let my offspring be worthy of a *dakṣiṇā*"; for this reason, the first *dakṣiṇā* in a sacrifice should be given to an Ātreya.[2]

In these passages once again, a tradition related of an individual Ṛṣi is explicitly connected with—and made relevant to—his descendants. Consequently, such passages may be said to reflect in some measure the status and interests of those descendants of the Ṛṣi : particularly since the extant form of many such passages constitutes an explanation or justification for the performance of a particular custom involving the descendants of that Ṛṣi.

In all of the cases noted in this sub-section, it can be seen that a conscious attempt is being made—by members of particular *gotras*—to increase, decrease, or simply account for the status and rank of both individual Ṛṣis and their *gotra*-descendants.

(e) *Conclusion*

We have seen in this section that certain traditions related of the Ṛṣis have been either formulated or manipulated for the express purpose of accounting for the status or rank both of the Ṛṣi himself and also of the descendants of that Ṛṣi. It is consequently clear that these traditions have developed largely under the influence of the Brahmin-members of particular *gotras*, seeking either to emphasise and enhance the status of their own Ṛṣi-ancestor (hence indirectly their own status as descendants of that Ṛṣi), or else to denigrate—or simply account for—the status of another Ṛṣi and his descendants : such a purpose being explicitly stated in certain of the passages noted in the last subsection. Thus the changes which occur in the status of any

1. *Pañcaviṃśa Brāhmaṇa* 6.6.8-11 : see also *Brahma Purāṇa* 13.9-11.
2. *Gopatha Brāhmaṇa* 1.2.17 : see also *Śatapatha Brāhmaṇa* 4.3.4.21.

individual Ṛṣi can be seen to reflect in some measure the changes in status of the descendants of that Ṛṣi; consequently, the changes which occur between the two main lists of the Seven Ṛṣis—where individual Ṛṣis are included in the one list but excluded from the other—may be said to reflect once again changes in the status of the descendants of such Ṛṣis.

The most notable changes which occur between the two main lists of the Seven Ṛṣis concern the omission of Viśvāmitra, Jamadagni, Bharadvāja, Gautama, and Kaśyapa from the second list, and the inclusion of Aṅgiras, Pulastya, Pulaha, Kratu, and Marīci—as also in some measure Bhṛgu—in that list. The process by which such changes occur has been noted especially in examining the lists of the seven main *gotras* in the Śrauta Sūtras, Epics and Purāṇas, and in examining the kinships and family-relationships which are said to exist between each of the individual Ṛṣis. In this respect, the omission of one Ṛṣi is invariably directly related to the inclusion of another Ṛṣi, and *vice versa*; in nearly every case where this process occurs, a Ṛṣi who is included in the first main list but excluded from the second is referred to in the Epics and Purāṇas as being the "son" of one of the Ṛṣis in the second main list—even though no such relationship is ever mentioned in Vedic literature. The very fact that such inclusions and omissions are evident in the context of listing Ṛṣi-*gotras* and Ṛṣi-*vaṃśas* implies that they are in some measure related to the changing status of the descendants of such Ṛṣis; and as we have seen, certain passages explicitly state that a myth or tradition has been related of a Ṛṣi precisely in order to illustrate or account for the status of the descendants of that Ṛṣi.

We may therefore conclude at this stage that the traditions of the Seven Ṛṣis—and especially the formulation of the second main list of the group—have been considerably influenced by the Brahmin *gotra*-descendants of particular Ṛṣis seeking to establish and consolidate their own status by manipulating the status ascribed either to their own Ṛṣi-ancestor or to other Ṛṣis. This in turn has given rise to the inclusion or omission of individual Ṛṣis in either of the two main lists of the Seven Ṛṣis. Thus the changes between the two main lists are directly related to changes in status among the descendants of individual Ṛṣis

TABLE 3

The Formulation of the Second Main List

(1)	Viśvāmitra	Jamadagni	Bharadvāja	Gotama	Atri	Vasiṣṭha	Kaśyapa	(Agastya)
(2)	Viśvāmitra	Bhṛgu	Aṅgiras		Atri	Vasiṣṭha	Kaśyapa	Agastya
(3)	(Bhṛgu)		Aṅgiras		Atri	Vasiṣṭha	Marīci	Pulastya, Pulaha, Kratu

(1) The first main list of the Seven Ṛṣis.
(2) The lists of the seven main *gotras*.
(3) The second main list of the Seven Ṛṣis.

during the periods of composition of these various texts. We shall examine further aspects of this conclusion in the general concluding section of this chapter.

C. Regional Factors

(a) *The Region of the Group*

(i) *Vedic Literature.* The region with which the Seven Ṛṣis are associated—as a group—throughout Vedic literature is invariably the north. The *Atharvaveda*, for example, speaks of the Seven Ṛṣis as guardians of the northern region, together with Viśvakarman :

> May Viśvakarman with the Seven Ṛṣis protect me from the northern region.... may those malignant ones who attack me from the northern region come upon Viśvakarman with the Seven Ṛṣis.[1]

A similar idea is also to be found in the early Iranian tradition, where Ahura Mazda is said to have created the Seven Stars (*haptoirngas*) to head the stars of the northern region and to protect the region against the demonic Yātus and Pairikas who sought to prevent the advance of Tishtrya or Sirius by hurling hostile shooting-stars.[2] Again in the *Hiraṇyakeśin Gṛhya Sūtra*, instructions are given to set up seats for the Seven Ṛṣis towards the north, and for Agastya towards the south :

> They prepare seats (for them) facing east, in a place inclined to the north, with north-pointing *darbha*-grass; in the space between Vasiṣṭha and Kāśyapa they prepare (a seat) for Arundhatī : and (a seat) for Agastya in the south, in a place inclined to the south.[3]

This association of the Seven Ṛṣis with the northern region is altogether predictable, given their identification with the

1. *Atharvaveda* 19.17.7, 19.18.7.
2. For example, *Sīrāzah* 1.13, 2.13: *Tīr Yashat* 6.12.
3. *Hiraṇyakeśin Gṛhya Sūtra* 2.8.19.2-7.

seven stars of Ursa Major which are closest to Dhruva or the northern celestial pole; the association of Agastya with the southern region is similarly predictable, given his identification with the southern star Canopus (as mentioned earlier in this chapter).

The association of the Seven Ṛṣis with the northern celestial pole is clearly implied by a passage in tha *Jaiminīya Upaniṣad, Brāhmaṇa*, which tells that the Seven Ṛṣis are located at the centre of the sky :

Where these Seven Ṛṣis are, there is the centre (*madhyam*) of the sky.[1] The "centre" may here be taken in the sense of the northern celestial pole, which constitutes the centre of the sky inasmuch as all other stars and constellations revolve around it : a view which is explicitly stated by the astronomer Varāhamihira[2]. Since the constellation of the Seven Ṛṣis or Ursa Major is that closest to the centre-point or "pivot" of the sky, the above passage may be seen as a poetic—if astronomically slightly imprecise—way of expressing their location. It is certainly not necessary to conclude with Tilak[3] and others that such references imply an observation being made from a circumpolar region directly beneath the northern celestial pole, since they are primarily intended—and interpreted by the astronomers—simply to indicate that region of the sky around which all the constellations and stars appear to be turning—hence the region which appears fixed or *dhruva*. The northern celestial pole is generally deemed to have been represented during the period presently in question by the star Thuban or Draconis, which is approximately mid-way between the present northern celestial pole (Polaris) and the Seven Ṛṣis or Ursa Major (see chapter 7). Consequently, the constellation of the Seven Ṛṣis would at this earlier period have been not only perhaps the most easily recognisable constellation in the northern hemisphere, but also unquestionably that closest to what was then the northern celestial pole.

1. *Jaiminīya Upaniṣad Brāhmaṇa* 4.26.12.
2. *Bṛhat-saṃhitā* 13.1-6.
3. B. Tilak, *The Arctic Home in the Vedas*, p. 55; see also his *Orion*.

Apart from relating that the Seven Ṛṣis are at the "centre" of the sky, other passages—as for example one in the *Śatapatha Brāhmaṇa*—relate that they rise in the north :

> They [the Kṛttikās or Pleiades, the wives of the Ṛṣis] were deprived of intercourse : for the Seven Ṛṣis rise in the north, and they in the east.[1]

It may be noted also that one passage in the *Ṛgveda* speaks of the Seven *vipras* or Ṛṣis as the Seven Oxen, who travel to the east for their enjoyment :

> The Seven *vipras,* along with the five Adhvaryus, [officiating priests], dearly protect the path of the bird [Agni] entrusted to them; the ageless oxen take their pleasure in the east—the divine ones take delight indeed in the observances of the gods.[2]

Similarly, the term "The Seven Oxen" is used to designate "The North" in many of the Latin languages, as for example in the Latin *septentriones.* Here once again, therefore, it would seem that the Seven Ṛṣis are implicitly associated with the northern region; such an association is parallel to that in further Indo-European contexts, and is also consistently followed throughout Vedic literature.

ii. *The Epics and Purāṇas.* In Vedic literature, the Seven Ṛṣis who are associated with the northern region are either explicitly or implicitly those of the first main list of the group : since, as we saw in Chapter I, this is the only list of the group which is known in that literature. The same association between this group of Seven Ṛṣis and the northern region is evident in a passage in the *Uttara Kāṇḍa* of the *Rāmāyaṇa* :

> Vasiṣṭha, Kaśyapa and Atri, Viśvāmitra and Gautama, Jamadagni and Bharadvāja—these are the Seven Ṛṣis; these seven constantly dwell in the northern region.[3]

---

1. *Śatapatha Brāhmaṇa* 2.1.2.4.
2. *Ṛgveda* 3.7.7; this passage is further discussed in Chapter 7.
3. *Rāmāyaṇa* 7.1.4-5 and 10.

Certain *parvans* of the *Mahābhārata* similarly retain this association. Thus a passage in the *Anuśāsana Parvan*, in recounting the deeds of Viśvāmitra, relates that he constantly resorts to the northern region :

He shines in the middle of the *brahma*-Ṛṣis and Dhruva, and always resorts to the northern region.[1]

The later *Śānti Parvan* again affords evidence of being a bridge between the two lists and traditions—as was seen also to be the case in Chapter I. One passage in this *parvan* lists the Seven Mind-born Sons of Brahmā and, while identifying them as the Seven Ṛṣis, nonetheless locates them in the east. It then refers to the Ṛṣis of the first main list; but it explicitly and perhaps purposely omits to call them the Seven Ṛṣis, while nonetheless still locating them in the northen region :

> These are the Seven Sons of Brahmā Svayambhū, the great-souled ones : Marīci, Atri, Aṅgiras, Pulastya, Pulaha, Kratu, and illustrious Vasiṣṭha, resembling Svayambhū; these are called the seven Brahmās in the Purāṇa, and have attained certainty. . . . they are the creators of the three worlds, O child, the seven Ṛṣis in the east. . . . Ātreya, Vasiṣṭha, and the great Ṛṣis Kaśyapa, Gautama and Bharadvāja, and Viśvāmitra Kauśika, and Jamadagni the lordly son of great-souled Ṛcīka —these seven resort to the northern region.[2]

It is noteworthy that in this passage "Atri" has now become "Ātreya" in the first main list of the group : a phenomenon comparable to that noted in the last section, where the Ṛṣis of the first main list become subordinated to those of the second by being termed their "sons". In the *Harivaṃśa*, a complete change in the regional associations of the groups is fully evident. A passage in this work lists the Ṛṣis of the second main list of group, calling them both the Sons of Brahmā and the Seven Ṛṣis, and also now locating them in the northern region :

> Marīci, lord Atrī, Aṅgiras, Pulaha, Kratu, Pulastya and Vasiṣṭha : these are the Seven Sons of Brahmā; these Seven Ṛṣis, are established in the northern region, O king.[3]

1. *Mahābhārata* 13.3.15.
2. Ibid., 12.201.1-35.
3. *Harivaṃśa* 7.7-8.

Just as this group of Ṛṣis has gradually—particularly throughout the *Mahābhārata*—come to replace the role of the Ṛṣis of the first main list, so too they have come to be located in that region which was previously ascribed to the Ṛṣis of the first main list. Thus while the Ṛṣis of the second main list are at one stage—in the *Mahābhārata*—said to live in the eastern region, they are at a later stage—in the *Harivaṃśa*—said to live in the northern region.

It is possible to discern a still earlier location ascribed to the Ṛṣis of the second main list, which is given in the *Rāmāyaṇa* version of the myth of Triśaṅku. In this myth, the attempts of Viśvāmitra to transfer Triśaṅku in bodily form to the sky are at first thwarted by Indra; but then Viśvāmitra in anger creates another group of Seven Ṛṣis together with another set of Nakṣatras[1]—and the *Rāmāyaṇa* version adds that these new Seven Ṛṣis, which the gods decree should remain for as long as the worlds endure, were created in the southern region :

> Filled with anger, he created another (group of) Seven Ṛṣis stationed in the southern region [*dakṣiṇamārgasthān*], and another garland of Nakṣatras.[2]

Thus this new group of Seven Ṛṣis created by Viśvāmitrā is said to be located in the southern region; and since Viśvāmitra himself is a member of the first main list of the Seven Ṛṣis—which, according to this same text, is located in the northern region—we may therefore conclude that this "new" group of Seven Ṛṣis in the southern region represents in effect the Ṛṣis of the second main list who, as we saw in Chapter I, are largely unknown to Vedic literature and first appear in the *Rāmāyaṇa*. Thus the Ṛṣis of the second main list are firstly (in the *Rāmāyaṇa* said to reside in the southern region, then (in the *Mahābhārata*) in the eastern region, and finally (in the *Harivaṃśa* and subsequently in the Purāṇas) in the northern region formely occupied by the Ṛṣis of the first main list.

---

1. For these creations, see the versions in *Mahābhārata* 1.65.20-42 : *Bhaviṣya Purāṇa* 4.130.9-39 : *Śiva Purāṇa* 5.2.38 : *Skanda Purāṇa* 6.7.1-19 : *Devībhāgavata Purāṇa* 7.13.1-62, 7.14.1-25.

2. *Rāmāyaṇa* 1.59.20-21.

At this point it should again be borne in mind that the northern location of the Seven Ṛṣis is demanded by their astronomical role, wherein they are identified with the seven stars of the constellation Ursa Major. Thus the fact that the second main list of the Seven Ṛṣis is first of all associated with the southern and eastern regions, and only subsequently with the northern region, is a further indication (complementary to that noted in Chapter I) that factors other than astronomical considerations have been operative in the origin, formulation and development of this second main list. From the *Harivaṃśa* onwards, however, the Ṛṣis of the second main list assume not only the title of the "Seven Ṛṣis" but also the geographical and astronomical significance of occupying the northern region; hence the astronomer Varāhamihira knows only of this second main list as constituting the Seven Ṛṣis, and he accordingly relates that it is they who inhabit the northern region.[1]

We may note here, on a more general level, that several of the myths related of the Seven Ṛṣis in the Purāṇas once again connect them with the northern region. One such myth, for example, relates that the Seven Ṛṣis divided the Gaṅgā into seven parts at Hardwar in the Himālayas;[2] while another myth, frequently encountered, relates how the Seven Ṛṣis persuaded Himālaya to give his daughter Pārvatī to Śiva.[3] In the latter myth, the Seven Ṛṣis are implicitly those of the second main list, since several versions relate that Aṅgiras acted as the spokesman for the group; similarly in further contexts it is this group of Ṛṣis, the Sons of Brahmā, who are said to live in the northern region.[4]

---

1. *Bṛhat-saṃhitā* 13.1-6.

2. *Bhāgavata Purāṇa* 1.14.50-51 : *Brahma Purāṇa* 172.15-19, 173.3ff. : *Bṛhaddharma Purāṇa* 2.22.1ff. : *Mahābhāgavata Purāṇa* 69.1 ff.

3. *Brahma Purāṇa* 34.17ff. : *Brahmavaivarta Purāṇa* 4.41.30—4.43.107 : *Kālikā Purāṇa* 10.1ff., 11.1ff. : *Mahābhāgavata Purāṇa* 24.1ff. : *Matsya Purāṇa* 154.311-425 : *Padma Purāṇa* 5.40.301-465 : *Saura Purāṇa* 57.44-80 : *Śiva Purāṇa* 2.2.19.26-76, 2.3.31.16—2.3.33.64, 2.3.39.51-55, 2.3.44.19-38 : *Skanda Purāṇa* 1.1.23.1-86, 6.245.16-17 : *Vāmana Purāṇa* 26.1-27.62 : *Kumārasambhava* 6.3-95.

4. For example, *Brahma Purāṇa* 5.8-9 : *Śiva Purāṇa* 5.34.9-10.

In order to further illustrate the regional associations of the two main lists of the Seven Ṛṣis, we shall next examine the regional associations of each of the individual Ṛṣis who are included in either of the two main lists.[1] It may be found helpful when examining these associations to refer to the map at the end of section C.

(*b*) *The Region of Ṛṣis in Vedic Literature*

The Vedic texts are centred primarily upon the region of the north Indian plain from the Panjāb and adjacent territories in the west to the Gaṅgā-Yamunā basin and central Gangetic region in the east (up to present-day Bīhar); they also take notice, to a lesser degree, of the eastern Gangetic region from Magadha to the lands of the Aṅgas, Kaliṅgas, Andhras and others (present-day Bīhar, West Bengal, Orissa and adjacent areas). These texts show little knowledge of regions to the south of the Vindhyas : it is indeed this very point which is of particular interest in the persent context, in examining the regions with which individual Ṛṣis in each of the two main lists of the Seven Ṛṣis are associated. It is therefore no surprise to find that, in Vedic literature, individual Ṛṣis are associated with regions which are generally well-known to the authors of those texts : namely with regions of northern India, particularly around the Panjāb and the Gaṅgā-Yamunā basin. We shall here cite a selection of examples in order to illustrate this point.

Both in the *Ṛgveda* and in subsequent texts, Vasiṣṭha is said to have crossed the Sindhu (Indus) river with Indra, and to have brought success to king Sudās through the help of Indra.[2] Both Vasiṣṭha and Viśvāmitra are referred to as being the Purohitas or family priests of king Sudās; with him they are associated especially with the region of Panjāb, particularly with

1. There are a number of useful works on the geography of early India : most helpful for the present context are S. M. Ali, *The Geography af the Purāṇas* : B. C. Law, *The Historical Geography of Ancient India* : and D. C. Sircar, *Studies in the Geography of Ancient and Medieval India.* It is interesting to note that in many of the places associated with the Ṛṣis, there exists to this day an Ashram named after such Ṛṣis.

2. For example *Ṛgveda* 7.33.3-7.

the rivers Vipāśā and Śutudrī (Vipas and Sutlej).[1] Similarly, Bharadvāja is spoken of as the Purohita of king Divodāsa the grandfather of Sudās;[2] he is also said to have taken part in the battle of the ten kings on the river Sindhu, alongside Mānuṣa.[3] Atri is also connected indirectly with that battle on the sindhu: for he is said to have received gifts from kings Trasadasyu and Tryaruṇa, both of whom were Puru kings with their capital on the Sarasvatī, and the former of whom was the son of Purukutsa who was killed in that battle.[4]

Viśvāmitra and Jamadagni are both said in one Brāhmaṇa context to have helped the Bharatas against the Ikṣvākus on the banks of the river Sindhu;[5] in a further context Viśvāmitra is said to have helped the Bharatas on the banks of either the Gaṅgā or the Yamunā.[6] According to the *Aitareya Brāhmaṇa*, the descendants of Viśvāmitra include those who live on the borders (of "civilised society"): including such peoples as the Andhras, Puṇḍras and others.[7]

Gotama is said to have accompanied king Māthava Videgha eastwards from the river Sarasvatī to the river Sadānīrā, which formed the boundary between the Kosalas and Videghas, and which had not been crossed by the Āryan peoples before the time of king Māthava.[8]

Just as Agastya remains throughout Vedic literature something of an outsider to the group of Seven Ṛṣis, so too his descendants are said to live "outside" or beyond the Kuru-Pañcālas—namely beyond the territory occupied by these tribes between the Panjāb and the Gaṅgā-Yamunā rivers.[9]

1. *Ṛgveda* 3.53.9-12, 7.33.3-7 : *Aitareya Brāhmaṇa* 8.21 : *Jaiminīya Brāhmaṇa* 3.23-24 : *Śāṅkhāyana Śrauta Sūtra* 16.11.13-14 : *Nirukta* 2.24, 9.29 : *Bṛhaddevatā* 4.105-119.
2. *Ṛgveda* 1.116.18, 6.31.4 : *Pañcaviṃśa Brāhmaṇa* 15.3.7.
3. *Jaiminīya Brāhmaṇa* 3.244-247.
4. *Bṛhaddevatā* 5.28-36.
5. *Jaiminīya Brāhmaṇa* 3.237-238.
6. Ibid., 3.183 : *Pañcaviṃśa Brāhmaṇa* 14.3.12-13.
7. *Aitareya Brāhmaṇa* 7.18.
8. *Śatapatha Brāhmaṇa* 1.4.1.10-20, 11.4.3.20.
9. *Jaiminīya Brāhmaṇa* 2.221.

It can therefore be seen from these examples that the individual Ṛṣis of the first main list are primarily associated in Vedic literature with regions lying especially around the main river-basins of north India : particularly around the Panjāb and around the Gaṅgā-Yamunā and eastern Gangetic regions, to the north of the Vindhyas.

(*c*) *The Region of Ṛṣis in the Rāmāyaṇa*

Within the *Rāmāyaṇa* the Gangetic valley and surrounding areas remain important localities insofar as each of the individual Seven Ṛṣis is concerned, and frequent references are made to their dwelling in these areas. Vasiṣṭha, for example, appears primarily in this work as the chief Purohita or family priest of king Daśaratha at Ayodhyā in the kingdom of Kosala.[1] Viśvāmitra is said to have his main abode on the banks of the river Kauśikī (a transformation of Satyavatī) close to the Himālayas;[2] it is also related of him that, while performing *tapas* in order to become a Brahmin, he travelled first to the southern region (where he created the "new" group of Seven Ṛṣis), then to Puṣkara in the western region, and then to the eastern region, before finally settling by the river Kauśikī in the northern region.[3] From there he also journeyed to visit king Daśaratha in Ayodhyā, to request that Rāma might accompany him to slay the Rākṣasas.[4]

Both Vasiṣṭha and Viśvāmitra are associated with several other Aikṣvāka kings of Ayodhyā, apart from Daśaratha : most notably with Triśaṅku,[5] and also in the case of Viśvāmitra with Ambarīṣa, at whose sacrifice Śunaḥśepa was rescued and adopted by Viśvāmitra.[6]

It is said that Gautama used to dwell with Ahalyā in an Ashram or hermitage near Mithilā, the capital of Videha, but that he later retired to the peaks of the Himālayas in order to

1. For example 1.69.17-32, 2.102.3-31, *etc.*
2. 1.33.10.
3. 1.50.1—1.64.18.
4. 1.56.10—1.59.33.
5. 1.60.5—1.61.27.
6. 1.60.5—1.61.27.

perform *tapas.*[1] Similarly, king Nimi is said to have founded the city of Vaijayanta close to the Ashram of Gautama on the slopes of the Himavat mountain.[2]

When Rāma sets out from Ayodhyā at the start of his banishment, he first visits the Ashram of Bharadvāja, near the confluence of the Gaṅgā and Yamunā (Prayāga, modern Allahabad).[3] From there he travels to the Citrakūṭa mountain (modern Citrakut, a short distance to the west of Allahabad), and thence arrives at the Ashram of Atri—where he is told of how in olden times Anasūyā, the wife of Atri, through her *tapas* caused the river Jāhnavī or Gaṅgā to flow in that place.[4]

It can thus be seen that the Ashrams or hermitages of all these Ṛṣis—namely Vasiṣṭha, Viśvāmitra, Gautama, Bharadvāja and Atri—are all considered in the *Rāmāyaṇa* to be predominantly in a region within or closely adjacent to the Gaṅgā-Yamunā river basins.

The consecration of Rāma, and his installation, as king of Ayodhyā, is said to have been performed by Vasiṣṭha, Kāśyapa and Gautama—together with other Ṛṣis not included in either of the two main lists of the Seven Ṛṣis.[5] The Kāśyapa Ṛṣyaśṛṅga is also said to have married the daughter of the king of Aṅga, and to have visited king Daśaratha to perform an *aśvamedha* sacrifice with Vasiṣṭha.[6] Thus although the Ṛṣi Kaśyapa is not explicitly involved in such accounts, it is clear that certain of his descendants are again associated with the northern region of India—in particular with the eastern Gangetic area. Noteworthy in the *Rāmāyaṇa* is the paucity of individual references to Jamadagni, who appears only once as the father of Paraśurāma,[7] and once in a list of Ṛṣis who come to visit Rāma after he has regained his kingdom. In this latter list [already cited in sub-section (a) ii. above], it is related that

1. 1.47.11-32.
2. 7. appendix 1 no. 8 lines 91-94.
3. 2.48.8-9.
4. 2.109.6-10.
5. 6.116.55.
6. 1.8.1—1.12.20.
7. 1.73.16 ff.

the Seven Ṛṣis Vasiṣṭha, Kaśyapa, Atri, Viśvāmitra, Gautama, Jamadagni, and Bharadvāja—namely those of the first main list—all came from the northern region in order to visit Rāma in Ayodhyā.[1] Thus it may be said that all of the Ṛṣi-members of the first main list of Seven Ṛṣis are consistently associated in the *Rāmāyaṇa*, both individually and as a group, primarily with the northern region of India.

Agastya is frequently mentioned throughout the *Rāmāyaṇa* as inhabiting the southern region. His Ashram is said to be at Pañcavaṭī, near the source of the river Godāvarī, where Rāma resides during his exile;[2] he is also famed as having made the Vindhya mountains bow before him, as he travelled to take up residence in the south.[3] It is near his Ashram in the south that he is said to have devoured the demon Vātāpi, whose name would appear to have been adopted as that of the Cālukya city Vātāpi or Bādāmi in the Western Deccan.[4] It is also related that he dwells on the summit of Mount Malaya, in the southernmost part of the Western Ghats: near the rivers Kāverī and Tāmraparṇī; and close to the city of the Pāṇḍyas.[5] Among the Ṛṣis who came from the southern region to pay homage to Rāma at his installation as king of Ayodhyā were Agastya, together in some textual recensions with Atri, as well as other Ṛṣis not included in either of the two main lists of the Seven Ṛṣis.[6] The "Atri" mentioned in this context is evidently to be distinguished from the "Atri" mentioned in the following verses of this passage as a member of the Seven Ṛṣis (of the first main list); who came to Ayodhyā from the northern region; the passage is therefore of particular interest, since Atri appears in both main lists of the Seven Ṛṣis rather than in only one. By associating Atri in this way with both the southern and northern regions, the passage again implies a point already noted earlier in this section—namely that the Ṛṣis of the second main list

1 7.1.4-5 and *10.
2. 3.12.1 ff., 1.3.11.
3. 3.10.81-92, 4.51.7.
4. 3.10.53-64.
5. 4.40.15-23.
6. 7.1.3 and 7.

are associated primarily (both individually and as a group) with the southern region.

In the case of Agastya, this Ṛṣi is unquestionably associated with the southern region; and as we saw earlier in this chapter, Agastya is variously said to be either the son of Pulastya or the father of Pulastya, Pulaha and Kratu—all three of whom appear only in the second main list of the Seven Ṛṣis. In the *Rāmāyaṇa*, the Yakṣas—the sons of Pulastya—are said to dwell near the Ashram of Agastya;[1] Agastya is also said to have cursed the Yakṣa Mārīca, descendant of Marīci, to become a Rākṣasa.[2] This latter Mārīca is the friend and ally of the Rākṣasa king Rāvaṇa, the opponent of Rāma, who together with other Rākṣasas is said to reside in Laṅkā (modern Sri Lanka) : and all of these Rākṣasas—such as Kumbhakarṇa, Vibhīṣaṇa and Indrajit—are said to be either sons or descendants of Pulastya.[3] Apart from being the ancestor of these Yakṣas and Rākṣasas of the southern region, Pulastya is also said to have gone to Māhiṣmatī on the banks of the river Narmadā—the capital of king Arjuna Kārttavīrya—in order to persuade Arjuna to release Rāvaṇa whom he had captured.[4] It is further related of Pulastya that he performed *tapas* on the slopes of Meru, and that through his curse was born Viśravas, who eventually gained as his wife the daughter of Bharadvāja—from whom was born Vaiśravaṇa or Kuvera. The latter is said to have dwelt originally in Laṅkā, but to have been expelled from there by his brother Rāvaṇa, whereafter he went to dwell on Mount Kailāsa in the Himālayas.[5] It can thus be seen that Pulastya, together with his descendants the Yakṣas and Rākṣasas is very much associated with the southern region, south of the Vindhyas and including Sri Lanka; while certain passages also connect him with the Himālayas.

Particularly in the case of Pulastya, a similar process is evidently occurring as has been seen to be operative with the second

1. 3.10.81-92.
2. 1.24.8-12.
3. 5.21.4-7, 6.49.9-23, 6.68.12, *etc.*
4. 7.32.1 – 7.33.23.
5. 7.2.4—7.17.31.

main list of the Seven Ṛṣis as a group : whereby they are associated firstly with the southern region, and then subsquently with the northern region. The latter association is likely to be due in part to an attempt to associate such Ṛṣis with those regions—particularly Kurukṣetra and the Himālayas—which were considered by the Vedic authors to be in a sense the most sacred of regions : as well as being the regions with which the Ṛṣis of the first main list were primarily associated, whose role and importance is gradually adopted by the Ṛṣis of the second main list. Thus by associating such Ṛṣis as Agastya and Pulastya with the northern region, their claims to at least equal status with the Ṛṣis of the first main list—who were previously associated, in Vedic literature, with the northern region—are thereby furthered : even though these Ṛṣis nonetheless othewise remain predominantly associated with the southern rather than the northern region.

Just as the demon-figure Mārīca is said to dwell in Laṅkā with Rāvaṇa and the other Rākṣasas, so too the Mārīcas as a group are spoken of as being the friends and allies of the monkey Sugrīva, who go to the western region in search of Sītā : travelling by implication from a region south of the Vindhyas to Avantī, Surāṣṭra, and the borders of the ocean.[1] Since Mārīca is said to have been originally a Yakṣa before being cursed by Agastya to be a Rākṣasa, therefore the Mārīcas as a whole might logically be termed Yakṣas—and thus sons of Pulastya, the father of both Yakṣas and Rākṣasas. The association of the Mārīcas or descendants of Marīci with the southern region is therefore complementary to the association of Pulastya himself with that region, and the various relationships which are said to exist between Agastya on the one hand and the three Ṛṣis Pulastya, Pulaha and Kratu on the other hand again complement the association of all of these Ṛṣis with the southern region, in view of the strong association of Agastya with the south. Since all four of the Ṛṣis Mārīci, Pulastya, Pulaha and Kratu appear in the second main list of the Seven Ṛṣis—along with Atri, who is said to have accompanied Agastya from the southern region—we may therefore conclude that the second

1. 4.41.1, 845, 4.41.3, 850.

main list as a whole is closely connected with the southern region of India, namely the region to the south of the Vindhyas and including Ṣri Lanka. This conclusion is therefore parallel to that reached earlier through studying the regional references to the group as a whole: where the "new" group of Seven Ṛṣis, first referred to in the *Rāmāyaṇa*, is created by Viśvāmitra in the south; it is further demonstrated by reference in subsequent Epic and Purāṇic contexts, as we shall now see.

(*d*) *The Region of Ṛṣis in the Mahābhārata and the Purāṇas*

The pattern of regional association which has been observed in the *Rāmāyaṇa* is very largely followed also in the *Mahābhārata* and in the Purāṇas. In order to illustrate this point, we shall cite a number of examples for each of the individual Ṛṣis who appear in either of the two main lists of the Seven Ṛṣis.

i. *Viśvāmitra* : Viśvāmitra is said to have his Ashram by the river Kauśikī or Parā,[1] to which he eventually retires after having first inherited the kingdom of Kānyakubja or Kanauj from his father Gādhi.[2] He is said to have favoured the country of Magadha[3], and to have a sacred river near the Vaidurya mountain in the west,[4] as well as another Ashram on the west bank of the river Sarasvatī where he quarrelled with Vasiṣṭha.[5] He is associated especially with the Aikṣvāka king Triśaṅku of Ayodhyā,[6] and with other Aikṣvāka kings:[7] while Kauśika Brahmins are said to dwell near Dvārakā.[8]

(ii) *Jamadagni* : Jamadagni is said to have performed sacrifices at Palāśaka, near the Sarasvatī and Dṛṣadvatī rivers;[9] he

1. *Mahābhārata* 1.65.20-42, 1.66.1-15, 3.82.113-114, 3.85.9-12, 3.109.18-20, 13.3.10,
2. Ibid., 1.165.1-44.
3. Ibid., 2.19.3-11.
4. Ibid., 3.87.7-12.
5. Ibid., 9.39.11 ff., 9.41.1 ff. : *Skanda Purāṇa* 6.172.1-22 : *Vāmana Purāṇa, saromāhātmya* 19.1-43.
6. Ibid., 1.65.20-42 : *Harivaṃśa* 10.1-20 : *Brahmāṇḍa Purāṇa* 2.3.63.113ff.: *Brahma Purāṇa* 7.105-109 : *Skanda Purāṇa* 6.4.1—6.8.9 : *Liṅga Purāṇa* 1.66.6-11: *Śiva Purāṇa* 5.37.47—5.38.18 : *etc.*
7. Ibid., 1.66.1—1.68.25. 13.3.6 ff.
8. *Mārkaṇḍeya Purāṇa* 6.24-25.
9. *Mahābhārata* 3.83.13-16.

is also said to have performed *tapas* at Bhṛgukaccha or Broach,[1] and to have a *tirtha* or sacred pool at the confluence of the river Narmadā and the ocean.[2] He was killed by the Haihaya king Arjuna Kārttavīrya, who had his capital at Māhiṣmatī on the river Narmadā;[3] while Arjuna was in turn killed—along with all the Kṣatriyas—by Jamadagni's son Rāma, who thereafter went to dwell either on Mount Mahendra (probably in the eastern region of modern Orissa),[4] or at Sūrpāraka or Rāmeśvaram by the shores of the southern ocean.[5] Jamadagni's wife Reṇukā is said to have desired either Citraratha, king of the Gandharvas, or Arjuna Haihaya—on account of which Jamadagni ordered Rāma to kill her.[6]

iii. *Bharadvāja* : Bharadvāja is said to dwell at the sources of the Gaṅgā[7]; so too his son Yavakrīta was killed at the Ashram of Raibhya near that of Bharadvāja, close to the Bhṛgutuṅga mountain in the Himālayas and to the rivers Tuṣṇī and Gaṅga[8]. He is further said to go to the Gaṅgā for his bath—which gives occasion for his cursing of Viṣṇu.[9] He is referred to as the Purohita of king Divodāsa of Kāśī or Banaras,[10] and as having given the *Āyurveda* to the king of Kāśī;[11] also as having been adopted by king Bharata,[12] as being the father of Droṇa—warrior in the

---

1. *Skanda Purāṇa* 5.3.218.1-57.
2. *Matsya Purāṇa* 194.30-35 : *Kūrma Purāṇa* 2.40.31-32.
3. *Mahābhārata* 3.116.1-18, 12.49.39ff. : *Agni Purāṇa* 4.14-20 : *Bhāgavata Purāṇa* 9.15.1—9.16.16 : *Brahmāṇḍa Purāṇa* 2.3.26-30 : *Brahmavaivarta Purāṇa* 3.24.1—3,27.50 : *Padma Purāṇa* 6.268.1-81 : *Skanda Purāṇa* 5.3.218-1-57, 6.66.1-61, 6.69.1-27 : *etc.*
4. Ibid., 1.121.12-18, 3.83.14-15, 3.85.14-17, 3.117.1-10 : *Harivaṃśa* 31.100-109 : *Agni Purāṇa* 4.14-20 : *Bhāgavata Purāṇa* 9.16.16-27 : *etc.*
5. Ibid., 3.86.7-11, 3.83.39-40, 12.49.56 ff. : *Skanda Purāṇa* 5.2.29.14-54.
6. Ibid., 3.116.5-14 : *Bhāgavata Purāṇa* 9.16.1-8 : *Kāñcipurāṇam* 46.1-34.
7. Ibid., 1.121.3-11.
8. Ibid., 3.135.7-9.
9. Ibid., 12.329.42.
10. Ibid., 13.31.22 ff.
11. *Brahma Purāṇa* 11.37-38.
12. *Mahābhārata* 1.89.17-19 : *Harivaṃśa* 23.49-53 : *Agni Purāṇa* 278.8-10 : *Brahma Purāṇa* 13.58-61 : *Bhāgavata Purāṇa* 9.20.34-39 : *Matsya Purāṇa* 49.13-35 : *Śiva Purāṇa* 5.4.38 : *Viṣṇu Purāṇa* 4.19.1 ff.

Bhārata war in Kurukṣetra[1], and as dwelling in Prayāga (modern Allahabad)[2]. Bhāradvājas are listed as peoples of northern countries,[3] and as dwelling near Dvārakā.[4]

iv. *Gautama* : Gautama is said to have cast his father Dīrghatamas into the Gaṅgā, whence he travelled downstream to found the realms of Aṅga, Vaṅga Kaliṅga, Puṇḍra and Suhma;[5] he is also said to have lived in Girivraja, the capital of Magadha near Gayā.[6] and to have protected king Bṛhadratha on the banks of the Gaṅgā.[7] He is said to be the father of Aśvatthāman and Kṛpa, warriors in the Bhārata war in Kurukṣetra,[8] and also to have performed *tapas* for 60,000 years in his Ashram on the Pāriyātra or western Vindhya hills.[9] Gautama Brahmins are additionally said to dwell in Dvārakā.[10]

v. *Atri* Atri is said to have his Ashram among the snows by the source of the river Airāvatī in the Himālayas,[11] and to have gone to Videha to instruct king Nimi on the performance of *śrāddha* rites.[12] He is also said to have performed *tapas* for obtaining a son on Mount Ṛkṣakala, on the banks of the river Nirvindhya,[13] on the banks of river Narmadā,[14] and in the Kamala forest in the south, by the Citrakūṭa mountain.[15] Ātreyas are additionally said to be peoples of northern countries.[16]

vi. *Vasiṣṭha*: Vasiṣṭha is associated with the rivers Vipāśā and Śutudrī or Śatadrū,[17] as also with the Sarasvatī and Sarayū[18]

1. *Mahābhārata* 1.57.88-96, 1.121.3-9.
2. *Rāmacaritamānasa* 1.43.1ff.
3. *Mārkaṇḍeya Purāṇa* 57.39 : *Vāmana Purāṇa* 13.41 ff.
4. Ibid., 6.24-25.
5. *Mahābhārata* 1.98.17-33.
6. Ibid., 2.19.3-11, 3.82.88-93.
7. Ibid., 12.49.56 ff.
8. Ibid., 1.57.88-90, 1.120.3-21.
9. Ibid., 12.127.3 ff.
10. *Mārkaṇḍeya Purāṇa* 6.24-25.
11. *Matsya Purāṇa* 119.55 ff.
12. *Mahābhārata* 13.91-18 ff.
13. *Śiva Purāṇa* 3.19.2-16.
14. *Skanda Purāṇa* 5.3.103.1-109.
15. *Śiva Purāṇa* 4.3.7-39, 5.2.18-19.
16. *Mārkaṇḍeya Purāṇa* 57.39 : *Vāmana Purāṇa* 13.41 ff.
17. *Mahābhārata* 1.167.1-20, 3.130.8-9, 13.3.12-13.
18. Ibid., 9.39.11ff., 9.41.1 ff., 13.140.15 ff. : *Vāmana Purāṇa, Saromāhātmya* 19.1-43 : *Skanda Purāṇa* 6.172.1-22.

and he is said to have made Kurukṣetra sacred by performing *tapas* there.[1] He is associated with Triśaṅku and with other Aikṣvāka kings of Ayodhyā—a city which he is himself said to have protected;[2] he is also spoken of as the Purohita of the Bharatas[3] and of the Aikṣvākas of Ayodhyā.[4] He is said to have an Ashram on the slopes of Mount Meru,[5] and to have cast himself in grief from the summit of Meru;[6] while a mountain in the Himālayas is said to bear his name,[7] and he is variously associated in further contexts with the Himalayas.[8] He is reputed to have introduced Vāmācāra Tantrism to Kāmarūpa or Assam,[9] and to have lived and died in the eastern region;[10] while Vāsiṣṭhas are said to live close to Mount Mahendra (in modern Orissa)[11]. He is additionally associated with the Arbudācala mountain (Mount Abu),[12] and is said to have obtained the city of Pratiṣṭhāna on the river Godāvarī for Sudyumna.[13]

(vii) *Kaśyapa* : Kaśyapa is said to have installed Varuṇa as lord of waters in the western region, where he himself also resides;[14] while Kāśyapa-dvīpa is said to be one of the seven divisions of Jambudvīpa, identified with Kashmir.[15] His sons are said to have first multiplied in the eastern region;[16] Kāśyapas

1. *Mahābhārata* 1.89.31-42.
2. Ibid., 1.168.15-25 : *Harivāṃśa* 9.88-100, 10.1-20 : *Agni Purāṇa* 5.14 : *Brahma Purāṇa* 7.48-58, 8.1-21 : *Brahmāṇḍa Purāṇa* 2.3.63.15-177 ; *Śiva Purāṇa* 5.38.1-18 : *Skanda Purāṇa* 6.2.1-23, 6.3.1-31 : *Devībhāgavata Purāṇa* 7.9.1-11. 7.10.1-58.
3. Ibid., 1.89.31-42.
4. Ibid., 1.164.1-14, 1.166.1—1.168.25, 12.75.1 ff., 13.77.1ff. : *Brahmāṇḍa Purāṇa* 2.3.48.29ff. : *Bhaviṣya Purāṇa* 1.118.19 : *Viṣṇu Purāṇa* 4.2.1ff. : *Śiva Purāṇa* 5.37.5.
5. Ibid., 1.93.6.
6. Ibid., 1.166.35-43.
7. Ibid., 1.207.2 ff.
8. Ibid., 3.81.155-157, 3.82.43-44, 3.130.14-16.
9. *Kālikā Purāṇa* 84.1 ff.
10. *Mahābhārata* 5.106.13.
11. Ibid., 3.115.1-4.
12. *Skanda Purāṇa* 7.3.1.1-35.
13. *Brahma Purāṇa* 6.21 : *Liṅga Purāṇa* 1.65.29 : *Śiva Purāṇa* 5.36.20; *Viṣṇu Purāṇa* 4.1.1 ff.
14. *Mahābhārata* 5.108.3-18.
15. Ibid., 6.6.57, 3.13.10-11 : *Bhaviṣya Purāṇa* 3.1.6.5-6.
16. Ibid., 5.106.6.

are said to dwell by Mount Mahendra (in Orissa),[1] while it was to Mount Mahendra that Kaśyapa banished Rāma.[2] He is said to have gone to Kāśī or Banaras to worship Śiva[3] : and he is famed as having been incarnated in Mathurā as Vasudeva, the father of Vāsudeva-Kṛṣṇa-Viṣṇu.[4]

It can be seen from these references to the regions associated with the individual Ṛṣis of the first main list that such Ṛṣis are generally thought of as residing in northern regions, as opposed particularly to residing in regions south of the Vindhyas. Three exceptions to this must be noted : namely in the cases of Atri (associated also with the rivers Nirvindhyā and Narmadā), of Vasiṣṭha (associated with Arbudācala, and with the city of Pratiṣṭhāna on the river Godāvarī), and of Jamadagni (associated with Bhṛgukaccha and the river Narmadā). In the cases of Atri and Vasiṣṭha, their association with regions to the south of the Vindhyas is clearly parallel to their inclusion also in the second main list of the Seven Ṛṣis which, as we have already seen, is itself closely connected with the southern region. In the case of Jamadagni, it would seem that the Jāmadagnyas tended to settle in this region of India which was, by and large, beyond the known limits of Vedic Aryan culture : this in turn helps to explain the relative paucity of references to the region of this Ṛṣi in Vedic literature. It is particularly relevant to note that, while in social terms the Jāmadagnyas are assimilated to the Bhārgava *gotra*, so too the region with which both Bhṛgu and the Bhārgavas are most closely associated is similarly that around Bhṛgukaccha and the river Narmadā (see below). This therefore helps to explain why Jamadagni—although associated with a region to

1. *Mahābhārata* 3.115.1 ff.

2. Ibid., 3.117.11 ff., 12.49.56ff. : *Agni Purāṇa* 4.14-29 : *Bhāgavata Purāṇa* 9.16.7-27 : *Harivaṃśa* 31.100-109.

3. *Śiva Purāṇa* 3.18.2-22.

4. *Harivaṃśa* 45.20-45 : *Agni Purāṇa* 276.1-2 : *Bhaviṣya Purāṇa* 4.55.34 : *Matsya Purāṇa* 47.8-10 : *Padma Purāṇa* 5.13.148-150 : *Brahmavaivarta Purāṇa* 2.49.50, 4.7.1 ff. ; *etc.*

the south of the Vindhyas, as well as with the northern region—was nonetheless excluded from the second main list of Seven Ṛṣis : namely because the Bhārgava *gotra* had expanded largely at the expense of the Jāmadagnya *gotra*, whence by reflection in the literature Bhṛgu came to undermine the status of Jamadagni and to be assimilated (and in some measure included) within the second main list of the Seven Ṛṣis.

We shall now examine references to the regions with which the individual Ṛṣis of the second main list are associated. It must firstly be noted that such references are hardly ever found for the Ṛṣis : Marīci, Pulaha and Kratu within these texts; furthermore, there are few individual myths related of these Ṛṣis, which might otherwise associate them with a particular region.[1] In the second place, we have already seen that Atri and Vasiṣṭha are the only two Ṛṣis who appear in both of the main lists of Seven Ṛṣis, and since the regional references associated with them have already been examined, we shall now deal accordingly with the two remaining Ṛṣis of the second main list—namely Aṅgiras and Pulastya together with Bhṛgu and Agastya, both of whom have been seen to be closely associated with this second main list.

viii. *Aṅgiras*: Aṅgiras is said to have been born at the *tīrtha* of Dadhīci on the banks of the river Sarasvatī.[2] He is said to dwell at Prayāga (modern Allahabad);[3] while Āṅgirases are said to dwell by Mount Mahendra (in Orissa).[4]

ix. *Pulastya*: Bhīṣma is said to have seen and discoursed with Pulastya at the sources of the Gaṅgā.[5] Pulastya is however said to have his Ashram at Vīranagara on the banks of the river Devikā[6]; he is said to have visited Arjuna Haihaya

---

1. One exception may be noted in the case of Pulaha, who is said in a previous birth to have been a mosquito in a Śaiva temple in Kurukṣetra—becoming after death a Son of Brahmā on account of his devotion to Śiva : *Saura Purāṇa* 67.13-15.
2. *Mahābhārata* 3.81.163-164, 3.98.12.
3. Ibid., 3.83.65-67.
4. Ibid., 3.115.1-4.
5. Ibid., 3.80.11-21 : *Padma Purāṇa* 5.2.46 ff.
6. *Viṣṇu Purāṇa* 2.15.6.

in Māhiṣmatī on the river Godāvarī to secure the release of Rāvaṇa[1], and to have given Kuvera lordship over Laṅkā, which was subsequently seized by Rāvaṇa.[2] He is said to have cursed the Yakṣa Vidyādhara to become a wild boar—the latter being released from the curse by king Rājarāja Pāṇḍya, and his body becoming Mount Panrimalai.[3] His wife Ilā, the daughter of king Tṛṇabindu, is said to have been a pupil of Agastya and to have performed *tapas* in Java.[4]

x. *Bhṛgu*: Bhṛgu is said to have practised tapas on Mount Puru, near Gaṅgādvāra (modern Hardwar), whence his Ashram there became known as Bhṛgutuṅga.[5] He is also said to have *tirthas* or sacred pools by the Bhāgirathī river,[6] and at the Daśāśvamedha Ghat.[7] Bhārgavas are said to reside in the Himavat mountains,[8] in the eastern region,[9] and by Mount Mahendra (Orissa):[10] as also near Dvārakā,[11] where Bhṛgu is said to have visited Kṛṣṇa.[12] Bhṛgu is also said to have an Ashram by the river Godāvarī,[13] and a *tirtha* by the river Narmadā which became known as Bhṛgukaccha (modern Broach):[14] while Bhārgavas are similarly said to live by the river Narmadā[15], and at Govardhana near Nasik and the sources of the river Godāvarī.[16]

xi. *Agastya* : Agastya is said to have both an Ashram and a mountain near Prayāga (modern Allahabad) in the eastern

1. *Brahma Purāṇa* 13.186-187 : *Matsya Purāṇa* 43.37-39.
2. *Mahābhārata* 3.258.11-16.
3. *Tiruvilayāṭarpurāṇam* 45.52-55.
4. *Agastyaparva* 394.1 ff.
5. *Mahābhārata* 3.88.18-20, 1.207.2 ff.
6. Ibid., 3.97.35-37.
7. *Matsya Purāṇa* 193.23-53 : *Padma Purāṇa* 1.20.23-82.
8. *Mahābhārata* 1.169.11-25.
9. *Mārkaṇḍeya Purāṇa* 57.44 : *Vāmana Purāṇa* 13.45.
10. *Mahābhārata* 3.115.1-4.
11. *Mārkaṇḍeya Purāṇa* 6.24-25.
12. *Kūrma Purāṇa* 1.26.5.
13. *Bṛhannāradīya Purāṇa* 15.2-46.
14. *Mārkaṇḍeya Purāṇa* 57.52, 58.22 : *Matsya Purāṇa* 113.50 : *Skanda Purāṇa* 5.3.181.1-65.
15. *Mahābhārata* 3.121.19-21 : *Skanda Purāṇa* 1.2.3.1 ff.
16. *Mārkaṇḍeya Purāṇa* 57.35.

region[1]; he is said to have cursed Kuvera on the banks of the river Yamunā,[2] and to have travelled to Gayaśiras near Gayā in order to visit Dharma.[3] He is said to have gained Lopāmudrā as his wife at the Sindhu *tīrtha* on the river Sarasvatī,[4] and to have practised *tapas* with her at Gaṅgādvāra (modern Hardwar)[5] where the Bhāgirathī flows past his Ashram[6]; as also to have a *tirtha* in the Himālayas.[7] He is also said to have gained Lopāmudrā from the king of the Vidarbhas, in the western Vindhyas[8]. It is related that he caused the Vindhyas to bow low as he travelled to the south[9], going from Kāśī (Banaras) to Kāñcī and Mount Potiyai in order to restore the balance of the earth, after the Seven Ṛṣis had gone to the Himālayas to attend the wedding of Śiva and Parvatī.[10] He is said to have performed *tapas* in Ujjayinī,[11] to have another Ashram on the Vaidūrya mountain[12], and to have *tīrthas* in the southern country of the Pāṇḍyas[13] and in the Draviḍa land south of the Godāvarī river.[14] He devoured the demon Vātāpi, associated with the city of Vātāpi or Bādāmi in the Deccan[15], and married the river Kāverī, which flowed from his overturned water-pot.[16] He also married

1. *Mahābhārata* 3.85.14-17.
2. Ibid., 3.158.51-59.
3. Ibid., 3.93.9-12.
4. Ibid., 3.130.5-6.
5. Ibid., 3.95.11.
6. Ibid., 3.97.32.
7. Ibid., 1.207.2 ff.
8. Ibid., 3.94.11-27.
9. Ibid., 3.102.2-15 : *Brahma Purāṇa* 118.2-8 . *Padma Purāṇa* 5.19.145-198 : *Skanda Purāṇa* 4.1.4.1—4.1.5.109 : *Vāmana Purāṇa* 19.21-36 : *Devībhāgavata Purāṇa* 10.2.1 ff. : *Viṣṇudharmottara Purāṇa* 1.213.1ff : *Bṛhat-saṃhitā* 12. 1-13 : *Kandapurāṇam* 2.22.1—2.25.13 : *Agastyaparva* 343.6-13.
10. *Kāñcipurāṇam* 63.185-288 : *Kandapurāṇam* 1.10.46-64.
11. *Skanda Purāṇa* 5.1.55.1-33, 5.2.1.1-59 : *Saura Purāṇa* 67.1ff.
12. *Mahābhārata* 3.86.12-16.
13. Ibid., 3.86.7-11.
14. Ibid., 3.118.4.
15. Ibid., 3.94.4—3.97.15 : *Agni Purāṇa* 206.1-12 : *Bhāgavata Purāṇa* 6.18.15 : *Skanda Purāṇa* 7.1.284.1-33 : *Devībhāgavata Purāṇa* 6.9.38 ff. : *Viṣṇudharmottara Purāṇa* 1.213.1 ff. : *Bṛhat-saṃhitā* 12.1-13 : *Kandapurāṇam* 2.20.1-31, 2.26.1-32.
16. *Kandapurāṇam* 2.23.1-28, 2.27.1-66 : *Kāverīpurāṇam* 5.1-49 : *Tulākāverīvāṅmayam* 5-6 : *Tiruvaiyārrupurāṇam* 4.1-25.

the daughter of a Draviḍa king[1], and cursed the Pāṇḍya king Indradyumna of the Draviḍa country[2]; while he was visited on Mount Potiyamalai by the Cera, Cola and Pāṇḍya kings.[3] He is additionally said to live on Mount Malaya[4], and to have defeated the Vaiṣṇavas in Tirukurrāla[5]; while he is famed as having taught the Tamil grammar to Nakkiran in Madurai[6], and is reputed to be the foremost *yogin* of Java[7].

It can therefore be seen that, with one or two notable exceptions, the regional associations of Ṛṣis evident in the *Rāmāyaṇa* are again generally followed in the *Mahābhārata* and in the Purāṇas : whereby the Ṛṣis of the first main list are associated predominantly with regions to the north of the Vindhyas, while the Ṛṣis of the second main list are associated predominantly with southern regions. One exception has already been discussed in the case of Jamadagni; a further qualification must be made in the case of Aṅgiras, whose inclusion in the second main list would seem likely to be due to reasons of a social or *gotra*-rather than regional-nature. Nonetheless, distinct patterns of the regional associations of Ṛṣis emerge from these texts, and we can now therefore draw certain conclusions on the basis of the material which has been surveyed in this section.

(*e*) *Conclusion*

Taking as a whole all of the references cited in this section, we can see that a definite pattern emerges overall: whereby the Ṛṣis who appear in the first main list of the Seven Ṛṣis are associated primarily—both individually and as a group—with regions of India to the north of the Vindhyas, while the

1. *Bhāgauata Purāṇa* 4.28.32.
2. Ibid., 8.4.7-10.
3. *Tiruvilaiyāṭarpurāṇam* 14.2-30.
4. *Bhāgavata Purāṇa* 6.3.35.
5. *Tirukkurrālattalapurāṇam* 2.3.33-171 : *Kandapurāṇam* 2.28.1-19.
6. *Tiruvilaiyāṭarpurāṇam* 54.7-22.
7. *Agastyaparva* 343.6-13. On the South Indian and South-East Asian traditions of Agastya, see also J. Gonda, 'The Old Javanese Agastyaparva' : R.M.Ng. Poerbatjaraka *Agastya in den Archipel* : K. A. N. Sastri, 'Agastya'. For an analysis of certain themes in the South Indian traditions of Agastya and other Ṛṣis, see D.D. Shulman, *Tamil Temple Myths*.

Ṛṣis who appear in the second main list are associated primarily—both individually and as a group—with southern regions of India, and also with Sri Lanka and Java.

This pattern is not exclusive : thus for example Viśvāmitra, who appears only in the first main list, is said on one occasion to have performed *tapas* in the southern region, where he also created the "new" group of Seven Ṛṣis; while both Pulastya and Agastya—the former of whom appears only in the second main list, and the latter of whom is closely connected with the Ṛṣis Marīci, Pulastya, Pulaha and Kratu who also appear only in the second list—are associated in places with the northern region. These, however, form only a minority of references to the regions with which such Ṛṣis are associated; the overall pattern is indicative of an association of the one list with the northern region, and of the other list with the southern region. Furthermore, the Ṛṣis Atri and Vasiṣṭha—who appear in both main lists of the Seven Ṛṣis—are also associated with both the northern and the southern regions: thereby tending once again to reinforce these patterns of the regional associations of the two main lists of the Seven Ṛṣis.

It is also necessary to note that Aṅgiras, in the small number of regional references related of him, is associated with northern rather than southern regions, even though he appears only in the second main list. On the other hand, however, both Aṅgiras and Vasiṣṭha—in distinction from any other Ṛṣis—share in certain myths with Agastya, who is clearly very much the Ṛṣi of the south. Thus for example both Agastya and Aṅgiras—and no other Ṛṣis—are said to have drunk the ocean through the powers of their *tapas*;[1] while both Agastya and Vasiṣṭha—and no other Ṛṣis—are said to have been born when the seed of Mitra-Varuṇa fell into a pot, whence both are on occasions termed "Pot-born" (*kumbhaja, kumbhayoni*).[2] The

1. For example *Mahābhārata* 3.101.1—3.103.19 : 13.138.3.

2. For example *Ṛgveda* 7.33.10-13 : *Nirukta* 5.13-14 : *Bṛhaddevatā* 5.143-160 : *Mahābhārata* 3.101.14, 12.291.7 ff., 13.143.18, 13.102.1ff. : *Agni Purāṇa* 206.1-12 : *Bhāgavata Purāṇa* 6.18.5-6 : *Matsya Purāṇa* 61.18-53, 201.1-39 : *Narasiṃha Purāṇa* 6.1 ff. : *Padma Purāṇa* 5.22.19-40 : *Śiva Purāṇa* 45·.23-26 : *Viṣṇu Purāṇa* 4.5.1 ff. : *Viṣṇudharmottara Purāṇa* 1.117.1 ff.

fact that such myths connect Aṅgiras and Vasiṣṭha with Agastya implies a certain community of tradition shared by these Ṛṣis, comparable to the community of being associated with the second main list of the Seven Ṛṣis. Furthermore, we have seen that Agastya is elsewhere closely linked with the Ṛṣis Marīci, Pulastya, Pulaha and Kratu, all of whom appear only in the second main list; hence his further association through myths with Aṅgiras and Vasiṣṭha is yet another factor linking all of the Ṛṣis of that list. In a similar manner, one passage in the *Ādi Parvan* of the *Mahābhārata* relates that when Parāśara sought to destroy the Rākṣasas, the Ṛṣis Pulastya, Pulaha, Kratu, Atri and Vasiṣṭha persuaded him against doing so.[1] Here once again, the fact that both Atri and Vasiṣṭha are associated with Pulastya, Pulaha and Kratu as in a sense the "saviours" of the Rākṣasas is again an indication of a community of tradition shared by these Ṛṣis.

We are now in a position to conclude that certain factors of a regional nature have been operative in the formulation of the second main list of the Seven Ṛṣis. Taking the references as a whole—and keeping in mind the necessary qualifications made above—it can be seen that a clear overall pattern emerges from the associations of Ṛṣis with particular regions: wherein the Ṛṣis of the first main list (both individually and as a group) are associated primarily with regions to the north of the Vindhyas, while the Ṛṣis of the second main list (both individually and as a group) are associated predominantly with regions of southern India, Sri Lanka and Java.

D. Conclusion

It now remains merely to bring together and summarise the various conclusions which have been reached in preceding sections of this chapter, and to draw certain further conclusions as to the nature and degree of both *gotra* and regional factors which have been operative in formulating the second main list of the Seven Ṛṣis—relating these conclusions to the period of composition of the texts in which the second main list is first formulated.

---

1. *Mahābhārata* 1.172.1-17.

We have seen that the changes which occur between the two main lists—whereby individual Ṛṣis are included in the one list but excluded from the other list—are related in some measure to the role of the Ṛṣis as the ancestors or founders of the seven main *gotras*. In this respect, the exclusion of the Ṛṣis Jamadagni, Bharadvāja and Gautama from the second main list is directly related to the inclusion therein of Aṅgiras and to the assimilation of Bhṛgu to that list, this being reflected in the subordination of the Jāmadagnya, Bhāradvāja and Gautama *gotras* to the Āṅgirasa and Bhārgava *gotras*. Similarly, the inclusion of Pulastya, Pulaha and Kratu (as also to a lesser degree Marīci) in the second main list is directly related to the changing status and increasingly important role of Agastya and the Āgastyas, and the inclusion of these Ṛṣis reflects a distinct importance being ascribed to the Āgastyas. Again, the exclusion of Viśvāmitra from the second main list is linked with his subordination to Bhṛgu, while the exclusion of Kaśyapa is directly connected with the inclusion of Marīci. In all of these cases, the Ṛṣis of the first main list who are excluded from the second come to be termed the 'sons' of their counterparts in the second main list.

We have further seen that the changes between the two main lists are cannected with the different regions with which the Ṛṣis of those lists are associated: those of the first main list being primarily associated with northern regions of India, to the north of the Vindhyas, and those of the second main list being predominantly associated with southern India, Sri Lanka and Java. Consequently, placing these two conclusions side by side, it can be said that one of the main factors operative in bringing about the changes between the two main lists rests in the influence of the members of particular Brahmin *gotras* living in regions of southern India, to the south of the Vindhyas, who were in a position to manipulate these lists and traditions so as to have their own Ṛṣi-ancestor included in the group of Seven Ṛṣis. In this respect, both *gotra* and regional factors can be seen to be operating contemporaneouly, each predominating in different degrees with each of the individual Ṛṣis.

We can now relate this overall conclusion—as to the influential role of members of particular Brahmin *gotras*, living to the south of the Vindhyas—to the period during which the second main list came to be formulated. We saw in Chapter 1 that the formulation of that list may be ascribed to the period between approximately 100 B.C. and A.D. 200; this same period is known to have been one during which fundamental changes were occurring in the social and political climate of India. During the Maurya period (c. 315-175 B.C.), for example, the Maurya empire extended its sway well to the south of the Vindhyas, as indicated most notably by the many Aśokan rock-edicts which are to be found as far south as present-day Karnataka, and Aśoka's son Mahinda is reputed to have introduced Buddhism into Sri Lanka during this period. It is only to be expected, therefore, that social and cultural influences not only extended from north to south at that time, but also flowed from south to north. The subsequent period, from the end of the Maurya dynasty to the start of the Gupta dynasty (c. 175 B.C. to A.D. 320), saw the advent of foreign invaders from the west and north, most notably the Yavanas or Indo-Greeks, the Śakas or Indo-Scythians, and the Kuṣāṇas; but it also witnessed the rise of dynasties and the expansion of cultures, particularly in the Deccan and southern India. In the extreme south, this period saw the composition of much of the Tamil Śangam literature, as also extensive trading relations with the Roman Empire, both of which indicate a high degree of social and cultural dynamism. It is particularly noteworthy in this connection that Agastya is regarded as the author of Tamil grammar and in particular of the *Agattiyam*—the grammar said to have been used for the first Śangam, and to have been the inspiration for the *Tolkāppiyam* of the second Śangam which was reputedly composed by his pupil Tolkappiyan. Between the Vindhyas and the extreme south, there arose during this period the dynasty of the Sātavāhanas (c. 50 B.C. to A.D. 240) with their capital at Pratiṣṭhāna on the river Godāvarī. Many later traditions are associated with the greatness of Sātavāhana or Śālivāhana, who drove the Śakas out of India;[1] the Sātavāhana legends are

1. The most notable of such traditions appear in works deriving from the now lost *Bṛhatkathā* of Guṇāḍhya : particularly in the *Bṛhatkathāśloka-saṅgraha* of Budhasvāmin, in the *Bṛhatkathāmañjarī* of Kṣemendra, and in the

also closely connected with the cycles of stories concerning the legendary king Vikrama or Vikramâditya of Ujjayinī, with whom Śâlivâhana had much friendship and rivalry.[1] In later times, Śâlivâhana is closely associated with the founding of the Śaka era of A.D. 78, which is even said in some contexts to date from either his birth or his accession,[2] thus witnessing to the significance ascribed to the Sâtavâhanas by later writers. The Sâtavâhana king Hâla was reputedly the author of the *Sattasai*, a Prakrit work giving mention of a *vikrama-carita* or eulogy of the deeds of Vikrama;[3] while Guṇâḍhya is said to have composed his *Bṛhatkathā*—containing the stories of Śâlivâhana and Vikrama—at the Sâtavâhana capital of Pratiṣṭhāna around the 1st or 2nd century A.D.[4] On a more general level the *Yuga-Purāṇa*—which was probably composed in Ujjayinī around this same period—implies that there was a flowering of culture in the Deccan and southern India at the start of the Christian era[5]—namely under the Sâtavâhanas, who in their inscriptions styled themselves the lords of the three oceans and

---

Kathāsaritsāgara of Somadeva. The original *Bṛhatkathā* is also cited in, for example, the *Kāvyādarśa* of Daṇḍin (1.38), the *Vāsavadattā* of Subandhu (verses 110, 147), and both the *Harṣacarita* (introd. verse 17) and *Kādambarī* (para. 106) of Bāṇa. Further traditions appear in the Kālaka cycle of stories (usefully collected in W. Norman Brown, *The Story of Kālaka* : see also H. Jacobi, 'Das Kālakācārya-kathānaka', *ZDMG* Vol. 34, pp. 247-318, and S. M. Nawab, *The Collection of Kālaka Story*) : also in the *Prabandhacintāmaṇi* of Merutuṅga (Chapter 1), in the *Vikramacarita* or *Siṃhāsanadvātriṃśakā* (especially no. 24), and in the *Bhaviṣya Purāṇa* (3.3.2.8-34, 3.3.3.1-32, 3.4.1.17-46).

1. For a general discussion and analysis of these legends, see J. E. Mitchiner, 'Legends concerning Vikrama and the origin of the Vikrama era', and 'The Śaka era of A.D. 78'.

2. For example *Ā'in-i-Akbari* Book 3 *ā'in* 1 ; *Muhūrtamārtaṇḍa, alaṅkāra* verse 3. For inscriptional use of the "*śālivāhana-śaka*" era, see the second article in the previous note.

3. See especially *Sattasaī* Book 5 verse 64.

4. See the accounts in works deriving from the *Bṛhatkathā*.

5. *Yuga-Purāṇa Ślokas* 98-113 : see the text and discussion in J. E. Mitchiner, 'The Yuga Purāṇa', pp. 922-924, and *The Yuga-Purāṇa*. For further details and more general discussion of social, political and cultural changes under the Sātavāhanas, see especially K. A. N. Sastri, *A History of South India*, pp. 92-114, also *The Mauryas and the Sātavāhanas* and *Sources of Indian History* : D. C. Sircar, In Majumdar & Pusalker (ed.), *The Age of Imperial Unity*, pp. 191-227; R. G. Bhandarkar, *The Early History of the Deccan* : P. T. S. Iyengar, *A History of the Tamils to* 600 *A.D.* : H. C. Raychaudhuri, *A Political History of Ancient India* : G. Yazdani, *The Early History of the Deccan.*

of the southern region (Dakṣiṇāpatha). Many Sātavāhana kings sought to revive Brahmin customs, upholding caste distinctions and performing such Vedic sacrifices as the *aśvamedha* and *rājasūya*;[1] Gautamīputra Satakarṇi, for example, was a notable performer of such sacrifices, and sought to emulate the deeds of such Epic heroes as Rāma and Arjuna. Not only Hinduism but also Buddhism flourished under Sātavāhana rule—as is evident especially from the cave-inscriptions and benefactions at Nāsik, Karle and Kanheri, and from the construction of the great railing at Amarāvatī. Nāgārjuna, the great luminary of Mādhyamika thought, most probably accomplished much of his work under Sātavāhana patronage; Indian, Tibetan and Chinese sources all agree that he was the close friend of a Sātavāhana emperor who constructed for him the monastery of Śrīparvata (Nāgārjunakonda), and that two of his works (the *Suhṛllekha* and the *Ratnāvali*) are dedicated to this Sātavāhana monarch.[2] We shall further see in the next chapter that one version of the Era of the Seven Ṛṣis is closely associated, in its origin and formulation, with the Sātavāhanas and with their Vākāṭaka successors. It might therefore be expected that it would be in such a cultural context that we should seek those Brahmin groups who formulated and developed the second main list of the Seven Ṛṣis, as also the many further traditions associated with the Ṛṣis.

We may thus conclude overall that the formulation of the second main list of the Seven Ṛṣis—and the change between the two main lists—was brought about in large measure by the members of particular Brahmin *gotras* between approximately 100 B.C. and A.D. 200, who resided in regions of southern India and were probably associated with such general cultural and social changes as were then taking place, particularly under the Sātavāhana dynasty in the region of the western Deccan.

1. Both sacrifices together with others, are listed for example in line 11 of the Nānāghat inscription of Nāgamnikā : see Sircar, *Select Inscriptions*, no. 82. See also many of the further inscriptions listed by Sircar, as well as the documentations in the CII, *Ep. Ind.* and elsewhere.

2. A useful little survey of the available evidence is that in K.S. Murty, *Nagarjuna* : note also S. Lévi, 'Kaniṣka et Sātavāhana'.

4

THE ERA OF THE SEVEN ṚṢIS

A. Introduction

The Era of the Seven Ṛṣis[1] is a type of chronological reckoning which is described especially in the Purāṇas and in subsequent contexts, and which remains in use up to the present day in certain parts of India. It is associated with the theory that the Seven Ṛṣis—as the stars of Ursa Major—remain "in" or conjoined with each of the 27 Nakṣatras or Lunar Mansions in turn for a period of 100 years, thus completing a full cycle over a period of 2700 years. Before discussing the Era in detail, it is useful to gain a general idea of this theory by referring to the main Purāṇic passage—found with minor variations in several Purāṇas—in which it is outlined :

> The Seven Ṛṣis remain for 100 (years) in turn through the entire circle of 27 Nakṣatras. This is the *yuga* [era] of the Seven Ṛṣis, known by Divine reckoning—there are known to be 6 divine months and 7 divine years; Divine time is set in motion for those (Nakṣatras) by those Seven Ṛṣis. When the two eastern (stars) of the Seven Ṛṣis are seen in the northern region, and in the middle of them is seen a Nakṣatra which is "the same" in the sky, the Seven Ṛṣis are known as being joined to that one in the sky, (remaining in) the same

1. For alternative attempts to reconstruct this Era, see especially A. Cunningham, *A Book of Indian Eras*, pp. 6-17 ; K. D. Sethna, 'Megasthenes and Indian Chronology'; S. B. Roy, *Ancient India, A Chronological Study*.

(relative position) for 100 (years). This is the teaching concerning the *bhoga* of the Nakṣatras and the Ṛṣis.[1]

The passage is, to say the least; somewhat curious, particularly since the stars of Ursa Major do not alter their position relative to the Lunar Mansions in the way supposed. The first item of information given in the passage emphasises that the Purāṇas are concerned with a total of 27 Nakṣatras—rather than with 28, including Abhijit, as listed in many contexts in Vedic literature.[2] The "six divine months and seven divine years" is simply another way of referring to 2700 years of men : since it is elsewhere stated, for example in the *Matsya Purāṇa*, that one divine year is equal to 360 years of men.[3] The two "eastern" stars of the Seven Ṛṣis represent—according to the interpretation of Varāhamihira[4]—the Ṛṣis Marīci and Vasiṣṭha, or the stars η and ζ Ursa Major : and since no Nakṣatra is ever seen literally "in the middle" of these two stars, many commentators interpret this as meaning the Nakṣatra which is to be seen on a line drawn at right-angles from between these two stars to the horizon. Even such an interpretation cannot, however, escape from the difficulty that the Lunar Mansions do not alter their positions in this way relative to the stars of Ursa Major; the theory therefore came to be accepted as a matter of faith rather than observation. Thus Kamalākara, for example, wrote in his *Tattvaviveka* that although no such motion of the stars was perceptible, nevertheless the authority of the Purāṇas which affirmed such a motion was irrefutable—hence the stars themselves might be fixed, but the Seven Ṛṣis must be invisible deities who perform such a motion in the specified period.[5]

Since the theory is astronomically and observationally incorrect, it is quite likely that it represents a synthesis of two originally

---

1. *Brahmāṇḍa Purāṇa* 2.3.74.231-235 : *Matsya Purāṇa* 273.40-44 : *Vāyu Purāṇa* 2.37.413-417 : compare *Bhāgavata Purāṇa* 12.2.27-31 : *Viṣṇu Purāṇa* 3.24.33-39.

2. For example, *Maitrāyaṇī Saṃhitā* 2.13.20 : *Taittirīya Saṃhitā* 3.1.1-2, 3.1.4.1 ff. : *Atharvaveda* 19.7.1, 19.8.2 : *Śāṅkhāyana Gṛhya Sūtra* 1.26 : *etc.*

3. *Matsya Purāṇa* 142.12.

4. *Bṛhat-saṃhitā* 13.1-6.

5. See H. T. Colebrooke, *Miscellaneous* Vol. 2. p. 316.

quite separate features : namely in the first place a method of chronological reckoning in terms of centennial cycles, associated with—and perhaps using the names of—the Nakṣatras, and in the second place the concept of the Seven Ṛṣis as the stars of Ursa Major in the sky. The subsequent association of the Seven Ṛṣis with the method of chronological reckoning may be seen as an elaboration of an idea which first occurs in the *Śatapatha Brāhmaṇa* : namely that the Seven Ṛṣis had at one time in the past been the husbands of the Kṛttikās (*i.e.* the Pleiades, one of the Lunar Mansions), but had subsequently moved away from or "divorced" their wives—who rose in the east of the sky, while they themselves rose in the north.[1] In the above-cited Purāṇic passage, two terms are used to describe the theory; firstly *yuga*—being yoked or joined to the Nakṣatras—and secondly *bhoga*. This latter term can mean—among other things—both "astronomical conjunction" and also "sexual pleasure" : hence there gradually evolved the theory—developed from such passages as that in the *Śatapatha Brāhmaṇa*—of a kind of "sacred marriage" between the Ṛṣis and the Nakṣatras, wherein the Ṛṣis remain for 100 years "in" each of the Nakṣatras in turn. The development of the theory as a whole must be presumed to have occurred upon conceptual and mythological rather than astronomical grounds : and it is noteworthy that in certain regions (for example in Kashmir) the theory of centennial cycles was known as the Lok-Kāl or Laukika ("The People's Era" or "The Popular Era") rather than by any name pertaining to the Seven Ṛṣis. This again suggests that the Seven Ṛṣis were not originally associated with this chronological reckoning.

The very fact that a centennial cycle is employed in this reckoning is a point well worthy of note : for it provides evidence both of a cyclical mode of reckoning (as opposed to further chronological reckonings based upon a particular non-recurrent date, such as Kali 3102 B.C., Saṃvat 58 B.C., and Śaka A.D. 78), and also of the currency of the concept of a century, both from a relatively early time in India. This method of chronological reckoning has remained in use from

1. *Śatapatha Brāhmaṇa* 2.1.2.1-5.

at least the early Purāṇas up to the present day; it is still used particularly in north-west India and in Kashmir, being known by such names as the Lok-Kāl. the Saptarṣi-Kāl, and the Pahāri-Saṃvat or Hill-Era. Further names by which it is known include the Pāṇḍu-Kāl (a term used especially by Albīrūnī), the Laukika (a term used by both Kalhaṇa and Albīrūnī, and found also in certain inscriptions), the Kollam Era (a term used primarily in Kerala, where use of the era seems to have been adopted following the founding of Quilon), and the Saptarṣi Yuga (as in the Purāṇas).

Two different versions of this era can be discerned, both in the early literary sources and also in later accounts and inscriptional uses; our primary aim in this chapter will therefore be to elucidate and clarify the precise natures of these two different versions.

B. The Views of the Astronomers on the Era

The astronomer Varāhamihira, writing most probably around A.D. 550, devotes a complete chapter to the Seven Ṛṣis in his *Bṛhat-saṃhitā* : during the course of which he relates that the Seven Ṛṣis were "in" the Nakṣatra Maghā while king Yudhiṣṭhira was reigning, which was some 2526 years before the commencement of the Śaka era :

> The *munis* were in Maghā when king Yudhiṣṭhira ruled the earth; the Śaka time is separated by 2526 (years) from that king.[1]

This same verse is cited almost word for word by such later writers as Kalhaṇa.[2] Taking the Śaka era as commencing in A.D. 78[3], the reign of Yudhiṣṭhira is thus here to be placed in 2448 B.C., at which time it is thought that the Seven Ṛṣis were

1. *Bṛhat-saṃhitā* 13.3.
2. *Rājataraṅgiṇī* 1.56.
3. It is to be noted that, with this and all subsequent dates, a margin of one year must be allowed for : due to the fact that such eras usually commence during the course of a year according to the Christian calendar—namely during the month of Caitra or March-April.

in the Nakṣatra Maghā. It is additionally stated in further contexts that the Mahābhārata war took place in 2449 B.C. (see below), thus indicating that the year 2448 B.C. was thought to represent the first year of Yudhiṣṭhira's reign.

At this point, however, there arises a difficulty. The Epics and Purāṇas all relate that the Mahābhārata war took place at the end of the Dvāpara Yuga, and that the Kali Yuga commenced in the 36th year after that war. Thus for example the *Mahābhārata* relates that in the 36th year after that war, Yudhiṣṭhira observed inauspicious omens portending the death of Kṛṣṇa and the start of the Kali Yuga :

> When the 36th year had been reached, Yudhiṣṭhira, the son of the Kurus, observed inauspicious omens (heralding the start of the Kali Yuga).[1]

A passage in the *Viṣṇu Purāṇa* further adds that the Kali Yuga commenced at the death of Kṛṣṇa, while the Seven Ṛṣis were in Maghā; and that Yudhiṣṭhira, upon seeing inauspicious omens, renounced his throne and consecrated Parīkṣit as king :

> Those (Seven Ṛṣis), O best of Twice-born men, were in Maghā in the time of Parīkṣit, and the Kali then commenced, consisting of 1200 years. When the portion of lord Viṣṇu, the increaser of the family of Vasudeva, had gone to heaven, O Twice-born, then indeed the Kali arrived .... The Pāṇḍava Yudhiṣṭhira, the son of Dharma, having seen inauspicious omens, abandoned his kingdom accompanied by his younger brother; after Kṛṣṇa had gone, he performed the *abhiṣeka* [coronation ceremony] on Parīkṣit.[2]

According to such passages, therefore, the Kali Yuga commenced some 35 years after the Mahābhārata war : at which time the Seven Ṛṣis were in Maghā. Varāhamihira—following his predecessors Āryabhaṭa and Parāśara—accepted the date of 3102 B.C. as denoting the start of the Kali Yuga. In doing so, however, he was consequently obliged to introduce a period of 653

1. *Mahābhārata* 16.1.1 : see also 16.2.2, 16.3.18.
2. *Viṣṇu Purāṇa* 4.24.34-38.

years as the interval separating the start of the Kali Yuga on the one hand (in 3102 B.C.) from the period of Yudhiṣṭhira and the Mahābhārata war on the other hand (in 2449/2448 B.C.). Kalhaṇa, closely following the theories of Varāhamihira, thus takes notice of this intervening period :

> After 653 years of the Kali had passed, the Kurus and Pāṇḍavas lived on the earth.[1]

Accordingly, given that the Seven Ṛṣis were in Maghā in 2449/2448 B.C. during the reign of Yudhiṣṭhira, and that they spend 100 years in each Nakṣatra, then they would have been in Kṛttikā at the start of the Kali Yuga in 3102 B.C., some 653 years earlier than this. Varāhamihira claims to be following the theories of his predecessor Vṛddha Garga (who probably lived around the start of the Christian era[2]) in describing the motion of the Seven Ṛṣis :

> I shall describe the motion of those (Seven Ṛṣis) after the opinion of Vṛddha Garga.[3]

Yet Vṛddha Garga himself held that at the twilight between the Dvāpara and Kali Yugas, the Seven Ṛṣis were in the Nakṣatra sacred to the Pitṛs or Ancestors :

> At the junction of the Dvāpara and the Kali, those *munis*, devoted to *dharma* and intent upon the protection of living beings, stood in that (Nakṣatra) sacred to the Pitṛs.[4]

Since Maghā is the Nakṣatra sacred to the Pitṛs, it would seem that Vṛddha Garga held to the theory that the Seven Ṛṣis were in Maghā at the start of the Kali Yuga; hence Varāhamihira in fact disagrees with his predecessor on this point, by proposing that although the Seven Ṛṣis were in Maghā at the time of Yudhiṣṭhira and the Mahābhārata war, they were nevertheless

---

1. *Rājataraṅgiṇī* 1.51.
2. See J. E. Mitchiner, 'The Yuga Purāṇa' : Kern suggested a date of 50 B.C., in his Introduction to the *Bṛhat-saṃhitā* pp. 34-40.
3. *Bṛhat-saṃhitā* 13.2.
4. Quoted by Bhaṭṭotpala on *Bṛhat-saṃhitā* 13.3.

in Kṛttikā at the start of the Kali Yuga, some 653 years before this.

The difficulty and confusion arises through the positing of two different dates for the start of the Kali Yuga—namely 3102 B.C., and 2414 B.C. (namely 35 years after the Mahābhārata war of 2449 B.C.); Varāhamihira is attempting to combine both of these dates, by accepting both that the Seven Ṛṣis were in Maghā at the time of the Mahābhārata war (which, according to him, was not the time of the start of the Kali Yuga) and also that the Kali Yuga commenced in 3102 B.C. Yet it would seem clear that there are two originally quite separate traditions : one of which places the Seven Ṛṣis in Maghā in 3102 B.C., the other of which places the Seven Ṛṣis in Maghā in 2448 B.C., corresponding to the different dates for the start of the Kali Yuga.

C. The Purāṇic Accounts of the Era

Accounts of the Era of the Seven Ṛṣis are principally contained in five verses in the *Brahmāṇḍa*, *Matsya*, *Vāyu*, *Viṣṇu*, and *Bhāgavata Purāṇas*[1]—these being the only Purāṇas which refer to the Era in any detail. In this section, we shall examine and discuss each of these verses individually.[2]

> (i) From the anointing of Mahāpadma Nanda to the birth of Parīkṣit : this (period) is to be known as (consisting of) 1050 years.

According to the *Mahābhārata*, the birth of Parīkṣit took place during the Mahābhārata war.[3] Supposing for the moment that the Purāṇas envisage this war as having occurred in 2449 B.C. (a point which will be discussed below)—rather than in 3137 B.C., namely 35 years before the start of the Kali Yuga in

1. These accounts are to be found at *Brahmāṇḍa Purāṇa* 2.3.74.227-236 : *Matsya Purāṇa* 273.36.45 : *Vāyu Purāṇa* 2.37.409-418 : *Viṣṇu Purāṇa* 4.24.32-40 and *Bhāgavata Purāṇa* 12.2.26-33.

2. A more detailed discussion of individual textual variants may be found in J. E. Mitchiner, 'The Saptarṣi Yuga : elucidation of a cyclical era', pp. 61-72.

3. *Mahābhārata* 10.16.1 ff. *et. al.*

3102 B.C.—this would give a date of 1399 B.C. for the accession of Nanda. Since this date is 1000 years—or 10 Nakṣatras—later than 2449 B.C. when the Seven Ṛṣis were in Maghā, the Seven Ṛṣis should accordingly have been in the Nakṣatra Pūrvāṣāḍhā in 1399 B.C. This is indeed stated to be the case in the *Viṣṇu* and *Bhāgavata Purāṇas* :

> When the great Ṛṣis will enter Pūrvāṣāḍhā, then from Nanda onwards the Kali will be at its height.

These same two texts also give a somewhat different account of the main verse :

> From the birth of Parīkṣit to the anointing of Nanda : this (period) is to be known as (consisting of) 1015 years.

Thus the interval between Parīkṣit and Nanda is here held to be 1015 years, rather than 1050 years; and the accession of Nanda is accordingly placed in 1434 B.C., rather than in 1399 B.C.

> (ii) The interval from Mahāpadma (Nanda) to Pauloma Andhra is said to be 836 years.

The intended meaning of this verse is apparently to the effect that an interval of 836 years elapsed after the time of Mahāpadma Nanda; while certain of these texts add that this interval was between Nanda and Pauloma Andhra. Given—from the first main verse—the date of Nanda in either 1399 B.C. or 1434 B.C., then an interval of 836 years after Nanda will give a date of either 563 B.C. or 598 B.C. : when the Seven Ṛṣis would be in either Bharaṇī or Aśvinī respectively. According to the individual chronologies given for each dynasty in the Purāṇas, such a period of 836 years would be consistent with the sum of the years for each of the dynasties from the Nandas through the Mauryas, Śuṅgas and Kaṇvas to the end of the Andhras. Yet at the same time it is known with reasonable certainty that the Andhras ruled especially during the early centuries of the Christian era, and not in the 6th century B.C. This must have been well-known also to the Purāṇic writers, who composed their accounts at a period probably not long after that of the

Andhra dynasty (see below); and the third main verse seemingly attempts to clarify the situation.

> (iii) The first and last (rulers) of the Andhras are said (to occupy) this same period of time in the future; these (rulers) have been reckoned by future *Śruta*-Ṛṣis learned in the Purāṇas.

This verse implies that the same interval of time as has just been referred to—namely the interval of 836 years—is to separate the time previously stated from that of the end of the Andhra dynasty. Consequently, a further period of 836 years after the previously given dates of either 563 B.C. or 598 B.C. would give a date of either A.D. 273 or A.D. 238 for the end of the Andhra dynasty, according to this chronological reckoning.

Several of these Purāṇas are generally held to have been composed at around this time of the end of the Andhra dynasty in the third century A.D.; it might therefore be expected that they would be reasonably accurately informed as to the precise date of the end of the Andhras,[1] and thus to favour the reading of 1015 years given in the *Viṣṇu* and *Bhāgavata Purāṇas* in the first of these main verses, rather than the reading of 1050 years given in the other three Purāṇas. The reason for the difference of 35 years between the two sets of texts may be traced to the probability that the *Viṣṇu* and *Bhāgavata Purāṇas* are here following the Epic tradition that the Kali Yuga commenced in the 36th year after the Mahābhārata war, while the *Brahmāṇḍa, Matsya* and *Vāyu Purāṇas* are in effect confusing the date of the commencement of the Kali Yuga with the date of the Mahābhārata war, during which occurred the birth of Parīkṣit—which is the event in question from which the intervals are being reckoned. In other words, the 1050 years in the latter texts already includes a period of 35 years, while such a period has been additionally added in the 1015 years of the former texts.

1. For discussions on the date of the end of the Andhras, see for example M. B. Mitchiner, *Indo-Greek and Indo-Scythian Coinage*, Vol. 9, pp. 853-883 : D. C. Sircar, *Ancient Mālwā and the Vikramāditya Tradition*, pp. 65-105 : *ibid.*, in R. C. Majumdar *et. al.* (*ed.*), *The Age of Imperial Unity*, pp. 191-211 : *etc.*

This accordingly gives rise to the difference of 35 years between the two groups of texts; while it is in fact the *Viṣṇu* and *Bhāgavata Purāṇas* which in this instance retain the correct mode of reckoning, thereby placing the end of the Andhra dynasty in A. D. 238. This reckoning will consequently be adopted in the following discussion.

> (iv) The Seven Ṛṣis completed 100 (years) in (the Nakṣatra) dedicated to the Pitṛs [namely in Maghā] in the time of (Janamejaya) Pārīkṣita; they will again be linked in the future (to Maghā) (at the time) of the Andhras after 2700 years.

The emendation suggested for this verse by Pargiter[1] is found in none of the texts, and although it has been followed by many later writers, it in effect adds still more to the confusion created by the several textual variants for the verse. This verse implies that while the Seven Ṛṣis completed their stay in Maghā during the time of Janamejaya Pārīkṣita, they will again be in Maghā at the end of the Andhra dynasty, which will be after a complete cycle of 2700 years. The *Viṣṇu Purāṇa* presents the first item of information in a slightly different form :

> Those (Seven Ṛṣis) were in Maghā in the time of (Janamejaya) Pārīkṣita, O best of Twice-born men.

Consequently, the three periods of 1015, 836 and 836 years together total 2687 years : thereby encompassing the 27 Nakṣatras—or 2700 years—which are thought to separate the period of Parīkṣit from the time of the end of the Andhra dynasty. The fifth main verse further confirms such an interpretation.

> (v) The Seven Ṛṣis were thus joined (to Maghā) in the time of Parīkṣit for 100 (years); they will be the same [namely in the same position, joined to Maghā] for 100 (years) in (the time of) the 24th part [*i.e.* ruler] of the Andhras.

Pargiter's suggested emendation to this verse once again adds

1. See F. E. Pargiter, *The Purāṇa Text of the Dynasties of the Kali Age*, pp. 59 (text+note 46) and 75 (translation).

further confusion to the reading of a difficult passage.[1] This verse again implies that the Seven Ṛṣis are in Maghā both at the time of Parīkṣit and also at the time of the 24th ruler of the Andhras; we must therefore next enquire as to who was this 24th Andhra king. The *Brahmāṇḍa*, *Vāyu*, *Viṣṇu* and *Bhāgavata Purāṇas* all state that there was a total of 30 Andhra kings, while the *Matsya Purāṇa* states their total number as 19. In the actual lists of individual rulers, however, the *Brahmāṇḍa Purāṇa* lists 16 kings, the *Vāyu Purāṇa* lists 17 kings, the *Viṣṇu Purāṇa* lists 24 kings, the *Bhāgavata Purāṇa* lists 23 kings, the *Matsya Purāṇa* lists 30 kings.[2] While all of these texts agree in stating that the end of the Andhra dynasty coincided with the Seven Ṛṣis being in Maghā, and the preceding verses have been referring to the end of the Andhras, it is fair to surmise that the expression "the 24th ruler of the Andhras" is similarly intended to denote in this context the last ruler of the Andhra dynasty; and this is particularly supported by the fact that the *Viṣṇu Purāṇa* lists precisely this total of 24 Andhra kings. Thus the information in this verse relates that the Seven Ṛṣis will again be in Maghā in the time of the 24th ruler of the Andhras, which is also the time of the end of the Andhra dynasty.

We may summarise the information presented in these five main verses in the following form :

(a) The Seven Ṛṣis were in Maghā in the time of Parīkṣit.

(b) The Seven Ṛṣis left Maghā in the time of Janamejaya Pārīkṣita.

(c) The Seven Ṛṣis will again be in Maghā at the end of the Andhra dynasty, which will be 2700 years after the time of Parīkṣit.

(d) The Seven Ṛṣis will be in Pūrvāṣāḍhā in the time of Nanda.

(e) The interval between the birth of Parīkṣit and the consecration of Nanda is 1015 years.

---

1. See Pargiter, *op. cit.*, pp. 61 and 75. For more detailed criticisms see 'The Saptarṣiyuga'.

2. See *Brahmāṇḍa Purāṇa* 2.3.7.161-170 : *Vāyu Purāṇa* 2.37.342-352 : *Viṣṇu Purāṇa* 4.24.12-13 : *Bhāgavata Purāṇa* 12.1.22-28 : *Matsya Purāṇa* 273.1-17; also J. E. Mitchiner, 'The Purāṇic Lists of Andhra Kings'.

(f) The interval between Nanda and the end of the Andhra dynasty is 2 × 836 years, or 1672 years.
(g) Hence the interval between the birth of Parīkṣit and the end of the Andhra dynasty is 1015+1672=2687 years.

We may further add the information given in the additional passages cited earlier from the *Viṣṇu Purāṇa.* :

(h) Yudhiṣṭhira was ruling before the start of the Kali Yuga.
(i) The Kali Yuga commenced at the death of Kṛṣṇa.
(j) When the Kali Yuga commenced, Yudhiṣṭhira renounced his throne and consecrated Parīkṣit.
(k) The Seven Ṛṣis were still in Maghā when Janamejaya Pārīkṣita was ruling.

All of these statements thus accord with the chronological scheme put forward by Varāhamihira, wherein the Mahābhārata war and the reign of Yudhiṣṭhira are placed in 2449-2448 B.C. If it were to be proposed—as Cunningham, and after him Roy[1] and others have done—that the Purāṇic writers accepted the date of 3102 B.C. for the start of the Kali Yuga, then it must similarly be held that they placed the times of Yudhiṣṭhira, Parīkṣit and the Mahābhārata war before this date : in other words, some 35 years earlier, namely in 3137 B.C. The consecration of Nanda would then have to be placed 1015 years later, namely in 2122 B.C.; and the end of the Andhra dynasty would have to be placed 1672 years later, namely in 450 B.C. Such dates would thus be some 650 years earlier than the known period of the end of the Andhras, close to which time these texts are usually held to have been composed; they would also contradict the statement of Varāhamihira that Yudhiṣṭhira was ruling in 2448 B.C.—a statement which witnesses that such a scheme of chronology as that followed in the above analysis was known in at least Gupta times, which is again at a period close

1. See A. Cunningham, *A Book of Indian Eras*, pp. 8-17 : S. B. Roy, *Ancient India*, p. 143—"The Kashmir Laukika abda begins with Rohiṇī in c. 3100 B.C. and its Maghā comes in c. 2500 B.C. It is different from Garga's scheme and cannot be applied to the Purāṇic scheme; the Purāṇas did not adopt the Kashmir Laukika abda but used—though very sparsely—the Vṛddha Garga system" (*sic*).

to which these texts are usually held to have been composed, and scarcely a century after the end of the Andhra dynasty which is itself mentioned in these very texts. We may accordingly safely conclude that the Purāṇas follow the same chronological scheme as that used by Varāhamihira : wherein the Mahābhārata war, the birth of Parīkṣit and the reign of Yudhiṣṭhira are placed in 2449-2448 B.C., but wherein the start of the Kali Yuga is placed not in 3102 B.C. (as postulated by Varāhamihira) but in 2414 B.C.—namely 35 years after the Mahābhārata war. The end of the Andhra dynasty is similarly to be placed, therefore, in A.D. 238; and as we shall see in greater detail later in this chapter, this latter date of A.D. 238 is also used in a Vākāṭaka inscription of A.D. 458 as the commencement of an era[1]—thereby tending to confirm the validity of this reconstruction and to emphasise the importance of the year A.D. 238 as the date regarded as signifying the end of Andhra rule and the commencement of Vākāṭaka rule.

The accounts of the Era of the Seven Ṛṣis in the *Brahmāṇḍa*, *Vāyu*, *Matsya*, *Viṣṇu* and *Bhāgavata Purāṇas* form the concluding section to the lists of Kings of the Kali Yuga. Since these accounts themselves refer to the ending of the Andhra dynasty in A.D. 238, they can clearly not have been composed before around A.D. 250. On the other hand, the lists of kings in these texts fail to make any noteworthy mention of the Gupta dynasty—the *Matsya Purāṇa* for example completely omits any mention of the Guptas; it is therefore apparent that these sections of the Purāṇas must have been composed at a period prior to or very shortly after the founding of the Gupta dynasty in A.D. 320—or, less likely, that they were composed in a region well beyond the influence of the Guptas. Since, however, the Purāṇic authors take note of even minor northern dynasties such as the Abhīras, it is highly unlikely that they would have made no mention of the Guptas, had they been composed during or after the period of the Gupta empire—irrespective of the region in which they were composed; and since several of these texts do list a small number of Gupta kings, we may conclude that their accounts

1. See J. E. Mitchiner, 'The System of Dating in the Hisse-Borala Inscription of Devasena'.

were composed only shortly after the founding of that dynasty. Consequently, the accounts of the Era of the Seven Ṛṣis must have been incorporated into the Purāṇas between approximately A.D. 250 and 350 : the former of these dates being perhaps the more likely, in view of the extent to which these accounts are closely connected with the ending of the Andhra dynasty in A.D. 238. This version of the Era is therefore likely to have been in use by at least the end of the 2nd century A.D.—in other words, by at least A.D. 200—prior to its incorporation within the Purāṇas.

D. The Commencement of Cycles of the Seven Ṛṣis

There are two separate points which we must discuss concerning the commencement of cycles of the Seven Ṛṣis. The first of these is the precise year—according to the Christian or other eras—in which each individual centennial cycle of the Seven Ṛṣis is thought to commence; while the second of these is the question of the Nakṣatra with which each complete cycle of 2700 years is thought to commence.

(*a*) *The Commencing Year of Individual Cycles*

The earliest evidence of the precise commencing year of Seven Ṛṣi or Laukika cycles is to be found in an inscription in the temple of Baijnāth in the district of Mandi : this records the twin dates of 89 Laukika and 735 Śaka, as also the twin dates of 80 Laukika and 725 Śaka.[1] In both cases, the year 1 Laukika will be equivalent to the year 647 Śaka, or to the year A.D. 725.[2] From this time up to the present day, the same commencing year of individual cycles is invariably given, namely in the year 25 of each Christian century A.D.; as may be seen from the following examples.

Kalhaṇa states at the start of the *Rājataraṅgiṇi* that he is writing in the year 24 Laukika, equivalent to 1070 Śaka :

1. See Cunningham, *A Book of Indian Eras*, p. 6.
2. One should note again the necessity of allowing a margin of 1 year in such calculations.

(We are) presently in the 24th Laukika year; of the Śaka time, more than 1000 years have passed, and 70 full years.[1]

He similarly states at the end of the *Rājataraṅgiṇī* that he completed the work in the year 25 Laukika, equivalent to 1071 Śaka.[2] In both cases, the year 1 Laukika will be equivalent to the year 1047 Śaka, and to the year A.D. 1125. Kalhaṇa first makes detailed use of the Laukika era from the fourth book of the *Rājataraṅgiṇī* onwards : the first reference being to the effect that the brothers-in-law of Lalitāpīḍa ruled unrestrained from the year 89 Laukika to the year 26 Laukika.[3] By totalling the lengths of reign for each of the kings of Kashmir between the time of Lalitāpīḍa and the time of Kalhaṇa's writing in Śaka 1071 or A.D. 1150, it is evident that the above-mentioned dates must fall within the 9th century A.D.; the former of them will in fact fall within the same Laukika cycle as that of the Mandi inscription. Thus the year 89 Laukika will in this instance refer to the Laukika cycle of A.D. 725-825, denoting the year A.D. 813; while the following year 26 Laukika will refer to the next Laukika cycle of A.D. 825-925, denoting the year A.D. 850.

Albīrūnī also gives a detailed account of how to compute the Era of the Seven Ṛṣis. Taking as an example the date of the fall of Somnath—which occurred in January of A.D. 1026—he says that he has seen Indians write down the figures 242, 606 and 99 which they add together to give the Śaka year of 947. Albīrūnī suggests that the figure 242 shows the number of Śaka years which preceded the period when the Indians first started to use this cycle, while the figure 606 shows the number of complete centennial cycles of 101 years each, and the figure 99 shows the number of years elapsed of the current cycle of the Seven Ṛṣis.[4] However, in opposition to this interpretation, we must note that all the Indian literary sources are unanimous in stating that each cycle of the Seven Ṛṣis is of only 100 years' duration—not of Albīrūnī's suggested 101 years' duration. We

1. *Rājataraṅgiṇī* 1.52.
2. Ibid., 8.3404.
3. Ibid., 4.703.
4. Albīrūnī's *India*, Ch. 49 : *trans.* E. Sachau, Vol. 23, pp. 9-10.

here follow Cunningham's suggestion[1] that the figure 6 in the above computation denotes the number of years which had elapsed between the establishment of the Gupta era in A.D. 319-320—some 242 years after the start of the Śaka era in A.D. 78—and the commencement of the new cycle of the Seven Ṛṣis in A.D. 325 : to which figure is added the total of 6 complete cycles elapsed, to A.D. 925, plus 99 years of the current cycle elapsed; and since the 99th year is said to have already elasped, therefore the cycle must be in its 100th year—namely in A.D. 1025-26.

Buhler, Cunningham and others have shown that the same reckoning was followed in Kashmir in the 19th century A.D., whereby the start of each centennial cycle of the Seven Ṛṣis was considered to correspond to the year 25 of each Christian century A.D. Buhler also indicated that the Kashmiri Brahmins of the 19th century A.D. reckoned that the Laukika era had commenced in the year 3076-3075 B.C.—namely some 25 years after the start of the Kali Yuga, which they placed in 3102-3101 B.C. In this connection he cited a verse—whose source he could not ascertain—which was related to him by a Kashmiri Brahmin :

> When the years of the Kali marked by the "arrows and eyes" [i.e. 5 and 2, or 25] had elapsed, the most excellent Seven Ṛṣis ascended to heaven. For in the calendar used in the world [namely the Laukika], the virtuous declare the computation of the Seven Ṛṣi (years to begin from that point).[2]

Cunningham independently obtained similar information through his enquiries in Kashmir; he was also informed by the Brahmins of Kangra that the Seven Ṛṣis had spent 75 years in one Nakṣatra at the start of the Kali Yuga, and remained in the same Nakṣatra for a further 25 years.[3] The Kashmiri Brahmins furthermore reckoned the start of each Laukika year from

1. Cunningham, *A Book of Indian Eras*, p. 16.
2. G. Buhler, *A Detailed Report of a Tour in Search of Sanskrit Manuscripts*, pp. 59-60.
3. Cunningham. *A Book of Indian Eras*, pp. 6-15.

the month of Caitra or March-April.[1] The commencing date of the Laukika era suggested in these contexts is most probably due to the more general reckoning of dates from the start of the Kali Yuga in 3102 B.C. It does not necessarily follow from such 19th century accounts that the same date was regarded as denoting the commencement of the Era of the Seven Ṛṣis in earlier times; and it is to be noted that such a date is not recorded by either Kalhaṇa or Albīrūnī, nor is it given in the Purāṇas or in the works of the astronomers. The astronomers, on the contrary, reckon the start of the Era from the dawn of the Kalpa, since which time the Seven Ṛṣis are said to have completed almost 730, 720 complete cycles down to the start of the Kali Yuga.[2]

We may conclude that in all of the above instances, from the 9th to the 19th centuries A.D., the individual cycles of the Seven Ṛṣis were thought to commence in the 25th year of each Christian century A.D., and in the 76th year of each Christian century B.C.

This conclusion may now briefly be set in the context of the Epic and Purāṇic statements examined earlier. As we saw in the last section, the Seven Ṛṣis are said to have been in Maghā both at the time of the Mahābhārata war in 2449 B.C. and at the start of the Kali Yuga in 2414 B.C., and to have left Maghā during the reign of Janamejaya Pārīkṣita. According to the *Mahābhārata*, Parīkṣit was born during the Mahābhārata war (namely in 2449 B.C.), and was thus 35 years old at his accession in 2414 B.C.; he is said to have died as the result of a snake-bite,[3] whereupon his son Janamejaya succeeded to the throne while still a child[4]—and the Brahmins at his court are said to have witnessed the Mahābhāraṭa war with their own eyes,[5] and to have related the entire *Mahābhārata* epic to him at his request. According to this chronology, therefore, both the death of Parīkṣit and the

1. Cunningham, *A Book of Indian Eras*, p. 13.
2. See for example *Mahā-siddhānta* 1.11, 1.15-16, 1.19,2.9-10.
3. For example *Mahābhārata* 1.3.188-189, 1.37.1—1.39.20, 1.46.14-22.
4. *Mahābhārata* 1.40.6-7.
5. Ibid., 1.54.18.

accession of Janamejaya might be placed close to c. 2400 B.C., when Parīkṣit would have been 48 years old and Janamejaya perhaps 10 years old, and the Brahmins in their seventies. Such an Epic view would be fully consistent with the further view that the Seven Ṛṣis were in Maghā both at the time of the Mahābhārata war (in 2449 B.C.) and also in the time of Janamejaya (c. 2400 B.C.), on the basis of the Seven Ṛṣis' having been in Maghā during the period 2476-2376 B.C. We may therefore infer that the Purāṇas, in setting forth their particular chronological scheme, also base their computations upon the Seven Ṛṣis' entering each Nakṣatra in the equivalent of the 76th year of each Christian century B.C.

(b) The Nakṣatra with which each Complete Cycle Commences

The Nakṣatra lists which appear throughout the Vedic *saṃhitās*, the Brāhmaṇas and the Sūtras invariably commence with Kṛttikā.[1] In his account of the Era of Seven Ṛṣis, Cunningham considered each complete cycle of the Seven Ṛṣis through the Nakṣatras as commencing with Aśvinī;[2] yet the commencement of the Nakṣatra lists with Aśvinī first appears only in the *Sūrya-siddhānta*,[3] and was not fully accepted until much later times. Varāhamihira variously lists the Nakṣatras in different contexts in his works as commencing with either Aśvinī or Kṛttikā[4] : thereby suggesting that the change in commencement from Kṛttikā to Aśvinī had still not been fully accepted or effected in the mid-6th century A.D. It is quite likely that the commencement of the Nakṣatra lists with Aśvinī was not adopted until around the 6th century A.D., at which time the vernal equinox coincided with the star ζ Piscium being on the borders of Revatī and Aśvinī[5]. Consequently, any reconstruction

1. For example *Taittirīya Saṃhitā* 4.4.10-13: *Maitrāyaṇī Saṃhitā* 2.13.20 : *Kāṭhaka Saṃhitā* 39.13 : *Atharvaveda* 19.7.1 ff. : *Taittirīya Brāhmaṇa* 1.5.1, 3.1.4 ff. : *etc.*

2. Cunningham, *A Book of Indian Eras*, pp. 8-17.

3. For example *Sūrya-siddhānta* 8.9 ff.

4. For example *Bṛhajjātaka* 16.1 ff. (Aśvinī) : *Bṛhat-saṃhitā* 14.1 ff., 15.1 ff. (Kṛttikā); see also G. R. Kaye, *Hindu Astronomy*.

5. See especially A.A. Macdonell and A. B. Keith, *A Vedic Index*, Vol. 1, p. 421 : H. T. Colebrooke, *Miscellaneous Essays*, Vol. 2, pp. 281 ff. : A. Weber, *Indische Studien*, Vol. 10, p. 234.

of the Era of the Seven Ṛṣis which seeks to trace ideas about the Era at a period earlier than the 6th century A.D. or thereabout should accordingly commence the list of Nakṣatras with Kṛttikā rather than with Aśvinī. Hence the accounts of the Era in the Purāṇas—which, as we have seen, may be ascribed to a period well before the 6th century A.D.—may accordingly be deemed at this stage to commence their complete cycles with Kṛttikā rather than with Aśvinī : as may also be the version of the Era used by Vṛddha Garga, the predecessor of Varāhamihira.

As we saw in section B, the positioning of two different dates for the start of the Kali Yuga (namely 3102 B.C. and 2414 B.C.) gives rise to—or is associated with—two different versions of the Era of the Seven Ṛṣis : wherein the Seven Ṛṣis are variously said to have been in Maghā at either the one or the other of these dates. Consequently, there will be two different dates given in each version for the commencement of the complete cycles—or conversely, each complete cycle in either version will commence at the same date but in different Nakṣatras. The latter of these two possibilities is in fact the case, as we shall now see.

In different contexts in both the Epics and the astronomical texts, three different Nakṣatras are mentioned as being the first in the Nakṣatra lists : namely Kṛttikā, Dhaniṣṭhā (called Śraviṣṭhā in the earlier Nakṣatra lists), and Śravaṇā (called Śroṇā in the earlier lists). Vṛddha Garga, at around the start of the Christian era, relates that Kṛttikā is called the first of the Nakṣatras in the context of sacrifices, whereas Dhaniṣṭhā (Śraviṣṭhā) is deemed to be the first in calculations :

> They declare Kṛttikā in the first place of all those Nakṣatras in sacrifices; but Śraviṣṭhā is the first of the *lagnas* from calculation.[1]

Varāhamihira similarly regards Dhaniṣṭhā as being the first of the Nakṣatras in several of his calculations :

1. Quoted by Somākara on *Vedāṅga-jyotiṣa* 5.

. . . . Multiply (the *ahargaṇa*) by 7, divide by 610, and deduct (the result from the *ahargaṇa*); the result is the lunar Nakṣatra, counting from Dhaniṣṭhā.[1]

. . . . The remainder, divided by 27, is that Nakṣatra (of birth), commencing with Dhaniṣṭhā.[2]

In the *Vana Parvan* of the *Mahābhārata* it is related that when the Kṛttikās are allotted a place in the sky by Skanda, they take the place formerly occupied by Abhijit—namely the place adjacent to Śravaṇā;[3] and in the same context it is related that Brahmā originally created the Nakṣatras as commencing with Dhaniṣṭhā :

Then Time was created by Brahmā, beginning with Dhaniṣṭhā.[4]

A further passage in the *Āśvamedhika Parvan* of the *Mahābhārata* once again considers Dhaniṣṭhā (Śraviṣṭhā) as the first of the Nakṣatras :

The Ṛkṣas [Nakṣatras] commence with Śraviṣṭhā, the seasons commence with Śiśira [the cold season, January to March].[5]

This passage is complicated by the fact that many manuscripts read Śravaṇā in place of Śraviṣṭhā : thus of the 28 manuscripts referred to for this passage in the BORI Critical Edition, 14 contain the reading *śraviṣṭhā*, while 12 contain the reading *śravaṇā*.[6] Hence there is equally good evidence in favour of both of these readings.

---

1. *Pañcasiddhāntikā* 12.3. The translation is in this instance taken from the interpretation of Thibaut and Dvivedin.
2. *Bṛhajjātaka* 26.15, 26.16.
3. For example *Mahābhārata* 3.219.1-11.
4. *Mahābhārata* 3.219.10.
5. Ibid., 14.44.2.
6. Mss. as follows : *śraviṣṭhā*—4 Kashmiri, 1 Bengali, and all 9 Southern recensions : *śravaṇā*—1 Śāradā, 4 Bengali, & 7 Devanāgarī : also *bhaviṣyā*—1 Kashmiri : *aviṣṭhā*—1 Devanāgarī; additionally, *aśvinyā* in margin of 1 Kashmiri and 1 Devanāgarī.

The myth of Triśaṅku as presented in the *Rāmāyaṇa* relates that Viśvāmitra, in his anger at being thwarted in his attempts to transfer Triśaṅku bodily to the sky, created another set of both Seven Ṛṣis and Nakṣatras in the southern region (as opposed to the original set in the northern region,[1] which the gods decree should remain as long as the worlds endure :

> Creating another (group of) Seven Ṛṣis established in the southern region, he, blind with anger, created another garland of Nakṣatras.[2]

The *Ādi Parvan* of the *Mahābhārata*, in its version of the same myth, adds that Viśvāmitra created these Nakṣatras as commencing with Śravaṇā :

> This one, in anger, created further hosts of Nakṣatras, by means of the glory of the (original) Nakṣatras; (he created) Nakṣatras headed by Śravaṇā.[3]

It is consequently evident from such passages as the above that, from around the start of the Christian era, the Nakṣatras were variously thought to commence with either Kṛttikā, Dhaniṣṭhā (Śraviṣṭhā), or Śravaṇā. The mention in the last of these passages of the creation of both new Nakṣatras and also a new group of Seven Ṛṣis suggests that the "new"—or different ordering of the—Nakṣatras was in some way associated with the Seven Ṛṣis : and indeed, the different versions of the Era of the Seven Ṛṣis—wherein the Seven Ṛṣis are said to be in Maghā in either 3102 B.C. or 2414 B.C.—may be seen to correspond to the different orderings of the Nakṣatras. For in order that such a correspondence should occur, it will be the case that the period of the Seven Ṛṣis being in Kṛttikā in the one version will correspond to the period of their being in either Dhaniṣṭhā (Śraviṣṭhā) or Śravaṇā in the other version.

On the basis that the Seven Ṛṣis were in Maghā in 2414 B.C. —as held by Varāhamihira and by the Purāṇic authors—and

1. On the northern location of the Seven Ṛṣis, see Chapter 3 section C.
2. *Rāmāyaṇa* 1.59.20-21.
3. *Mahābhārata* 1.65.34.

thus entered Maghā in 2476 B.C., they would accordingly have entered Kṛttikā in 3176 B.C., Dhaniṣṭhā in 3876 B.C., and Śravaṇā in 3976 B.C. Conversely, on the basis that the Seven Ṛṣis were in Maghā in 3102 B.C.—as held by Vṛddha Garga—and thus entered Maghā in 3176 B.C., they would accordingly have entered Kṛttikā in 3876 B.C., Dhaniṣṭhā in 1876 B.C., and Śravaṇā in 1976 B.C. It can therefore be seen that there occurs an exact correspondence between the period of the Seven Ṛṣis being in Kṛttikā in the version held by Vṛddha Garga, and in Dhaniṣṭhā (Śraviṣṭhā) in the version held by Varāhamihira and the Purāṇic authors (namely the period 3176-3076 B.C.) : and that this is the only such correspondence to occur between these two versions. We may therefore conclude that the version of the Era in which the Nakṣatras are said to commence with Dhaniṣṭhā (Śraviṣṭhā) is that which was adopted in practice by Varāhamihira and the Purāṇic authors; as opposed to the version used by Vṛddha Garga, in which the Nakṣatras—and the complete cycles of the Seven Ṛṣis—commence with Kṛttikā.

We must next enquire whence arose the apparent confusion between the commencement of the "new" list of Nakṣatras—or the correspondence of the new version to the original version—with either Dhaniṣṭhā or Śravaṇā, as corresponding to Kṛttikā in the "old" version followed by Vṛddha Garga. It will be observed that, in both versions, the Seven Ṛṣis are in Śravaṇā during the century preceding that in which they are in Dhaniṣṭhā : and that they are thus in Śravaṇā in the "new" version during the century preceding that in which they are in Kṛttikā in the "old" version. However, we have so far established dates for only one complete cycle of the Seven Ṛṣis : namely for that in which they are in both Kṛttikā and Dhaniṣṭhā in 3876 B.C., as based on the dates at which they are in Maghā at the start of the Kali Yuga according to each of the two different versions. It is consequently apparent that the correspondence between the seven Ṛṣis being in Kṛttikā in the one version at the same time as they are in Śravaṇā—rather than Dhaniṣṭhā—in the other version arises from the fact that there occurs a difference of 100 years, or one Nakṣatra, between the two versions during a complete cycle of the Seven Ṛṣis. In other words, one of the versions uses a total of 27 Nakṣatras, while the other version uses a total of 28 Nakṣatras. We have already seen that the version followed by Varāhamihira and by the Purāṇic authors uses a total of 27 Nakṣatras;[1] we may therefore infer that the version followed by Vṛddha Garga uses a total of 28 Nakṣatras, with the addition of Abhijit. Such an inference is indeed implied in the statement of Vṛddha Garga that the list of Nakṣatras commencing with Kṛttikā is that used in connection with sacrifices : since the Nakṣatra lists in the sacrificial literature of the Vedic *saṃhitās*, the Brāhmaṇas and the Sūtras invariably commence with Kṛttikā, and generally use a total of 28 Nakṣatras—in common with the Chinese *sieou* and Arabic *manāzil* systems.[2] Similarly, Vṛddha Garga's use of the term *śraviṣṭhā* (as it appears in the early Nakṣatra lists) rather than *dhaniṣṭhā* (as it appears in the later Nakṣatra lists, and as is used by Varāhamihira) may be taken to imply that he is speaking with reference to the earlier or sacrificial lists of Nakṣatras. It may further be noted that, of the later astronomers, Āryabhaṭa continues to use in places all 28 of the Nakṣatras in his calculations, with the inclusion of Abhijit;[3] while, as noted earlier, Varāhamihira generally uses only 27. Moreover, Brahmagupta in one passage in his *Brāhmasphuṭa-siddhānta* refers to a Jain tradition of there being 2 suns, 2 moons and 54 Nakṣatras :

> It is said by the Jains that there are 54 *bhas* [Nakṣatras], also 2 suns and 2 moons.[4]

Yet while Brahmagupta refers to a total of 54 $(=2\times27)$ Nakṣatras, it is noteworthy that most Jain cosmographical texts refer to there being 56 $(=2\times28)$ Nakṣatras in Jambūdvīpa.[5]

---

1. For example the passage cited at the start of this chapter.
2. For example *Kāṭhaka Saṃhitā* 39.13 : *Maitrāyaṇī Saṃhitā* 2.13.20 : *Taittirīya Saṃhitā* 3.1.1-2, 3.1.4.1 ff., 4.4.10-13 : *Atharvaveda* 19.7.1, 19.8.2 : *Taittirīya Brāhmaṇa* 1.5.1, 3.1.4 ff. : *Śāṅkhāyana Gṛhya Sūtra* 1.26 : *etc.*
3. For example *Āryabhaṭīya* 12.1-8.
4. *Brāhmasphuṭa-siddhānta* 11.3.
5. For example *Jīvābhigama Sūtra* 875 ff. : see especially W. Kirfel, *Die Kosmographie der Inder*, pp. 270 ff.

We may therefore infer that Brahmagupta (writing in A.D. 628) —as also Varāhamihira—was here attempting to assert that the number of Nakṣatras was 27, rather than the 28 of the Vedic texts : the 28 accepted also by his predecessors Vṛddha Garga and Āryabhaṭa, the latter of whom came in for severe criticism in many other respects by Brahmagupta.[1]

On the basis that the version of the Era followed by Vṛddha Garga uses a total of 28 Nakṣatras, it can be seen that the complete cycle wherein occurs the start of the Kali Yuga will commence with Kṛttikā in 3876 B.C., corresponding to Dhaniṣṭhā in the "new" version; while the preceding complete cycle will commence with Kṛttikā some 2800 years earlier, namely in 6676 B.C., corresponding to Śravaṇā in the "new" version; and the following complete cycle will commence with Kṛttikā in 1076 B.C. Thus the Seven Ṛṣis will have been in both Kṛttikā and Śravaṇā in the "old" and "new" versions respectively in 6676 B.C.; while at the start of the next complete cycle there will be a difference of 100 years between the two versions (with Kṛttikā now corresponding to Dhaniṣṭhā) and a difference of 200 years at the start of the next complete cycle after that. This conclusion implies that the date of 6676 B.C. was in some sense regarded as being a starting-point of Indian chronology : and this is indeed confirmed in part in the works of Greek and Roman authors. Pliny, for example, makes the following observation :

> From Father Liber [Bacchus] to Alexander the Great, they reckon the number of their kings to have been 154, and they reckon (the time as) 6451 years and 3 months.[2]

Since Alexander entered the Panjāb in 326 B.C. and left again at the end of the same year, Pliny's statement therefore indicates that the first king—symbolised by the figure of Father Bacchus —was thought to have reigned in India in $6451\frac{1}{4}+326 = 6777$ B.C. Solinus also makes a similar observation : stating that 6451 years and 3 months were reckoned from Father

1. See for example *Brāhmasphuṭa-siddhānta*, Chapter 11.
2. *Naturalis Historia* 6.59-60.

Bacchus—the first who invaded India—to Alexander the Great, and that 153 kings were thought to have reigned during that intermediate period.[1] Arrian again makes a comment on such chronology. The text is unfortunately somewhat corrupt at this passage, but reads as follows :

> From Dionysos to Sandrocottos the Indians count 153 kings, and more than 6042 years; and during this time, thrice for liberty * * * this for 300 years, the other for 120 years.[2]

Although the text is somewhat unclear as to which represents the total number of years to be counted between Dionysos (namely the first king) and Sandrocottos (namely Candragupta Maurya), we may infer that in Arrian's account the first king was thought to have reigned in India either 6042 years before Sandrocottos, or 6042+300+120=6462 years before Sandrocottos. Taking again the date of 326 B.C. as the provisional date of Sandrocottos—corresponding to the date of Alexander, as mentioned by Pliny and Solinus—the first king was therefore thought to have reigned in either 6368 B.C. or 6788 B.C. It is noteworthy that the latter date of 6788 B.C. is only some 11 years earlier than the date of 6777 B.C. mentioned by both Pliny and Solinus. It might therefore be suggested that, since Arrian reckons to Sandrocottos rather than to Alexander (as do Pliny and Solinus), Arrian may here be preserving a tradition wherein Sandrocottos or Candragupta Maurya was thought to have come to the throne some 11 years after the campaigns of Alexander in 326 B.C., namely in 315 B.C.—a tradition which would most probably derive from the eye-witness account of Megasthenes. In this event, all three writers would be in agreement on the point that the first king was thought to have reigned in India in 6777 B.C.; but the present state of preservation of the *Indica* makes it impossible to draw any more definite conclusions on this point. It can, however, be seen that the date of 6777 B.C. which is given at least by Pliny and Solinus is

---

1. *Compendium* 52.5 : cited in J. W. McCrindle, *Ancient India as described by Megasthenes and Arrian*, and in R. C. Majumdar, *Classical Accounts of India.*
2. *Indica* 9.9.

only a single century in advance of the date of 6676 B.C. which is suggested in the Indian texts to represent a starting-point of Indian chronology, as based upon the Era of Seven Ṛṣis. We may therefore conclude that such a date was indeed regarded—from at least the 4th century B.C.—as being a starting-point of Indian chronology : at which date the Seven Ṛṣis, in the original version of Era, were thought to have commenced their complete cycle in Kṛttikā, the first Nakṣatra. Subsequently, with the formulation of the "new" version around the start of the Christian era, this commencement of the complete cycle in Kṛttikā in the "old" version was taken (on the basis of the different dates given for the start of the Kali Yuga) to correspond to the Seven Ṛṣis being in Śravaṇā in the "new" version; thereafter, when dates were more generally reckoned from the start of the Kali Yuga (which in both versions fell within the next complete cycle of the Seven Ṛṣis), the starting-point of the chronological reckoning was accordingly transferred to the next complete cycle (as related in the 19th century by the Brahmins of Kashmir), when the Seven Ṛṣis were in Kṛttikā in the "old" version and in Dhaniṣṭhā (Śraviṣṭhā) in the "new" version. This accordingly accounts for the different reckonings of the start of the Nakṣatra lists with either Kṛttikā, Śravaṇā, or Dhaniṣṭhā (Śraviṣṭhā) within the context of the Era of the Seven Ṛṣis.

E. The Origins of the Two Versions of the Era

The original version of the Era of the Seven Ṛṣis was apparently associated in some measure with the sacrificial cult : as is indicated by Vṛddha Garga's reference to its use in sacrifices, and as is suggested through its employment of a list of 28 Nakṣatras as frequently occurs in Vedic—as opposed to most Epic, Purāṇic and astronomical—literature. The "new" version, by contrast, was apparently used in more popular and astronomical circles : as is indicated through its common designation as the Lokakāla or Laukika—namely the people's era or the era used in the world—and through its appearance in Epic, Purāṇic and astronomical texts, and also through Vṛddha Garga's reference to its use in calculations.

The original version was seemingly in use by at least the 4th century B.C., when Megasthenes compiled his accounts of India; while the "new" version was noted by Vṛddha Garga around the start of the Christian era, and was incorporated within the Purāṇas by the end of the 3rd century A.D. (as discussed in Section C). Moreover, the formulation of the "new" version is closely linked with both the reduction of the number of Nakṣatras from 28 to 27, and also with the change in the date of the Kali Yuga from 3102 B.C. to 2414 B.C. : all of which were consequently most probably introduced from the same—essentially non-Vedic—cultural milieu.

It would seem most likely that the "new" version originated in a cultural context situated in a more southern region than that generally associated with Vedic literature, and more specifically in the western Deccan. Three main indicators point to this conclusion, and we shall take each of these individually.

(i) The first indication occurs in the Epic and Purāṇic versions of the myth of Triśaṅku : wherein, as we have seen in this and the previous chapter, it is related that Viśvāmitra created "new" sets of both Seven Ṛṣis and Nakṣatras in the southern region—which in this context may be taken to denote simply a region to the south of the Vindhyas—in addition to those in the northern region. As we noted especially in Chapter 3, Section C, this may be set alongside the fact that there appears in the Epics and Purāṇas a "new" or second main list of Seven Ṛṣis, whose members are associated with regions of southern India to the south of the Vindhyas, and who come to replace in importance the Seven Ṛṣis of the first main list which appears primarily in Vedic literature. We concluded at the end of the last chapter that the formulation of this "new" list of Seven Ṛṣis was primarily brought about by the members of particular Brahmin *gotras* between approximately 100 B.C. and A.D. 200, who resided in regions of southern India and were probably associated with such cultural changes as were then taking place under the Sātavāhana or Andhra dynasty in the western Deccan; we may therefore infer at this stage that the formulation of the "new" version of the Era of the Seven Ṛṣis—together with the reduction in the number of Nakṣatras, and the new date of the Kali Yuga—which, as we have seen, similarly occurred around the start of the Christian era, was once again effected within this same cultural milieu of the western Deccan, in the "southern" or trans-Vindhyan region of India.

(ii) The second indication appears in the Purāṇic accounts of the Era of the Seven Ṛṣis : which have been seen to use as one of their key dates that of the ending of the Andhra dynasty, which they place in A.D. 238. From this it would appear that the Purāṇic writers were well-acquainted both with the date of the end of the Andhras, and also with the Andhra dynasty itself, which was established primarily in the region of the western Deccan—to the south of the Vindhyas, and between the Narmadā and Godāvarī rivers.

(iii) The third indication appears in the earliest inscriptional use of the Era of the Seven Ṛṣis : namely in the Hisse-Borālā inscription of the Vākāṭaka king Devasena, dated to A.D. 458, which comes once again from the region between the Narmadā and Godāvarī rivers in the western Deccan. This inscription is now unfortunately broken into three pieces, making full interpretation difficult, particularly for the missing two or three syllables at the very start of the inscription. Taking this lacuna into account, the first line of the inscription may be read as follows :

> (In the year) 220 of * * * having passed, the Seven Ṛṣis being in Uttarā Phālgunī : (in the year) 380 of the Śakas, (in the year) of Śrī Devasena of the Vākāṭakas.[1]

We have elsewhere discussed various aspects of this inscription and its interpretation;[2] attention will here be drawn to two

---

1. The inscription was first edited by S. Gokhale, 'Hisse-Borala Inscription of Devasena, Saka 380'; it has also been discussed by V. B. Kolte, and by G. S. Gai and S. Sankaranarayan. For a criticism of their views and further discussion of the inscription, see J. E. Mitchiner, 'The System of Dating in the Hisse-Borala Inscription of Devasena'.

The first line of the inscription reads as follows : *siddham* || * * * *tasya vri* [*vṛ*] *ttasya* 220 *saptarṣaya uttarāsu phālgunīṣu śakānāṃ* 380 *vākāṭakānāṃ śrī devasenasya.*

2. See the article last mentioned, also 'The Saptarṣi Yuga', esp. pp. 90-92.

aspects of the inscription. In the first place, it can be seen that the inscription uses the "new' version of the Era of the Seven Ṛṣis, as followed also by Varāhamihira and the Purāṇic writers: wherein the Seven Ṛṣis are in Uttarā Phālgunī during the period A.D. 425-525, which is the period within which the inscription is elsewhere dated (namely Śaka 380=A.D. 458). In the second place, the inscription once again refers to the date of A.D. 238 (A.D. 458—220), using it as the commencing date of an era; and we may infer that, while the Purāṇic authors speak of this date as that of the end of the Andhras or Sātavāhanas, this Vākāṭaka inscription may well use the date as that of the establishment of Vākāṭaka rule in the western Deccan, in direct succession to Sātavāhana rule.

Taking together all three of these indications, we may conclude that the "new" version of the era of the Seven Ṛṣis both originated and was first used in the region of the western Deccan, south of the Vindhyas and between the Narmadā and Godāvarī rivers; and that it was originated and first used during the early centuries of the Christian era, under the Sātavāhana and Vākāṭaka dynasties.

F. Conclusion

We may conclude that the older and original version of the Era of the Seven Ṛṣis commenced with the Seven Ṛṣis in Kṛttikā in 6676 B.C., used a total of 28 Nakṣatras, and placed the start of the Kali Yuga in 3102 B.C. This version was in use in northern India from at least the 4th century B.C., as witnessed by the statements of Greek and Roman writers; it was also the version used by Vṛddha Garga, at around the start of the Christian era. At a period prior to that of Vṛddha Garga, there came into use a new version of the Era, which used a total of 27 Nakṣatras and placed the start of the Kali Yuga in 2414 B.C. The commencement of the older version with Kṛttikā in 6676 B.C. corresponded to the period of the Seven Ṛṣis being in Śravaṇā in the new version; while the start of the next complete cycle in the older version with Kṛttikā in 3876 B.C. corresponded to the Seven Ṛṣis being in Dhaniṣṭhā (Śraviṣṭhā) in the new version. The basis for the formulation of the new version arose from the postulation of a new date for the start of the Kali Yuga—since in both versions, the Seven Ṛṣis are said to be in Maghā at the start of the Kali Yuga. The new version originated and was first used in the western Deccan, particularly under the Sātavāhana and Vākāṭaka dynasties; it was also followed by the Epic writers, and incorporated into the Purāṇas.

The later astronomers—most notably Varāhamihira—subsequently attempted to harmonise the two versions, by accepting the date of 3102 B.C. as the start of the Kali Yuga (as given in the older version) while yet in practice making use of the new version of the Era. They were consequently obliged to introduce a period of 653 years as the interval separating the start of the Kali Yuga from the Mahābhārata war—a feature which is clearly totally at variance with both Epic and Purāṇic traditions. This latter "compromise" solution is that which is generally to be found in all subsequent contexts: notably in the *Rājataraṅgiṇī*, and also in such present-day uses of the Era as that followed in Kashmir.

Table 4

The Era of the Seven Ṛṣis, "original" version

1.	Kṛttikā	6676 B.C.	3876 B.C.	1076 B.C.
2.	Rohiṇī	6576	3776	976
3.	Mṛgaśiras	6476	3676	876
4.	Ārdrā	6376	3576	776
5.	Punarvasu	6276	3476	676
6.	Puṣya	6176	3376	576
7.	Āśleṣā	6076	3276	476
8.	Maghā	5976	3176	376
9.	Pūrvā Phālgunī	5876	3076	276
10.	Uttarā Phālgunī	5776	2976	176
11.	Hastā	5676	2876	76
12.	Citrā	5576	2776	25 A.D.
13.	Svātī	5476	2676	125
14.	Viśākhā	5376	2576	225
15.	Anurādhā	5276	2476	325
16.	Jyeṣṭhā	5176	2376	425

17.	Mūlā	5076	2276	525
18.	Pūrvāṣāḍhā	4976	2176	625
19.	Uttarāṣāḍhā	4876	2076	725
20.	Abhijit	4776	1976	825
21.	Śravaṇā	4676	1876	925
22.	Dhaniṣṭhā	4576	1776	1025
23.	Śatabhiṣā	4476	1676	1125
24.	Pūrvā Bhādrapadā	4376	1576	1225
25.	Uttarā Bhādrapadā	4276	1476	1325
26.	Revatī	4176	1376	1425
27.	Aśvinī	4076	1276	1525
28.	Bharaṇī	3976	1176	1625

TABLE 5

The Era of the Seven Ṛṣis, "new" version

1.	Śravaṇā	6676 B.C.	3976 B.C.	1276 B.C.
2.	Dhaniṣṭhā	6576	3876	1176
3.	Śatabhiṣā	6476	3776	1076
4.	Pūrvā Bhādrapadā	6376	3676	976
5.	Uttarā Bhādrapadā	6276	3576	876
6.	Revatī	6176	3476	776
7.	Aśvinī	6076	3376	676
8.	Bharaṇī	5976	3276	576
9.	Kṛttikā	5876	3176	476
10.	Rohiṇī	5776	3076	376
11.	Mṛgaśiras	5676	2976	276
12.	Ārdrā	5576	2876	176
13.	Punarvasu	5476	2776	76
14.	Puṣya	5376	2676	25 A.D.
15.	Āśleṣā	5276	2576	125
16.	Maghā	5176	2476	225

17.	Pūrvā Phālgunī	5076	2376	325
18.	Uttarā Phālgunī	4976	2276	425
19.	Hastā	4876	2176	525
20.	Citrā	4776	2076	625
21.	Svātī	4676	1976	725
22.	Viśākhā	4576	1876	825
23.	Anurādhā	4476	1776	925
24.	Jyeṣṭhā	4376	1676	1025
25.	Mūlā	4276	1576	1125
26.	Pūrvāṣāḍhā	4176	1476	1225
27.	Uttarāṣāḍhā	4076	1376	1325

CONCLUSION TO PART ONE

The feature which has emerged above all others from the traditions examined in this part of the book concerns the period and region in which many of these traditions were formulated. Thus we have seen that the second main list of the Seven Ṛṣis came to supersede the first primarily in later-Epic and early-Purāṇic literature, or around the early centuries of the Christian era: it was similarly during this same period that both the Manvantara traditions and also the second version of the Era came to be formulated. In the case of the lists, the reasons for the change can be traced to influences exerted by members of particular Brahmin *gotras* from southern regions of India; in a complementary manner, the second version of the Era uses as a key date the year A.D. 238 as representing the end of the Sātavāhana dynasty in the western Deccan, and this version was first used inscriptionally by the Vākāṭaka successors of the Sātavāhanas in that same region. Thus the overall conclusion from examining these traditions is that they were almost certainly formulated and promulgated in large measure around the region of the western Deccan—or present-day Maharashtra—during the rule of the Sātavāhanas and their successors, especially during the first three to four centuries of the Christian era.

This conclusion in its turn implies that a relatively high and dynamic degree of cultural change was then occurring in that region; this we have sought to illustrate briefly at the end of Chapter 3, although a fuller treatment of social, cultural and political changes under the Sātavāhanas in particular must remain beyond the scope of the present work. This period of early Indian history has long been something of a "dark age", with all too little being known for certain about it; yet the conclusions which we have drawn in this part of the book—alongside continuing archaeological discoveries and further studies on the political, architectural and cultural heritage of the Sātavāhanas—will, it is hoped, help to throw further light upon this dynamic and formative period in the development of Indian thought and culture.

PART TWO

MYTHOLOGICAL, PHILOSOPHICAL AND MYSTICAL TRADITIONS

5

THE SEVEN ṚṢIS ON EARTH I

Cultic and Ascetic Roles

A. Introduction

In this part of the book we shall be examining the main traditions concerning the activities and achievements of the Seven Ṛṣis, together with ideas about their nature and status. The first theme which we shall examine in this and the next chapter centres upon the activities of the Ṛṣis on earth : their composition of Vedic hymns and performance of sacrifice, their withdrawal from society in pursuit of ascetic practices, their relation with and degree of involvement in society, and the apparent conflict between their ascetic pursuits and their role as the progenitors of mankind. In general terms, ideas concerning their activities tend to remain reasonably constant from the Vedas onwards, right up to the present day; our aim in these chapters will consequently be to survey the main types of activities ascribed to the Ṛṣis throughout the mainstream of Hindu literature, while at the same time taking note of such changes in emphasis as may occur in different periods.

B. Cultic Role

(a) *Seers and Composers*

The role of the Ṛṣis as seers and composers of hymns is especially prominent in the *Ṛgveda,* as also throughout subsequent Vedic literature; much the same idea is continued in later times in thc ascriptions of various works to the authorship of one of the Ṛṣis. All of the hymns throughout the ten books or *maṇḍalas* of the *Ṛgveda* are said to have been composed by Ṛṣis, and in many cases by one of the Seven Ṛṣis. These hymns were reputedly not so much composed—in the sense of having been created —by the Ṛṣis as their own works, as rather to have been "seen by" and revealed to them in the sense of divine or supramental revelation : in much the samé way as the Bible, the Koran and other scriptures are held by some to be direct revelations of God, the Word of God brought to men through the medium of certain individuals. Thus, according to the most prevalent Hindu view, the Ṛṣis were essentially the vehicles or means whereby these "eternal revelations" of the hymns were made known to mankind. It is not our aim to give an exhaustive catalogue of the hymns and their authorships; but special note may be taken of certain important ascriptions of authorship, particularly where these are specifically mentioned in further Vedic texts.

Viśvāmitra is reputed to be the composer of a large number of *Ṛgveda* hymns, especially in the third and fourth *maṇḍala*— the entire third *maṇḍala* being ascribed in composition to him and his descendants. These include *Ṛgveda* 3.12, 3.21, 3.28, 3.30, 3.31, 3.33, 3.34, 3.36, 3.38, 3.47, 3.48, 3.51, 3.62, 4.19, 4.22, and 4.32[1] — *Ṛgveda* 3.62.10 being the sacred *gāyatri* hymn which is repeated daily by every Brahmin at his morning and evening devotions ("We meditate on that pre-eminent brilliance of the god Savitṛ, may he inspire our minds"[2]). To Vasiṣṭha's composition are ascribed the *āpri* verses (for royal consecration) *Ṛgveda* 7.2,[3] together with various other hymns especially in the seventh *maṇḍala*, whose composition in its entirety is ascribed to him and his descendants :

1. *Aitareya Brāhmaṇa* 6.18, 6.20, 8.3 : *Kauṣītaki Brāhmaṇa* 15.1, 23.3, 28.2 : *Aitareya Āraṇyaka* 1.2.2 : *Bṛhaddevatā* 4.104–119.

2. *tat savitur vareṇyam bhargo devasya dhīmahi dhiyo yo naḥ pracodayāt*; see also *Agni Purāṇa* 2.5.16 : *Garuḍa Purāṇa* 35.1 ff.

3. *Kauṣītaki Brāhmaṇa* 25.10 : *Śāṅkhāyana Śrauta Sūtra* 11.13.7.

notably *Ṛgveda* 3.66, 3.94, 7.19, 7.23, 7.24 and 7.82.[1] Bharadvāja is reputedly the composer of *Ṛgveda* 6.17, 6.18, 6.22, 6.30, and 6.69[2]—as indeed, with his descendants, of the entire sixth *maṇḍala*. To Jamadagni's composition are ascribed the *vihavya* hymn *Ṛgveda* 10.128, which he "saw" while he and Viśvāmitra were once quarrelling with Vasiṣṭha[3] : as also the *virāj* metre,[4] the *āpri* verses *Ṛgveda* 10.110 for consecration,[5] and *Vājasaneyi Saṃhitā* 29.25-36.[6] Agastya is said to be the composer of the *kayāśubhīya* hymn,[7] and the seer of the *udgitha* or chant of the immortal *gāyatri* which was revealed to him by Indra and enabled him and the other Ṛṣis to attain heaven;[8] he is also reputedly the composer of *Ṛgveda* 10.60.6,[9] and of various spells and incantations.[10] Atri is reputedly the composer, with his descendants, of the entire fifth *maṇḍala* of the *Ṛgveda*, as also of certain verses set to the *uṣṇiḥ*-metre;[11] similar general references appear to the composition of *vyāhṛtis* or sacred utterances and of verses set to the *triṣṭubh*-metre by Viśvāmitra[12], of the *ājya* and other chants and metres by Vasiṣṭha,[13] and of various verses by Bhṛgu.[14] Among the most common ascriptions of metres to a Ṛṣi, Vasiṣṭha is said to be the composer of the *rathantara*, which he received from Savitṛ and Viṣṇu, and Bharadvāja the composer of the *bṛhat*, received from Agni[15] : the *rathantara* being identified with

---

1. *Aitareya Brāhmaṇa* 6.18, 6.20, 8.3 : *Kauṣītaki Brāhmaṇa* 15.1, 23.3, 28.10, 29.2-3, 30.3 : *Aitareya Āraṇyaka* 1.5.2.
2. *Aitareya Brāhmaṇa* 6.18, 6.20, 8.3 : *Kauṣītaki Brāhmaṇa* 15.1, 23.3. 29.3, 30.9 : *Pañcaviṃśa Brāhmaṇa* 12.10.23 : *Aitareya Āraṇyaka* 1.2.2 : *Śāṅkhāyana Śrauta Sūtra* 10.11.8, 11.9.3, 14.32.7.
3. *Taittirīya Saṃhitā* 3.1.7.3 : *Pañcaviṃśa Brāhmaṇa* 9.4.14.
4. *Taittirīya Saṃhitā* 3.3.5.
5. *Aitareya Brāhmaṇa* 4.26 : *Bṛhaddevatā* 5.25.
6. *Śatapatha Brāhmaṇa* 13.2.2.14.
7. *Taittirīya Saṃhitā* 7.5.5 : *Pañcaviṃśa Brāhmaṇa* 9.4.17, 21.14.5.
8. *Jaiminīya Upaniṣad Brāhmaṇa* 4.14.5-8, 4.15.1ff.
9. *Bṛhaddevatā* 7.97-98.
10. *Atharvaveda* 2.32.3.
11. *Kauṣītaki Brāhmaṇa* 22.3, 24.5 : *Śāṅkhāyana Śrauta Sūtra* 10.4.4.
12. *Śāṅkhāyana Āraṇyaka* 1.6, 2.7.
13. *Kauṣītaki Brāhmaṇa* 22.7, 25.2, 26.15.
14. *Aitareya Brāhmaṇa* 2.20.
15. *Ṛgveda* 10.181.1-2 : *Aitareya Brāhmaṇa* 1.21, 8.3 : *Pañcaviṃśa Brāhmaṇa* 7.7.18 : *Aitareya Āraṇyaka* 1.4.2, 3.1.6.

either breath or speech and the earth, the *bṛhat* with mind and the sky.[1] On occasions, Viśvāmitra is similarly associated with the *vairūpa* and the eye, and Jamadagni with the *vairāja* and the ear;[2] while a somewhat different tradition associates Viśvāmitra with *uktha* or speech, and Vasiṣṭha with *brahman* or thought.[3]

Most of the hymns "seen" and sung by the Ṛṣis contain praises of various gods—especially for their deeds in helping men or in having helped the singer—together in many instances with pleas that the gods may further bestow aid and prosperity. In the case of the Seven Ṛṣis, noteworthy examples are in the hymns of Gotama and the Gautamas in praise of Agni (*Ṛgveda* 1.78.2, 8.88.4); of Agastya in praise of the Aśvins (*Ṛgveda* 1.117.11, 1.184.5); of Aṅgiras and the Āṅgirasas in praise of Indra (*Ṛgveda* 1.162.2ff., 1.71.2, 2.15.8, 2.17.1, 2.20.5, 3.31.19, 4.16.8, 10.62.1-6); of Atri and the Atris in praise of Agni (*Ṛgveda* 5.15.5, 5.22.4) and of Indra (5.39.5, 5.40.5-9, 8.36.6-7, 8.37.7, 8.38.8); of Bharadvāja in praise of Indra (*Ṛgveda* 6.23.10, 6.25.9, 6.31.4) and of Uṣas (6.65.6); of Vasiṣṭha in praise of Indra (*Ṛgveda* 7.18.4, 7.22.3, 7.23.1ff., 7.26.5, 7.33.1-14), of Agni (7.42.6, 10.122.8), of the Aśvins (7.73.3), of Varuṇa (7.86.5, 7.88.1-4, *Bṛhaddevatā* 6.11-15), and of all the gods (10.65.15, 10.66.14-15); of Vasiṣṭha and Jamadagni in praise of Sarasvatī (*Ṛgveda* 7.96.1-3); of Bhṛgu and the Bhṛgus in praise of Indra (*Ṛgveda* 8.3.9, 8.6.18); of Jamadagni in praise of Soma (*Ṛgveda* 9.62.24, 9.65.25); and of Kaśyapa in praise of Soma (*Ṛgveda* 9.114.2). In all of these hymns, the Ṛṣi is specifically mentioned by name as praising the god for a particular deed or quality : while additionally in several of them—as also in a large number of further instances—mention is made of the praises of the descendants of that Ṛṣi. Just as on one occasion it is said that the powerful words of Viśvāmitra were protected by the Bharata peoples,[4] so it may be inferred that many

1. *Aitareya Brāhmaṇa* 4.28 : *Śatapatha Brāhmaṇa* 1.7.2.17, 1.8.1.19.

2. *Maitrāyaṇī Saṃhitā* 2.7.19 : *Taittirīya Saṃhitā* 4.3.2 : *Vājasaneyi-Saṃhitā* 13.54-57

3. *Kauṣītaki Brāhmaṇa* 10.5, 29.3 : *Pañcaviṃśa Brāhmaṇa* 15.5.24 : *Ṣaḍviṃśa Brāhmaṇa* 1.5.1-3 : *Jaiminīya Upaniṣad Brāhmaṇa* 3.15.1-3.

4. *Ṛgveda* 3.53.12.

hymns, traditionally held to have been first sung by one of the Ṛṣis, were subsequently preserved and handed down by the descendants and followers of the Ṛṣi.

We shall next look at certain instances in post-*Ṛgveda* literature in which the practical effectiveness of hymns is illustrated: that is to say, in which a Ṛṣi is able to bring about a desired goal by "seeing" a hymn. Several such instances are related of Vasiṣṭha. In several contexts it is said that, when all the Ṛṣis sought to see Indra face to face, Vasiṣṭha alone did so—and as a reward, Indra revealed a *brāhmaṇa* or the *virāj* to him alone, for which reason his descendants multiplied and became Brahmins and Purohitas.[1] So too it is said that when his sons were slain, Vasiṣṭha saw a hymn and thereby gained offspring and cattle;[2] that he won the favour of Indra through a hymn;[3] and that when he was reproached by the other Ṛṣis for being a Vaiśya rather than a Brahmin, he gained deliverance through a hymn.[4] Jamadagni is similarly said to have gained deliverance from his enemies through a hymn;[5] while several different passages relate that Viśvāmitra either alone or with Jamadagni won a victory for the Bharatas against the Vṛcīvats by means of two hymns.[6] Bharadvāja is also said to have gained victories for various kings by means of a hymn in praise of Indra,[7] and we shall be looking at further such examples later in this chapter. It is related that by means of hymns, Gautama obtained *manas* or mind,[8] as also power and greatness;[9] and that through a hymn, Atri repelled the darkness of Svarbhānu which was covering the sun.[10] In addition to these somewhat worldly gains,

1. *Taittirīya Saṃhitā* 3.5.2 : *Gopatha Brāhmaṇa* 2.2.13 : *Pañcaviṃśa Brāhmaṇa* 15.5.24 : *Śatapatha Brāhmaṇa* 12.6.1.38 ff. : *Bṛhaddevatā* 5.143-160.
2. *Jaiminīya Brāhmaṇa* 1.14.7 : *Pañcaviṃśa Brāhmaṇa* 4.7.3, 8.2.4, 19.3.8 : *Bṛhaddevatā* 6.28, 6.34.
3. *Pañcaviṁśā Brāhmaṇa* 12.12.10.
4. *Jaiminīya Brāhmaṇa* 3.195.
5. Ibid., 1.152.
6. Ibid., 3.183, 3.237-238 : *Pañcaviṃśa Brāhmaṇa* 14.3.12-13.
7. Ibid., 3.244-247 : *Pañcaviṃśa Brāhmaṇa* 15.3 7 : *Bṛhaddevatā* 5.124-142.
8. Ibid., 1.149.
9. *Pañcaviṃśa Brāhmaṇa* 13.12.8.
10. Ibid., 6.6.8, 14.11.14 : *Gopatha Brāhmaṇa* 1.2.17.

various Ṛṣis are said to have attained heaven by means of hymns : as for example Vasiṣṭha,[1] Gautama,[2] and all the Ṛṣis together;[3] while Viśvāmitra is similarly said to have won the abode dear to Agni by means of a hymn.[4]

This same idea of the efficacy of sacred speech is to be found also, although to a lesser extent, in Epic and Purāṇic literature: as for example where Vasiṣṭha is said, by means of hymns, to have restored the strength of Indra when the god was afflicted by Vṛtra.[5] We shall be looking at further examples of the power of the Ṛṣis' speech later in this chapter. A slightly different feature which is found in later literature is the ascription of works to the authorship of one of the Ṛṣis. Just as the Seven Ṛṣis—particularly in the context of the Manvantara tradition—are said to be the teachers and promoters of *dharma* ("truth", "righteousness", "law"), so various Dharma Śāstras or law-books are said to be the work of individual Ṛṣis, notably Vasiṣṭha, Gautama, Atri, and Aṅgiras.[6] Bharadvāja is said to be the author of a *rāja-śāstra*, or treatise on the duties of kings,[7] and various other works—ranging from ritual to astronomical treatises—are nominally ascribed to one of the Ṛṣis, thereby associating them with the promulgation of such varied branches of learning.

We can see from these examples that the role of the Ṛṣis as seers and composers of both hymns and other works is one to which considerable importance is attached—especially throughout Vedic literature, but also in many post-Vedic contexts. Such importance arises in part from the very nature of sacred speech or *vāc*, which is seen as a form of breath (*prāṇa*) and also as a form of both fire and the sun: whence the use of *vāc*—

1. *Pañcaviṃśa Brāhmaṇa* 5.4.5, 7.7.18, 11.8.14, 12.3.15.

2. Ibid., 11.5.21-22.

3. *Jaiminīya Brāhmaṇa* 3.269-276 : *Pañcaviṃśa Brāhmaṇa* 8.2.6 : *Jaiminīya Upaniṣad Brāhmaṇa* 4.14.5-8, 4.15.1-5.

4. *Taittirīya Saṃhitā* 5.2.3.4.

5. *Mahābhārata* 12.272.21 ff.

6. *Mānava Dharma Śāstra* 3.16,8.140 : *Nārada Dharma Śāstra* 1.99 : *Yājñavalkya Dharma Śāstra* 1.4-5 : *Agni Purāṇa* 162.1-2 : *Garuḍa Purāṇa* 93.1 ff.

7. *Mahābhārata* 12.58.3.

particularly in chanting hymns—enables the chanter both to attain heaven and also to defeat his enemies (especially, in later contexts, through the power of a spoken curse). We shall have cause to examine the nature and symbolism of *vāc* in several subsequent contexts, in both this and later chapters.

(b) *Sacrificers*

The role of the Ṛṣis as sacrificers is by no means to be entirely separated from their role as seers of hymns, since in several—especially post-*Ṛgveda*—contexts such hymns are said to have been "seen" by them during the course of sacrifices. As in the case of the recitation of hymns, the main motive underlying the performance of a sacrifice was to gain a particular aim or desire, as is related in one Brāhmaṇa passage :

> In olden times, the Ṛṣis used to hold sacrifices for certain objects—"such is our aim, may that be fulfilled".[1]

One of the principal aims of the Ṛṣis is depicted in Vedic literature as being to gain sons and cattle. When Vasiṣṭha's sons were slain by the sons of Saudāsa, he desired more sons to defeat the Saudāsas; he "saw" a rite and sacrificed with it, and thereby gained his wish—whence the sacrifice came to be known thereafter as one for obtaining children.[2] When Kaśyapa desired children and cattle, he saw a sacrifice, offered it, and gained his wish;[3] similarly, through a four-day sacrifice, the descendants and cows of Jamadagni increased,[4] and Atri gained four excellent sons through another sacrifice.[5] Bharadvāja obtained long life through a sacrifice;[6] while Viśvāmitra, as king of the Jahnus,

1. *Śatapatha Brāhmaṇa* 6.9.24.

2. *Taittirīya Saṃhitā* 7.4.7 : *Jaiminīya Brāhmaṇa* 2.289 : *Kauṣītaki Brāhmaṇa* 4.8 : *Pañcaviṃśa Brāhmaṇa* 21.11.2 : *Mānava Śrauta Sūtra* 9.4.2.11 ff. : *Vaitāna Sūtra* 43.26.

3. *Jaiminīya Brāhmaṇa* 2.81-82.

4. Ibid., 2.285 : *Pañcaviṃśa Brāhmaṇa* 21.10.5-6, 22.7.2 : *Āpastamba Śrauta Sūtra* 22.18.16 : *Mānava Śrauta Sūtra* 9.4.2.1 : *Śāṅkhāyana Śrauta Sūtra* 16.23.7-8.

5. *Pañcaviṃśa Brāhmaṇa* 21.9.2 : *Āpastamba Śrauta Sūtra* 22.18.16 : *Mānava Śrauta Sūtra* 9.4.2.1 : *Śāṅkhāyana Śrauta Sūtra* 16.23.7-8.

6. *Śāṅkhāyana Śrauta Sūtra* 14.12.2.

conquered the Vṛcīvats and gained their kingdom by means of a sacrifice.[1] The Seven Ṛṣis also—when together seeking to go to heaven—saw some sacrificial verses and performed sacrifice with them, thereby gaining their various desires for offspring, cattle and wealth.[2] In virtually all of these cases, men are urged to perform the same sacrifice in order to fulfil the same aim.

Not all sacrifices are said to have been performed by the Ṛṣis in order to attain such desires for themselves alone. In many cases, the Ṛṣis are said to have performed sacrifices for kings—in many cases acting in their role as Purohitas or family priests [see Chapter 6 section A(a)]. Vasiṣṭha thus performed the sacrificial anointing of Daśaratha[3] and sacrificed for Saudāsa,[4] while both he and Ṛṣyaśṛṅga performed the *aśvamedha* sacrifice for Daśaratha.[5] Bharadvāja obtained a son for king Bharata by means of a sacrifice;[6] while Viśvāmitra, Jamadagni, Vasiṣṭha and Agastya all took part in a sacrifice for Hariścandra in which Śunaḥśepa was to be offered.[7] Many of the Seven Ṛṣis took part in a sacrifice for king Nimi, where Vasiṣṭha, angry that the sacrifice had been conducted without him since he had then been sacrificing elsewhere for Indra, cursed the king.[8] Further examples of the performance of sacrifices by the Ṛṣis on behalf of others will be noted during the course of this and later chapters. In many such cases, the Ṛṣis are said to have been offered a *dakṣiṇā* or sacrificial fee for their services : thus for example, in some accounts, it is related that Kaśyapa first officiated in the sacrifice of Viśvakarman, at which he was given the earth as his *dakṣiṇā*;[9] while in other accounts, he was given the earth

1. *Pañcaviṃśa Brāhmaṇa* 21.12.2 : *Āpastamba Śrauta Sūtra* 22.20.2 : *Mānava Śrauta Sūtra* 9.4.2.11 ff.
2. *Jaiminīya Brāhmaṇa* 2.218-221 : *Āpastamba Śrauta Sūtra* 22.22.13 : *Śāṅkhāyana Śrauta Sūtra* 14.61-67.
3. *Rāmāyaṇa* 1.7.3.
4. *Viṣṇu Purāṇa* 4.4.1 ff.
5. *Rāmāyaṇa* 1.8-12.
6. *Mahābhārata* 1.89.17-19.
7. *Aitareya Brāhmaṇa* 7.15-18 : *Bhāgavata Purāṇa* 9.7.22-23.
8. *Bhāgavata Purāṇa* 9.13.1-11 : *Devībhāgavata Purāṇa* 6.14.10-69 : *Matsya Purāṇa* 201.1-39 : *Viṣṇu Purāṇa* 4.5.1 ff.
9. *Śatapatha Brāhmaṇa* 13.7.1.15 : *Śāṅkhāyana Śrauta Sūtra* 16.16.3-4 : *Mahābhārata* 3.114.17-22.

after the sacrifice of Paraśurāma the son of Jamadagni, which was performed after the latter had rid the earth of Kṣatriyas.[1] In further instances, the Ṛṣis are depicted as performing sacrifices for gods : as for example, on behalf of Brahmā,[2] and on behalf of Dakṣa—in which Śiva, angry at not being given his share, destroyed the sacrifice and assaulted several of the Ṛṣis.[3] Similarly, Marīci and other Ṛṣis performed an *aśvamedha* sacrifice in order to rid Indra of the sin of *brahmahatyā* (killing a Brahmin) after the slaying of Vṛtra,[4] and Jamadagni performed a sacrifice in praise of the rivers at Palāśaka.[5] It can be seen that in many of these cases also, the principal aim was to bring about a specific desired aim for the person on behalf of whom the sacrifice was offered.

In other instances, a sacrifice is said to have been performed by the Ṛṣis not to bring about any specific desire on earth, but in order to attain heaven (Svarloka, Svargaloka and similar—see Chapter 7). The example most frequently met with in Vedic literature is the sacrifice of the Āṅgirasas and Ādityas (gods), both of whom were seeking to attain that goal. Some accounts simply state that they both offered sacrifice with Agni or Fire, and thereby went to heaven;[6] but other accounts go into somewhat greater detail, the main features of which may be summarised as follows :

> The Ādityas and Āṅgirasas contended as to who should go first to the world of heaven. The Āṅgirasas first saw the *soma*-sacrifice [or simply the sacrifice], and announced that they

---

1. *Rāmāyaṇa* 1.74.8 ff. : *Mahābhārata* 1.121.19-23, 3.117.1-15, 9.48.8, 12.49.55-80, 13.61.34 : *Harivaṃśa* 31.100-109, 42.39-47 : *Agni Purāṇa* 4.14-20: *Bhāgavata Purāṇa* 9.16.16-27 : *Brahma Purāṇa* 213.113-123 : *Brahmāṇḍa Purāṇa* 2.3.47.46-60 : *Devībhāgavata Purāṇa* 3.30.53, 4.16.14-15 : *Padma Purāṇa* 6.268.18 : *Skanda Purāṇa* 5.2.79.14-16 : *Varāha Purāṇa* 15.15.

2. *Padma Purāṇa* 5.16.11, 5.16.97, 5.29.4 ff.

3. See especially the accounts in *Bhāgavata Purāṇa* 4.4.31 ff. : *Brahma Purāṇa* 39.10 ff. : *Śiva Purāṇa* 2.2.27.1-56, 2.2.29.22-4, 2.2.30.22 ff. : *Vāmana Purāṇa* 2.8-5.6.

4. *Bhāgavata Purāṇa* 6.13.21.

5. *Mahābhārata* 3.88.13-16.

6. *Taittirīya Saṃhitā* 3.5.1, 5.3.9 : *Aitareya Brāhmaṇa* 1.16 : *Āpastamba Śrauta Sūtra* 24.12.7.

would offer it on the next day; but the Ādityas offered it on that same day, with Agni [Fire] as their Hotṛ [sacrificial priest], and thereby went to heaven. They gave to the Āṅgirasas as *dakṣiṇā* first Vāc [Speech] or the earth, which took the form of a lioness and separated the gods from the demons; then they gave the sun in the form of a white horse. Whoever offers this sacrifice will go to heaven, and leave his neighbour behind.[1]

Various sub-themes are developed from this account : relating especially how the Āṅgirasas, or individual Āṅgirasas, went to heaven either through performing sacrifice or through chanting hymns which enabled them to perceive and offer the sacrifice; in many such instances once again, men are likewise urged to perform the same sacrifice in order to attain the same goal.[2] A number of further passages correspondingly relate that when the gods went to heaven, they hid the traces of the sacrifice in the *yūpa* or sacrificial post, fearing lest men should discover the sacrifice and follow them; but the Ṛṣis discovered the *yūpa* and its hidden secret, and thereby attained heaven.[3] The law-books similarly emphasise that by performing particular sacrifices, men will attain heaven;[4] while in the Epics and Purāṇas, the myth of Triśaṅku again illustrates how a Ṛṣi accomplished—this time on behalf of another—the transference from earth to heaven by means of a sacrifice :

---

1. *Aitareya Brāhmaṇa* 4.17, 6.34-35 : *Jaiminīya Brāhmaṇa* 2.115-117, 2.122-124, 3.187-188 : *Kauṣītaki Brāhmaṇa* 30.6 : *Pañcaviṃśa Brāhmaṇa* 16.12.1-4, 16.14.2, 24.2.2, 25.16.2 : *Śatapatha Brāhmaṇa* 3.5.1.13-23, 12.2.2.9ff.: *Taittirīya Brāhmaṇa* 3.9.21.1 : *Mānava Śrauta Sūtra* 9.3.2.14, 9.5.3.1 ff. : *Śāṅkhāyana Śrauta Sūtra* 12.19.1-5, 14.40.1.

2. *Taittirīya Saṃhitā* 2.6.3.2-4, 3.1.9, 5.2.8.4-5, 5.4.2, 5.7.2, 6.1.1, 6.1.3, 6.2.6, 7.1.4 : *Atharvaveda* 18.1.61 : *Aitareya Brāhmaṇa* 3.24, 4.32, 5.14 : *Jaiminīya Brāhmaṇa* 1.183, 1.224, 2.235, 3.56, 3.76-77, 3. 216 : *Kauṣītaki Brāhmaṇa* 18.10 : *Pañcaviṃśa Brāhmaṇa* 8.9.5, 12.3.23, 12.5.16, 12.6.12, 12.11.10-11, 13.11.2. 14.5.25, 14.10.9, 15.5.11, 20.11.3-4, 25.2.2.

3. *Taittirīya Saṃhitā* 6.3.4 : *Jaiminīya Brāhmaṇa* 3.216 : *Śatapatha Brāhmaṇa* 1.6.2.1-4.

4. For example *Viṣṇu Dharma Śāstra* 78.8 : *Yājñavalkya Dharma Śāstra* 3.184.

King Triśaṅku sought to attain heaven in bodily form. He requested Vasiṣṭha to accomplish this for him, but the Ṛṣi refused and cursed him. Then the king made the same request to Viśvāmitra, who performed a great sacrifice and thereby raised Triśaṅku to the sky. Indra became alarmed at this, and started to hurl Triśaṅku back to earth; but Viśvāmitra threatened to burn the worlds with the fire of his anger, and the gods permitted Triśaṅku to remain in bodily form in the heavens.[1]

We shall be further examining the processes by which the Ṛṣis attained heaven in Chapter 7: but we may note here that the performance of sacrifice by a Ṛṣi—like the seeing and chanting of hymns—was frequently looked upon as being a means to bring about this end, either for the Ṛṣi himself or on behalf of another.

Although sacrifice continued to be regarded as an efficacious means of bringing about a desired goal, greater emphasis is laid upon its performance by the Ṛṣis in Vedic literature than in the Epics and Purāṇas. One of the main reasons underlying this change in emphasis arises from the increasing "ritual interiorisation"[2] of the sacrificial cult, whereby the external generation of heat in sacrifice comes to be replaced by the internal generation of heat through ascetic austerities—a topic which we shall be examining in a moment. The change is especially evident in the Brāhmaṇas and Upaniṣads : it is well-illustrated in one Purāṇic myth, wherein the Ṛṣis performed a sacrifice for king Vasumanas and were then questioned by the king as to the relative merits of sacrifice (*yajña*), asceticism (*tapas*), and renunciation (*sannyāsa*). The Ṛṣis replied that the path of asceticism was the

1. *Rāmāyaṇa* 1.56.10—1.59.33 : *Mahābhārata* 1.65.20-42, 13.3.1 ff. : *Harivaṃśa* 9.88-100, 10.1-20 : *Bhāgavata Purāṇa* 9.7.5-6 : *Bhaviṣya Purāṇa* 4.130.9-39 : *Brahma Purāṇa* 7.105-109 : *Brahmāṇḍa Purāṇa* 2.3.63.73-114 : *Devībhāgavata Purāṇa* 7.10.1—7.14.25 : *Liṅga Purāṇa* 1.66.6-11 : *Śiva Purāṇa* 5.2.38, 5.37.47—5.38.18 : *Skanda Purāṇa* 6.4.1—6.8.9 : *Vāyu Purāṇa* 2.26.84-115 : *Viṣṇu Purāṇa* 4.3.1 ff. : *Kathāsaritsāgara* 6.28.1 ff.

2. On the concept of ritual interiorisation. see especially M. Eliade, *Yoga : Immortality and Freedom*, pp. 111 ff.

best of all;[1] and indeed, in the Epics and Purāṇas it is generally this path which the Ṛṣis are primarily depicted as pursuing in order to achieve their goals.

(*c*) *Teachers*

The teaching role of the Ṛṣis—as distinct from their role as seers and composers—emphasises their activity in passing on and handing down the knowledge and revelation which they have received, rather than their actual reception of such knowledge. The two are by no means entirely separate from one another; but it is interesting to note that while their role as seers is especially prominent in Vedic literature, their role as teachers is emphasised more in the Epics and Purāṇas—while their activity in teaching the Vedas and *dharma* to mankind in each of the fourteen Manvantaras (see Chapter 2) is an idea which is encountered almost exclusively in the Purāṇas.

We meet with a number of instances in which individual Ṛṣis are said to give instruction to others on particular topics. It is related, for example, that Vasiṣṭha took Bhīṣma the son of Śāntanu as his pupil, and taught him the Vedas and Vedāṅgas,[2] and that he also instructed him on false ascetics and heretics, on Buddhists and Jains.[3] He is further said to have given instruction to king Karāla,[4] to king Saudāsa Aikṣvāka,[5] and to Rāma.[6] Pulastya is said to have instructed Bhīṣma on the merits of visiting *tirthas* and places of pilgrimage;[7] and Kaśyapa is said to have instructed the son of Aila on the relative superiority of Brahmins and Kṣatriyas, on the origins of Rudra and Vāyu, and other matters.[8] Gautama is said to have taught the *Dhanurveda*, a treatise on archery, to his son Kṛpa;[9] while Bharadvāja

1 *Kūrma Purāṇa* 1.19.31-43.
2. *Mahābhārata* 1.94.33-35, 12.38.10-11, 12.46.15.
3. *Viṣṇu Purāṇa* 3.17.1 ff.
4. *Mahābhārata* 12.291.7 ff.
5. Ibid., 13.77.1 ff.
6. Ibid., 13.83.37 ff.
7. Ibid., 3.80.1—3.83.115.
8. Ibid., 12.74.1 ff.
9. Ibid., 1.120.2-21.

is said to have taught the same treatise to Drupada,[1] as well as to have taught the *Āyurveda*, a treatise on medicine, to the king of Kāśī.[2] Many further lengthy passages occur throughout the Epics and Purāṇas in which a Ṛṣi gives instruction to an enquirer or pupil : thereby emphasising the role of the Ṛṣi as one who passes on knowledge of both sacred and secular matters—both being ultimately included under the heading of *dharma*, or the proper ordering and well-being of the universe. Several Purāṇas in their entirety are said to be narrated by or passed on to one of the Ṛṣis in this way : thus for example the *Brahmāṇḍa* was revealed by Brahmā to Vasiṣṭha, who handed it down to his grandson Parāśara;[3] the *Bhāgavata* and *Viṣṇu* are related by Parāśara to Maitreya;[4] the *Agni* was revealed by Agni to Vasiṣṭha, and handed down to Vyāsa the son of Parāśara;[5] the *Garuḍa* was revealed by Garuḍa to Kaśyapa;[6] the *Kūrma* was revealed by Nārāyaṇa-Viṣṇu to Nārada, and handed down to Gautama and thence to Parāśara;[7] the *Padma* was revealed by Brahmā to Pulastya, who handed it down to Bhīṣma;[8] the *Vāmana* was handed down from Pulastya to Nārada;[9] while the *Tiruviḷaiyāṭar* was handed down from Agastya to the other Ṛṣis.[10] In a similar manner, the lists of teachers in the Upaniṣads indicate how knowledge was passed on—usually from a divine source—from one Ṛṣi to another.[11] We have already noted that the Seven Ṛṣis are said to periodically teach and renew *dharma* and knowledge of the Vedas among men within each Manvantara and Mahāyuga; so too the Seven Ṛṣis are also said to have given instruction to Dhruva on the correct

---

1. *Mahābhārata* 5.149.13.
2. *Brahma Purāṇa* 11-37-38.
3. *Brahmāṇḍa Purāṇa* 1.1.1. 8-9.
4. *Bhāgavata Purāṇa* 3.8.9 : *Viṣṇu Purāṇa* 1.1.1. ff.
5. *Agni Purāṇa* 1.8 ff.
6. *Garuḍa Purāṇa* 1.1 ff.
7. *Kūrma Purāṇa* 2.44.141.
8. *Padma Purāṇa* 5.2.46-47.
9. *Vāmana Purāṇa* 1.1 ff.
10. *Tiruviḷaiyāṭarpurāṇam* 1.1 ff.
11. For example *Bṛhadāraṇyaka Upaniṣad* 2.6, 4.6 : *Muṇḍaka Upaniṣad* 1.1.1-2.

performance of *tapas* or asceticism, when he sought their advice on commencing his austerities.[1] Agastya is further renowned as having taught Tamil grammar to Nakkīran in Madurai, which had been revealed to him by the favour of Śiva;[2] and Vasiṣṭha is said to have introduced Vāmācāra Tantrism into Assam.[3] We can thus see that, in these and in many further instances, prominent emphasis is given to the passing on of knowledge—frequently received from a divine source—by the Ṛṣis.

In considering the role of the Ṛṣis as teachers, we may also note the relationships between the Ṛṣis and their pupils. Little detailed information is given on this subject, and very rarely is any mention made of individual pupils who are taught by one of the Seven Ṛṣis. Mention has already been made of Bhīṣma's pupilage under Vasiṣṭha: we shall refer to two other notable instances, in the cases of Viśvāmitra and Gautama. Viśvāmitra is said to have accepted a certain Gālava as his pupil (although many Purāṇas term Gālava the son of Viśvāmitra); and the story of Gālava—as based upon the *Mahābhārata* account—may by summarised as follows :

> Gālava was the son of a poor Brahmin, who entrusted him to the care of Viśvāmitra. Gālava studied at the feet of his *guru* [teacher], and waited upon him for 100 years; at the end of that time, Viśvāmitra achieved Brahmin-hood, and told Gālava that he could depart. Gālava asked what gift he might present, to which Viśvāmitra replied that his service during 100 years had been his gift; but Gālava insisted, and with slight anger Viśvāmitra replied that he should present him with 800 cows as white as the moon-rays and each with one black ear. Gālava thereupon fell to despair, not knowing how to obtain such animals, and prepared to die: he sought the protection of Viṣṇu, who sent Garuḍa to help him—and together they visited various kings in their quest. King Yayāti gave them his daughter Mādhavī, so that they might find a

1. *Skanda Purāṇa* 4.1.19.101 ff. : *Viṣṇu Purāṇa* 1.11.29-56.
2. *Kāñcipurāṇam* 63.202-288 : *Tiruviḷaiyāṭarpurāṇam* 54.7-22.
3. *Kālikā Purāṇa* 84.1 ff.

suitor and gain a dowry of cows : and by that means they obtained 600 cows, 200 each from kings Haryaśva Aikṣvāka, Divodāsa, and Uśīnara. Gālava then took the 600 cows together with Mādhavī to Viśvāmitra, who was delighted with his pupil's gift.[1]

The account furnishes some idea of the lengthy service paid by the pupil to his Ṛṣi-teacher : as also of the almost impossible nature of the task set by the teacher to test the sincerity and genuineness of feeling of his pupil. The same themes are met with in the case of Gautama and his pupil Uttaṅka, the account of which may be summarised as follows :

Gautama was highly pleased with the devotion of his pupil Uttaṅka, and insisted that he should stay on at the Āśrama after his period of pupilage was completed. Uttaṅka spent many years at the Āśrama; but one day, sadly realising that he was growing old, he asked Gautama's permission to depart. Gautama agreed to his pupil's request, whereupon Uttaṅka asked what gift he might give to his *guru*; but Gautama replied that he was already pleased with him, and he transformed him into a youth of 16 and gave him his own daughter as wife. Uttaṅka then asked Gautama's wife Ahalyā what *dakṣiṇā* or gift he might give to Gautama, to which she replied that his presence and devotion had been sufficient gift; but Uttaṅka insisted, and Ahalyā told him to bring the golden ear-rings worn by Madayantī the wife of king Saudāsa. When Ahalyā told Gautama of her request, the Ṛṣi feared for his pupil's life, but Uttaṅka had by then already departed. Uttaṅka made his request to Madayantī and Saudāsa, who gave him the ear-rings wrapt in a black deer-skin; on his way back to the Āśrama he was hungry and climbed a tree to pick fruits, and while he was eating, the deer-skin—which he had hung from the tree—fell to the ground, and a snake took the ear-rings into ant-hill. Uttaṅka in his anger pierced the ant-hill for thirty-five days, causing the Earth to become anxious and distressed; eventually Indra came and regained the ear-rings

1. *Mahābhārata* 5.104.1—5.117.20, 13.18.38 : *Śiva Purāṇa* 5.3.69-77.

from the snake. Thus Uttaṅka was finally able to present them to Ahalyā, the wife of his *guru*.[1]

Here we are once again presented with the lengthy period of stay with the Ṛṣi-teacher, the insistence on presenting a gift, the seemingly impossible task set and its eventual resolution by the pupil. Both of these accounts illustrate certain aspects of the relationship between the Ṛṣi-teacher and his pupil, which generally conform to the usual pattern of *guru-śiṣya* (teacher-pupil) relationships as set out in further contexts. A number of further passages refer in a general manner to the several or many pupils of each of the Seven Ṛṣis, who resided with them at their Āśramas; and the Āśramas of Ṛṣis are sometimes depicted as being the residences and meeting-places of many Ṛṣis or Brahmins. Thus it is said, for example, that many Ṛṣis came to dwell at the Āśrama of Gautama during a twelve-year drought,[2] and that the Dānavas—when seeking to destroy Brahmins—in a single night slew 100 *munis* residing in the Āśrama of Vasiṣṭha and 12 Brahmins residing in the Āśrama of Bharadvāja.[3] Thus we may conclude that the Ṛṣis were not actively involved in attracting followers to their teachings, but were more concerned with imparting such teachings to those who came to visit or reside with them in their Āśramas—and especially with passing on their knowledge to only a single or a few close pupils, who would in most cases reside with their Ṛṣi-teacher for a considerable period of time.

C. Ascetic Role

(a) *The Nature of tapas*

The performance of *tapas* might rightly be termed one of the most characteristic pursuits of the Ṛṣis. *Tapas* is a word with many shades of meaning. It is derived from the Sanskrit root *tap*, which conveys the basic meaning of heat : the performance

1. *Mahābhārata* 14.55ff. : *Skanda Purāṇa* 7.3.2.1-56.
2. *Brahma Purāṇa* 74.21—75.50 : *Devībhāgavata Purāṇa* 10.9.1-97 : *Kūrma Purāṇa* 1.15.93-104 : *Śiva Purāṇa* 4.25.1—4.27.22 : *Varāha Purāṇa* 71.1-62.
3. *Mahābhārata* 3.100.1-24.

of *tapas* consequently conveys the basic idea of inwardly heating oneself, through the performance of various religious and ascetic practices. Whether such practices involve the performance of sacrifice, the recitation of sacred texts, the adoption of certain physical postures, the performance of meditation, the worship of deities or any further pursuits is of somewhat secondary importance, since the emphasis in *tapas* lies not so much in the thing done as rather in the way in which it is done—on the inner state of the practitioner, whereby through these various means he increases his inner store of mystical heat. The aim in performing *tapas* is thus invariably to bring about some change within the performer—a change in both physical, mental and spiritual states; *tapas* as such represents a condition of change and transition, a dynamic state of movement and flux, whereby ultimately the purely gross and material gives way to and evolves into the spiritual and divine, and man becomes equal to the gods or realises his own divinity.

The concept of tapas is found in several *Ṛgveda* hymns, and is repeatedly met with throughout Vedic and subsequent literature. The universe itself is said to have originated from the tapas of Prajāpati or Brahmā, who by heating himself set in motion the entire cycle of creation. *Tapas* itself is a dynamically creative power, which enables the *tapasvin* or practitioner of *tapas* to change both himself and his environment; but just as fire is both a purifying and a destructive element, so too the fire of *tapas* can be used also for destructive ends, particularly through the power of a curse. The very meaning of the word *tapas* is itself closely connected in many respects with the meaning of the term *ṛṣi* : for the Sanskrit √*ṛṣ* denotes movement and exertion, and the Ṛṣis are those who—by their motion and self-exertion—brought the universe into being.[1] Another word which is frequently used—from the *Ṛgveda* onwards—as a synonym of the term Ṛṣi is *vipra*, and the Seven Ṛṣis are frequently referred to as the Seven *vipras* or *vipra*-Ṛṣis, especially in connection with the singing of hymns and the performance of the *soma*-sacrifice.[2] Here

1. *Śatapatha Brāhmaṇa* 6.1.1.1-5 : see also Chapters 7 and 8.
2. For example *Ṛgveda* 1.62.4, 3.31.5, 6.22.2, 9.92.2.

again the same meaning of movement is implied, particularly inner motion and change : for the Sanskrit root √*vip* denotes the idea of trembling, shaking or vibrating, and the Seven Ṛṣis as *vipras* are those who shake or vibrate inwardly—who are inwardly excited and inspired, being in a state of constant inner movement and change. Thus the Ṛṣi is essentially one who is undergoing transformation, who vibrates like a power-house of energy; his powers are amassed through the building-up of inner heat, which ultimately enables him to take the place of both Fire and the sun—transforming his whole being, as it were, into pure energy—and to attain heaven and conquer the realms of the gods.[1]

The ascetic practices said to be undertaken by the Ṛṣis in amassing their stores of *tapas* are closely similar in a great many respects to the austerities performed by the Syrian and Egyptian "Desert Fathers" and others in the Christian tradition, by the early Ṣūfīs in the Islamic tradition, and by many other ascetics in further traditions. But a probably far more archaic figure who is similarly comparable to the Ṛṣi—as also to the Christian and Muslim ascetic—is the Shaman, a figure who is met with in many cultures and among many peoples throughout the world and most prominently in Central and North Asia. Both the Ṛṣi and the Shaman were especially involved in the production of "mystical heat" : both underwent some form of symbolic death for the attainment of their office—that of the Ṛṣi being well-illustrated in the ascetic practices of Viśvāmitra, performed in order to attain the status of a *brahma*-Ṛṣi (see below). Similarly, both had the ability to fly through the air and assume different bodily forms; and both made the mystical ascent to heaven—although the Ṛṣi rarely acted as a Psychopomp or descended to the nether worlds, preferring instead to consign others to that world through his curse. The Shaman is perhaps closer to the Ṛṣi than to any other figure in Indian literature, including the *yogin*; this in turn raises the likelihood that many ideas and practices present in the Ṛṣi traditions are by no means narrowly Indian or Indo-European in origin, but may be traced back to a far greater antiquity

---

1. On the concepts of mystical heat and *tapas*, useful reference may be made to C. Blair, *Heat in the Rig Veda and Atharva Veda*, and D. Knipe, *In the Image of Fire*.

well beyond the confines of "Indo-European" and "Dravidian", where we are dealing with ideas and practices which may well have been developed from the pre-historic Shamanic cults of Asia. In the case of the Ṛṣi, such features were absorbed, moulded and re-interpreted in conformity with the religious complex of Hinduism; but it is noteworthy that many Shamanic features are still preserved among the "Aboriginal" tribes of India, as well as on more popular levels of Hinduism.[1]

Throughout this section, we shall necessarily be concerned only with those aspects of asceticism which are specifically associated with one of the Seven Ṛṣis, and not with the ascetic practices of other Ṛṣis or with Indian asceticism in general—a complete survey of which would in itself occupy many volumes. In examining the various ascetic practices which the Seven Ṛṣis are said to have performed, we shall be looking at them under a number of different headings; but it should not be assumed that these headings are distinct from one another, or that they represent different stages or levels of ascetic pursuit. On the contrary, in many contexts they overlap one another and are said to be pursued concurrently by the Ṛṣis; but they may nonetheless be conveniently analysed under the headings into which they naturally divide themselves—namely, after certain basic considerations shared by all paths, those of *karma* or meritorious action, *jñāna* or spiritual knowledge and meditation, and *bhakti* or devotion. All of these paths of *tapas* are present throughout the Ṛṣi traditions, although the emphasis on and manifestations of each differ somewhat in different periods and due notice will be taken of such differences as they occur.

(*b*) *The Paths and Goals of Asceticism*

(*i*) *General Considerations*. The places chosen by the Ṛṣis for the practice of *tapas* were invariably isolated and almost inaccessible,

1. On Shamanism generally, see especially M. Eliade, *Shamanism*; on Shamanic ideas and practices among the Indo-Europeans and the tribes of India, see ibid., pp. 375-427 : E. M. Loeb, 'Shaman and Seer' : W. Ruben, 'Schamanismus in alten Indien' : R. Rahmann, 'Shamanistic and related phenomena in Northern and Middle India'. On *tapas* and mystical heat in relation to both Yoga and Shamanism, see especially *Shamanism*, pp. 407-421, and Eliade, *Yoga : Immortality and Freedom*, pp. 106-114, 318-341. Note also the correspondence between the Shaman and the Ṛṣis as *śramaṇas* (for example *Jaiminīya Brāhmaṇa* 2.218 : *Śatapatha Brāhmaṇa* 1.6.2.1-7) : see N. D. Mironov & S. M. Shirokogoroff, 'Śramaṇa-Shaman'.

as for example in the cases of Atri's Āśrama in the midst of the Himālayan snows and mountains,[1] and of Agastya's inaccessible Āśrama on mount Vidyutman[2]—free from the disturbances and distractions of the world around. Their Āśramas or hermitages were situated especially in forests or in hills and mountains, frequently close to the banks of a river; the Ṛṣi might perform his *tapas* either within or away from the Āśrama, depending on the particular type of *tapas* being performed. In the case of extremely severe ascetic practices, the Ṛṣi might abandon the Āśrama altogether and live in the open air—as especially in the case of Viśvāmitra while performing austerities to become a *brahma*-Ṛṣi. We have already examined in Chapter 3 many of the localities of such Āśramas—the most frequently-mentioned region being in the Himālayas around the sources of the river Gaṅgā; another place in which the Ṛṣis are frequently said to have resided is the Naimiṣāraṇya or Dāruvana, the great Pine Forest near the southern slopes of the Himālayas which remains to this day a favourite haunt of ascetics. This forest figures prominently in accounts of Śiva's seduction of the Ṛṣis' wives,[3] and in certain accounts of the Ṛṣis' stay at Gautama's Āśrama during a drought[4] while in a similar manner the region of the Seven Ṛṣis (in the sky) is said to be reserved for ascetics who live in forests.[5] Along with physical withdrawal from the world went the renunciation of all worldly attachments. Thus when Agastya took Lopāmudrā the daughter of a king—as his wife, he instructed her to abandon her ornaments and finery, and to dress instead in rags.[6] The Ṛṣis are most frequently said to wear clothes of deer-skin or bark-cloth, to smother their bodies with ashes, and to have their hair uncut, matted and tied in a knot[7] : in other words, they are

1. *Matsya Purāṇa* 119.55 ff.
2. Ibid., 163.75-82.
3. For example *Brahmāṇḍa Purāṇa* 1.2.27.1-129 : *Kūrma Purāṇa* 2.37.2-162: *Liṅga Purāṇa* 1.29.1—1.31.45 : *Śiva Purāṇa* 2.2.29.22-24.
4. For example *Kūrma Purāṇa* 1.15.93-104.
5. *Garuḍa Purāṇa* 49.1 ff. : *Kūrma Purāṇa* 1.2.69 : *Mārkaṇḍeya Purāṇa* 49.77-80.
6. *Mahābhārata* 3.95.1-12.
7. For example *Liṅga Purāṇa* 1.34.24-26 : *Matsya Purāṇa* 154.311-425.

depicted as being in appearance much as many other—especially Śaiva—ascetics, scantily clad in clothes made from the natural surroundings. One passage even describes Aṅgiras, Gautama and Vasiṣṭha in terms of those who wander over the earth disguised as madmen while imparting wisdom.[1] Kālidāsa gives a more poetic and idealised account of their dress, and describes the Seven Ṛṣis as "wearing sacred threads of pearls, dressed in golden bark-clothes, carrying jewel rosaries, and looking like heavenly trees which have adopted an ascetic mode of life".[2] Certain further passages imply that they wear beards—as in the case of Bhṛgu, whose beard is torn out and then replaced with a goat's beard at the destruction of Dakṣa's sacrifice by the hosts of Śiva;[3] other passages describe them as possessing *kamaṇḍalus* or water pots for performing their ritual ablutions—as in the cases of Agastya, who carried the river Kāverī in his water-pot,[4] and of Bharadvāja, who caught his seed in his water-pot when it fell at the sight of the Apsaras Ghṛtācī.[5] The Ṛṣis are frequently spoken of as shunning meat and as being vegetarian : thus the Seven Ṛṣis gathered fruits and roots to live on[6] and praised abstention from meat,[7] while Viśvāmitra cursed Śiva for serving him meat,[8] and Vasiṣṭha similarly cursed king Saudāsa for offering him meat (or in some versions, human flesh).[9] Even the animals around Atri's Āśrama are said to be vegetarian and friendly to one another, due to the influence of the Ṛṣi.[10] The practice of fasting is another common ascetic pursuit undertaken by the Ṛṣis. During

1. *Bhāgavata Purāṇa* 6.15.11-15.
2. *Kumārasambhava* 6.3 ff.
3. For example *Bhāgavata Purāṇa* 4.5.19, 4.6.51, 4.7.5 : *Śiva Purāṇa* 2.2.30.53, 2.2.41.49, 2.2.42.9.
4. *Kandapurāṇam* 2.23.1-28, 2.27.1-66 : *Kāveripurāṇam* 4.1-49 : *Tiruvaiyārrupurāṇam* 4.1-25 : *Tulākkāverimānmiyam* 5-6.
5. *Mahābhārata* 1.57.88-90, 1.121.3-9, 1.154.1-12, 5.54.47-48.
6. Ibid., 9.47.27-53.
7. Ibid., 13.116.11.
8. *Padma Purāṇa* 6.147.56-68.
9. For example *Rāmāyaṇa* 7.57.10-33: *Bhāgavata Purāṇa* 9.9.18-39 : *Viṣṇu Purāṇa* 4.4.1 ff.
10. *Matsya Purāṇa* 119.55ff.

the course of his austerities, Viśvāmitra is said to have taken no food for 3,000 years, living only on air (*vāyubhakṣa*) : he is also said to have lived on water and the leaves of trees (*jalāhāra*, *parṇāhāra*),[1] and to have attained Brahmin-hood by taking only one meal a day for 1,000 years.[2] Anasūyā the wife of Atri obtained three sons by fasting for 300 years;[3] while Jamadagni, Viśvāmitra, Gautama and Bhṛgu are all said to have attained heaven by fasts.[4] Similarly, Ṛṣis are depicted on several occasions as giving discourses on the merits of fasting—as in the case of Aṅgiras;[5] and it is said that if one eats a meal only every third day, one will atain the region of the Seven Ṛṣis.[6] The length of time spent in such pursuits is frequently said to be of extremely long duration, as in the examples just noted. Even in one Brāhmaṇa, Kaśyapa is said to have stood on one foot for 1,000 years in the forest of the Ṛṣis, to have supported the waters of immortality on his head for a further 1,000 years, and to have then heated himself for 48,000 Brahmā-years on top of the waters.[7] Many similar examples of the lengthy pursuit of *tapas* are met with in the Epics and Purāṇas, as for example in the case of Gautama who performed *tapas* for 60,000 years at his Āśrama in the Pāriyātra hills,[8] and for 10,000 years on the Brahmagiri mountain.[9]

The Ṛṣis are in many cases depicted as leading lives of total sexual abstention in their Āśramas—especially during the course of particular vows or ascetic pursuits. In several cases they were accompanied by their wives—as Agastya by Lopāmudrā, Vasiṣṭha by Arundhatī, Atri by Anasūyā, Gautama by Ahalyā, and Jamadagni by Reṇukā; but in such cases, the wives either aided them in their *tapas* and themselves became ideals of

---

1. *Rāmāyaṇa* 1.62.13—1.63.15 : *Mahābhārata* 1.65.21 ff., 9.39.23-24 : *Devībhāgavata Purāṇa* 1.14.65 ff.
2. *Mahābhārata* 3.109.64 ff.
3. *Śiva Purāṇa* 5.2.18-19.
4. *Mahābhārata* 3.109.64 ff.
5. Ibid., 3.109.8 ff.
6. Ibid., 3.110.14-15.
7. *Gopatha Brāhmaṇa* 1.2.8.
8. *Mahābhārata* 12.127.1 ff.
9. *Śiva Purāṇa* 4.24.2 ff.

chastity and adepts at *tapas* (as with Lopāmudrā, Arundhatī and Anasūyā),[1] or else succumbed to sexual desires and were cursed or killed by their husbands (as with Ahalyā, Reṇukā, and the six wives of the Seven Ṛṣis). The Ṛṣis themselves were on occasions overcome by sexual desires, which destroyed the power of their *tapas* (as especially Viśvāmitra, Bharadvāja and Gautama);[2] however, even in such cases, the succumbing to sexual desires together with the subsequent loss of ascetic merit merely serves to highlight the emphasis placed in the Ṛṣi traditions upon the uncompromising—if precarious—pursuit of total sexual abstention during the performance of *tapas*.

(ii) *Meritorious Deeds* : The first and foremost of all meritorious actions performed by the Ṛṣis was sacrifice. The Ṛṣis are depicted as being frequent performers of sacrifice throughout Vedic, Epic and Purāṇic literature; although it is generally not until the later literature that sacrifice comes to be looked upon as one of the paths of *tapas*, and Vedic literature generally tends to draw a distinction between the performances of sacrifice and *tapas*. Sacrifice itself is sometimes viewed in the later literature as a means whereby the Ṛṣi—in kindling external heat—correspondingly kindles heat within himself, enabling him to achieve his desired goals. Since the role of the Ṛṣis as sacrificers has already been discussed earlier in this chapter, it need not detain us here.

Another type of action which the Ṛṣis are frequently depicted as performing is ritual bathing. Mention is often made of the *tīrthas* or sacred pools which are associated with each of the Ṛṣis, and the locations of several of these were noted in Chapter 3. Such pools or tanks—used for the purpose of ritual purification—are often mentioned as being at or near the Āśramas of Ṛṣis, serving as places to perform ritual ablutions either in, adjacent to or in place of a river.[3] Lengthy praise is often given throughout the Epics and Purāṇas to the merits of

1. For example *Mahābhārata* 1.191.5-6, 3.113.22-23, 4.20.6-11 : *Kūrma Purāṇa* 2.37.42-44 : *Vāmana Purāṇa* 6.58-67.

2. See further in Chapter 6 section B.

3. For example *Mahābhārata* 1.121.3-9 : *Brahma Purāṇa* 96,1-22 : *Śiva Purāṇa* 3.18.2-23 : *Kāñcipurāṇam* 14.1-13.

tirtha-yātrā, or making pilgrimage to such tanks, as also of making pilgrimage to the Āśramas of the Ṛṣis.[1] The Ṛṣis themselves are sometimes said to have undertaken such pilgrimages, in addition to visiting such sacred centres as Kāśī (Banaras) or Kāñcī. On one occasion, the Ṛṣis are said to have performed a *tirtha-yātrā*, commencing by bathing in the river Kauśikī; while the Seven Ṛṣis also tell Śiva that they have performed three types of *tapas*—namely studying the Vedas, performing sacrifice, and visiting holy places.[2] Gautama similarly in one context speaks of three types of *tapas*, namely of spirit, word and body—of which the latter is the best, particularly in the form of pilgrimage or bathing.[3] Thus the internal (as well as external) heat generated by and during the performance of both pilgrimage and ritual bathing added still further to the store of the Ṛṣis' *tapas*.

A third type of meritorious action engaged in by the Ṛṣis was the offering of hospitality to visitors. In the Ṛṣi traditions, such visitors were frequently of royal connection : thus for example Atri and Agastya both entertained Rāma—together with Lakṣmaṇa and Sītā—when he visited their Āśramas during the period of his banishment from Ayodhyā,[4] while Bharadvāja similarly entertained Bharata and his army when Bharata was searching for Rāma.[5] Jamadagni entertained king Arjuna Kārttavīrya and his army,[6] and Vasiṣṭha entertained king Viśvāmitra and his army[7] : in both cases, the food was provided miraculously by the Ṛṣi's *Kāmadhenu* or wish-granting cow, and each time with dire results, since the kings in both instances subsequently tried to steal the *Kāmadhenu*. The Āśramas of Ṛṣis on occasions became the refuges for kings and princes : thus

1. See especially *Mahābhārata* 3.80 ff., the 28 *saromāhātmya* chapters of the *Vāmana Purāṇa*, and in many parts of the *Skanda Purāṇa*.

2. *Mahābhārata* 13.96.1 ff.

3. *Tiruviḷaiyāṭaṟpurāṇam*.

4. *Rāmāyaṇa* 2.84.1—2.85.77, 2.109.1 ff., 3.11.1 ff.

5. Ibid., 2.84.1—2.85.77.

6. *Mahābhārata* 12.49.39 ff. : *Agni Purāṇa* 4.14.20 : *Bhāgavata Purāṇa* 9.15.23-41 : *Brahmāṇḍa Purāṇa* 2.3.26.43 ff. : *Brahmavaivarta Purāṇa* 3.24.1 ff. : *Padma Purāṇa* 268.1-81 : *Skanda Purāṇa* 5.3.218.1-57, 6.66.1-61.

7. *Rāmāyaṇa* 1.50.17—1.55.24 : *Mahābhārata* 1.165.1-44 : *Devībhāgavata Purāṇa* 3.17.7-22 : *Skanda Purāṇa* 3.1.39.22-32, 6.167.1-74, 6.214.19 ff,

Bharadvāja sheltered the *yuvarāja* or crown-prince Sudarśana and his mother when Sudarśana had been chased from his kingdom by his brother,[1] and Bhṛgu sheltered king Vītahavya when the latter was being pursued by king Pratardana—saving his life by making him a Brahmin through the power of his own word.[2] Further details of the relations between Ṛṣis and kings—and of the degree of political involvement of Ṛṣis—will be examined in Chapter 6. Aside from entertaining kings, the Ṛṣis also offered shelter and hospitality to other Ṛṣis and Brahmins—as in the cases of Gautama and other Ṛṣis noted earlier—and also to the gods. Thus for example, Gautama fed the Trimūrti at the shrine in his Āśrama;[3] while Dharma, in order to test the strength of Viśvāmitra's tapas, took the form of Vasiṣṭha and asked for food, and when the food was cooked he asked Viśvāmitra to wait, and went away—he returned only after 100 years, and when he found that the food was still hot he thanked Viśvāmitra, on account of which merit the latter achieved his goal of becoming a *brahma*-Ṛṣis.[4] The task of offering hospitality frequently acquired merit also for the wives of the Ṛṣis. Thus on one occasion during a drought, when Atri was performing *tapas*, Anasūyā served and supported him, and by her merits the Gaṅgā came and remained in that place.[5] Similarly, when the Seven Ṛṣis had once left Arundhatī performing *tapas* in the Āśrama while they went to search for food in the Himālayas, Śiva came disguised as a Brahmin and begged for hospitality, and Arundhati cooked for him for twelve years—listening to his discourses, and herself eating nothing; when the Seven Ṛṣiṣ returned to the Āśrama after that period, Śiva announced that the merits of Arundhatī's *tapas* in performing that act were superior even to their own *tapas* acquired through rigid austerities.[6] Thus we can see that the offering of hospitality becomes not merely a form of service but an act of *bhakti* or devotion towards the visitor : the

1. *Devibhāgavata Purāṇa* 3.15.49-61.
2. *Mahābhārata* 13.31.22 ff.
3. *Padma Purāṇa* 4.110.1 ff.
4. *Mahābhārata* 5.104.1 ff.
5. *Śiva Purāṇa* 4.3.7—4.4.61.
6. *Mahābhārata* 9.47.27-53.

emphasis lies—as in the cases of all such meritorious deeds—not so much upon the person to whom hospitality is offered or the nature of the deed done, but rather upon the degree of fervour and inner self-abnegation with which it is done. For it is this inner fervour and devotion which constitutes the *tapas* of meritorious deeds, the inner self-heating which transforms the performer and enables him to achieve his goals.

(iii) *Spiritual Knowledge and Meditation* : One of the main foundations of spiritual knowledge (*jñāna*) is mental knowledge (*vidyā*), acquired through study—particularly of the Vedas and of other sacred literature. The Seven Ṛṣis are not often referred to as studying the Vedas : on the contrary, they are frequently described as being those who composed, are most conversant with and supremely knowledgeable in the Vedas—as makers of the Vedas (*vedakṛts*), knowers of the Vedas (*vedavids*), and masters of the Vedas (*vedācāryas*.[1] One notable exception to this is in the case of Bharadvāja and his son Yavakrīta, who acquire mastery of the Vedas only through *tapas* : although in this case also, Vedic knowledge is acquired by the Ṛṣi not through study but through the revelation of the Vedas by Indra.[2] As we saw earlier, the Seven Ṛṣis are said to be composers of Vedic hymns, and are thought to come to the earth periodically in order to renew Vedic knowledge among men; they are further depicted as teaching the Vedas and other sacred works to various individuals and pupils, and as praising the learning, study and recitation of the Vedas.

The next stage in the acquisition of spiritual knowledge—and perhaps the most characteristic feature of the *tapas* performed by the Ṛṣis—is the practice of meditation, involving the concentration of the mind in a single direction and towards a single goal (*ekāgratā*) in order to achieve ultimate union with the Supreme or Absolute (*yoga*). In order to achieve such concentration of the mind and energies, it is first necessary to completely subdue and still the body, and specific forms of

1. For example *Mahābhārata* 12.327.61 ff., and innumerable further instances, especially in accounts of the creation of the Ṛṣis by Brahmā where they are said to be born endowed with perfect knowledge of the Vedas.

2. *Mahābhārata* 3.135.1—136.18.

bodily posture (*āsana*) are frequently mentioned as being practised by the Ṛṣis. In the *Ṛgveda*, the Seven Ṛṣis are said to have been seated in their performance of *tapas*;[1] Bhṛgu similarly performed *tapas* while seated at the Daśāśvamedha, the length of his *tapas* being such that he became covered in ant-hills[2]—the latter being a prominent motif also in certain accounts of the *tapas* of his son Cyavana.[3] In other cases, the Ṛṣis performed their self-heating by standing still in one place for great lengths of time, taking on the appearance of inanimate objects or of their natural surroundings—as in the cases of Viśvāmitra, who in performing *tapas* became like a stick or log of wood (*kāṣṭha*) and like a rock (*śaili*),[4] and of Bhṛgu's son Cyavana, who while performing *tapas* in a river took on the appearance of a post or pillar covered in moss and was inadvertently netted by some fishermen.[5] Several Ṛṣis performed *tapas* standing on one leg : as for example Kaśyapa, who stood on one leg for 1,000 Brahmā-years,[6] and his wife Aditi, who similarly stood on one leg for many years in order to gain the wish of having Viṣṇu born as her son.[7] Among the further practices undertaken by Viśvāmitra for 1,000 years at a time were those of keeping the arms raised above the head until they became atrophied and withered (*ūrdhvabāhu*), of observing the five fires in summer (*pañcatapas*—lighting four fires around the body, in addition to the scorching heat of the summer sun), of remaining in the open air during the rainy season, and of remaining in water or wet clothing both day and night during winter—as well as emaciating his body by fasts and other self-subduing austerities (*niyamas*), as noted earlier.[8] The principal aim underlying all such practices

1. *Ṛgveda* 10.109.4 : *Atharvaveda* 19.41. The term used is *tapase upaniṣedur* : which may be linked with the name *Upaniṣad* given to the spiritual treatises composed by the forest Ṛṣis, denoting being seated both as a form of *tapas* and also (by extension) at the feet of a teacher.
2. *Matsya Purāṇa* 193.23-53 : *Padma Purāṇa* 1.20.23-82.
3. For example *Mahābhārata* 3.122.1-27.
4. *Mahābhārata* 1.63.10-15.
5. Ibid., 13.50.1 ff.
6. *Gopatha Brāhmaṇa* 1.2.8.
7. *Mahābhārata* 13.82.24 ff.
8. See especially *Rāmāyaṇa* 1.62.18—1.63.15 : *Mahābhārata* 1.65.21 ff., 9.39.23-24.

was essentially to completely subdue the body and bring about the total cessation of all bodily movement—in order to concentrate all the energies and heat of the body inwards, along with the inward direction of the mind. The same aim lay behind another common ascetic pursuit of the Ṛṣis, namely that of *mauna* or silence : as was performed both by Viśvāmitra for 1,000 years,[1] and also by Atri for 3,000 Deva-years whereby his body burned with heat and illumined the world in place of the sun.[2] A further common practice was *prāṇāyāma*, or the control of breathing, which was again regarded as an effective means of building up bodily heat and of stilling the lower senses : thus Atri performed *yoga* and *prāṇāyāma* for 100 years during a drought, while meditating on Śiva,[3] and he is also said to have tormented the three worlds with the fire of his *prāṇāyāma*.[4] Such forms of bodily discipline are specifically intended to bring about the conquest of the fires of desire and anger; and the Ṛṣis are frequently described as those who have mastered their passions and subdued themselves,[5] as those who have freed themselves of the lower qualities of *rajas* and *tamas*,[6] and as those who have liberated themselves from sins and past deeds (*karma*) by *tapas*—as in the case of Viśvāmitra, who burnt the sin of stealing and eating dog-flesh through his *tapas*.[7] They are similarly depicted as having been taught *yoga* because of the power of their *tapas* : thus Vasiṣṭha received *yoga* from Rudra after performing severe *tapas*,[8] while the Ṛṣis received *sāṅkhya-yoga* from Śiva[9] and are also on occasions termed *mahā-yogeśvaras* or masters of the art of *yoga*.[10]

1. *Rāmāyaṇa* 1.64.1.
2. For example, *Harivaṃśa* 20.1-14.
3. *Śiva Purāṇa* 4.3.7—4.4.61.
4. *Bhāgavata Purāṇa* 4.1.15-33. On the performance and significance of such practices, see especially Eliade *Yoga*, Chapter 2.
5. For example *Mahābhārata* 1.164.1-14, 3.183.1-32 : *Liṅga Purāṇa* 1.34.24-26.
6. *Bhāgavata Purāṇa* 6.3.14-15.
7. *Mahābhārata* 12.139.12 ff.
8. *Kūrma Purāṇa* 1.24.37.
9. Ibid., 2.37.122-126.
10. For example *Mahābhārata* 13.92.19-20.

A further prominent theme in the performance of *tapas* by the Ṛṣis is the building-up of heat and power through the sublimation of sexuality : but this is an idea which will be examined in detail in the next chapter.

The building-up of heat through such ascetic practices was often accompanied by a specific object on which the mind was focused and concentrated. This most usually took the form of meditation on a particular Vedic *mantra* or set of words, on a deity, or on the nature of *ātman* or the real Self. Thus Dīrghatamas became cured of his blindness by constantly repeating the name of Keśava (one of the many names of Viṣṇu), and thereafter became known as Gautama;[1] while Gautama, Atri, Viśvāmitra, Aṅgiras and Bhṛgu are said to be the Ṛṣi-seers of each of the five syllables of the "*namaḥ śivāya*" *mantra*.[2] Atri is said to have meditated on Śiva as part of his *tapas*,[3] as did also the Seven Ṛṣis on the instruction of Brahmā,[4] and Kaśyapa in order to defeat the demon-Asuras.[5] The Seven Ṛṣis—like the Ṛṣis of the Upaniṣads—are also said to have achieved through *tapas* and renunciation (*nivṛtti*) the destruction of individuality (*ahaṅkāra*) and the realisation of *ātman*.[6] We shall be examining in a moment the various goals which the Ṛṣis achieved through such ascetic and meditational practices.[7]

(iv) *Devotion*: As was noted earlier, the path of devotion is by no means separate from those of meritorious deeds and meditation. We have seen that the performance of sacrifice in honour

---

1. *Mahābhārata* 12.328.50.
2. *Liṅga Purāṇa* 1.85.45-54 : *Śiva Purāṇa* 7.2.13.46-47.
3. *Śiva Purāṇa* 4.3.7—4.4.61.
4. *Kāñcipurāṇam* 14.1-13.
5. *Śiva Purāṇa* 3.18.2-23.
6. See for example *Mahābhārata* 12.285.14 ff. : *Brahmāṇḍa Purāṇa* 1.2.32.90 ff. : *Matsya Purāṇa* 145.81-91 : *Vāyu Purāṇa* 1.59.79-105.
7. For more general information on ascetic practices and modes of conduct, see *Mānava Dharma Śāstra* Chapter 6 and other law-books, as also various Upaniṣadic, Epic and Purāṇic contexts (for example the *Śānti Parvan* of the *Mahābhārata*). A useful survey is that of H. P. Chakraborti, *Asceticism in Ancient India* (on Hindu, Buddhist, Jain and Ājivika ascetics); see also J. C. Oman, *Mystics, Ascetics and Saints of India* : A. S. Geden, 'Asceticism (Hindu)' : A. Hayley, 'Aspects of Hindu Asceticism'.

of a particular deity, the offering of hospitality, and the performance of pilgrimage and bathing were all essentially forms of devotional practice; and the same may be said of meditating on or repeating the name of a particular deity. So too the singing and chanting of hymns by the Ṛṣis in praise of a deity is a form of devotion which is found from the *Ṛgveda* onwards, as we saw earlier in this chapter.

Devotional prayer and worship as a form of *tapas* sometimes appears as a means for attaining a desired goal. Thus Gautama, when parted from his wife, regained her by praying to Śiva for 100 Deva-years, and Viśvāmitra was similarly delivered from the loss of his wife, son and kingdom by worshipping Śiva;[1] Anasūyā, by serving her husband Atri and worshipping Śiva, surpassed in merit the *tapas* of Atri himself;[2] and Aṅgiras, by worshipping Śiva in his tapas, obtained the supreme *yoga*.[3] In a similar manner, Viśvāmitra, Bhṛgu and Vasiṣṭha are all said to have worshipped the goddess Devī;[4] while on many further occasions, the Ṛṣis are depicted as worshipping and reciting the praises of gods—particularly Brahmā, Viṣṇu and Śiva. So too the Ṛṣis frequently obtain—through their *tapas*—the favour of particular gods, who bring about their goals : as for example in the cases of the Seven Ṛṣis[5] and of Bhṛgu.[6] On further occasions, a more specific form of worship is mentioned as having been performed by the Ṛṣis. Viśvāmitra is in one context said to have achieved Brahmin-hood by offering the Gaṇapati-*pūjā*, or worship to Gaṇeśa;[7] while Vasiṣṭha became an adept in *yoga* by worshipping the Śiva *liṅga* and reciting the *gāyatri mantra*,[8] and in several further instances Ṛṣis are depicted as attaining the favour of (and boons from) Śiva by setting up and worshipping a Śiva-*liṅga* after taking a ritual bath.[9] We

1. *Brahmavaivarta Purāṇa* 4.46.45 ff.
2. *Śiva Purāṇa* 4.3.7—4.4.61.
3. *Kūrma Purāṇa* 2.39.30-31.
4. *Devībhāgavata Purāṇa* 3.30.23-24.
5. *Mahābhārata* 12.281.13 ff.
6. *Padma Purāṇa* 1.20.23-82.
7. *Skanda Purāṇa* 6.214.19-72.
8. *Agni Purāṇa* 218.1-2.
9. For example *Śiva Purāṇa* 3.18.2-13 : *Kāñcipurāṇam* 14.1-13.

may note that this particular form of devotional *tapas* is mentioned only in later Purāṇas; although the idea of purely devotional *tapas*—while never as characteristic a path in the Ṛṣi traditions as that of physical asceticism and the pursuit of spiritual knowledge—is nonetheless to be found also in a somewhat different form in the practices of offering sacrifice, chanting hymns, offering hospitality, performing pilgrimage, and ritual bathing. In all of these, as we have seen, the emphasis rests not so much on the act performed as rather on the inner fervour of the performer; for all of these paths had the potential of enabling the performer to augment his reserve of inner heat, whereby he might achieve his goals.

(v) *Goals* : Several of the goals which the Ṛṣis strove for and attained through their *tapas* have already been noted. Sometimes these were immediate and material goals : as in the cases—especially in Vedic literature—where they obtained sons and wealth, or the defeat of enemies. There were also attainments which represented stages on the path towards the ultimate goal : such as the destruction of past sins and deeds (*karma*), the destruction of the lower elements of *rajas* and *tamas* and of the false conception of the individual self (*ahaṅkāra*), and the conquest of desires and anger—all of which were purged and burnt by the fires of *tapas*. A further attainment was the acquisition of various powers, occasioned by the performance of *tapas* : these are very characteristic features of the Ṛṣi traditions, and we shall be looking at them in detail in a minute; but in most cases, such powers were obtained not so much for their own sake (although in some instances this was indeed the goal of a Ṛṣi's *tapas*) but rather as incidental achievements on the path to the ultimate goal.

One of the principal ultimate goals of *tapas*—characteristic especially of Vedic literature—was the attainment of heaven or the abode of the gods. We have seen many examples of how the Ṛṣis attained this goal through sacrifice and through the "seeing" and recitation of hymns; by extension, the Ṛṣis are also said to have attained heaven by performing *tapas*, whereby they see hymns and thereby attain this goal—as in the cases of the Āṅgirasas[1]

1. For example *Jaiminīya Brāhmaṇa* 1.224, 2.235 : *Pañcaviṃśa Brāhmaṇa* 15.9.9, 20.11.3.

and of the Seven Ṛṣis.[1] The attainment of heaven was also the goal achieved by the Seven Ṛṣis in other contexts through *tapas* alone (in the form of ascetic austerities),[2] and by Bhṛgu through correct understanding of the nature of *brahman.*[3] It is this same idea which underlies the transference of the Seven Ṛṣis to the sky, where they become the stars of Ursa Major—as we shall see in greater detail in Chapter 7. A further goal—by no means separate from the last—was the attainment of the presence of a deity. This might be achieved on the one hand through attaining the realm of that deity : as for example in the cases of Vasiṣṭha and Viśvāmitra who by *tapas* attained the realm of Indra,[4] and of the Seven Ṛṣis who in many other contexts attain the presence of Brahmā, Śiva or Viṣṇu and attend upon them in their realms. On the other hand, it might be achieved through summoning the presence of that deity on earth : as in the many cases, especially throughout the Epics and Purāṇas, where a god—being pleased with the *tapas* of a Ṛṣi—appears before the Ṛṣi and grants him his desire. The third principal goal of the Ṛṣi in performing *tapas*—mention of which has already been made—was to achieve the dissolution of the individual self, and thereby to realise and merge with *brahman* or the Supreme. In many instances the Ṛṣis are said to achieve *siddhi*, and are referred to as being *siddhas* : the term may in some contexts mean that they achieved some form of power (see below), but in many instances it implies that they achieved perfection and fulfilment, together with complete emancipation.[5] They are similarly said to attain *mokṣa* or liberation from the narrow confines of individual consciousness and from rebirth, and to merge with and dissolve into the Highest, Supreme or Absolute (*mahat*, *parama*, *paramasatya*, *brahman*).[6]

1. *Jaiminīya Brāhmaṇa* 2.218-221 : *Śatapatha Brāhmaṇa* 1.6.2.1-4 : *Mahābhārata* 3.44.22-28.

2. For example *Mahābhārata* 13.94-95 : *Padma Purāṇa* 5.15.344-345.

3. *Taittirīya Upaniṣad* 3.1-6.

4. *Aitareya Brāhmaṇa* 6.20 : *Jaiminīya Upaniṣad Brāhmaṇa* 3.3.7-10 : *Mahābhārata* 1.165.135-145. 3.85.9-12.

5. See for example *Devībhāgavata Purāṇa* 7.18.1 ff. : *Padma Purāṇa* 1.20.23-82.

6. For example *Brahmāṇḍa Purāṇa* 1.2.32.90 ff. : *Matsya Purāṇa* 145.81-91 : *Vāyu Purāṇa* 1.59.79-105.

The nature of the goals achieved by the Ṛṣis is inevitably closely linked with the nature of the Ṛṣis themselves, and we shall again be looking at their goals in this light in Chapter 9.

(*c*) *Ascetic Rivalries*

On several occasions, we find references to disputes and rivalries between Ṛṣis. In some cases, these arise due to a difference of opinion. Atri on one occasion went to gain wealth from king Vainya to distribute to his sons and servants before retiring to the forests, and praised the king as the foremost of all sovereigns : but Gautama objected to this, saying that such a title was reserved only for Indra—and the dispute was only finally resolved by Sanatkumāra in Atri's favour, whereupon he gained the desired wealth from the delighted king.[1] Disputes between Ṛṣis are referred to even in Vedic literature, and are often associated with both Vasiṣṭha and Viśvāmitra. On one occasion, Viśvāmitra and Jamadagni were both disputing with Vasiṣṭha and Jamadagni by means of a hymn appropriated the power and strength of Vasiṣṭha;[2] on another occasion, Viśvāmitra was rendered unconscious by the sons of Vasiṣṭha, but revived by the Jamadagnis;[3] while Vasiṣṭha was once reproached by the other Ṛṣis for being a Vaiśya rather than a Brahmin—a situation from which he delivered himself by means of a hymn.[4]

The most celebrated instances of ascetic rivalry in the Epics and Purāṇas once again take place between Vasiṣṭha and Viśvāmitra : usually while Viśvāmitra is striving—as a Kṣatriya to achieve the status of a *brahma*-Ṛṣi and to equal the *tapas* of Vasiṣṭha. On the first occasion, Viśvāmitra as king of the Jahnus visited Vasiṣṭha's Āśrama with his army, and was miraculously entertained by the Ṛṣi's wish-granting cow; he then sought to steal the cow, but Vasiṣṭha created warriors and demons from the cow's body and destroyed the army of Viśvāmitra, who thereupon devoted himself to *tapas* in order to become a *brahma*-

1. *Mahābhārata* 3.183.1-32.
2. *Taittirīya Saṃhitā* 3.1.7, 5.4.11.
3. *Bṛhaddevatā* 4.105-119.
4. *Jaiminīya Brāhmaṇa* 3.195.

Ṛṣi.[1] During the course of his austerities, he transferred king Triśaṅku to the sky in bodily form—after the king had been cursed by Vasiṣṭha for making the same request of him—against the wishes of both Vasiṣṭha and Indra;[2] he also urged king Saudāsa to eat and destroy the sons of Vasiṣṭha, after the king had been cursed to become a demon by Vasiṣṭha.[3] In another incident, when both were performing *tapas* on opposite banks of the river Sarasvatī, each would daily challenge the other as to the relative superiority of their *tapas*; one day, Viśvāmitra determined to kill Vasiṣṭha, and ordered the river to transport the Ṛṣi to him—but the river, afraid of the curse of either Ṛṣi first carried Vasiṣṭha on her current to Viśvāmitra's Āśrama, and then while Viśvāmitra was searching for a weapon to kill his rival she carried Vasiṣṭha back again to his own Āśrama.[4] On a further occasion, Viśvāmitra made a bet with Vasiṣṭha to disprove the virtues of king Hariścandra, and subjected the king to numerous trials, including the loss of his wife, son and kingdom; thereupon Vasiṣṭha, enraged at this treatment which merely highlighted the virtues of the king, cursed Viśvāmitra to become a heron, and Viśvāmitra in return cursed Vasiṣṭha to become a maina-bird—and in such forms they then fought each other for 10,000 years with their nails and beaks.[5] On yet other occasions, Viśvāmitra created a demon Dhārā to destroy Vasiṣṭha,[6] and they also fought each other with divine Brahmā-weapons.[7]

1. *Rāmāyaṇa* 1.50.17—1.55.24 : *Mahābhārata* 1.165.1-44, 9.39.11 ff. : *Devībhāgavata Purāṇa* 3.17.7-22 : *Garuḍa Purāṇa* 181.1 ff. : *Skanda Purāṇa* 3.1.39.23-32, 6.167.1-74, 6.214.19 ff.

2. *Rāmāyaṇa* 1.56.10—1.59.33 : *Mahābhārata* 1.65.20-42, 13.3.1 ff. : *Harivaṃśa* 9.88-100, 10.1-20 : *Bhāgavata Purāṇa* 9.7.5-6 : *Bhaviṣya Purāṇa* 4.130.9-39 : *Brahma Purāṇa* 7.105-109 : *Brahmāṇḍa Purāṇa* 2.3.63.73-114 : *Devībhāgavata Purāṇa* 7.10.1-58, 7.12.11—7.14.25 : *Liṅga Purāṇa* 1.66.6-11 : *Śiva Purāṇa* 5.2.38, 5.37.47—5.38.18 : *Skanda Purāṇa* 6.4.1—6.8.9 : *Vāyu Purāṇa* 2.26.84-115 : *Viṣṇu Purāṇa* 4.3.1 ff. : *Kathāsaritsāgara* 6.28.1 ff.

3. *Mahābhārata* 1.166.1—1.167.21, 13.3.1 ff. : *Liṅga Purāṇa* 1.64.2-8 : *Kāñcipurāṇam* 15.1 ff.

4. *Mahābhārata* 9.41.1 ff. : *Skanda Purāṇa* 6.172.1-22.

5. *Bhāgavata Purāṇa* 9.7.7 : *Devībhāgavata Purāṇa* 6.12.25—6.13.48, 7.17.38—7.27.43 : *Mārkaṇḍeya Purāṇa* 7.1—9.30.

6. *Skanda Purāṇa* 6.168.30—6.169.36.

7. Ibid., 6.171.1-28.

Such ascetic rivalries, it need scarcely be pointed out, clearly indicate a lack of control of the passions and anger. In some cases, the principal offence is explicitly shown to be on the part of Viśvāmitra—who is then only on the path seeking to become a *brahma*-Ṛṣi. Vasiṣṭha frequently appears in a more passive role in such rivalries : thus when his sons were slain by king Saudāsa, he is said to have borne no anger at this offence, and to have instead tried unsuccessfully to kill himself;[1] and when Viśvāmitra sought to kill him on the Sarasvatī, he simply let himself be borne to and fro by the river while singing her praises. So too, after cursing the Apsaras Rambhā for disturbing his *tapas*, Viśvāmitra realised that he had to abandon both lust and anger in order to attain his goal of becoming a *brahma*-Ṛṣi.[2] In several instances, however—especially in later Purāṇas both Ṛṣis clearly show anger and hatred to each other, thereby releasing and wasting in destructive forms the inner heat which they had amassed through *tapas*. Commenting upon this during the course of a passage denouncing the efficacy of bathing in water in order to purify the mind, one relatively late text expresses wonder at this lack of self-control :

> If the waters of *tirthas* could purify minds, why did the *munis* residing on the banks of the Gaṅgā always have jealousy and envy towards each other ? Humble *munis* like Vasiṣṭha and Ṛṣis like Viśvāmitra were always entangled in love and hatred, always impatient in anger.[3]

It should perhaps be pointed out here that we are dealing not so much with an ethical as with a magical point : in showing anger and hatred, the Ṛṣis do not so much hurt or offend others, but destroy their own fiery powers amassed through *tapas*—thereby setting further from themselves the goals for which they are striving. Their anger—like their lust—directed the force of their *tapas* away from their goals of heaven and *brahman*, directing them outwards rather than inwards : thus seeming to contradict

1. *Mahābhārata* 1.166.1—1.168.25 ; *Liṅga Purāṇa* 1.64.8-9.
2. For example *Rāmāyaṇa* 1.63.10-15.
3. *Devībhāgavata Purāṇa* 6.12.26 ff.

the purpose of their ascetic pursuits. We shall have further cause to discuss this apparent contradiction in subsequent contexts.

(*d*) *The Powers of the Ascetic*

The Ṛṣis—like many other ascetics both in India and in other traditions and cultures—are said to have gained a number of miraculous powers through their austerities. In the Buddhist tradition, the powers of becoming invisible, walking on water and flying through the air are among those most frequently said to be obtained by performing *tapas*;[1] while in the *Yoga-sūtras*, a large number of such powers or *siddhis* are listed as being attained through the practice of *yoga*—including, in addition to such "physical" powers, various types of mental knowledge such as of previous existences and of the thoughts of others.[2] Hiuen Tsiang relates an interesting account of how a man might become a Ṛṣi by suppressing his breathing, remaining speechless, reciting magical prayers, and concentrating his sight and hearing within himself : whereafter he would be able to fly through the air, issue orders, be gratified in his desires, escape from feebleness, old age, sickness and death, and live eternally.[3] Hiuen Tsiang is here doubtless reflecting popular views on the attainments and powers of the Ṛṣis which were narrated to him at the time of his visit to Banaras in the seventh century A.D., and such powers are indeed attributed to the Ṛṣis throughout Indian literature. We shall here examine them under the two headings of creative and destructive powers.

(i) *Creative* : We have already seen that the basic transformation brought about by the Ṛṣi in his performance of *tapas* was the production of heat in the body; the fire of his *tapas* became such that he was transformed into Fire itself, burning the worlds with his heat and illuminating them with the light that radiated from his body (see Chapter 7 for a more detailed account and

1. For example *Majjhima Nikāya* 1.34, 1.69, 1.494, 3.11-12, 3.98.
2. See especially *Yoga-sūtras* 3.16 ff.
3. *Si-yu-ki* Book 7 : trans. S. Beal, *Buddhist Records of the Western World*, Vol. 2 pp. 55-59.

examples of this achievement of the Ṛṣis). Consequently, one of the powers acquired by the Ṛṣis was to bring light to the world, and to take the place of either the sun or the moon. It is frequently related of Atri that when the demon Svarbhānu enveloped the sun in darkness, Atri either found and replaced or else himself took the place of the sun or the moon, illuminating the world with the brilliance of his own body—and he is similarly termed the father of Soma or the moon.[1] Atri's wife Anasūyā is also said to have dispelled darkness by her *tapas*;[2] and Aṅgiras is said to have once taken the place of Agni, himself heating and illumining the world.[3] Many further instances occur where the brilliance of the Ṛṣis' bodies is spoken of as shining like fire and the sun and as illumining or burning the worlds, and it was this same strength of *tapas* which gave the Ṛṣis the power to become stars in the sky. This entire tradition will, as noted above, be examined in Chapter 7.

A further power of the Ṛṣis was that of creating rain or water. When Indra—the god of rain—caused a twelve-year drought, Agastya threatened to transform himself into another Indra by *tapas*; Indra, seeing the power of the Ṛṣi's asceticism, thereupon poured rain.[4] Viśvāmitra similarly forced Indra to rain by performing rites while cooking during a drought[5]; and Vasiṣṭha ended a twelve-year drought by bringing king Saṃvaraṇa and his wife back to the city from the hills and forests where they had been making love[6]—a motif which may be compared with that in the accounts of Ṛṣyaśṛṅga, whose abandonment of *tapas* in the forests, love-making and subsequent

1. *Ṛgveda* 5.40.6-9 : *Atharvaveda* 13.2.4-36 : *Gopatha Brāhmaṇa* 1.2.17 ff.: *Kauṣītaki Brāhmaṇa* 24.3 : *Pañcaviṃśa Brāhmaṇa* 6.6.8-11, 14.11.14 : *Śatapatha Brāhmaṇa* 4.3.4.21 : *Bṛhaddevatā* 5.12 : *Mahābhārata* 1.114.40-41, 13.141.1 ff. : *Harivaṃśa* 20.1-14 : *Brahma Purāṇa* 13.9-11 : *Brahmāṇḍa Purāṇa* 2.3.8.76-79 : *Liṅga Purāṇa* 1.63.71-73 : *Matsya Purāṇa* 23.3-6 : *Skanda Purāṇa* 7.1.20.42-44 : *Vāyu Purāṇa* 2.9.70-73.

2. *Rāmāyaṇa* 2.109.6-8.

Mahābhārata 3.207.6-20.

4. Ibid., 14.95.11 ff.

5. Ibid., 12.139.12 ff.

6. Ibid., 1.162.10—1.163.21.

move to the city bring about the desired effect of creating rain.[1] In further instances, Ṛṣis are attributed with the power to sustain themselves and others during droughts, through the creation of water. During a 100-year drought, Atri's wife Anasūyā caused the river Jāhnavī or Gaṅgā to flow past their Āśrama in the Citrakūṭa mountain through her *tapas*;[2] during a similar drought, Gautama created water at his Āśrama in the forests, so that the other Ṛṣis came and lived with him.[3] Similarly, during a drought caused by the Tāraka-war, Vasiṣṭha by his *tapas* sustained people by creating water with which to cook rice, roots, fruits and herbs.[4] The contrary power to destroy water was also possessed by the Ṛṣis : thus it is related of both Aṅgiras and Agastya (the latter in particular) that, due to the powers of their *tapas*, they drank the entire ocean in a single gulp—whereafter the gods had to find a way of bringing more water to the earth.[5]

Brief mention may be made here of the Ṛṣis' power to create and obtain sons. This power has already been noticed in connection with their performance of sacrifice and seeing of hymns, and it will be examined in greater detail in the next Chapter.

The Ṛṣis possessed further powers over life itself : powers of rejuvination, of curing illnesses, and of restoring the dead to life. Even in the *Ṛgveda*, Vasiṣṭha is said to have been made ageless by the Aśvins[6]; and throughout subsequent literature, one of the aims of the Ṛṣis in performing *tapas* was to attain the realm of the immortals and to obtain immortality—even as it is said that the gods and demons themselves performed *tapas* in order to escape death.[7] The most recurrent example of rejuvination is

1. *Rāmāyaṇa* 1.8.1—1.9.32 : *Mahābhārata* 3.110.1—3.113.22 : *Bhāgavata Purāṇa* 9.23.8-9.
2. *Rāmāyaṇa*, 2.109.6-8 : *Śiva Purāṇa* 4.3.7—4.4.61, 5.2.18-19 : *Tirumūrttimalaipurāṇam* 3.
3. For example *Śiva Purāṇa* 4.24.2-33.
4. *Liṅga Purāṇa* 1.63.79-84.
5. *Mahābhārata* 3.101.1—3.103.19, 13.138.3-4, 13.139.9 ff. : *Agni Purāṇa* 206.1-12 : *Brahmavaivarta Purāṇa* 2.56.1 ff. : *Devībhāgavata Purāṇa* 6.9.38 ff. : *Matsya Purāṇa* 61.36-43 : *Padma Purāṇa* 5.19.159-186 : *Saura Purāṇa* 47.63 ff. : *Skanda Purāṇa* 6.34.1-59 : *Viṣṇudharmottara Purāṇa* 1.213.1 ff. : *Bṛhat-saṃhitā* 12.1-5 : *Rāmacaritamānasa* 1.31.3, 1.255.4 : *Tiruviḷaiyāṭarpurāṇaṃ* 1.15-58.
6. *Ṛgveda* 1.112.9.
7. *Mahābhārata* 5.42.1 ff.

in the case of Bhṛgu's son Cyavana, who when aged and decrepit performed *tapas* and was given new life and young body by the Aśvins.[1] In these instances, the Ṛṣis concerned were rejuvinated by gods; but in other instances, a Ṛṣi is himself depicted as having the power to rejuvinate others. Thus Gautama, when pleased with the devotion of his aged pupil Uttaṅka, made him into a youth of sixteen.[2] They were similarly able to rid themselves of illnesses : thus when Bhṛgu was once afflicted with leprosy, he worshipped Viṣṇu and thereby both destroyed the sickness and gained unparalleled health.[3] Just as in these examples a Ṛṣi prolonged, renewed or improved the quality of life, so also he held the power to bring the dead back to life. When Rāma had killed his mother Reṇukā on the orders of his father Jamadagni, he obtained from Jamadagni the favour that she be brought to life again;[4] similarly, on account of her chastity, Atri's wife Anasūyā was able to restore to life a Brahmin who had died due to the curse of Varāha.[5] When Bharadvāja was immolating himself on the funeral-pyre of his son Yavakrīta, he prophesied that his rival Raibhya—who had killed Yavakrīta—would himself be killed by his own son; when this occurred, Raibhya's son through *tapas* obtained from the gods the favour that Bharadvāja, Yavakrīta and Raibhya might all be restored to life.[6] In this latter example, it is the gods who actually restore the Ṛṣi to life : but it is nonetheless on account of the *tapas* of Raibhya's son that they are obliged to grant this

1. *Ṛgveda* 1.116.10, 1.117.13, 1.118.6, 5.74.5, 7.68.6, 7.71.5, 10.39.4, 10.59.1 : *Jaiminīya Brāhmaṇa* 3.120-128 : *Pañcaviṃśa Brāhmaṇa* 14.6.10 : *Śatapatha Brāhmaṇa* 4.1.5,1 ff. : *Mahābhārata* 3.122.1—3.123.23, 4.20.6-11 : *Bhāgavata Purāṇa* 9.3.1-26 : *Bhaviṣya Purāṇa* 1.19.1-88 : *Devībhāgavata Purāṇa* 7.2.31—7.5.58 : *Padma Purāṇa* 4.14.1—4.16.54 : *Skanda Purāṇa* 7.1.280.1—7.1.281.25.

2. *Mahābhārata* 14.55.1 ff : *Skanda Purāṇa* 7.3.2.1-56.

3. *Vāmana Purāṇa* 53.9.

4. *Mahābhārata* 3.116.1-18 : *Bhāgavata Purāṇa* 9.16.1-18 : *Devībhāgavata Purāṇa* 2.5.41 : *Kāñcipurāṇam* 45.1-3, 46.1-34 : Elmore, pp. 82-86, 94-96 : Whitehead, p. 116.

5. *Śiva Purāṇa* 2.3.54.79.

6. *Mahābhārata* 3.138.1—3.139.24.

favour. While in these examples a Ṛṣi or his associate was able to bring a dead person back to life, Vasiṣṭha on the other hand discovered an unlooked-for power in being unable to deprive himself of life. When trying to do so in grief at the deaths of his sons, he bound himself with ropes and jumped into the river Vipāśā—but rose from it unfettered; he climbed to the top of mount Meru and hurled himself down—but the earth caught him with lotus-like hands, and cushioned his landing; and he plunged into the torrential and crocodile-filled river Śatadrū—but the river mistook him for Agni or Fire, and fled from him in a hundred different directions.[1] Thus in this instance the wealth of power amassed by the Ṛṣi in the form of heat or *tapas* was so great that, of its very nature, it preserved the life of the Ṛṣi—even against his own will.

The very words and speech of the Ṛṣi constituted yet another type of power. We have already noted earlier the role played by *vāc* or sacred speech, particularly in the context of the Ṛṣis' "seeing" and reciting hymns; and especially in the Epics and Purāṇas, the Ṛṣi comes to be viewed as a kind of oracle, an infallible speaker whose speech alone literally carries power and authority—a fiery utterance from a receptacle of fire and *tapas*. Merely by uttering the words "may all be well with you" (*svasti te 'stu*), Atri stopped the sun from falling from the sky;[2] and merely by the authority of his word, Bhṛgu transformed the Kṣatriya Vītahavya into a Brahmin.[3] Vasiṣṭha released king Saudāsa Kalmāṣapāda from his curse by saying "*om*" and sprinkling him with water;[4] while, when Pulastya predicted that Parāśara would understand all the scriptures and would have a son who would compile the Purāṇas, Vasiṣṭha assured Parāśara that whatever was spoken by the great Ṛṣi Pulastya would surely come to pass.[5]

The last example cited may also be considered under the heading of a further power possessed by the Ṛṣis : namely that

1. *Mahābhārata* 1.166.1—1.168.25, 3.130.8-9 : *Liṅga Purāṇa* 1.64.1-9.
2. *Brahma Purāṇa* 13.9-11 : *Liṅga Purāṇa* 1.63.71-73 : *Skanda Purāṇa* 7.1.20.42-44.
3. *Mahābhārata* 13.31.22 ff.
4. For example *Mahābhārata* 1.168.1-25.
5. *Liṅga Purāṇa* 1.64.114-123.

of knowing the past and future, and being able to read the minds of others. This type of knowledge is often manifested when a Ṛṣi is able to discern through *tapas* that his wife has been unfaithful to him : as in the cases of Jamadagni and Reṇukā, Gautama and Ahalyā, and the Seven Ṛṣis and their wives.[1] So too, by performing *tapas*, Kaśyapa came to know that the life-span of king Parīkṣit was at an end.[2] By extension, such knowledge of past and future encompassed also past and future lives. Thus Vasiṣṭha told Ajapāla of his former birth as a Śūdra,[3] and also related the previous lives of king Dharmamūrti,[4] as well as those of Somaśarma;[5] while Pulastya narrated both the former and the future births of a parrot.[6]

Another power obtained through *tapas* was that of assuming different bodily forms. Transformation of physical appearance is, as we have seen, fundamental to his performance of *tapas*, where the entire being is transmuted into a mass of fiery heat and energy which has the potential to heat and illumine the worlds; the same idea underlies the ability to attain rejuvination and renewal of bodily form. The changing of bodily appearance at will is illustrated in the case of Viśvāmitra, who variously came to Hariścandra as a young and an old Brahmin when testing the king;[7] while the ability to enter and take possession of the body of another is illustrated in the case of Bharadvāja, who by the power of *yoga* entered into Pratardana in order to gain a military victory for him.[8] The Ṛṣis also had the power to transform the bodily forms of others through their curse—examples of which we shall be looking at in a moment.

One final instance of ascetic powers may be mentioned : namely the ability to fly through the air. This power is already attested in the *Ṛgveda* in the case of another ascetic, the long-haired ascetic (*keśin*, *muni*), who mounted on the wind and

1. For references, see Section E.
2. *Devībhāgavata Purāṇa* 2.9.42 ff.
3. *Skanda Purāṇa* 7.3.9.1-61.
4. *Matsya Purāṇa* 92.21 ff.
5. *Padma Purāṇa* 2.17.1-40.
6. *Kathāsaritsāgara* 10.59.1 ff.
7. For example *Devībhāgavata Purāṇa* 7.18.1—7.27.43.
8. *Mahābhārata* 13.31.32 ff.

flew through the air,[1] and it also frequently appears in the Ṛṣi traditions. Thus the Seven Ṛṣis are said to have travelled through the sky to visit Himālaya, in order to seek Pārvatī as the bride of Śiva;[2] Vasiṣṭha similarly ascended to the sun, in order to obtain the sun's daughter for king Saṃvaraṇa.[3] The idea of flight through the sky also underlies the frequent movement in each Mahāyuga of the Seven Ṛṣis between the earth and Maharloka (see Chapter 2), as also the ascent of the Seven Ṛṣis to the sky where they become the stars of Ursa Major (see Chapter 7).

ii. *Destructive*

We have already seen in the rivalries of Viśvāmitra and Vasiṣṭha certain aspects of the potentially destructive power of *tapas* amassed by the Ṛṣis; and while certain destructive powers were somewhat incidentally acquired—such as the ability or threat to burn the worlds, on account of the severity of *tapas* being performed—other destructive powers were more consciously directed, and are encompassed under the heading of the Ṛṣis' power to curse. Their curses—usually resulting from righteous anger at some injustice or misdeed—were directed at times against all orders of beings: creatures, men, demons and gods; and we shall examine each of these in turn.

In addition to the cases of Viśvāmitra and Vasiṣṭha cursing each other (see Rivalries above), a further example of a Ṛṣi cursing another Ṛṣi appears in the case of Gautama. After he had been sheltering the Ṛṣis at his Āśrama for some time during a drought, the Ṛṣis wished to leave, but Gautama was unwilling to let them go; so in order to effect their goal, the Ṛṣis created (or variantly, persuaded Gaṇeśa to become) a feeble cow which wandered into the Āśrama and then fell down dead as soon as Gautama touched it with a blade of grass to move it away. The Ṛṣis thereupon accused Gautama of the

1. See especially *Ṛgveda* 10.136. 1-5.
2. For example *Brahma Purāṇa* 34.17 ff.: *Mahābhāgavata Purāṇa* 24-28: *Matsya Purāṇa* 154.311-425: *Śiva Purāṇa* 2.2.19.26-76, 2.3.31.16—2.3.33.14: *Skanda Purāṇa* 1.1.23.1-86: *Vāmana Purāṇa* 26.1—27.62: *Kumārasambhava* 6.3-95: *Kandapurāṇam* 1.7.1-20.
3. *Mahābhārata* 1.162.10-19: *Vāmana Purāṇa* 22.26-61.

sin of killing a cow, and left the Āśrama (or variantly, banished Gautama from his own Āśrama) ; but when Gautama discovered the deception, he cursed the Ṛṣis to be excluded from the Vedas and to be reborn as non-Śaivite Caṇḍālas.[1] Aside from cursing other Ṛṣis, several examples appear where Ṛṣis curse their own sons : thus Viśvāmitra cursed his fifty eldest sons to be Dasyus (demons), Caṇḍālas or other outcastes for refusing to accept his adoption of Śunaḥśepa;[2] and Jamadagni cursed his four eldest sons to lose their senses and become like beasts and birds in conduct (or, to be killed by Rāma) for refusing to obey his order to kill Reṇukā for her transgression.[3] As we have seen in the case of Viśvāmitra and Vasiṣṭha's sons, Ṛṣis would also on occasions curse and bring about the destruction of the sons of other Ṛṣis. On many further occasions, Ṛṣis are depicted as cursing both kings and women; both of these categories will be looked at in the next chapter, in connection respectively with the political and family roles of the Ṛṣis.

When a Ṛṣi wished to curse a god or a human being, he might reduce him to the status of an outcaste or demon; but when the wrath of a Ṛṣi fell on a demon, this usually resulted in the demon's destruction. Thus the Seven Ṛṣis destroyed Rākṣasas for obstructing their sacrifices,[4] and it was for the same reason that Viśvāmitra set out with Rāma to destroy Rākṣasas in the southern regions;[5] while Vasiṣṭha through his *tapas* caused a host of Rākṣasas to be slain for having destroyed king Mucukunda's army.[6] While the Rākṣasas were demons noted especially for obstructing sacrifices and eating flesh, other demons—particularly the sons of Diti (Daityas) and of Danu (Dānavas), both of whom are on occasions termed Asuras—frequently attacked and fought with the gods, and the gods

1. *Brahma Purāṇa* 74.21—75.50: *Devībhāgavata Purāṇa* 12.9.1-97: *Kūrma Purāṇa* 1.15.93-104: *Śiva Purāṇa* 4.25.1—4.27.22, 4.27.23-46: *Varāha Purāṇa* 71.1-62.

2. For example *Aitareya Brāhmaṇa* 7.18: *Rāmāyaṇa* 1.61.14-16: *Mahābhārata* 13.308.1 ff.: *Bhāgavata Purāṇa* 9.16.28-37.

3. *Mahābhārata* 3.116.1-18: *Bhāgavata Purāṇa* 9.16.1-8.

4. *Brahma Purāṇa* 134.1-16.

5. *Rāmāyaṇa* 1.18.1—1.20.19.

6. *Mahābhārata* 12.75.1 ff.

would on such occasions often seek the help of the Ṛṣis to save them. When the gods were once oppressed, they were rescued by Vasiṣṭha who burnt the demons with his *tapas*;[1] Agastya similarly once burnt the demons with his anger.[2] Agastya is especially noted as a destroyer of demons : it was to help the gods destroy demons that he drank the ocean in which the demons had been hiding,[3] and when the Asura Krauñca transformed himself into a mountain to hinder and mislead Agastya, the Ṛṣi in his anger cursed Krauñca to remain in that form and to be killed eventually by Skanda.[4] In a further incident, the demon Vātāpi—with the help of his brother Ilvala—was fond of destroying Brahmins by disguising himself as a ram cooked for their benefit and then bursting out of their stomachs when eaten; but when he tried to do this with Agastya, the Ṛṣi ate and digested Vātāpi with a satisfied belch, and burnt Ilvala to ashes with a single fiery glance.[5]

While the Ṛṣis were thus able to curse the lowest of the demons, they were also capable of cursing the highest of the gods. One account relates that Bhṛgu once tested the Trimūrti by insulting both Śiva and Brahmā and by kicking Viṣṇu, and concluded that Viṣṇu was superior to the other two gods since when kicked he merely caressed the Ṛṣi's foot and asked whether it was hurt[6] : an account which illustrates the degree of familiarity with which the Ṛṣis might on occasions approach the gods. Brahmā is said to have been cursed by Nārada to be unworshipped, after the god had unjustly cursed the Ṛṣi for being reluctant to create offspring,[7] and Atri's wife Anasūyā

1. *Mahābhārata* 13.140.15 ff.
2. Ibid., 13.140.1 ff.
3. For example *Mahābhārata* 3.101.1—3.103.19.
4. *Kandapurāṇam* 2.24.1-13.
5. *Rāmāyaṇa* 3.10.53-64, 3.41.39-44: *Mahābhārata* 3.12.37, 3.94.4—3.97.25, 3.197,.26: *Agni Purāṇa* 206.1-12: *Bhāgavata Purāṇa* 6.18.15: *Devībhāgavata Purāṇa* 6.9.38 ff.: *Skanda Purāṇa* 7.1.284.1-33: *Viṣṇudharmottara Purāṇa* 1.213.1 ff. *Bṛhat-saṃhitā* 12.1-3: *Kandapurāṇam* 2.20.1-31, 2.26.1-32.
6. *Bhāgavata Purāṇa* 10.89.1-19: *Liṅga Purāṇa* 1.29.34: *Padma Purāṇa* 2.282.8-93: *Tiruppatistalapurāṇam* 10 ff. For the *Padma* account, see O'Flaherty, *Hindu Myths*, pp. 149-154.
7. *Brahmavaivarta Purāṇa*. 1.8.1-68, 1.23.1—1.24.5.

in anger cursed all three gods to become her sons, after they had tried to rape her.[1] Viṣṇu was especially cursed by Bhṛgu to undergo his ten *avatāras* or rebirths on earth, for having killed the wife of the Ṛṣi when searching for demons which had taken refuge in the Ṛṣi's Āśrama.[2] Śiva was cursed by the Seven Ṛṣis in the Pine Forest to be deprived of his *liṅga* or phallus, when he had seduced the wives of the Ṛṣis;[3] he was also cursed by Viśvāmitra to be hidden in the Kali Yuga, for having served meat to the Ṛṣi;[4] and he was again cursed by Kaśyapa that his son should lose his head, for having struck the sun with his trident and thereby plunged the world into darkness.[5] Agni was cursed to be omnivorous, both by Aṅgiras—for having desired the wives of the Seven Ṛṣis[6]—and also by Bhṛgu—for not having prevented the abduction of the Ṛṣi's wife Pulomā.[7] Indra was cursed by Gautama to be deprived of his *liṅga* (or variantly, that his body should be covered with 1,000 *yonis* or vaginas) for having seduced Ahalyā the wife of the Ṛṣi;[8] he was

1. *Bhaviṣya Purāṇa* 3.4.17.67-78: *Cucīntirastalapurāṇam* 2.1—7.26: *Tirumūrttimalaipurāṇam* 6-7: Dubois, pp. 543-544. For the *Bhaviṣya* account, see O'Flaherty, *Hindu Myths*, pp. 53-55. This is a late form of the myth: earlier versions relate that they became her sons since pleased with her *tapas*—see Chapter 6 section B (b).

2. *Rāmāyaṇa* 1.24.18: *Brahmāṇḍa Purāṇa* 1.2.27.22-23, 2.3.72.62-149: *Devībhāgavata Purāṇa* 4.11.37—4.12.17: *Kūrma Purāṇa* 1.23.72 : *Liṅga Purāṇa* 1.29.25-29, 1.69.48, 2.48.30-32: *Matsya Purāṇa* 47.88-113: *Padma Purāṇa* 5.2.13, 5.4.89-113, 5.13.175-256: *Śiva Purāṇa* 7.2.31.129 : *Skanda Purāṇa* 7.2.17.3-4: *Kāñcipurāṇam* 21.1-20: *Kandapurāṇam* 6.21.32.

3. *Brahmāṇḍa Purāṇa* 1.2.27.1-129 : *Devībhāgavata Purāṇa* 4.20.36-37 : *Kūrma Purāṇa* 2.37.2-162: *Liṅga Purāṇa* 1.29.1—1.31.45: *Sāmba Purāṇa* 16.1 ff. : *Śiva Purāṇa* 2.2.29.22-24: *Skanda Purāṇa* 1.1.6.1-87, 6.1.1-72 : *Vāmana Purāṇa* 6.58-67 : *Kathāsaritsāgara* 3.20.1 ff.: *Kāñcipurāṇam* 40.5-26 : *Kandapurāṇam* 6.13.30-127.

4. *Padma Purāṇa* 6.147.56-68.

5. *Brahmavaivarta Purāṇa* 3.18.1.23.

6. Ibid., 4.18.75 ff.

7. *Mahābhārata* 1.5.11—1.7.6, 9.46.16 ff., 12.329.43: *Brahmavaivarta Purāṇa*.

8. *Rāmāyaṇa* 1.47.13—1.48.10, 7.30.16-37: *Mahābhārata* 12.329.14, 13.41.21, 13.138.6: *Brahma Purāṇa* 87.1-70: *Brahmāṇḍa Purāṇa* 1.2.27.22-23: *Brahmavaivarta Purāṇa* 3.21.8-10, 4.18.75 ff., 4.47.19-45, 4.61.1—4.62.1 ff.: *Liṅga Purāṇa* 1.29.25-29: *Mārkaṇḍeya Purāṇa* 5.12-13: *Padma Purāṇa* 2.56.16-18, 5.51.4-50:

also cursed by Bhṛgu, to be Rākṣasa, for having desired the Ṛṣi's daughter.[1] Dharma was also cursed by Bhṛgu for having assumed the form of a bull and thrown the Ṛṣi to the ground while the latter was practising *tapas*;[2] while the Vasus were cursed by Vasiṣṭha to be born among men, for having insulted him or for having stolen his wish-granting cow.[3] Vasiṣṭha additionally cursed several Gandharvas to become Rākṣasas;[4] while Agastya cursed the Yakṣa Mārīca to become a Rākṣasa, for having attempted to kill him,[5] and also cursed the Yakṣa-king Kuvera that his army of Yakṣas—together with his Rākṣasa friend and companion Manimān—would be destroyed, after Manimān had discharged excrement on the Ṛṣi's head.[6]

In all of these instances where a Ṛṣi cursed a man, demon or god, the motive for the curse was invariably some fault or transgression on the part of the one cursed. As in the case of their other powers, the Ṛṣis' power to curse—and the dynamically effective nature of their curses—was directly derived from their performance of *tapas* and their self-transformation into fiery heat; and just as this heat was in other contexts directed inwards, so too it might be directed outwards in a destructive blaze of anger which in some cases literally burnt and destroyed those who crossed their path. This *tejas*—or external manifestation of fiery ascetic energy—consequently assists the Ṛṣis in another of their roles: for by cursing the *adhārmic* or unrighteous actions of their transgressors, they once again preserve *dharma* and maintain the corrcet ordering of the universe.

Śiva Purāṇa 2.4.9.28, 5.4.18: *Skanda Purāṇa* 5.3.136.1-24, 6.207.5—6.208.96: *Viṣṇudharmottara Purāṇa* 1.128.1 ff.: *Kathāsaritsāgara* 3.17.1 ff.: *Rāmacaritamānasa* 1.210.1-4: *Mṛcchakaṭika* Act 5: *Irāmāvatāram* 1.9.75-77: Bedi, p. 18: see also, K. V. Zvelebil, *The Smile of Murugan*, pp. 212-213. For the *Rāmāyaṇa* account, see O'Flaherty, *Hindu Myths*, pp. 94-96.

1. *Tirumūrttimalaipurāṇam* 9.10.
2. *Matsya Purāṇa* 193.23-53.
3. *Mahābhārata* 1.61.68, 1.91.11—1.93.46: *Devībhāgavata Purāṇa* 2.3.15-46 : *Liṅga Purāṇa* 1.29. 5-9.
4. *Skanda Purāṇa* 2.1.24.1-49, 3.1.4.2-35.
5. *Rāmāyaṇa* 1.24.8-12.
6. *Mahābhārata* 3.158.51—3.159.35.

Viewed from another angle, however, the cursing power of the Ṛṣis poses the same dilemma as was noted earlier in the case of their rivalries; for it implies a degree of anger towards the one who is cursed, which is the very passion which in other contexts they themselves strive to eradicate. We shall be returning to this apparent dilemma in later contexts.

6

THE SEVEN ṚṢIS ON EARTH II

Political and Family Roles

A. Political Role

In this chapter, we shall see that several further roles ascribed to the Ṛṣis are developed from themes examined in the last chapter : especially in respect of the contexts in which they perform sacrifice or "see" hymns, and the uses which they make of their powers acquired through *tapas*. Such roles represent in one respect the interaction between the sacred and the secular; and since secular power was usually invested in a single individual—namely the king—the Ṛṣis are often depicted as interacting in various ways with kings.

(a) *Performing Ceremonies for Kings*

The Ṛṣis frequently appear as the Purohitas or hereditary family-priests of kings—the term *purohita* meaning literally "one who is placed in front", hence the foremost or principal priest at the king's court. In this role, they are depicted as performing all of the sacrifices, rites and ceremonies for a king, his family and his descendants, and as residing either in their own Āśrama or at the court of the king. The tasks of the Purohita extended from the initial *abhiṣeka* or consecration of a king to the performance of *śrāddha* or funeral rites for him : thus for example when king Dhruvasandhi died, his Purohita Vasiṣṭha performed his funeral rites and anointed his son Śatrujit as king.[1]

1. *Devībhāgavata Purāṇa* 3.14.16—3.16.3.

Vasiṣṭha is above all consistently associated throughout Vedic, Epic and Purāṇic literature with the Aikṣvāka dynasty of Ayodhyā, and is termed the Purohita both of Ikṣvāku himself[1]—the founder of the dynasty—and also of the Aikṣvākas in general. In Vedic literature he is especially said to have been the Purohita of king Sudās the son of Pijavana, and to have anointed him king;[2] while in the Epics and Purāṇas, most notably of all in the *Rāmāyaṇa*, one of the most frequently-mentioned Aikṣvāka kings for whom he acted as Purohita is Daśaratha and his son Rāma. In this role, he is depicted as having performed sacrifices for Daśaratha, and as having advised him on various matters;[3] he also persuaded the king to allow his son Rāma to accompany Viśvāmitra in order to destroy the Rākṣasas,[4] and could recite the *vaṃśa* or line of descent of all the Aikṣvāka kings.[5] Upon Daśaratha's death, Vasiṣṭha himself offered the throne to Bharata;[6] and when Rāma eventually returned to Ayodhyā after the period of his banishment, Vasiṣṭha officiated in anointing him as king.[7] In a similar manner, Aṅgiras acted as Purohita both for king Karandhama[8] and for Karandhama's son Avikṣit;[9] while Atri instructed his *gotra*-descendant king Nimi Ātreya in the performance of the *śrāddha* ceremony.[10]

The Ṛṣis are also depicted in a more general manner as paying homage to kings, and as performing or taking part in sacrifices for kings. When Rāma was consecrated as king of Ayodhyā, various Ṛṣis—including the Seven Ṛṣis—came to visit and pay homage to him;[11] the Seven Ṛṣis also attended an

1. For example *Bhaviṣya Purāṇa* 1.118.19.
2. *Aitareya Brāhmaṇa* 8.21: *Jaiminīya Brāhmaṇa* 3.23-24 : *Śāṅkhāyana Śrauta Sūtra* 16.11.13-15.
3. See especially *Rāmāyaṇa* Book 1, the *Bāla Kāṇḍa*: *Mahābhārata* 3.261-275: *Agni Purāṇa* 5.6 ff.: *Bhāgavata Purāṇa* 9.10.1 ff.
4. *Rāmāyaṇa* 1.18.1—1.20.19 & ff.
5. Ibid., 1.69.17-32, 2.102.3-31.
6. Ibid., 1.1.28 *etc.*
7. Ibid., 6.116.55.
8. *Mahābhārata* 14.5.7-8.
9. Ibid., 14.4.22.
10. Ibid., 13.91.18-91.
11. *Rāmāyaṇa* 7.1.1-6.

aśvamedha sacrifice of the Aikṣvāka king Purukutsa,[1] while Viśvāmitra, Jamadagni and Vasiṣṭha (and in some accounts also Agastya) all officiated in the sacrifice of the Aikṣvāka king Hariścandra in which Viśvāmitra adopted Śunaḥśepa as his son.[2] In such instances, the presence of the Ṛṣis was both a necessity—for the performance of sacrifice—and an honour for the king : thus king Dārbhya Rathavīti, when wanting to sacrifice, went to Atri to propitiate him and to ask for Atri's son Arcanāṇas to officiate in his sacrifice.[3] On many occasions the performance of sacrifice for a king would result in the king bestowing copious gifts on the Ṛṣi, as we shall see in a moment.

(b) *Obtaining Conquests for Kings*

This role of the Ṛṣis was also frequently performed while acting as the Purohitas of kings. On occasions, a Ṛṣi would destroy the enemies of a king by sacrifice, hymns or a curse; he would frequently accompany a king on his military expeditions often taking an active part in any conflicts. Thus for example Gautama accompanied king Māthava on his eastward expedition from the Sarasvatī to the Sadānīrā;[4] while when king Mucukunda's army was destroyed by Rākṣasas, the king appealed to his Purohita Vasiṣṭha who slew the Rākṣasas through his *tapas* and curse and then instructed the king at great length as to how a king depends on his Purohita for success.[5] Even in the *Ṛgveda* the Ṛṣis are depicted as achieving secular and military goals through sacred means : Vasiṣṭha is said to have aided the Aikṣvāka king Sudās by the power of his *brahman*, and to have made a way for the Tṛtsus in the Battle of the Ten Kings by his hymns of praise;[6] while Viśvāmitra is also said to have led king Sudās as the latter's Purohita and to

1. *Ṛgveda* 4.42.8: *Śatapatha Brāhmaṇa* 13.5.4.5.

2. *Aitareya Brāhmaṇa* 7.16: *Śāṅkhāyana Śrauta Sūtra* 15.17-27: *Vāsiṣṭha Dharma Sūtra* 17.31-35: *Mahābhārata* 13.3.6-8: *Bhāgavata Purāṇa* 9.7.22-23: *Brahma Purāṇa* 104.1-90: *Devībhāgavata Purāṇa* 6.12.37 ff.

3. *Bṛhaddevatā* 5.50.

4. *Śatapatha Brāhmaṇa* 1.4.1.10.

5. *Mahābhārata* 12.75.1ff.

6. *Ṛgveda* 7.33.3-7.

have conducted a sacrifice for him at the confluence of the Vipāśā and Śutudrī rivers, imploring in his hymns that the rivers might become fordable for the king.[1] Viśvāmitra is further referred to as the patron of the Bharatas;[2] on one occasion he (together, in some accounts, with Jamadagni) was with the Bharatas when they were being attacked by either the Aikṣvākas or Mahāvṛṣas on the banks of a river (variously named as the Sindhu, Gaṅgā or Yamunā), whereupon by means of a hymn he made the river fordable and allowed the Bharatas to cross it and gain cattle.[3] Vasiṣṭha, like Viśvāmitra, is similarly associated with the Bharatas; he is said to have revived their fortunes when they were in exile by agreeing to become the Purohita of their king Saṃvaraṇa and by installing prince Bharata as the lord of all Kṣatriyas—whereafter the Bharatas flourished and multiplied, and defeated the Pañcālas.[4] Bharadvāja is said to have either become or obtained a son for Bharata (see below); he is also referred to as the Purohita of king Divodāsa, and when Divodāsa was defeated by the Vaitahavyas Bharadvāja obtained a son Pratardana for the king, and by entering Pratardana through the power of his *yoga* he slew the Vaitahavyas and Ailas.[5] Bharadvāja further appears as the Purohita of king Kṣatra the son of Pratardana, for whom the Ṛṣi gained victory in the Battle of the Ten Kings by means of a hymn to Indra;[6] and again as the Purohita of kings Abhyāvartin Cāyamāna and Prastoka Sṛñjaya, for whom he gained a victory over the Varaśikhas by the same means.[7] Another Aikṣvāka king with whose victories Vasiṣṭha is associated is Sagara : when the king routed the Haihayas—together with their Śaka, Yavana and

---

1. *Ṛgveda* 3.53.12: *Nirukta* 2.24: *Bṛhaddevatā* 4.105-119.

2. *Ṛgveda* 3.53.12.

3. *Jaiminīya Brāhmaṇa* 3.237-238: compare *Jaiminīya Brāhmaṇa* 3.183: *Pañcaviṃśa Brāhmaṇa* 14.3.12-13.

4. *Ṛgveda* 7.33.7: *Pañcaviṃśa Brāhmaṇa* 15.5.24: *Mahābhārata* 1.89.31-42, 1.162.10—1.163.20.

5. *Ṛgveda* 1.116.18, 6.31.4: *Pañcaviṃśa Brāhmaṇa* 15.3.7: *Mahābhārata* 13.31.32 ff, 13.34.16.

6. *Jaiminīya Brāhmaṇa* 3.224-227.

7. *Bṛhaddevatā* 5.124-142.

other allies—the latter fled for refuge to Vasiṣṭha, who tricked them and handed them over to the king.[1] It is even said that the Aikṣvākas were able to conquer the entire earth by obtaining Vasiṣṭha as their Purohita[2] : a further indication of the high value placed upon obtaining such a Ṛṣi as Purohita. We can see from these examples that when the Ṛṣis obtained such conquests for kings, they invariably did so in a manner analogous to their activity in cursing others: for in such instances they were concerned to destroy not their own enemies but the enemies of others—and the power for such defeat and destruction derived once again from the fiery speech of the Ṛṣis, either in praising the gods to accomplish conquests (especially in Vedic contexts) or in burning foes with the fire of their curse. The very presence of a Ṛṣi was like that of a smouldering and threatening fire, ready to blaze forth and consume the worlds; and when a king or people obtained the favour of a Ṛṣi, well might their enemies tremble.

In several instances, the Ṛṣis are depicted as offering not merely hospitality but aid and shelter to exiled or cursed kings. When king Triśaṅku had been cursed by Vasiṣṭha, Viśvāmitra agreed to become his Purohita and eventually transferred him to the sky in gratitude for the king having earlier sheltered his wife and son.[3] As we saw earlier, Atri and Agastya both gave shelter and hospitality to the exiled Rāma, and Bharadvāja sheltered the exiled prince Sudarśana.[4] In a similar manner, when Paraśurāma was destroying the Kṣatriyas, Gautama protected king Bṛhadratha on the banks of the Gaṅgā; and at the end of Paraśurāma's slaughter, Kaśyapa banished him and re-established Bṛhadratha as king.[5] Thus we see here that the primary concern of the Ṛṣis in their relation with kings—as indeed in many other contexts—was once again with the preservation of *dharma*, the upholding of

1. *Brahma Purāṇa* 8.45-51: *Brahmāṇḍa Purāṇa* 2.3.63.126-140: *Nārada Purāṇa* 1.8.29-53: *Śiva Purāṇa* 5.38.42-44: *Vāyu Purāṇa* 2.26.125-139: *Viṣṇu Purāṇa* 4.3.1 ff.
2. *Mahābhārata* 1.164.1-14.
3. See sub-section (f) below.
4. For further examples and references, see Chapter 5 section C (b) ii.
5. *Mahābhārata* 12.49.56-80.

righteousness and the maintenance of a correct balance of power in the universe. When kings were threatened by enemies, the Ṛṣis saved them; and conversely, when kings or warriors went beyond the bounds of righteousness in their conquests, the Ṛṣis stepped in to restore the balance.

(c) *Ruling Kingdoms*

The role of the Ṛṣi as Purohita in many cases gave the Ṛṣi a powerful say in the running of the kingdom, especially through the advice—as *guru* or spiritual guide to the king—which he would offer to the king. This is particularly evident in the case of Vasiṣṭha who, by his diplomacy, was able for example to persuade the reluctant Daśaratha to allow Rāma to accompany Viśvāmitra on the latter's Rākṣasa-slaying expedition,[1] to have Vikukṣi installed on the throne upon the death of Ikṣvāku,[2] and to obtain the city of Pratiṣṭhāna for Sudyumna and his son Purūravas despite the fact that Sudyumna had earlier been deprived of inheritance by his father Manu.[3] On one occasion, Vasiṣṭha is himself said to have ruled over a kingdom in the absence of the king : for after the Ṛṣi had obtained Tapti the daughter of the sun as the bride of king Saṃvaraṇa, the king proclaimed his Purohita Vasiṣṭha regent in his capital and kingdom, while he himself went away to the hills for twelve years to make love to his wife.[4] Such an occurrence is, however, somewhat untypical; and in this particular case, the absence of the king and his abandonment of politics in favour of love-making resulted in a twelve-year drought, which was only ended when Vasiṣṭha brought the king and his wife back to the city. The structure in this account may be compared with that in an example that we noted at the end of the last sub-section : when Paraśurāma destroyed the Kṣatriyas, the earth—being without kings—started to sink in distress, whereupon Kaśyapa supported the earth and found new kings for her.[5] In both instances the

1. *Rāmāyaṇa* 1.18.1—1.20.19—ff.
2. *Śiva Purāṇa* 5.37.5.
3. *Brahma Purāṇa* 6.21: *Devībhāgavata Purāṇa* 1.12.1 ff.: *Liṅga Purāṇa* 1.65.29: *Śiva Purāṇa* 5.36.20: *Viṣṇu Purāṇa* 4.1.1 ff.
4. *Mahābhārata* 1.162.10—1.163.21.
5. Ibid., 12.49.39-80.

Ṛṣi rules or supports the earth on a temporary basis, in the absence of the rightful ruler, and in both cases it is the Ṛṣi himself who restores the ruler to his proper place.

In several instances, Ṛṣis are depicted as giving instruction on the necessity for and duties of kings. Thus Bharadvāja is said to have composed a *rāja-śāstra*, or treatise on the duties of kings;[1] in a similar manner, Vasiṣṭha instructed king Mucukunda on the interrelations between kings and their Purohitas—to the effect that a king depends on his Purohita for success, while a kingdom depends on a king.[2] This question of the political involvement of the Ṛṣis generally conforms to—and may be considered in connection with—the more general theory of Brahmin-Kṣatriya relations, where it is the duty of the king or Kṣatriya to rule and to protect the Brahmin, while it is the duty of the Brahmin to legitimate and sanctify the power of the king.[3]

One further example which we shall consider in this context is that of Viśvāmitra who, as a Kṣatriya, inherited the kingdom of Kānyakubja from his father Gādhi, ruled as king of the Jahnus, and defeated and gained the kingdom of the Vṛcīvats.[4] In this instance, however, Viśvāmitra ruled as king before he renounced both his kingdom and his Kṣatriya-hood; in order to become a *brahma*-Ṛṣi, it was indeed essential for him that he should renounce these. Here once again, therefore, we see the moral that it is not the proper course of events for a Ṛṣi—or a Brahmin—to exercise political authority.

(d) *Obtaining Sons for Kings*

There are two main ways in which the Ṛṣis are depicted as having obtained sons for the kings. The first of these was by

1. *Mahābhārata* 12.58.3.
2. Ibid., 12.75.1 ff.
3. On Brahmin-Kṣatriya relations, see especially J. C. Heesterman, 'Power and Authority in Indian Civilisation': L. Dumont, *Homo Hierarchicus*: A. K. Coomaraswamy, *Spiritual Authority and Temporal Power in the Indian Theory of Government*.
4. *Pañcaviṃśa Brāhmaṇa* 21.17.2: *Rāmāyaṇa* 1.50.17—1.55.24: *Mahābhārata* 1.165.1-44, 9.39.11 ff.: *Devībhāgavata Purāṇa* 3.17.7-22: *Garuḍa Purāṇa* 181.1 ff.: *Skanda Purāṇa* 3.1.39.23-32, 6.167.1-74, 6.214.19 ff.

prescribing some form of ritual or devotion for the king and his wife to perform. Vasiṣṭha, for example, advised king Hariścandra to obtain a son by worshipping Varuṇa,[1] and Gautama instructed king Yuvanāśva to worship Nārāyaṇa-Kṛṣṇa (one of the forms of Viṣṇu) in order to gain a son;[2] Kaśyapa prescribed the *putreṣṭi* or son-desiring sacrifice for Mālinī the wife of king Priyavrata,[3] while Vasiṣṭha gave the king of the Gandharvas a hymn, a *mantra* and an amulet for worshipping Śiva to obtain a son.[4] Bhṛgu prescribed for the wife of king Gādhi and her daughter Satyavatī a ritual involving bathing, embracing particular types of trees, and drinking specially-prepared libations—which resulted in the births of Viśvāmitra to the king's wife, and of Jamadagni to Satyavatī.[5] Aṅgiras instructed king Citraketu to perform a sacrifice to Tvaṣṭṛ,[6] while Bharadvāja similarly obtained through sacrifice a son Pratardana for king Divodāsa,[7] and through a sacrifice to the Maruts he either obtained or himself became a son for king Bharata.[8] Bhṛgu, when pleased with the *tapas* of king Sagara, gave him the boon of obtaining a son;[9] and Vasiṣṭha instructed Sagara to obtain a son by approaching the *muni* Aurva.[10]

There was, however, another—somewhat simpler and more practical—way for a Ṛṣi to obtain a son for a king : namely by having sexual intercourse with the king's wife. In several of the accounts just cited, such an interpretation may indeed be implied. Thus, for example, in the case of Bharadvāja and king Bharata, the earliest version in the *Mahābhārata* relates that

1. *Devībhāgavata Purāṇa* 7.14.26 ff.
2. *Kūrma Purāṇa* 1.19.12-18.
3. *Devībhāgavata Purāṇa* 9.46.8 ff.
4. *Brahmavaivarta Purāṇa* 1.12.7-10.
5. *Mahābhārata* 3.115.9-30, 12.49.1-30,13.4.1-48: *Bhāgavata Purāṇa* 9.15.5-15: *Brahma Purāṇa* 10.28-53: *Brahmāṇḍa Purāṇa* 2.3.66.35-63: *Kālikā Purāṇa* 85.1 ff.: *Skanda Purāṇa* 6.165.1—6.166.48: *Vāyu Purāṇa* 2.29.64-90: *Viṣṇu Purāṇa* 4.7.1 ff.
6. *Bhāgavata Purāṇa* 6.14.9-31.
7. *Mahābhārata* 13.31.22 ff.
8. Ibid., 1.89.17-19: *Harivaṃśa* 2.3.49-53: *Agni Purāṇa* 278.8-10: *Bhāgavata Purāṇa* 9.20.34-39: *Brahma Purāṇa* 13.58-61: *Matsya Purāṇa* 49.14-35.
9. *Rāmāyaṇa* 1.37.2 ff.
10. *Brahma Purāṇa* 78.3-11.

Bharata performed a great sacrifice, and received a son Bhumanyu from Bharadvāja :

> Then Bharata offered great sacrifices, and received from Bharadvāja a son called Bhumanyu; when that scion of the Purus learned that he himself was the father of a son, he consecrated Bhumanyu as prince-regent; thereafter Vitatha was born as the son of Bhumanyu.[1]

In subsequent versions, however, no mention is made of Bhumanyu : the *Harivaṃśa* and the *Brahma Purāṇa* both relate that Bharadvāja performed a great sacrifice for Bharata, and that Vitatha became the son of Bharata from Bharadvāja (*bharadvājāt suto 'bhavat*); while the *Matsya Purāṇa*, evidently not liking the implications of the passage, relates that Bharadvāja *became* Vitatha (*bharadvājo nṛpo 'bhavat*), and thereafter adds a lengthy myth—adapted directly from the Dīrghatamas myth—about his birth and adoption by the Maruts in order to explain how he was then given to Bharata by the Maruts and thus became his son. This latter idea of Bharadvāja "becoming" Vitatha is then adopted in other texts;[2] yet the earlier versions evidently imply that Bharadvāja himself was quite literally the procreative means whereby Bharata obtained a son. In further contexts, the idea of a Ṛṣi begetting a son for a king is made explicit. When Gautama-Dīrghatamas, for example, arrived in the realm of king Bali, the king—being desirous of obtaining a son—sent his wife to have intercourse with the Ṛṣi. In one version, the queen at first sent her Śūdra-nurse in her place : the Ṛṣi had intercourse with her, and Kākṣīvat and other sons were born. Then, when Bali insisted that she herself should go, the queen went and licked all of the Ṛṣi's body apart from his phallus—whereupon the Ṛṣi cursed her to give birth to a son without a phallus; and finally the Ṛṣi touched her womb, and she bore the five sons Aṅga, Vaṅga, Kaliṅga, Puṇḍra and Suhma.[3] This same version thereafter relates that the divine cow Surabhi cured Dīrghatamas of his blindness and old age—

1. *Mahābhārata* 1.89.17-19.
2. For references, see four notes above.
3. *Matsya Purāṇa* 48.32-79.

whence he became known as Gautama—through being pleased that the Ṛṣi had earlier followed the law of cows in raping his daughter-in-law,[1] and we need have little doubt about the sexual connotations of the account, which are similarly clear in further versions.[2] Quite unambiguous is the case of Vasiṣṭha, who begot a son Aśmaka on Madayantī the wife of king Mitrasaha ("Kalmāṣapāda") Saudāsa. Vasiṣṭha cursed the king to become a Rākṣasa, but subsequently released him from the curse after twelve years; and his queen, through intercourse with the Ṛṣi, bore a son Aśmaka. Many versions relate that the king himself commanded his wife to raise offspring for him and sent her to the Ṛṣi[3]: although one version attempts to evade the difficulty by saying that, since Vasiṣṭha had intercourse with the queen while the king was under a curse, there was no sin involved.[4] Further versions expand upon this theme, and relate that the king was again cursed by another Brahmin to die if he ever engaged in sexual intercourse : and so after the termination of Vasiṣṭha's curse, the king renounced sex and instead asked the Ṛṣi to beget a son on his wife.[5] All versions agree on one point, namely that the Ṛṣi had sexual intercourse with the king's wife; and the story was used by Pāṇḍu, who wanted his wife to propagate sons for him through an ascetic, and told her that she would not incur any sin by doing so—since he had heard that in olden times king Saudāsa obtained a son in that way through Vasiṣṭha.[6] We must therefore conclude that the Ṛṣis were often called upon to obtain sons for kings, and that in several instances they achieved this task not—as on many occasions—by prescribing some form of devotional or sacrificial rite to be performed, but rather through a far more straightforward and time-honoured method. In doing so, they

1. *Matsya Purāṇa* 48.80-84.
2. For example *Brahmāṇḍa Purāṇa* 2.3.74.47-88: *Vāyu Purāṇa* 2.37.47-87: *Bṛhaddevatā* 4.11-25.
3. For example *Mahābhārata* 1.113.21-22, 12.226.30.
4. *Mahābhārata* 1.173.1-24.
5. *Bhāgavata Purāṇa* 9.9.19-40: *Viṣṇu Purāṇa* 4.4.1 ff.: see also *Mahābhārata* 1.168.16-25: *Brahmāṇḍa Purāṇa* 2.3.63.175 ff.: *Kūrma Purāṇa* 1.20.12-14: *Liṅga Purāṇa* 1.66.26-28.
6. *Devībhāgavata Purāṇa* 2.6.49-52.

demostrate the sexual and erotic powers which are attributed to the ascetic, and which are indeed a very consequence of his asceticism : a theme to which we shall be returning towards the end of this chapter.

Several tribal myths throw an interesting light upon this additional role of the Ṛṣi in his capacity as the *guru* or spiritual guide of kings. These concern especially the seven Samduria sisters, and in particular the youngest of them :

> One day, the youngest sister found Nanga Baiga (the originator of mankind) sitting eating berries. She touched his feet and said, "Come, I'll make you my *guru*". "What are you talking about ?" asked Nanga Baiga. "What do you want with a *guru* ? Tell me what you really want". "I want you to give me a child", she said at last. "That is easy", said Nanga Baiga. Soon there was a child in the girl's belly, and she went back to her sisters.[1]

Thus we see here on a more popular level much the same basic idea as is presented in the Epics and Purāṇas : to the effect that the role of the Ṛṣi as *guru* was by no means limited to merely spiritual concerns.

(e) *Obtaining Gifts from Kings*

The Ṛṣis are depicted as being the recipients of various kinds of gifts from kings. On many occasions, they are said to be presented with wealth. Thus for example Bharadvāja received gifts and wealth from kings Prastoka Sṛñjaya, Abhyāvartin Cāyamāna and Bṛbu Takṣan, for whom he had—as Purohita—obtained

1. See V. Elwin, *The Baiga*, p. 328. For further myths of the seven Samduria sisters—who parallel in many respects the Kṛttikās as the wives of the Seven Ṛṣis—as also of the seven Brothers, see especially V. Elwin, *Myths of the North-East Frontier of India*, pp. 107, 128-130: *Myths of Middle India*, pp. 10-11, 29 ff., 114-115, 119-120, 176: *Tribal Myths of Orissa*, pp. 83, 523: C. von Führer-Haimendorf, *The Raj Gonds of Adilabad*, p. 224: L. B. Day, *Folk-Tales* of Bengal, pp. 113-118, 119-131, 227. Compare also the tribal myths of Baba Vasishtha Muni who, as the *guru* of Bhagavan, becomes the father of Nanga Baiga: see *The Baiga*, pp. 312:-313: *Myths of Middle India*, pp. 15-16.

victory in battle.[1] Atri obtained gifts of 10,320 cows and a golden wagon with two oxen from king Tryaruṇa Aikṣvāka, of 100 oxen from king Aśvamedha, and of much wealth from king Trasadasyu;[2] while Vasiṣṭha was presented with cattle by king Saudāsa, after he had pleased the king with a discourse on the sacred nature of cattle.[3] When Atri wished to retire to the forests, he first sought and gained wealth from king Vainya to distribute among his sons and servants by pleasing the king with praise.[4] In a similar manner, the pupils of Ṛṣis are also depicted as having received gifts from kings to present to their teachers. Uttaṅka obtained the golden ear-rings of queen Madayantī the wife of Saudāsa for Gautama's wife Ahalyā;[5] while Gālava obtained Mādhavī the daughter of king Yayāti together with 600 cows—200 each from kings Haryaśva Aikṣvāka, Divodāsa, and Uśīnara king of the Bhojas—to present to his teacher Viśvāmitra.[6] Viśvāmitra is also said to have obtained wealth from a king in a somewhat different way: being once insulted and threatened while performing *tapas* by king Hariścandra Aikṣvāka, he threatened to curse the king, and the latter in fear and propitiation gave the Ṛṣi his entire kingdom and wealth; but Viśvāmitra sternly demanded a further sacrificial fee, and steadily reduced the king to the level of a Caṇḍāla or outcaste, forcing him to sell even his wife and son—and the king was only saved from the clutches of the angry Ṛṣi through the intervention of the gods, who appeased Viśvāmitra and transferred the king with his wife, son and subjects to heaven.[7] In several further instances, Ṛṣis sought and received the gift of a king's daughter as their wife. Thus for example king Prasenajit gave his daughter Reṇukā to Jamadagni,[8] and in some accounts king Tṛṇabindu gave his

1. *Śāṅkhāyana Śrauta Sūtra* 16.11.10-12: *Bṛhaddevatā* 5.124-142.
2. *Bṛhaddevatā* 5.28-36.
3. *Mahābhārata* 13.77.1 ff.
4. Ibid., 12.183.1-32.
5. Ibid., 14.55-57.
6. Ibid., 5.104-117.
7. *Mārkaṇḍeya Purāṇa* 7.1—8.268: *Śiva Purāṇa* 2.4.1.35-37: for a version of this incident in the form of a test, see *Devībhāgavata Purāṇa* 7.1.18.1-7.1.27.43.
8. *Mahābhārata* 3.116.1-4.

daughter Ilvalā to Pulastya;[1] while Agastya, when requested by his ancestors to raise offspring, obtained a daughter Lopāmudrā for the king of the Vidarbhas and then asked the king to bestow her on him as his wife – and the king, somewhat unwilling but fearful of the Ṛṣi's curse, acceded to his request.[2] In such instances, therefore, the Ṛṣis received gifts from kings not merely due to the benevolence of the king, but also due to his gratitude for services rendered or to his fear of in any way incurring the displeasure or wrath of the Ṛṣi; thus the Ṛṣis benefitted materially from the patronage, benevolence and awed respect of kings.

(f) *Cursing Kings*

The relations between Ṛṣis and kings were not always of a benevolent and harmonious nature. One Brāhmaṇa passage relates that when Jamadagni was the Purohita of the Māhenas, they tried to kill him—a situation from which the Ṛṣi gained release through a hymn;[3] but relations are not usually depicted as being quite as dire as this. In later literature, if a king ever offended a Ṛṣi in any way he could expect a fiery curse in reply; and the main offences which kings are depicted as committing to incur the wrath of a Ṛṣi are invariably in the manner of either a personal insult or a ritual transgression. King Hiraṇyakaśipu once dismissed Vasiṣṭha as his Purohita and installed Triśiras in his place : whereupon the Ṛṣi cursed the king that his sacrifices should be incomplete and that he would be killed by an unknown being, and the king was subsequently slain by Viṣṇu as Narasiṃha or the Man-lion.[4] Vasiṣṭha similarly cursed king Nimi Aikṣvāka to die, for having employed another Ṛṣi to officiate in the sacrifice while he himself was absent performing a sacrifice for Indra; the king, who had been asleep

1. *Liṅga Purāṇa* 1.63.55-68: *Skanda Purāṇa* 7.1.20.17-36.
2. *Mahābhārata* 3.94.11—3.95.5.
3. *Jaiminīya Brāhmaṇa* 1.152.
4. *Mahābhārata* 12.329.20.
3. *Bhāgavata Purāṇa* 9.13.1-11: *Devībhāgavata Purāṇa* 1.19.20-27, 6.14.10-2 : *Matsya Purāṇa* 201.1-39: *Viṣṇu Purāṇa* 4.5.1 ff.

when cursed, then awoke and in return cursed Vasiṣṭha to die—whence the Ṛṣi came to be born again from the seed of Mitra-Varuṇa. Agastya on several occasions cursed a king for his insulting and irreverent behaviour : he once hurled Nahuṣa from heaven and cursed him to become a snake on earth, for having kicked him on the head with his left foot;[1] and he also cursed Indradyumna Pāṇḍya to become a stupid elephant, for having failed to offer water and worship on meeting the Ṛṣi and his pupils.[2] Gautama similarly reduced two kings to the status of animals by his curses : one to become a snake,[3] the other to become a lion.[4] Just as we have seen that Vasiṣṭha is often depicted as the Purohita of the Ikṣvākus or Aikṣvākas, so too he appears in the role of a chastiser of his Aikṣvāka patrons in several further contexts. On one occasion he cursed Vikukṣi Aikṣvâka and banished him to the forests, after the latter—while gathering animal-flesh for the sacrifice—had eaten a hare and thereby made the sacrifice unclean.[5] In another incident, Satyavrata the son of king Tryaruṇa—who had previously been exiled by his father to live among Caṇḍālas or outcastes for having taken another man's wife (and been angry then against his *guru* Vasiṣṭha for not having prevented his father from exiling him), and who had also used things unsprinkled by sacred water—killed Vasiṣṭha's *kāmadhenu* or wish-granting cow in order to feed Viśvāmitra's son during a drought; enraged at this third transgression, Vasiṣṭha cursed Satyavrata—whence he became known as Triśaṅku or the Thrice-transgressed. But Viśvāmitra, pleased that the prince had fed his son, thereafter installed Triśaṅku in his father's kingdom, acted as his Purohita, and finally transferred him bodily to heaven.[6] A further Aikṣvāka

1. *Mahābhārata* 3.101.14, 3.176.1—3.178,50, 5.17.1ff., 12.329.30 ff., 13.101-102: *Devībhāgavata Purāṇa* 3.29.49-52, 6.9.38-57: *Liṅga Purāṇa* 1.29.25-29: *Tiruviḷaiyāṭarpurāṇam* 1.59-65.
2. *Bhāgavata Purāṇa* 8.4.7-10.
3. *Kathāsaritsāgara* 10.61.1 ff.
4. *Skanda Purāṇa* 3.1.32.31-34.
5. *Brahma Purāṇa* 7.48-50: *Brahmāṇḍa Purāṇa* 2.3.63.11-25: *Devībhāgavata Purāṇa* 7.9.1-11: *Vāyu Purāṇa* 2.26.14 ff. : *Viṣṇu Purāṇa* 4.2.1 ff.
6. *Rāmāyaṇa* 1.56.10—1.59.33: *Mahābhārata* 1.65.20-42, 13.3.1 ff.: *Harivaṃśa* 9.88—10.20: *Bhāgavata Purāṇa* 9.7.5-6: *Bhaviṣya Purāṇa* 4.130.9-39:

king cursed by Vasiṣṭha was Mitrasaha Saudāsa who, when tricked by a Rākṣasa, offered flesh to Vasiṣṭha (or, in another version, struck Śakti the son of Vasiṣṭha with his whip) and was cursed to be a flesh-eating Rākṣasa; the king took a bowl of water to curse Vasiṣṭha in return, but relented and dropped it instead on his own feet—whence he became known as Kalmāṣapāda or Variegated-feet. Thereupon Vasiṣṭha, discerning the trick, limited the curse to twelve years; and at the instigation of Viśvāmitra, the transformed king commenced his flesh-eating habits by devouring the 100 sons of Vasiṣṭha.[1] Another example of Vasiṣṭha's wrath excited against a king appears in the case of Viśvāmitra who—as king of Kānyakubja—visited Vasiṣṭha's Āśrama, was miraculously fed by the Ṛṣi's *kāmadhenu* or wish-granting cow, and then sought to drag away the cow : whereupon the Ṛṣi created demons and warriors from the cow who destroyed Viśvāmitra's army.[2] In a similar incident, king Arjuna Kārttavīrya Haihaya visited Jamadagni's Āśrama, was fed by the Ṛṣi's *kāmadhenu*, and seized it; on this occasion, Jamadagni's son Rāma regained the *kāmadhenu* and cut off Arjuna's arms, and in return Arjuna killed Jamadagni—for which reason Rāma destroyed all Kṣatriyas.[3] This last account does not explicitly involve the curse of the Ṛṣi himself; yet it nonetheless vividly illustrates the potentially destructive power

---

Brahma Purāṇa 7.105—8.21: *Brahmāṇḍa Purāṇa* 2.3.63.73-104: *Devībhāgavata Purāṇa* 7.10.1-58, 7.12.11—7.14.25: *Liṅga Purāṇa* 1.66.6-11: *Śiva Purāṇa* 5.37.47—5.38.18 : *Skanda Purāṇa* 6.2.1—6.3.31, 6.4.1—6.8.9: *Vāyu Purāṇa* 2.26.84-116: *Viṣṇu Purāṇa* 4.3.1 ff.: *Kathāsaritsāgara* 6.28.1 ff.

1. *Rāmāyaṇa* 7.57.10-33: *Mahābhārata* 1.166.1—1.168.65: *Bhāgavata Purāṇa* 9.9.18-39: *Brahmāṇḍa Purāṇa* 2.3.63.175 ff.: *Liṅga Purāṇa* 1.64.2-123: *Nārada Purāṇa* 1.9.1-47: *Śiva Purāṇa* 4.10.1-31: *Skanda Purāṇa* 3.2.1-141, 5.2.80.1-63, 6.53.1-102: *Vāyu Purāṇa* 2.26.174 ff.: *Viṣṇu Purāṇa* 4.4.1 ff.: *Bṛhaddevatā* 6.34: *Kāñcipurāṇam* 15.1-27.

2. *Rāmāyaṇa* 1.50.17—1.55.24: *Mahābhārata* 1.165.1-44, 9.39.11 ff.: *Devībhāgavata Purāṇa* 3.17.7-22: *Garuḍa Purāṇa* 181.1 ff.: *Skanda Purāṇa* 3.1.39.-23-32, 6.167.1-74, 6.214.19 ff.

3. *Mahābhārata* 3.116.1—3.117.15, 12.49.39-80: *Agni Purāṇa* 4.14-20: *Bhāgavata Purāṇa* 9.15.23—9.16.27: *Brahmāṇḍa Purāṇa* 2.3.26.43—2.3.30.76: *Brahmavaivarta Purāṇa* 3.24-40: *Devībhāgavata Purāṇa* 4.18.36-41: *Kālikā Purāṇa*. 86.1 ff.: *Padma Purāṇa* 268.1-81: *Skanda Purāṇa* 5.3.218.1-57, 6.66.1—6.69.27: *Kāñcipurāṇam* 45.4-61: Elmore, pp. 82-86: Whitehead, p. 116.

which might be released through in any way offending or harming the Ṛṣi. In such contexts, the Ṛṣi comes to be seen not merely as an upholder and teacher of *dharma* who strives to maintain righteousness and proper conduct among men, but as the very embodiment of *dharma* itself : manifesting *dharma* in his words and deeds, and purging with his curse the *adhārmic* actions of others. It is consequently not surprising to find that kings were inclined to be wary of and respectful towards these fiery ascetics, and to be eager to enlist their services—particularly to bring success and prosperity to their kingdoms and destruction to their enemies.

B. Family Role

(a) *Asceticism and Sex*

Sexuality has proved to be a somewhat thorny problem to the ascetic in many different religious traditions. In several cases—as for example with the Christian monk or recluse, the early Moslem Sūfī-ascetic and the Buddhist and Jain monk—the complete renunciation of all sexual and family life is demanded of the ascetic; and the same is the case with many Hindu ascetics, where the virtues of being *ūrdhvaretas* or "having the seed drawn upwards" are applauded. The idea underlying the practice of being *ūrdhvaretas* is that the seed possesses a mystical potency which—when it is retained within the body—can be directed by various stages from the *liṅga* or phallus upwards through the different *cakras* or centres of power in the body, until it reaches the crown of the head and occasions the full enlightenment and liberation of the ascetic : this being an idea which was especially developed in Tāntric schools of thought. Consequently, the loss of seed meant also a loss of power; while its retention meant an amassing of potent energy and heat which would eventually enable the ascetic to conquer even heaven and the gods in attaining release from the material realm and realisation of his real Self as the Absolute.

This idea appears very prominently in the Ṛṣi traditions, wherein the Ṛṣis build up their powers of *tapas* by renouncing sexuality in favour of remaining *ūrdhvaretas*. Through their amassment of fiery energy, they frequently threaten to burn the worlds or become equal to the gods; consequently in several instances Indra or the gods in general—fearful both for the well-being of the worlds and also for the preservation of their own status—send to the Ṛṣis a beautiful Apsaras or water-nymph to tempt and seduce them, and to thereby destroy the powers of their *tapas*. Sometimes, due to the strength of his *tapas*, a Ṛṣi was able to resist the temptation—and consequently cursed the Apsaras. Thus when Indra sent the Apsaras Rambhā to seduce Viśvāmitra and turn him from his pursuit of *tapas*, her allurements failed to sway the resolve of the Ṛṣi, who cursed her to be turned to stone.[1] In a comparable manner, Pulastya cursed the Yakṣa Vidyādhara to become a wild boar for having disturbed his performance of *tapas* by singing;[2] he also cursed the daughter of king Tṛṇabindu to become pregnant for having disturbed his *tapas* by playing with her friends on the nearby hillside.[3] On many other occasions, however, Ṛṣis succumbed to the charms of an Apsaras. When Viśvāmitra was performing the severest *tapas*, Indra became alarmed and—fearing to be thrown from heaven—summoned the Apsaras Menakā and ordered her to seduce the Ṛṣi; the reluctant Menakā fearfully obeyed the order and succeeded in seducing Viśvāmitra, who abandoned his *tapas* at the sight of her beauty and had intercourse with her—whereafter was born Śakuntalā.[4] One account also relates that he became attached to the Apsaras Ghṛtācī and made love to her for ten years, failing to perceive the passing of time.[5] Gautama was once sexually aroused at the sight of a naked Apsaras (variously named as either Jānapadī, Urvaśī, Śāradvatī or Rambhā) : he tried to resist the temptation, but his seed fell into a clump of reeds, whence were born the twins

1. *Rāmāyaṇa* 1.63.1-15: *Mahābhārata* 13.3.1 ff.: *Brahma Purāṇa* 147.9-23: *Skanda Purāṇa* 3.1.39.23-69: see also *Kathāsaritsāgara* 2.10.1 ff.
2. *Tiruviḷaiyāṭarpurāṇam* 45.52-55.
3. *Rāmāyaṇa* 7.2.4-29.
4. *Rāmāyaṇa* 1.62.1-26: *Mahābhārata* 1.65.20—1.66.15: *Brahma Purāṇa* 147.5-9: *Devībhāgavata Purāṇa* 1.14.65 ff.: *Padma Purāṇa* 1.56.16-18: *Śiva Purāṇa* 5.4.35-36: *Skanda Purāṇa* 6.42.1—6.44.30: *Abhijñānaśākuntalam* 1.26: *Kathāsaritsāgara* 6.27.1 ff., 6.28.1 ff., 6.32.1 ff.
5. *Rāmāyaṇa* 4.34.6-8.

Kṛpa and Kṛpī.[1] Bharadvāja, when he once went to the river Gaṅgā for ablutions after performing an Agnihotra sacrifice, caught sight of the large-eyed and beautiful Apsaras Ghṛtācī : in his sexual excitement, his seed fell into the water-pot which he was carrying, whence was born Droṇa (or, in one account, Śrutavatī).[2] In such instances, the succumbing to temptation on the part of the Ṛṣi is regarded as a fault and failing : not so much in any moral or ethical sense, but rather because it destroys the power of his *tapas*. Thus it is said that Kāma or lust destroyed Viśvāmitra's *tapas* when he had intercourse with Menakā;[3] similarly, that even Vasiṣṭha—though an elder in age and wisdom—was duped by a woman's love and female charms;[4] and that Kaśyapa, Gautama and Viśvāmitra were all deluded by Śiva's *māyā* or power of illusion when they had intercourse with women.[5] Seen in this light, women are thus cast in the role of evil seductresses, sent to distract the Ṛṣis from their performance of *tapas* : just as it is elsewhere said that Brahmā created women through a magical Atharvan rite in order to make men unrighteous,[6] and that he created not four but five orders of beings—namely, in order of precedence, Brahmins, Kṣatriyas, Vaiśyas, Śūdras, and women.[7] Within these contexts, therefore, the pursuits of ascetic *tapas* and of sexual activities are seen to be mutually opposed and incompatible : for by succumbing to sexual desires and thus directing their energies outwards rather than inwards, the Ṛṣis destroy the powers of their *tapas* and render worthless the merits of their asceticism.

(b) *Asceticism and Marriage*

All of the Ṛṣis married, and in most cases had many wives and children. This at first sight seems a strange contradiction

---

1. *Mahābhārata* 1.57.89-90, 1.120.2-21, 5.54.48, 5.163.20-21: *Bhāgavata Purāṇa* 9.21.34-36: *Śiva Purāṇa* 5.4.32-33: *Kathāsaritsāgara* 6.32.1 ff.
2. *Mahābhārata* 1.57.88-90, 1.121.3-9, 1.154.1-12, 5.54.47-48, 9.47.54.
3. *Padma Purāṇa* 1.56.16-18.
4. *Agni Purāṇa* 353.11.
5. *Śiva Purāṇa* 5.4.28 ff.
6. *Mahābhārata* 13.40.7; see 13.40-49 on women generally.
7. For example *Bhaviṣya Purāṇa* 1.103.24.

to their role as ascetics; Kālidāsa indeed portrays the Seven Ṛṣis as being ashamed of having wives, saying that when Śiva—the foremost of ascetics—became inclined towards marrying Pārvatī and asked the Ṛṣis to obtain her for him, they thereupon gave up their own shame at being married.[1] Another passage similarly relates that the Ṛṣis resorted to the *gārhasthya* or householder state in preference to the ascetic life of the Āśrama *despite* being of great wisdom.[2] The motive for the Ṛṣis' marrying is, however, in nearly every instance not in order to obtain wives or enjoy sexual pleasure, but in order to gain children—just as Agastya obtained Lopāmudrā as his wife only upon the request of his ancestors for offspring.[3] The question of why the ascetic Ṛṣis married and had children must be considered in the light of their being the Mind-born Sons of Brahmā.[4] Brahmā is the god of creation who, by his *tapas*, brought the universe into existence; his very nature is to increase and expand, to propagate and set in motion the cycles of creation. The Ṛṣis, created by him as his Mind-born Sons, share in his nature and are created for the express purpose of continuing and expanding the creative process. Thus, when Brahmā first creates offspring who do not increase or take wives, he curses and abandons them and instead creates the Seven Ṛṣis as Prajāpatis or lords of creation; and at his command, the Ṛṣis marry and beget sons and grandsons.[5] Hence the Ṛṣis—whose very nature is that of movement and change (√ṛṣ), and who even in the Brāhmaṇas are depicted as having brought Prajāpati-Brahmā into existence through their motion and toil[6]—are impelled by their own nature to take part in and continue the cycle of creation. Seen in this light, therefore, their role as *gṛhasthas*—whereby they take wives and beget children, returning to the earth in each Mahāyuga for this very

1. *Kumārasambhava* 6.34.
2. *Devībhāgavata Purāṇa* 1.14.50. ff.
3. *Mahābhārata* 9.94.11-27.
4. For references, see throughout Chapter 1.
5. See for example *Brahmavaivarta Purāṇa* 1.8.1—1.24.10, 4.30.30-35; for more detailed discussion, see Chapter 9.
6. For example *Śatapatha Brāhmaṇa* 6.1.1.1-6, 7.2.3.5, 9.1.2.21, 10.2.2.1; see also Chapter 8.

purpose[1]—is merely an extension of their role as Ṛṣis and Sons of Brahmā.

The same conflict between asceticism and sexuality as we saw in the last sub-section is evident at times also in the married lives of the Ṛṣis.[2] We saw ealier that in many instances the Ṛṣis' wives helped and supported their husbands' performance of *tapas*; and in several instances—especially in the cases of Anasūyā, Ahalyā, Lopāmudrā and Arundhatī—the wives themselves became adepts in *tapas* and even rivalled their husbands in this pursuit. In order to fulfil their sexual role and beget children, however, the Ṛṣis had to leave aside their performance of *tapas*; this could result in a conflicting situation, particularly if the wife wished for intercourse against the inclinations of her Ṛṣi-husband. The case of Agastya and Lopāmudrā is illustrated in a *Ṛgveda* hymn, which is somewhat ambiguous as to whether the wife persuaded the Ṛṣi to have intercourse or whether the Ṛṣi himself desired intercourse[3]—although later versions make it clear that the Ṛṣi himself sought intercourse with his wife,[4] and all versions agree that the Ṛṣi's desire was for children rather than sexual pleasure. Diti, however, once insisted on having intercourse with her husband Kaśyapa before dusk and while the Ṛṣi was still performing *tapas* : Kaśyapa eventually gave in to her wishes, but afterwards cursed that she would give birth to a pair of evil sons—whence she bore Hiraṇyakaśipu and Hiraṇyākṣa.[5] In a number of further instances, sexual conflicts took the form of unfaithfulness on the part of the wife; in such cases the Ṛṣis divorced, cursed or killed their wives for even the slightest suspicion of unchastity. Reṇukā once felt desire for Citraratha the king of the Gandharvas when she saw him bathing and sporting with his wives; she curbed her desire, but her

1. See Chapter 2.
2. On the themes of asceticism and sexuality, particularly in the context of Śaiva mythology, see especially W. D. O'Flaherty, *Asceticism and Eroticism in the Mythology of Śiva*.
3. *Ṛgveda* 1.179.1-6. Discussed in P. Thieme, 'Agastya und Lopāmudrā'.
4. *Bṛhaddevatā* 4.57-58: *Mahābhārata* 3.95.1—3.97.25.
5. *Bhāgavata Purāṇa* 3.14.7—3.17.31.

husband Jamadagni perceived her slight lapse from wifely chastity and angrily ordered his son Rāma to cut off her head—Rāma obeyed, considering his father's word to be more important than his mother's life, but subsequently obtained from Jamadagni the favour that she be brought back to life.[1] In another case, Indra once took the form of Gautama in order to deceive and have intercourse with the Ṛṣi's wife Ahalyā (or, in some versions, he raped her against her will); thereupon the Ṛṣi abandoned Ahalyā and cursed her to be turned to stone, and also cursed Indra to lose his *liṅga*.[2] In both instances, the motive for the Ṛṣis' reaction arises once again from their being upholders and embodiments of *dharma*, whence even the slightest lapse of chastity poses an intolerable threat; thus in one version of the second account, Gautama ordered his son to kill Ahalyā but then relented, ascribing blame to neither her, himself or Indra but rather to the weakness of *dharma*.[3] In similar manner, the Seven Ṛṣis also abandoned their unfaithful wives—in some versions, merely for the suspicion of unchastity. Thus one version tells that when Agni was desirous of having intercourse with the wives of the seven Ṛṣis, Svāhā impersonated six of the wives in turn—excepting Vasiṣṭha's chaste wife Arundhatī—and in that way had intercourse with Agni; thereupon the Ṛṣis, hearing rumours that their wives had been unfaithful, promptly divorced and abandoned the six wives, despite protestations of their innocence by Viśvāmitra who had witnessed the impersonations of Svāhā.[4] In this version, Svāhā subsequently threw the seed of Agni into a lake or river, whence

1. *Mahābhārata* 3.116.1-18: *Bhāgavata Purāṇa* 9.16.1-8: *Devībhāgavata Purāṇa* 2.5.41: *Kāñcipurāṇam* 45.1-3, 46.1-34: Elmore, p. 82-86,94-96: Oppert, pp. 466-467: Whitehead. p. 116; Biardeau (1968) pp. 563-572 & (1970) pp. 286-303.

2. *Rāmāyaṇa* 1.47.13—1.48.10, 7.30.16-37: *Mahābhārata* 12.329.14, 13.138.6: *Brahma Purāṇa* 87.1-70: *Brahmāṇḍa Purāṇa* 1.2.27.22-23: *Brahmavaivarta Purāṇa* 4.47.19-45, 4.61.1-50: *Mārkaṇḍeya Purāṇa* 5.12-13: *Padma Purāṇa* 2.56. 16-18, 5.51.4-50: *Skanda Purāṇa* 5.3.136.1-34, 6.207.5—6.208.96: *Viṣṇudharmottara Purāṇa* 1 28.1 ff.: *Kathāsaritsāgara* 3.17.1 ff.: *Rāmacaritamānasa* 1.210.1-4: *Mṛcchakatika* Act 5: *Irāmāvatāram* 1.9.75-77: Bedi, p. 18: Zvelebil, pp. 212-213.

3 *Mahābhārata* 12.258.7-59.

4. *Śatapatha Brāhmaṇa* 2.1.2.1-5; *Mahābhārata* 3.213.1—3.215.12: *Skanda Purāṇa* 1.2.29.89-123. For the *Mahābhārata* account, see O'Flaherty, *Hindu Myths*, pp. 194-115.

Skanda was born; while in another version, the six wives of the Ṛṣis saw or received Agni's (or Śiva's) seed.[1] In a considerably different and later version, Śiva entered the Pine-Forest in the form of a beautiful youth and seduced the wives of the Ṛṣis—usually with the exceptions of Arundhatī and Anasūyā—whereupon the Ṛṣis divorced their wives and cursed Śiva to lose his *liṅga*.[2] Thus in each of these versions, the wives are accorded varying degrees of innocence or guilt, which in all cases lead to their abandonment by the Ṛṣis.

In several further contexts, the Ṛṣis are depicted as having rebuked or cursed their wives for non-sexual offences. Even the chaste Aruṅdhatī once doubted the word of her husband Vasiṣṭha, because of which she became only a small and sometimes invisible star next to him in the sky;[3] while Marīci cursed his wife Dharmavratā to be turned to stone, when she once stopped massaging his feet in order to honour and worship their visitor Brahmā.[4] In one instance, the opposite state of affairs is said to have occurred : Anasūyā once abandoned her husband Atri in a fit of anger and refused to live under his subjection, and after a *tapas* of fasting and sleeping on wooden boards for 300 years she obtained from Śiva the wish of having a son without sexual intercourse with her husband.[5] This last example again reveals the conflict between the ascetic and married states: where the wife abandons her married state in favour of asceticism yet achieves by doing so the same goal of children as she would otherwise gain through marriage. Once again we see

1. *Brahma Purāṇa* 82.1-15, 123.1-84: *Brahmavaivarta Purāṇa* 4.18.75-131: *Matsya Purāṇa* 158.26-41: *Śiva Purāṇa* 2.4.2.55-67: *Skanda Purāṇa* 1.1.27.44-102, 5.1.34.1-98. *Paripāṭal* 5.26-44. For the *Śiva* account, see O' Flaherty, *Hindu Myths*, pp. 159-168.

2. *Brahmāṇḍa Purāṇa* 1.2.27.1-129: *Devībhāgavata Purāṇa* 4.20.36-37: *Kūrma Purāṇa* 2.37.2-162: *Liṅga Purāṇa* 1.29.1-83, 1.31.21-45: *Sāmba Purāṇa* 16.1 ff.: *Śiva Purāṇa* 2.2.29.22-24: *Skanda Purāṇa* 1.1.6.1-87, 6.1.1-72- *Vāmana Purāṇa* 6.58-67: *Kathāsaritsāgara* 3.20.1 ff.: *Kāñcipurāṇam* 40.5-26: *Kandapurāṇam* 6.13.30-127: *Titruviḷaiyāṭarpurāṇam* 32.1-17. For the *Brahmāṇḍa* account, see O'Flaherty, *Hindu Myths*, p. 141—149: for detailed discussion and further examples, see O'Flaherty, *Asceticism and Eroticism*, pp. 93-110 & 172-209.

3. *Mahābhārata* 1.224.27-31.

4. *Agni Purāṇa* 114.7-25.

5. *Mahābhārata* 13.14.65 ff.: *Śiva Purāṇa* 7.2.15.67-68.

here the dual emphasis both upon the essentially anti-sexual pursuit of asceticism and also upon the wish and need to procreate children, which is resolved in this instance through non-sexual procreation.

A motif which frequently appears is that of the Ṛṣis' receiving wives as gifts. As we saw earlier, kings sometimes gave their daughters to Ṛṣis : as for example king Prasenajit gave Reṇukā to Jamadagni, king Tṛṇabindu gave Ilvalā to Pulastya, and the king of the Vidarbhas gave Lopāmudrā to Agastya. We may also consider in this context the "giving" to a Ṛṣi of a king's wife, in order to procreate offspring—a practice illustrative of the ascetic's supposed sexual potency, derived from the inner heat and power amassed through *tapas*. One passage praises kings who made such donations to the Ṛṣis, including king Marutta son of Karandhama who attained heaven by giving his daughter to Aṅgiras, and king Mitrasaha Saudāsa who similarly attained heaven through giving his wife Madayantī to Vasiṣṭha;[1] and as we saw earlier, this act of Mitrasaha in "giving" his wife to Vasiṣṭha was done expressly in order that the Ṛṣi might beget on her a son for the king. The gift of wives also came about in other ways : thus Viśvāmitra was presented with Mādhavī—on whom the delighted Ṛṣi begot a son Aṣṭaka—by his pupil Gālava;[2] while Pulastya was presented with three Rākṣasa wives—Puṣpotkaṭa, Rākā and Mālinī—by his son or grandson Kuvera, when the latter wished to appease the Ṛṣi's wrath.[3] Above all, however, Dakṣa the son of Brahmā is reputed to have given his daughters to the Ṛṣis. One account relates that he begot sixty daughters, and gave twenty-seven to Soma, thirteen to Kaśyapa, ten to Dharma, four to Ariṣṭanemi, two to Aṅgiras, and two to Kṛśāśva (although slightly different accounts appear on occasions as to the last ten of these).[4] Another account relates that he also

1. *Mahābhārata* 12.226.28.
2. Ibid., 5.117.10-23.
3. Ibid., 3.259.1-8.
4. *Mahābhārata* 1.60.1-15, 12.200.17-28, 12.329.46: *Harivaṃśa* 2.4.7, 3.23-25: *Agni Purāṇa* 18.29-31: *Bhāgavata Purāṇa* 6.6.1-2; *Bhaviṣya Purāṇa* 4.2.24-27: *Brahma Purāṇa* 3.25-28: *Brahmāṇḍa Purāṇa* 1.2.37.44: *Brahmavaivarta Purāṇa*

begot eleven daughters, and gave one to each of the Ṛṣis Marīci, Atri, Aṅgiras, Pulastya, Pulaha, Kratu, Vasiṣṭha, Bhṛgu, and also to Bhava (Śiva), Agni, and the Pitṛs or Ancestors.[1] All of the Purāṇas contain lengthy accounts of the various descendants of each of these Ṛṣis and their wives, and we shall be noting the names of the principal wives and offspring of the Ṛsis in a minute. It need scarcely be pointed out that the very existence of such lengthy accounts of their wives, children and descendants indicates the importance attached to this role of the Ṛṣis as progenitors : a role which we also saw in Chapter 3 to be of great importance in the context of the *gotra* organisation, wherein the Seven Ṛṣis are regarded as the progenitors of the seven main Hindu family-lineages.

The children who were born to the Ṛṣis were sometimes of an evil or disobedient nature : in which cases they incurred the wrath of the Ṛṣi's curse. Thus Viśvāmitra cursed his fifty eldest sons to be outcastes, when they refused to accept his adoption of Śunaḥśepa;[2] while Jamadagni cursed his four eldest sons to be turned to stone (or variantly, to be killed by Rāma) when they refused to obey his command to kill Reṇukā.[3] In many further cases, however, the offspring born to the Ṛṣis were not limited to humans, but included the entire animate creation : gods and demigods, the various classes of demons, birds and beasts, fishes, trees, plants and vegetables. The principal progenitors of such beings were Marīci's son Kaśyapa, and also Pulastya and Pulaha; the names of such offspring will be noted below. We may once again observe here that the bewildering

---

1.9.1-8: *Devībhāgavata Purāṇa* 7.1.34-38: *Garuḍa Purāṇa* 6.1 ff.: *Kūrma Purāṇa* 1.15.4-6: *Liṅga Purāṇa* 1.63.11-15: *Matsya Purāṇa* 4.52-55, 5.12-14, 146.15-17: *Śiva Purāṇa* 2.1.16.26-28, 2.2.14.2-8: *Skanda Purāṇa* 6.22.4-5, 7.1.21.3-5: *Vāyu Purāṇa* 2.40-42: *Viṣṇu Purāṇa* 1.15.1 ff.

1. *Agni Purāṇa* 20.8-17: *Bhāgavata Purāṇa* 3.24.9-25: *Garuḍa Purāṇa* 5.1 ff.: *Kūrma Purāṇa* 1.8.16-19: *Liṅga Purāṇa* 1.5.18-26, 1.70.284-292: *Mārkaṇḍeya Purāṇa* 50.20-25: *Padma Purāṇa* 5.3.175-179: *Śiva Purāṇa* 2.1.16.19-24, 7.1.17.9ff.: *Viṣṇu Purāṇa* 1.7.23-25.

2. *Aitareya Brāhmaṇa* 7.18: *Rāmāyaṇa* 1.61.14-16: *Mahābhārata* 13.3.8: *Bhāgavata Purāṇa* 9.16.28-37; for a general curse, see *Brahma Purāṇa* 104.1-90 *et. al.*

3. *Mahābhārata* 3.116.1-18: *Bhāgavata Purāṇa* 9.16.1-8.

diversity of such offspring is but an extension of the idea that the Ṛṣis are those created by Brahmā in order to continue the cycle of creation which he himself had set in motion : we shall be examining this idea in greater detail in Chapter 9. All of the Trimūrti or three main gods—Brahmā the god of creation, Viṣṇu the god of preservation, and Śiva the god of destruction—are said to have been on one occasion or another either born or reborn of the Ṛṣis. Kaśyapa begot Viṣṇu as one of the twelve Ādityas on his wife Aditi; and just as Jamadagni's son Rāma was one of the *avatāras* or descents among men of Viṣṇu, so too Kaśyapa and Aditi gave birth to Viṣṇu in several of his *avatāras*. Pleased with their *tapas* for a son to destroy the demon Bali, Viṣṇu agreed to become their son as the Vāmana or dwarf;[1] while Kaśyapa and Aditi are said to have been reborn as Vasudeva and Devakī in order to bear Viṣṇu as Vāsudeva-Kṛṣṇa[2] and as Daśaratha and Kauśalyā in order to bear him as Rāma.[3] At Kaśyapa's request, Śiva also agreed to become his son, and was reborn as the eleven Rudras through Kaśyapa's wife Surabhi.[4] When Atri and Anasūyā sought through *tapas* to obtain a son, the Trimūrti were pleased with their asceticism and consented to become their sons—whence were born Brahmā as Soma, Viṣṇu as Datta son of Atri or Dattātreya, and Śiva as Durvāsas.[5] In giving birth to such divine sons—as well as to all other levels and orders of creation—the Ṛṣis are not merely

1. *Mahābhārata* 12.326.75: *Agni Purāṇa* 4.6-7, 276.14: *Bhāgavata Purāṇa* 8.16.19: *Brahmāṇḍa Purāṇa* 2.3.3.117-118: *Devībhāgavata Purāṇa* 3.16.43-44, 4.16.12-13: *Kūrma Purāṇa* 1.16.41 ff.: *Matsya Purāṇa* 244.41-52: *Nārada Purāṇa* 1.10.4, 1.11.70-80: *Padma Purāṇa* 5.25.1-70, 6.266-267: *Vāmana Purāṇa* 50.46 ff., *saromāhātmya* 3.6—9.44: *Vāyu Purāṇa* 2.5.131: *Kāñcipurāṇam* 56.2-3.

2. *Harivaṃśa* 45.20-45: *Agni Purāṇa* 276.1-2: *Bhaviṣya Purāṇa* 4.55.34: *Brahmāṇḍa Purāṇa* 2.3.71.237-238: *Brahmavaivarta Purāṇa* 2.49.50, 4.7.1 ff.: *Devībhāgavata Purāṇa* 4.2.41—4.3.17, 4.10.33-37, 4.20.60-62: *Matsya Purāṇa* 47.8-10, 47.30-35: *Padma Purāṇa* 5.13.148-150 : *Mahābhāgavata Purāṇa* 50.1 ff.

3. *Rāmacaritamānasa* 1.122.2.

4. *Śiva Purāṇa* 3.18.2-29.

5. *Bhāgavata Purāṇa* 1.3.11, 2.7.4, 4.1.15-33: *Devībhāgavata Purāṇa* 4.16.6-9: *Mārkaṇḍeya Purāṇa* 16.70—17.11: *Śiva Purāṇa* 3.19.2-27, 5.2.18-19: *Skanda Purāṇa* 5.3.103.1-109. For the later version where they are born as a curse, see Chapter 5 section C (d) ii.

portrayed as being of supreme virtue and merit. For it is indeed on account of the purity and strength of the Ṛṣis' *tapas* that the gods consent to become their sons : and we have here once again the idea that it is only through rigid and single-minded devotion to asceticism—involving the denial and sublimation of all sexual activities in order to build up the maximum amount of inner heat—that the greatest creative potency and power can be obtained.

(c) *The Principal Wives and Children of the Ṛṣis*

All of the main Purāṇas—as well as several passages in the Epics—go into considerable detail in listing the genealogies of the Ṛṣis; like the similar genealogies in Vedic literature, these in many cases seek to trace lines of descent right down to the period of their composition in the early centuries of the Christian era. The task of charting all such descendants would itself virtually require writing another Purāṇa;[1] but we shall here limit ourselves to the more moderate task of listing the names of the wives of the Ṛṣis, together with those of the children born to them. The sources from which these are taken are primarily the Epics and Purāṇas : many of the names have already been met with earlier in this chapter, and others may be found especially in the contexts cited in the last sub-section. A number of differences occur between different texts, but in the following account, in order not to overburden the reader with a plethora of names and variants, we shall simply note the names of the wives and children which appear most frequently.

Marīci married Sambhūti the daughter of Dakṣa, and begot on her a son Pūrṇimāsa (or a daughter Pūrṇimā). He also married Dharmavratā, whom he later cursed, and Urṇā, who bore him six sons who were cursed by Brahmā. He also married Kālā, and according to some accounts, it was on her that he begot his son *Kaśyapa*.

1. For attempted reconstructions, see especially F. E. Pargiter, *Ancient Indian Historical Tradition*: V. Rahurkar, *The Seers of the Ṛg Veda*: P. Bhargava, *India in the Vedic Age*, pp. 166-192: D. C. Sircar (ed.), *The Bharata War and Purāṇic Genealogies*.

Kaśyapa married thirteen daughters of Dakṣa. Their names, together with their offspring, are usually given as follows : 1. Aditi begot the twelve Ādityas (gods : Viṣṇu, Indra, Vivasvat—whose son Manu Vaivasvata was the progenitor of the human race—Mitra, Varuṇa, Pūṣan, Tvaṣṭṛ, Bhāga, Aryaman, Dhātṛ, Vidhātṛ or Savitṛ, and Aṃśa); 2. Diti begot the Daityas (demon-enemies of the gods), foremost among whom were Hiraṇyakaśipu, Hiraṇyākṣa and Ilvala; 3. Danu begot the Dānavas (demon-enemies of the gods); 4. Vinatā begot the celestial birds Garuḍa and Aruṇa; 5. Kadrū begot the Nāgas or snakes, foremost among whom was Vāsuki; 6. Surabhi begot buffaloes and cattle, as also the eleven Rudras; 7. Krodhavaśā (or Krodhā) begot snakes, Piśācas (goblins), and sharp-toothed creatures; 8. Ariṣṭhā (or Variṣṭhā) begot Gandharvas (celestial musicians); 9. Muni begot Apsarases (celestial water-nymphs); 10. Irā (or Ilā) begot vegetables and trees; 11. Tāmrā begot hawks, moths, vultures, parrots and other birds; 12. Surasā (or Suravā, or Siṃhikā) begot demons, including Namuci and Vātāpi; 13. Timi begot water-creatures. The names of the 12th and 13th wives in particular are often altered : other names which appear in their place are Saramā, Kālā, Viśvā, Khoṣā, Tviṣā, Kāṣṭā, Idaśā, Pradhā, Khagā, Svadhā, Danāyu, Anāyu, and Adāyu.

Kaśyapa was also the progenitor of two sons Vatsara and Asita; and several accounts relate that he also married Asiknī the daughter of Vīraṇa, on whom he begot Nārada.

Aṅgiras married Smṛti the daughter of Dakṣa, and begot four daughters Sinīvālī, Kuhu, Rākā and Anumati. He also married Śubhā (Śraddhā, Svadhā), and begot variously six, seven or eight offspring, foremost of whom were two sons Bṛhaspati and Utathya. Bṛhaspati had intercourse with Utathya's wife Mamatā, and begot Dīrghatamas who became *Gautama* (or variantly, Dīrghatamas the father of Gautama); while Bṛhaspati was also the father of *Bharadvāja* (in some accounts, also through intercourse with his brother's wife).

Gautama married Ahalyā, and begot a son Śatānanda. He also begot the twins Kṛpa and Kṛpī, when his seed fell at the sight of an Apsaras.

Bharadvāja married Vīrā, and begot a son Vīra or Yavakrīta. He also begot a son Droṇa and a daughter Śaradvatī (who became the wife of Indra) when his seed fell at the sight of the Apsaras Ghṛtācī.

Bhṛgu married Khyāti the daughter of Dakṣa, and begot two sons Dhātṛ and Vidhātṛ, and also a daughter Śrī or Lakṣmī who became the wife of Viṣṇu. He also married Pulomā, and begot a son Cyavana; according to some accounts, Cyavana begot Aurva who was the father of Ṛcīka : Ṛcīka married Satyavatī the daughter of Gādhi, and through Bhṛgu's help Satyavatī begot *Jamadagni* while her mother begot *Viśvāmitra.*

Jamadagni married Reṇukā, and begot five sons, of whom Paraśurāma ("Rāma with the axe") or Rāma was the youngest.

Viśvāmitra in some accounts married Dhṛti, although more usually the name of his wife is not given. He begot 101 sons, and adopted Śunaḥśepa or Devarāta; in some accounts, Gālava also appears as one of his sons. He also married Mādhavī, and begot a son Aṣṭaka; and he additionally begot Śakuntalā on the Apsaras Menakā.

Atri married Anasūyā the daughter of Dakṣa, and begot three sons Soma, Datta (Dattātreya) and Durvāsas. He also married a further ten wives including Bhadrā (in some accounts, Soma is the son of Bhadrā), and begot on them the Svastyātreyas.

Vasiṣṭha married Ūrjā the daughter of Dakṣa, and begot seven sons known as the Seven Vāsiṣṭha Ṛṣis (see Chapter 2). He also married Arundhatī, and begot 100 sons, the eldest of whom was Śakti; Śakti in turn begot Parāśara, whose son was Kṛṣṇa Dvaipāyana or Vedavyāsa. He also begot a son Aśmaka on Madayantī the wife of Mitrasaha Saudāsa.

Pulastya married Prīti the daughter of Dakṣa, and begot a son Dattoli (who in a previous birth had been *Agastya*). He also married Havirbhū (who in some accounts is the mother of both Dattoli and Viśravas) and Ilavilā; in some accounts he begot Vaiśravaṇa on Ilavilā, while in most accounts he begot Viśravas, who married Iḍaviḍā and begot Vaiśravaṇa or Kuvera (the god of wealth), from whom the Yakṣas (rural demi-gods) were descended. He also married three wives Puṣpotkaṭā, Rākā and Mālinī, from whom were descended the Rākṣasas (flesh-eating demons), the foremost of whom was Rāvaṇa (begotten on Puṣpotkaṭā). In several accounts he also begot Gandharvas, Piśācas, Kinnaras (creatures half-man half-beast), monkeys, snakes, and ghosts.

Pulaha married Kṣamā the daughter of Dakṣa, and begot three sons Kardama (Karman), Sahiṣṇu, and Arvavīra (Varīyas). In some accounts, he married Gati who bore him these three sons; while he also begot such offspring as Kinnaras or Kiṃpuruṣas, Piśācas, ghosts, snakes, monkeys, wolves, elephants, lions, tigers, bears, and deer.

Kratu married Sannati the daughter of Dakṣa, and begot the 60,000 Vālakhilyas (attendants of the sun's chariot). Some accounts give his wife as Kriyā; and some relate that he remained *ūrdhvaretas* with neither wife nor children, although this is usually related of the Vālakhilyas.

Agastya married Lopāmudrā, and begot a son Dṛḍhāsyu or Dṛḍhacyūta. According to some accounts, he had further sons including Idhmabāhu, who were adopted by Pulastya, Pulaha and Kratu.

(d) *Conclusion*

Having now surveyed the main types of activities in which the Ṛṣis engaged on earth, we are in a position to assess the significance of the different roles ascribed to the Ṛṣis, in an attempt to define the very meaning of the term *ṛṣi*. First and foremost, a Ṛṣi is one who seeks to bring about a change—a transformation both of himself and also of his environment. He is one who devotes himself to rigorous ascetic pursuits in order to build up his inner reserves of energy and heat, and who becomes like a power-house of potent energy, throbbing and vibrating through the heat of his austerities. He becomes an embodiment of fire, rivalling and surpassing even Agni himself: this is the direct result of his self-heating through *tapas*, and it gives him particular power which he uses in two ways. On the one hand, he uses it to achieve contact with the divine: by constantly and resolutely directing the power inwards, he becomes equal to the gods and conquers their realms—just as he also uses the external heat of sacrifice to attain heaven, and "sees" and chants hymns like *mantras* of inner potency to enable him to reach this goal. In attaining this contact with the divine, he merges with the divine and realises his own true nature or Self: which for the Ṛṣi is the realisation of his nature as a son of Brahmā, the creator. This in turn leads to his other use of his inner power: for as a son of the creator, his role is to continually create and re-create, to expand and transform the worlds; it is for this task that he marries and procreates children, giving birth to the entire animate creation. In doing so, his powers are directed outwards towards the world: he is concerned not merely with procreation, but with the maintenance of *dharma*, the correct ordering of the worlds—he instructs men in *dharma* or the correct performance of the duties allotted to them, and when the limits of *dharma* are overstepped by either gods, demons or men, he himself redresses the balance with his fiery curses. Thus even this seemingly destructive power is ultimately used by the Ṛṣi for creative ends: the destruction of evil being in such cases necessary for the creation and preservation of good. He indulges in sexual activities in order to expand the creative process; yet he derives his power for sexual creation from his pursuit of asceticism and *tapas*, and it is only because he is an ascetic that he can also generate creation. For in this respect he combines within himself both the ascetic and the erotic, the divine and the worldly: his pursuit of asceticism is ultimately not a denial but an affirmation of the world, since both the ascetic and the erotic are but different aspects of his own dynamically creative and transformative nature, shared with and inherited from the creator himself. Only by turning inwards and generating power through *tapas* within himself can the Ṛṣi then direct this power towards either heaven or earth; thus when the Ṛṣi turns his back on the world to pursue *tapas*, his aim is to increase his own powers which enable him not merely to attain contact with the divine for its own sake but also to establish divine order throughout the worlds. The Ṛṣi is thus one whose attention is towards both heaven and earth, gods and men: through his *tapas* he seeks both attainment of the divine and also—as a son of the creator—fulfilment of his own nature as an integral and necessary actor in the creative process. For the Ṛṣi these two aims are not opposed but complementary—only through the renunciation of sexuality and the pursuit of asceticism does he attain the divine, while conversely it is only through the pursuit of asceticism and the subsequent realisation of unity with the creator that he is enabled to act as the supreme sexual progenitor of all animate creation.

7

THE SEVEN ṚṢIS IN THE SKY

A. Introduction

The idea of the Seven Ṛṣis as stars in the sky is—as we noted in Chapter 5—but an extension of the idea that, through performing sacrifice and *tapas*, they attained Svarga-loka (heaven, the sky) or Brahmaloka (the realm of Brahmā). It is once again through their fiery nature—through the fire of *tapas* amassed from ascetic austerities—that they attain such a goal: just as fire itself ascends from earth to the sky, and Agni (the fire personified) conveys the sacrifices of men to the gods, thereby acting as a mediator between earth and heaven, between men and the gods. In this chapter we shall therefore examine firstly the means whereby the Seven Ṛṣis attain their place in the sky, and then look at various other topics associated with their role as stars in the sky.

B. Transference to the Sky

(a) *Transference through Sacrifice or Agni*

In Vedic literature—especially in the Vedic *saṃhitās* and the Brāhmaṇas—Agni or Fire not only conveys the sacrifices of men to the gods: he is also the means whereby first the gods and then the Ṛṣis attain a place in the sky or heaven (Svar, Svargaloka, Suvargaloka, Div, Devaloka, and similar). Thus it is related in various places that the gods went to heaven by means of Agni or Fire,[1] or by means of sacrifice;[2] while the myth—cycle of the Ādityas (gods) and the Aṅgirases relates in many varied forms how first the gods and then the Aṅgirases or Ṛṣis attained heaven through performing sacrifice. The basic account simply states that they both attained heaven through this means:

> The Ādityas and Aṅgirases used to be here (on earth); they formerly offered sacrifice with Agni to Agni, and went to Svarga Loka.[3]

A great many variant themes appear in different contexts. Several accounts relate that the Ādityas, having attained heaven through sacrifice, gave to the Aṅgirases as *dakṣiṇā* or sacrificial fee the sun in the form of a white horse— this being yet another form of fire,[4] through which the Aṅgirases themselves might attain heaven :

> The Ādityas and the Aṅgirases contended over going to Svarga Loka; the Ādityas performed sacrifice with Agni, giving the sun which had become a white horse: and so the Ādityas went to Svarga Loka, and the Aṅgirases were left behind.[5]

Such accounts frequently add that "he who offers this sacrifice will himself attain heaven". A great many further accounts expand upon this same basic theme,[6] and also relate how individual Aṅgirases attained heaven or the sky.[7] In other places it is

---

1. For example *Taittirīya Saṃhitā* 5.3.9: *Atharvaveda* 4.11.6.
2. For example *Taittirīya Saṃhitā* 6.3.4: *Śatapatha Brāhmaṇa* 1.6.2.1.
3. *Aitareya Brāhmaṇa* 1.16: *Āpastamba Śrauta Sūtra* 24.12.7: *Āśvalāyana Śrauta Sūtra* 1.3.28.
4. See *Śatapatha Brāhmaṇa* 2.6.3.9, 7.3.2.12 ff.
5. *Aitareya Brāhmaṇa* 6.34-35: *Jaiminīya Brāhmaṇa* 2.115-117, 2.122-124: *Kauṣītaki Brāhmaṇa* 30.6: *Pañcaviṃśa Brāhmaṇa* 16.12.1-4: *Śatapatha Brāhmaṇa* 3.5.1.13-23: *Taittirīya Brāhmaṇa* 3.9.21.1: *Śāṅkhāyana Śrauta Sūtra* 12.19.1-5.
6. *Maitrāyaṇī Saṃhitā* 3.6.7, 3.8.4: *Taittirīya Saṃhitā* 2.6.3.2-4, 3.1.9, 5.2.8.4-5, 5.4.2, 5.4.3, 5.7.2, 6.1.1, 6.1.3, 6.2.6: *Atharvaveda* 18.1.61: *Aitareya Brāhmaṇa* 4.17, 4.32, 5.14: *Jaiminīya Brāhmaṇa* 1.224: *Kauṣītaki Brāhmaṇa* 18.10: *Pañcaviṃśa Brāhmaṇa* 16.14.2, 24.2.2, 24.16.2: *Śatapatha Brāhmaṇa* 12.2.2.9 ff.: *Śāṅkhāyana Śrauta Sūtra* 14.40.1.
7. *Taittirīya Saṃhitā* 7.1.4: *Aitareya Brāhmaṇa* 3.24: *Jaiminīya Brāhmaṇa* 1.183, 2.235, 3.56, 3.76-77, 3.216: *Pañcaviṃśa Brāhmaṇa* 8.9.5, 12.3.23, 12.5.16,

related how the Ṛṣis in general attained heaven through fire or sacrifice—the two being virtually synonymous, inasmuch as the central feature of sacrifice was the kindling of sacred fire. Sometimes it is said that when the gods went to heaven they hid the sacrifice in the *yūpa* or sacrificial post, where it was subsequently found by the Ṛṣis:

> The gods went to Svarga Loka through sacrifice; they thought "Men will follow us", and so they hid it in the *yūpa* and went to Svarga Loka. The Ṛṣis discovered that sacrifice through the *yūpa*.[1]

On other occasions, the Ṛṣis discovered the sacrifice in a different form:

> The gods went to heaven through sacrifice; thinking, "How can we hide this from men ?" they hid the essence [*rasa*] of the sacrifice as a bee hides its honey, they concealed the sacrifice in the *yūpa* and became invisible. The Ṛṣis chanted and exerted themselves, seeking to follow the gods to heaven. They saw the sacrificial offering crawling in the form of a tortoise [*kūrma*], and thought, "This is the sacrifice"; they commanded it to stand still in honour of Agni, which it did, and they sacrificed it and thereby gained their wish.[2]

Fire itself is compounded of both heat and light; and in some cases it is said to be through light that the Ādityas and Aṅgirases attained heaven.[3] One passage similarly relates that heaven is attained through light:

> When the Aṅgirases were going to heaven, the fulfilment of sacrifice was taken by the Ṛṣis; that became gold, and it is through golden light that he [the sacrificer] goes to heaven.[4]

12.6.12, 12.11.10-11, 13.11.22, 14.5.25, 14.10.9, 15.5.11, 20.11.3-4. It is to be noted that in such accounts, the form "Aṅgirases" usually appears in place of "Āṅgirasas".

1. *Taittirīya Saṃhitā* 6.3.4.
2. *Śatapatha Brāhmaṇa* 1.6.2.1-7.
3. For example *Taittirīya Saṃhitā* 5.7.2.2.
4. *Taittirīya Saṃhitā* 5.4.2.3-4.

As we saw in Chapter 5, the Ṛṣis attain heaven not only through the external fire of sacrifice, but also through the amassing of internal fire and heat through *tapas*. One passage thus relates that the Ṛṣis attained heaven through the performance of various ascetic pursuits;

> The Ṛṣis strove for Svargaloka through exertion [*śrama*], tapas, and the performance of vows [*vratacaryā*]; they desired "When we have created children in this world, may we go to Svargaloka"; and when they had created children, they went to Svargaloka.[1]

In many cases, the attainments of Svargaloka or Brahmaloka are synonymous: the latter frequently being their goal in post-Vedic literature. Vedic literature generally conceives of there being only three worlds or lokas, namely Bhūr (the earth), Bhuvar (the atmosphere), and Svar (the sky), of which Svar or Svarga is the highest world. The Epics and Purāṇas, on the other hand, visualise another four worlds as being above these three, namely Mahar, Jana, Tapas, and Brahma Lokas; thus giving a total of seven worlds, of which Brahmaloka is the highest.[2] In both canceptions, therefore, the Ṛṣis are visualised as attaining the highest of all the worlds—although as stars, they are always said to reside in Svargaloka or the sky. Thus one Purāṇic passage relates that the Seven Ṛṣis went to Div or the sky at a *tīrtha* called *svargamārgaprada*, or "that which bestows the path to Svarga";[3] while an Epic passage seemingly compounds the two highest Lokas, in relating that the Seven Ṛṣis performed *tapas* on earth in order to attain Brahmaloka, and finally achieving their goal they went to Svarga.[4] In further contexts throughout the Epics and Purāṇas, the Seven Ṛṣis are frequently depicted as having their abode in Brahmaloka;[5] and as we saw in Chapter 2, they are also said (within

1. *Jaiminīya Brāhmaṇa* 2.218-221.
2. On Indian cosmogony in general, see especially R. Gombrich, 'Ancient Indian Cosmologies', and W. Kirfel, *Die Kosmographie der Inder*; on astronomy, G. R. Kaye, *Hindu Astronomy*, and O. Neugebauer, 'Tamil Astronomy'.
3. *Brahmāṇḍa Purāṇa* 2.3.13.62: *Vāyu Purāṇa* 2.15.60.
4. *Mahābhārata* 13.94.2—13.95.86.
5. For example *Rāmāyaṇa* 7.33.20: *Mahābhārata* 7.164.86-89.

the Manvantara tradition) to reside in Maharloka and to move to Janaloka during the fire and flood at the end of each Kalpa.[1]

It is not only the Seven Ṛṣis who—like the gods—are said to have attained transference to the sky through sacrifice and *tapas*. The same goal is also said to have been attained by others—either by performing the same sacrifice as the Ṛṣis, or through *tapas*, or through performing good deeds. Thus when Arjuna travelled through Svarga or the sky, he realised that what are seen from the earth as stars were in fact the self-illumined bodies of Ṛṣis and heroes—their bodies illumined by the fires of their ascetic merit :

> Those who have attained virtue shine there (in the sky) through their own radiance, and are seen here (on earth) in the form of shining stars. Arjuna saw hundreds of royal Ṛṣis, *siddhas*, and heroes killed in battle, who had conquered Svarga through *tapas*, and who were illumined by their own powers and lustre. O Pārtha, these men of good deeds are established through their own powers, and they are seen on earth in the form of stars.[2]

Further passages similarly relate that a man who performs a particular sacrifice will go to Svarga and become a bright and shining object, and that it is the bodies of men of good deeds and *tapas* which shine brightly in the sky.[3] We may again recall here that Viśvāmitra, by means of a sacrifice, transferred king Triśaṅku to Svarga in bodily form : where he now shines as the constellation Orion.[4] All such instances therefore illustrate that the Ṛṣis attained their transference to the sky through Fire : either (especially in Vedic literature) in the external form of sacrifice, or (especially in the Epics and Purāṇas) in the internal form of *tapas*.

---

1. See also section C (c) of this chapter.
2. *Mahābhārata* 3.43.29-35.
3. For example *Taittirīya Saṃhitā* 5.3.9: *Āpastamba Dharma Sūtra* 2.9.24. 12-14.
4. See Chapter 5 section C (c) and Chapter 6 sections A (b) and (f).

(b) *Tapas as Fire*

An association between the Ṛṣis and Agni/Fire is evident from the very earliest times. In the *Ṛgveda*, the birth and kindling of Agni is frequently ascribed to Aṅgiras,[1] Bhṛgu,[2] Atharvan[3] and their descendants; it is similarly related that the Seven Ṛṣis kindled and gave birth to Agni[4]—all of which may be associated with the ritual kindling of fire in the context of the sacrificial cult. Conversely, both Bhṛgu and Aṅgiras are said to have been born from the sacrificial fire into which the seed of Prajāpati had been shed[5]—just as all the Ṛṣis are said in later literature to have been born in this way.[6] Agni is said to "possess" the Seven Ṛṣis, as he possesses seven tongues and seven dear abodes;[7] he is also frequently identified with Aṅgiras, and called both a Ṛṣi and the first Aṅgiras.[8] In a Brāhmaṇa passage, the Seven Ṛṣis are said to constitute the very essence of Agni :

> The Ṛṣis, as the *prāṇas* [vital airs[9]], formerly made up [*samaskurvan*] Agni; because in the beginning they made a share [*bhāgam*] in him, for that reason they were formerly the parts [*bhāgāḥ*] of him.[10]

All of these examples are taken from early Vedic literature; and they imply an early identification and connection between

1. *Ṛgveda* 1.83.4, 5.11.6.
2. Ibid., 1.58.6, 1.143.4, 2.4.2, 3.5.10, 4.7.1, 6.15.2, 10.46.2-9.
3. Ibid., 6.15.17, 6.16.13-14, 10.21.5.
4. *Atharvaveda* 11.1.1-3.
5. *Aitareya Brāhmaṇa* 3.34: *Jaiminīya Brāhmaṇa* 3.263: *Śatapatha Brāhmaṇa* 4.5.1.8.
6. *Mahābhārata* 13.85.15 ff.: *Brahmāṇḍa Purāṇa* 2.3.1.34-46: *Matsya Purāṇa* 195.6-16: *Vāyu Purāṇa* 2.4.34-47: *Nirukta* 3.17: *Bṛhaddevatā* 5.97-101.
7. *Maitrāyaṇī Saṃhitā* 1.6.2: *Taittirīya Saṃhitā* 1.5.3: *Vājasaneyi Saṃhitā* 17.79.
8. *Ṛgveda* 1.31.1, 1.31.17, 1.75.2, 4.3.15, 4.9.7, 5.8.4, 5.10.7, 5.11.6, 5.21.1, 6.2.10, 6.16.11, 8.60.2, 8.74. 11, 8.75.5, 8.84.8, 8.102.17 : *Maitrāyaṇī Saṃhitā* 1.7.1, 2.7.4, 2.7.6, 2.7.8, 2.13.7, 3.1.3: *Taittirīya Saṃhitā* 1.2.12, 1.3.14, 2.5.8, 2.6.11, 4.1.4, 4.2.1, 4.4.4, 5.1.5, 6.2.7: *Vājasaneyi Saṃhitā* 11.45, 12.117, 15.28, 34.12: *Śatapatha Brāhmaṇa* 1.4.1.25, 3.5.1.32, 6.1.4.4, 6.3.1.38-41, 6.3.3.3-4, 6.4.1.1-2, 6.4.4.14, 6.7.3.6, 7.3.2.8: *et. al.*
9. See Chapter 8.
10. *Śatapatha Brāhmaṇa* 7.2.3.5, 9.1.2.21.

Agni and the Ṛṣis, wherein Agni/Fire is seen as a constituent element within the nature of the Ṛṣis.

As we have already seen in Chapters 5 and 6, the same is the case in the Ṛṣis' performance of *tapas*. There frequently occur incidents—particularly throughout the Epics and Purāṇas—which demonstrate explicitly the nature of the Ṛṣis as embodiments of Fire through *tapas*; and while it is impossible to deal here with all of these, we shall refer to a limited number of examples which will serve to illustrate the fiery nature of the Ṛṣis.

On many occasions, reference is made to the *tejas*—the glaring fiery energy—of the Ṛṣis, produced from and an external manifestation of their *tapas*. When Viśvāmitra performed severe *tapas* in order to become a *brahma*-Ṛṣi, the gods went in distress to Brahmā to voice their fears to him :

> "The three worlds are troubled, and the sun in dimmed by Viśvāmitra, who has become brilliant and taken the form of Agni; just as the three worlds were in former times burnt by Kālāgni ["The Fire of Time", the fire which destroys the worlds at the end of each Kalpa], so too in our opinion will Viśvāmitra destroy the realm of the gods."[1]

In a similar manner, when Indra asked the Apsaras Menakā to seduce Viśvāmitra in order to destroy the powers of the Ṛṣi's *tapas*, she fearfully reminded him of the Ṛṣi's fiery nature :

> "He is one possessed of great *tapas* and *tejas*; he can burn the worlds with his fiery energy, and shake the earth with his foot; he can hurl down great Mt. Meru, and repidly move around it. How can a girl like me touch such a one who, engaged in *tapas*, has conquered his senses and burns like fire—who has a mouth radiant with fire, and the sun and moon for his eyes ?"[2]

Viśvāmitra's arch-rival Vasiṣṭha was similarly possessed of a fiery nature from his ascetic pursuits : so much so that when

1. *Rāmāyaṇa* 1.64.5-18.
2. *Mahābhārata* 1.65.27-38.

he sought in grief to kill himself after his sons had been slain by king Mitrasaha Saudāsa, his own nature prevented this :

> Having kindled a fire in the forest, Vasiṣṭha entered it; but although the flames were strong, Agni/the fire did not burn him, but became cold in his presence. Then the Ṛṣi saw a river flowing from the Himālayas, filled with fierce crocodiles, and threw himself into its torrential current; but the river, thinking that the Ṛṣi was Agni, fled away in a hundred directions [*śatadhā*]—that is why it is called the Śatadru.[1]

The river Śatadru was not the only one to mistake a Ṛṣi for Agni. Aṅgiras is said to have once taken the place of Agni in the latter's absence; and on his return, Agni thought that a second Agni had been created by Brahmā :

> Once Agni went in anger to a wood to perform *tapas*. Then lord Aṅgiras himself became Agni, heating the worlds through his radiance and destroying darkness—the Āśrama-dweller even excelled Agni, and illumined the whole world. While performing *tapas*, Agni was heated by the Ṛṣi's *tejas*; he thought that Brahmā had installed another Agni in the worlds, and that his own Agni-hood had been destroyed while he was performing *tapas*. Wondering how he could again become Agni, he saw the Ṛṣi heating the worlds like Agni; he slowly crawled towards him in fear, but Aṅgiras told him that he should again become Agni and resume his former place.[2]

We noted earlier that Agni—in his form as Kālāgni—burns the worlds and consumes the waters of the earth during the dissolution of the three worlds at the end of each Kalpa. In a similar manner it is related of Agastya that through his *tapas* he drank the waters of the oceans at the request of the gods, digesting them in a single gulp;[3] as did also Aṅgiras, drinking them by the

1. *Mahābhārata* 1.166.42—1.167.9.
2. Ibid., 3.207.6-20: compare also 3.212.1-30.
3. Ibid., 3.101.1—3.103.19: *Agni Purāṇa* 206.1-12: *Brahmavaivarta Purāṇa* 2.56.1 ff. : *Devībhāgavata Purāṇa* 6.9.388: *Matsya Purāṇa* 61.36-43: *Padma Purāṇa*

power of his *tejas* as if they were milk, and not even sating his thirst after doing so.[1] The Ṛṣis are also depicted on several occasions as literally burning their enemies—especially demons—with the fire of their anger, and reducing them to ashes. Thus Agastya burnt Ilvala to ashes with a single fiery glance,[2] and burnt the Dānavas with the fire of his wrath;[3] while Vasiṣṭha similarly burnt the Dānavas in order to rescue the gods,[4] and Bhṛgu's son Cyavana at birth consumed the demon Puloman to ashes at the very sight of him.[5] In all such instances, the fire which bursts forth from the Ṛṣis is that which has been amassed through their *tapas*; and their building-up of ascetic heat through austerities is seen to radiate from them as *tejas* or fiery energy—powerful enough to heat or burn the worlds, as also to illumine them and to lighten their darkness.

(c) *The Ṛṣis as the Sun*

We have already noted several examples where Ṛṣis are said to take the place of the sun: notably in the cases of Aṅgiras—who, taking the place of Agni, heated the worlds and destroyed their darkness—and of Viśvāmitra—who is said to have the sun and moon for his eyes, and to dim the brilliance of the sun with his own lustre. In many further instances, the brilliance of the Ṛṣis is likened to that of the sun, and they are described as burning like the sun. Thus Viśvāmitra is said to have gained the brilliance of the sun with his *tejas*,[6] and Vasiṣṭha, when ascending to the sun in order to obtain the sun's daughter for king Saṃvaraṇa, is himself described as possessing the brilliance of the sun and as even transcending the splendour of the sun.[7] We may

---

5.19.159-166: *Saura Purāṇa* 47.63ff.: *Skanda Purāṇa* 6.34.1-59: *Viṣṇudharmottara Purāṇa* 1.213.1 ff.: *Bṛhat-saṃhitā* 12.1-5: *Rāmacaritamānasa* 1.31.3, 1.255.4: *Tiruviḷaiyāṭarpurāṇam* 1.15-58.

1. *Mahābhārata* 13.138.3-4, 13.139.9-30.
2. *Rāmāyaṇa* 3.10.53-64.
3. *Mahābhārata* 13.140.1-14.
4. Ibid., 13.140.15 ff.
5. Ibid., 1.5.11—1.6.13.
6. Ibid., 9.39.26-27.
7. Ibid., 1.162.10—1.163.10: see also 12.291.7-9, 12.337.47.

also recall here that each of the twelve main Ṛṣis is depicted as occupying a place in the sun's chariot during one of the twelve months of the year;[1] while Yāska identifies the Seven Ṛṣis with the rays of the sun,[2] and a further passage relates that the sun becomes Aṅgiras in the after-part of the night and Bhṛgu at the time of the Agnihotra.[3] In all such contexts, therefore, the Ṛṣis are either identified or closely associated with the sun; and since the sun itself is often visualised as but another form of Agni or fire, the identification of the Ṛṣis with the sun is merely complementary to their identity with Agni —the essence of both Agni and the sun being identical with that of the Ṛṣis themselves.

In further contexts, two Ṛṣis in particular—namely Atri and Kaśyapa—are said to have either become or taken the place of the sun. In the *Ṛgveda*, the Aṅgirases are said to have discovered day and let the sun climb to heaven;[4] while Atri is similarly said to have found and replaced the sun when it was afflicted by Svarbhānu (the demon of eclipses):

> The demon Svarbhānu struck the sun with darkness; Indra destroyed him, and Atri found the hidden sun—Atri placed the eye of the sun in the sky.[5]

Other Vedic versions similarly relate that Atri conducted the sun back to the sky, and repelled the darkness by his speech.[6] Some later versions in the Purāṇas relate Atri's rescue of the sun in a similar way, often adding that Atri himself spread brilliance, and that he stopped the sun from falling by uttering the words "may all be well with you" (*svasti te'stu*).[7] In other versions, however, it is said that Atri himself took the place

1. See Chapter 1 section E.
2. *Nirukta* 4.27, 12.37.
3. *Jaiminīya Upaniṣad Brāhmaṇa* 4.5.3.
4. *Ṛgveda* 1.62.5, 1.71.2, 10.62.3.
5. Ibid., 5.40.6-9.
6. *Atharvaveda* 13.2.4-36: *Gopatha Brāhmaṇa* 1.2.17: *Kauṣītaki Brāhmaṇa* 24.3: *Pañcaviṃśa Brāhmaṇa* 6.6.8-10, 14.11.14: *Śatapatha Brāhmaṇa* 4.3.4.21.
7. *Brahma Purāṇa* 13.9-11: *Brahmāṇḍa Purāṇa* 2.3.8.76-79: *Liṅga Purāṇa* 2.63.71-73: *Skanda Purāṇa* 7.1.20.42-44.

of the sun, and became the sun. One Epic passage relates that Atri is he who, when the sun was destroyed, himself ascended upwards;[1] while another passage relates that he became both the sun and the moon:

> Svarbhānu pierced the sun and moon with arrows, whereupon the gods were engulfed in darkness and began to be struck down by the demons. They caught sight of Atri performing *tapas* in a wood, and asked him to help them; Atri asked how he could protect them, and they replied, "Become for us the moon, the destroyer of darkness, and the sun, the destroyer of demons". Thereupon Atri created light through his *tapas*, and made the worlds bright and without darkness; he overcame hosts of the gods' enemies through his own *tejas*, and the gods saw that the demons were being burnt by Atri.[2]

Further versions relate that, because of the length and power of his *tapas*, Atri's body assumed the brilliance of the moon: his lustre spread over the sky and flooded the worlds with light whence ten goddesses conceived and gave birth to his son Soma.[3] In another version it is said that through his *tapas* the moon flooded forth from his eyes and illumined the universe with its lustre.[4] The associations in these latter versions of Atri with the moon rather than with the sun may be derived from his role—especially in the Purāṇas—as the father of Soma: *soma* being yet another name for the moon.

While Atri is thus famed as the father of the moon, Kaśyapa is equally famed—particularly once again in the Epics and Purāṇas—as the father of the sun (Vivasvat, Savitṛ) through his wife Aditi. We may also recall that he is himself termed the son of Marīci: this in turn associates him with solar symbolism, since the word *marici* has the meaning of a ray of light. The word *kaśyapa* means a tortoise, and in the

1. *Mahābhārata* 1.114.39-42.
2. Ibid., 13.141.1-11.
3. *Harivaṃśa* 20.1-14.
4. *Matsya Purāṇa* 23.3-6.

Brāhmaṇas he is identified in this role both with Prajāpati and also with the sun:

> Having assumed the form of a tortoise [*kūrma*], Prajāpati created beings. Because he created, he made [*akarot*]: for that reason he is the tortoise. Now *Kaśyapa* is *kūrma* [*i.e.* both have the same meaning "tortoise"]: and that is why all beings are called descendants of Kaśyapa. This one [Kaśyapa] and this tortoise are (the same as) this sun.[1]

We may note that in his role as the tortoise, Kaśyapa is connected with yet further *avatāras* or descents among men of Viṣṇu, in addition to those noted in Chapter 6: namely with both the Kūrma (Tortoise) and Varāha (Boar) forms assumed by Viṣṇu in order to bear and rescue the earth. He is similarly connected with the archaic myth of the tortoise who rescues the earth from the waters: for in some accounts, when he had received the earth as *dakṣiṇā* from Paraśurāma, the earth started to sink into the waters and he himself rescued her and held her on his lap.[2] A still earlier passage in the *Atharvaveda* again speaks in terms of solar symbolism in connection with Kaśyapa:

> That which is radiant [*candraṃ*: also a name of the moon] in you, O Kaśyapa, and possessed of brilliance; that which is placed together and eminent, O one of bright light [*citrabhānu*: also a name of the sun]; that in which the seven suns are set together.[3]

This somewhat enigmatic passage is expounded in another work:

> Āroga, Bhrāja, Paṭara, Pataṅga, Svarṇaro, Jyotiṣīmat and Vibhāsa: all of these radiate heat in the sky for this world. It is said that they do not withdraw, and that they yield

1. *Śatapatha Brāhmaṇa* 7.5.1.1-6.
2. For example *Śatapatha Brāhmaṇa* 13.7.1.15: *Śāṅkhāyana Śrauta Sūtra* 16.16.3-4: *Mahābhārata* 3.114.17-22, 12.49.55-80; compare also *Mahābhārata* 13.139.1 ff, where Kaśyapa himself became the earth for 30,000 years.
3. *Atharvaveda* 13.3.10.

> strength. Kaśyapa is the eighth; he does not depart from great Mt. Meru. There is this verse about them: "That which is skilful in you, O Kaśyapa; possessed of brilliance, possessed of strength and eminent, O Citrabhānu; that in which the seven suns are set together; by that may he [the sacrificer] obtain kingship". All of those (seven suns) receive light for this world from Kaśyapa; the moon purifies them (deriving its light or power) from Kaśyapa. The seven *prāṇas* are in the head; the Ācāryas [spiritual teachers] say that they are the suns.[1]

As we shall see in the next chapter, the Seven Ṛṣis are also identified in a number of places as the seven *prāṇas* or vital airs in the head; this again implies a homology or mystical equation of the Ṛṣis and the sun or suns. In the case of Kaśyapa, the identification is explicit: in this passage he is clearly the supreme sun, who gives light to the seven suns—as also to the moon—with which they in turn illumine this world. The concept of the seven suns reappears in the Purāṇas, where it is often said to be the seven suns which burn the worlds to ashes at the end of each Kalpa;[2] while several myths relate that there used to be – in addition to the sun and moon – seven other suns which were the sons of the sun, but the moon saw that creatures on earth were being burnt and oppressed by the heat and so persuaded the sun to eat the seven suns.[3] In both cases, the seven suns clearly play a subordinate role to that of the supreme sun—which in the above passage is none other than the Ṛṣi himself.

Here once again, therefore, we meet with an idea which pervades the Ṛṣi traditions—namely that the essence of the Ṛṣis' nature is fire. It is by reason of this fiery nature that they themselves radiate both heat and light, equal to or surpassing even that of the sun; it is also through fire—particularly through the internalised form of *tapas*—that

1. *Taittirīya Āraṇyaka* 1.7.1-5.
2. See Chapter 2 section A.
3. See V. Elwin, *Tribal Myths of Orissa*, pp. 10-11: *Myths of the North-East Frontier of India*, p. 55: *The Baiga*, p. 332.

they attain transference to the sky, radiating their *tejas* or fiery energy from there as stars—or even as the sun itself.

C. The Ṛṣis as Ursa Major

(a) *The Ṛṣis and the Bears*

The constellation Ursa Major—which is commonly known in the West as the Great Bear, the Plough, the Haywain or the Dipper—is generally known in India as the *sapta*-Ṛṣis or *saptarṣi-maṇḍala*, or in other words as the Seven Ṛṣis. The Ṛṣis have been identified with these seven stars for several millenia; but one passage in the *Śatapatha Brāhmaṇa*—probably composed around the eighth century B.C. —relates that in earlier times the Ṛṣis in the sky were known as the *ṛkṣas* or Bears:

> The Kṛttikās [Pleiades] are Agni's Nakṣatra [Lunar Mansion]. Other Nakṣatras have one, two, three or four stars, but they have the most [*i.e.* six] stars; and they do not wander away from the eastern region, whereas all the other Nakṣatras do wander from the eastern region. They were formerly the wives of the Bears—for indeed, the Seven Ṛṣis were in earlier times called the Bears; but they were prevented from having intercourse, since the Seven Ṛṣis rise in the north while they rise in the east.[1]

We shall be examining in the next sub-section the role of the Kṛttikās as the wives of the Ṛṣis. The idea of this constellation as Bears almost certainly appears also in one *Ṛgveda* hymn, which speaks of the *ṛkṣas* which are seen in the sky by night but shine elsewhere by night; the commentator Sāyaṇa among others states that the *ṛkṣas* in this hymn are indeed to be interpreted as the Seven Ṛṣis.[2] In later times—especially in the Epics and Purāṇas—the term *ṛkṣa* came to be given a more general meaning, denoting either any star or shining object or sometimes more specifically stars which are in conjunction with

1. *Śatapatha Brāhmaṇa* 2.1.2.1-5.
2. *Ṛgveda* 1.24.10+Sāyaṇa's commentary.

the moon;[1] this more general meaning is, however, in all probability derivative from its original and more specific meaning denoting the shining stars of the Bears or Ursa Major.

Why, then, was this constellation originally called the Bears—and why was its name subsequently changed to the Ṛṣis ? In order to answer the first of these questions, we must examine parallels among other peoples and in other cultures. The Latin term *ursa major* means the Greater Bear, and the Romans knew of two Bears in the sky, namely the Greater Bear and the Lesser Bear (*ursa minor*). Their ideas in this field were largely borrowed from the Greeks, among whom the constellation was known as the Bear (*árktos*) from at least the time of Homer around the eighth century B.C.[2] Associated with this name was the myth of Callisto, one of the companions of Artemis :

> Zeus one day seduced Callisto, and she became pregnant; when Artemis came to know of this, in her jealousy she transformed Callisto into a bear and set a pack of hounds on her. Callisto would have been hunted to death [and in some versions, she is killed], but Zeus took her up into the sky and set her image among the stars.

This account is related by the Greek writer Apollodorus,[3] as also by the Roman writers Hyginus and Ovid.[4] The same idea of the constellation as a Bear is met with among many Central Asian, Siberian, and also North American Indian peoples; particularly among the latter, the constellation is also often seen as a bear (four stars) being pursued by the three hunters (three stars)—an idea comparable to the Greek conception of

---

1. For example *Brahmāṇḍa Purāṇa* 1.2.23.52, 1.2.24.80 & 91-92: *Liṅga Purāṇa* 1.56.14-18, 1.61.36.
2. For example *Iliad* 18.487: *Odyssey* 5.273.
3. Apollodorus, *Bibliotheke* 3.8.2.
4. Hyginus, *Poetica Astronomica* 2.1: Ovid, *Metamorphoses* 2.450 ff. On these myths, see especially R. Graves, *The Greek Myths,* Vol. 1 section 22: and M. Grant, *Myths of the Greeks and Romans*; on Greek astronomy and astrology, A. Bouché-Leclerq, *L'Astrologie Grecque.*

Callisto being pursued by hounds.[1] Common myths and traditions frequently reappear among various Asian and North American Indian peoples; when considered together, these are strongly suggestive of being ultimately derivative from a common cultural source as far as many features are concerned—although widespread borrowing is also evident in places, especially in the case of many Central Asian ideas. Aside from ideas of the constellation as a bear, several Indian Plains-tribes of North America see it as seven brothers who either climbed to heaven by means of a spider's web or were chased there by a bear—the latter being an inversion of the Greek account, where it is the bear who is chased to heaven by hounds. In Central Asia, several peoples see the constellation as a stag (four stars) being pursued by three hunters (three stars)—similar to the bear and three hunters throughout North America. The Kirghis see it as either seven watchmen who guard the horses of the little bear from a wolf, or as seven wolves who are pursuing the horses; the Ugrians and Ostiaks also see it as seven animals, while the Kirghis additionally see it as seven thieves—an idea shared with the Buriats, who see it as seven old men who steal a star from the Pleiades. We shall note in the next sub-section this similarity to the Indian conception, wherein the Seven Ṛṣis also "steal" or "rescue" Arundhatī from the other six Kṛttikas. One further idea, which is found among several Indian Plains-tribes of North America, is that the constellation represents a bier being carried by mourners; this idea reappears among the Baiga in India, who see it as a bed on which a corpse is being carried—in Bihar it is also seen as a bed, of which one leg was broken by a king who sprang too violently from it on seeing his queen running off to kill herself.[2] Thus we see in these examples a number of ideas which reappear throughout Asia and North America, particularly as to the constellation representing or being associated with a bear; one

1. See for example U. Holmberg, *Finno-Ugric and Siberian Mythology*, pp. 83 ff., 425 ff. : H. B. Alexander, *North American Mythology*, pp. 9, 26, 96 ff., 278. Such ideas are found among the Eskimos, Iroquois, Plains Tribes, and many others throughout North America.

2. See Alexander, p. 96, and V. Elwin, *The Baiga*, p. 335.

further Central Asian context in which this appears is in the Khotanese term "The Seven Bears" (*hauda richa—*), in which we may see a direct link with the *Ṛgveda* and Brāhmaṇa idea of the Seven Ṛṣis as the Seven Bears.[1]

By way of contrast, we may note that three other major civilisations held quite different traditions about this constellation. The Chinese, from at least the eighth century B.C., termed it the Northern Dipper or Ladle (*pei tou*)[2]—a name by which it is also known in contemporary North America; while the Egyptians called it the Hippopotamus[3]—a name which it retains in Egypt to the present day. In Mesopotamia, it was commonly known as the Chariot or Wain (*mar. gid. da*);[4] this idea was also adopted by the Greeks—thus Homer refers to both names for the constellation,[5] and Democritus noted this probable origin of the Greek idea when describing the Babylonian system of astronomy.[6] Thus we have clear distinctions between the ideas about the constellation in China, Egypt and Mesopotamia on the one hand and in the European, Asian and North American contexts noted earlier on the other hand.

We have already noted in Chapter 3 that the Seven Ṛṣis—as Ursa Major— are consistently associated with the northern region, and with the symbolic "centre" of the sky or northern celestial pole. In one *Ṛgveda* hymn they are also called the Oxen (*ukṣan*) who take their enjoyment in the east—a possible reference to the Kṛttikās (Pleiades) or wives of the Ṛṣis, who as we have seen are said to reside and rise in the east :

> Accompanied by the five Adhvaryu-priests, the Seven *vipra*-Ṛṣis dearly protect the path of the bird [? Agni] which has been set out; they take their pleasure in the east, those Oxen

---

1. See the fragment *Kha.* 1.131a: *Saṅghāta-sūtra* 25 a 1: *Siddhasāra* 3 .v. 5; H. W. Bailey, 'Gāndhārī', p. 771, and 'Indo-Iranica 3', pp. 405-406.
2. H. Chatley, 'Ancient Chinese Astronomy'.
3. W. Peek, *Constellations*, pp. 1 ff.; see also R. H. Allen, *Star Names, Their Lore and Meaning.*
4. F. X. Kugler, *Sternkunde und Sterndienst in Babel*, Book 2 pp. 249-251.
5. *Iliad* 18.487.
6. *Vitruvius* 9.4.1—9.5.3.

who do not waste away, those gods who delight in the rituals of the gods.[1]

Just as the Seven Ṛṣis are here called the Seven Oxen, so too in many Latin languages the term "Seven Oxen" denotes "The North"—as for example in the Latin *septentriones*. We may also note that the Khotanese term "The Seven Bears" similarly denotes "The North"[2]—a meaning derivative from association of the Seven Bears (as Ursa Major) with the northern celestial pole; for as we have already seen in Chapter 3 and shall see again below,[3] the association with the north and with the celestial pole is demanded by the position of the constellation Ursa Major. The designations of the Seven Ṛṣis both as Oxen and more especially as Bears implies that such designations—in view of their parallels, particularly among Indo-European peoples—are not specifically Indian in origin, but were brought to India; and it would seem extremely likely that their designation as Bears is ultimately of Central Asian origin, and was brought to India—as similarly to Greece and Rome—on one of the several waves of Indo-European migration to the subcontinent.

We may now seek for reasons why the name of the constellation was changed—at some period before the eighth century B.C.—from the Bears to the Ṛṣis. Here once again we may seek part of the answer in extra-Indian contexts. We have already noted in Chapter 5 a number of similarities between the phenomena of Ṛṣi-hood and Shamanism, and the bear is another motif which often appears prominently in the context of Shamanism. Among many peoples throughout Asia and North America, the bear is regarded as a sacred animal—and more specifically as the guardian-spirit of Shamans, as for example among the Thompson Indians and among the Ostyaks, Yakuts and Vasyugen;[4] the Cahuilla and Paviotso Indians of North America believe that Shamanic power is transmitted from the Creator to the Shaman through the medium of a bear;[5]

1. *Ṛgveda* 3.7.7. See also discussion in Chapter 3.
2. Bailey, 'Gāndhārī', p. 771.
3. See sub-section (c) below.
4. M. Eliade, *Shamanism*, pp. 89-90, 106.
5. Ibid., pp. 103, 105.

while the Eskimo believe that the great Spirit himself appears in the form of a white bear which devours and vomits up (denoting symbolic death and rebirth) an individual, thereby initiating him as a Shaman.[1] If we are indeed—as would seem likely—dealing here with ideas which may be traced back to archaic and pre-historic roots,[2] then the same may equally be the case with the idea of Ursa Major as a bear or bears—which was similarly held by many peoples throughout Asia and North America among whom the Shamanic cult was most prominent. In this event, we may see here one possible explanation for the change of the constellation's name from the Bear or Bears to the Ṛṣis : for while the Ṛṣis inherited many features from their Shamanic predecessors or counterparts,[3] nonetheless by the period of the Brāhmaṇas the Ṛṣi came to be regarded as a direct recipient and generator of sacred power—thereby replacing the role of the bear as the guiding spirit and mediating power between the Shaman and the Divine. The constellation Ursa Major is, as we have seen, that closest to the symbolic "centre" of the sky, which is the point the Shaman must pass through in order to communicate with the Divine.[4] It may well be that the bear was originally identified with this constellation in his role as mediator and guide to the Shaman, enabling him to communicate with the Divine; but in any event, when—in the later Vedic *saṃhitās* and in the Brāhmaṇas—the Ṛṣi came to be seen as one who not only praised and offered sacrifice to

1. W. Thalbitzer, 'The Heathen Priests of East Greenland', p. 454, and 'Les Magiciens esquimaux', p. 78: T. Lehtisalo, 'Der Tod und die Wiedergeburt', pp. 20 ff. See also M. Barbeau, 'Bear-Mother': N. P. Dyrenkova, 'Bear Worship among Turkish Tribes of Siberia': A. I. Hallowell, 'Bear Ceremonialism in the Northern Hemisphere': C. Hentze, 'Le Culte de l'ours et du tigre et le t'ao-t'ié'.

2. See especially K. J. Narr, 'Bärenzeremoniell und Schamanismus in der Ālteren Steinzeit Europas'.

3. See Chapter 5.

4. We may also note that the Shaman often makes his ascent to this "centre" (as also his descent to the underworld) by the World-Pillar or central axis, which appears prominently in the *skambha* hymns of the *Atharvaveda* (10.7, 10.8) where the Ṛṣis are said to be established in the *skambha* or pillar (10.7.14 &ff.). On the Shamanistic ascent, see Eliade, *Shamanism*, pp. 259-287.

the gods, but who himself ascended to heaven and attained a place among the gods, the place ascribed to him would quite naturally have been that closest to the symbolic "centre", and thereafter it would have been the Ṛṣis, rather than the bear or bears, who were associated with and gave their name to the constellation. The roots for this development lay indeed in the *Ṛgveda* itself, where the Ṛṣis are above all seers of *ṛks* or hymns; for the Sanskrit root $\sqrt{}$*ṛc* means both to praise (as the Ṛṣis praise the gods in their hymns) and also to shine (as they shine in the sky), and we may see here the embryonic concept which was developed in subsequent contexts into the idea of the Seven Ṛṣis as shining through their speech, and thence as shining stars in the sky.

The question of the change in name may also be considered in connection with a further feature of early Indian astronomy, namely the system of Nakṣatras or Lunar Mansions. There is little doubt that the Indian system—like the corresponding Chinese *sieou* and Arabic *manāzil* systems—is fundamentally independent of the Greek system, and is essentially of non-Indo-European origin.[1] Yet even by the period of the *Yajurveda*, this system had been fully accepted and integrated within the Indo-Aryan cult.[2] A further possibility is, therefore, that the name and idea of "The Ṛṣis" for this constellation similarly derived from the same non-Indo-European source, and that it was subsequently adopted by the Indo-Aryans and came to replace the earlier name "The Bears". The most likely source of origin in this respect is the Indus Valley Civilisation which, whether its language was Indo-European or non-Indo-European,[3] clearly produced a culture exhibiting many

1. See Macdonell & Keith, *Vedic Index*, Vol. 1 pp 428-430: H. Oldenberg, Nakṣatra und Sieou' L. de Saussure, 'Les Origines de l'Astronomie Chinoise': A. Weber, *Die Nachrichten von den Nakṣatra*, pp. 267 ff.: W. D. Whitney, 'Jacobi and Tilak on the Age of the Veda'.

2. For example *Kāṭhaka Saṃhitā* 8.15, 29.13: *Maitrāyaṇī Saṃhitā* 1.7.2, 2.13.20: *Taittirīya Saṃhitā* 1.5.1.4, 4.4.10.1-3: *Atharvaveda* 19.7.1, 19.8.1.

3. For an interpretation of the language as Summerian, see J. V. Kinnier Wilson, *Indo-Sumerian*; as Proto-Dravidian, A. Parpola *et. al.*, *The Decipherment of the Proto-Dravidian Inscriptions of the Indus Civilisation* and other works, and Yu. V. Knorozov *et. al.*, *Proto-Indica*; as Indo-Aryan, J. E. Mitchiner, *Studies in the Indus Valley Inscriptions.*

non-Indo-European features. We may in particular refer to those seals which depict seven individuals with ritual head-dress standing before a deity in a Pīpal tree to whom offerings are being made,[1] wherein the seven figures may well be interpreted as sacred seers or wise men. These figures may in turn be compared with the Seven Sages or *apkallus* of the Sumerians, Babylonians and Assyrians, who ensured the correct functioning of heaven and earth, taught civilisation to mankind, survived the great flood, and ascended to heaven.[2] Many traditions can be seen here which were subsequently associated with the Seven Ṛṣis—such as their role in the flood myth,[3] and their roles in teaching men, ordering society, and ascending to heaven;[4] and it is quite likely that the Indus Valley Civilisation acted as a cultural intermediary, whereby such Mesopotamian ideas were subsequently absorbed into the Indian Ṛṣi traditions.

We may therefore conclude that the idea of Ursa Major as "The Bears" derived originally from Central Asian origins, and was brought to India on one of the several waves of Indo-European migration. The idea of the constellation as Seven Sages or Seers may well have been current among the peoples of the Indus Valley Civilisation—elaborated from the Mesopotamian idea of the Seven *apkallus*; and this idea was adopted by the new migrators at an early stage in the development of the Indo-Aryan cult, along with such other astronomical features as the Nakṣatra system. These Seven Sages thence came to be identified as the Seven Ṛṣis, who by the later Vedic *saṃhitās* had come to be regarded not only as seers of hymns who communicated with the gods but as those who had attained heaven and dwelt with the gods. Seen in this light, therefore, the change in the constellation's name from "The Seven Bears" to "The Seven Ṛṣis" may be traced to the development of ideas within the early Vedic cult itself; while such development was

---

1. See J. Marshall, *Mohenjo Daro and the Indus Civilisation*, Vol. 1 plate XII no. 18 and vol. 3 plate CXVIII no. 7: E. J. Mackay, *Further Excavations at Mohenjo Daro*, plate XCIV no. 430.
2. See especially E. Reiner, 'The Etiological Myth of the Seven Sages'.
3. See Chapter 9.
4. See Chapters 2, 5 and 6.

in turn prompted and stimulated through the absorption of further ideas from the cultures and peoples with which the Vedic Aryans came into contact.

(b) *The Ṛṣis and the Kṛttikās*

It would seem that the Kṛttikās—the six stars of the Pleiades—were in early Vedic times visualised as men rather than women. One passage, for example, relates that it was the gods who became the Kṛttikās :

> The gods went to Svarga Loka through Agni : they became those Kṛttikās yonder.[1]

One *Ṛgveda* hymn, after speaking of the Seven Ṛṣis, takes note of these two different ideas :

> They tell me that those virtuous women are men; he who has eyes sees this, not he who is blind.[2]

In all other contexts, however, the Kṛttikās are regarded as being women—and as being the wives of the Seven Ṛṣis. As we saw at the start of the last sub-section, the *Śatapatha Brāhmaṇa* relates that the Kṛttikās—who are Agni's Nakṣatra or Lunar Mansion—used to be wives of the Seven Ṛṣis, but were prevented from having intercourse with their husbands. The idea of "divorce" or prevention of intercourse is evident in the very name of the Kṛttikās, which is derived from the Sanskrit root √*kṛt* meaning to cut, cut off or divide : hence the Kṛttikās are, strictly speaking, those who are cut off from their husbands. Explanations for this state of affairs are given especially in the Epics and Purāṇas, the earliest and most complete account of which may be summarised as follows :

> Agni desired the wives of the Seven Ṛṣis, and Svāhā, realising this and seeking to have intercourse with Agni, impersonated in turn each of the wives of the Ṛṣis—excepting the chaste Arundhatī, whose virtue was too great for her to

1. *Taittirīya Saṃhitā* 5.3.9.
2. *Ṛgveda* 1.164.16.

> impersonate. From the union of Agni and Svāhā in this way, Skanda was born having six heads; and the Ṛṣis, hearing rumours that their wives had been unfaithful, divorced and abandoned the six wives. The six wives then sought the protection of Skanda (also called Kārttikeya, or the son of the Kṛttikās), and adopted him as their son; and when Indra informed him that Abhijit had abandoned her place among the Nakṣatras, Skanda assigned the Kṛttikās a place in the sky.[1]

Thus the six wives of the Ṛṣis became the Kṛttikās or Pleiades in the sky, abandoned by and cut off from their husbands through the suspicion of unfaithfulness. In this version, the wives are depicted as being quite innocent of the charge brought against them : it is indeed essential that they should be so—for as we have seen earlier, the attainment of becoming a star in the sky was due to supreme virtue, whereby the individual shone brilliantly through his own inner merits. In other accounts of their abandonment by their husbands, less emphasis is placed upon their innocence: they are either inadvertently impregnated by the seed of Agni or Śiva, or else willingly succumb to the seductions of Śiva and are consequently cast off by their husbands.[2] Yet in the case of their seduction by Śiva, they are not called the Kṛttikās but only the wives of the Ṛṣis; this again illustrates the point that in order to attain a place in the sky, the wives must remain innocent and virtuous throughout.

As we have noted, the Kṛttikās are properly the wives who are cut off; but in many texts, the wives are called the Kṛttikās before they have been abandoned by their husbands—and Arundhatī, the chaste wife who was not abandoned, is then included as one of the Kṛttikās. Due to her chastity, Arundhatī ascended to the sky with the Seven Ṛṣis, to become the small star (Alcor) next to her husband Vasiṣṭha (ζ Ursa Major, the sixth star of the constellation). One Sūtra passage thus refers to

1. *Mahābhārata* 3.213.1—3.219.11: *Skanda Purāṇa* 1.2.29.89-210.
2. See Chapter 6 section B (b).

Arundhatī as the Kṛttikā who was "rescued" by the Seven Ṛṣis :

> The Seven Ṛṣis led to firmness Arundhatī, the foremost of the Kṛttikās; may she, the eighth (among the Seven Ṛṣis), shine upon us, as she sustains the pre-eminent conjunction of the six Kṛttikās (? with the moon).[1]

Thus Arundhatī is regarded as being distinguished above her sisters or sisters-in-law : as the wife who, because of her virtue and chastity, was not abandoned by her husband when the Ṛṣis parted from their wives. Several Central Asian accounts see the seventh Pleiad as having been not so much "rescued" as rather stolen from the other six : it is often said that the Pleiades was a single large insect which was trodden underfoot by a cow, and a bear took one part to the sky while the others pursued the bear; and the Buriats recount that the stars of Ursa Major are seven old men who have stolen a star from the Pleiades.[2] In all cases, Ursa Major is connected with the Pleiades, and one of the stars of the Pleiades is said to reside among the stars of Ursa Major.

Just as the Kṛttikās had to remain innocent and virtuous in order to become stars, so too Arundhatī remained with the Seven Ṛṣis because of her supreme chastity. Yet she became only a small star, sometimes invisible to the naked eye; this is said to have been due to a loss of virtue on her part, in having once doubted the word of her husband :

> Arundhatī doubted Vasiṣṭha, the best of Ṛṣis—she slighted that *muni*, who is of exceedingly pure form; because of that evil thought, her light is like reddish smoke—and she is sometimes visible and sometimes invisible, of small form and observed only occasionally.[3]

1. *Hiraṇyakeśin Gṛhya Sūtra* 1.7.22.14.

2. Holmberg, *Finno-Ugric and Siberian Mythology*, pp. 427, 430 ff. The motif of six unvirtuous and one virtuous sister frequently appears (without astronomical connotations) in Indian tribal myths: see Chapter 6 section A(d).

3. *Mahābhārata* 1.224.27-31.

Thus a loss of virtue automatically brought for Arundhatī a diminution of her brilliance and lustre. To shine brightly in the sky is thus synonymous with excelling in virtue; and just as the virtue and *tapas* of the ascetic increases his own sexual and erotic potency,[1] so too the sight of the stars shining brightly in the sky is deemed auspicious for sex and procreation. Thus the sight of Dhruva (the Pole star), Arundhatī and the Seven Ṛṣis is said to be auspicious for gaining children for a young bride and long life for her husband;[2] while the sight of these together with the Nakṣatras and the moon is described as the consummation of pleasure for a couple after they have had intercourse.[3]

We may also take note here of a further idea which appears only in the Purāṇas, wherein the Seven Ṛṣis—as the stars of Ursa Major—are considered to move their position in relation to each of the twenty-seven Nakṣatras : being conjoined or united with each Nakṣatra for a period of 100 years, and thus being as it were "married" to each one in turn. Since the Kṛttikās are one of the Nakṣatras, we may perhaps see in this idea a further attempted explanation for why the Seven Ṛṣis parted from the Kṛttikās who had earlier been their wives. Further discussion of this topic may be found in Chapter 4.

(c) *The Position of the Ṛṣis in the Sky*

We shall first deal with the question of the position of each of the Ṛṣis in relation to the others. We noted in Chapter 1 verses in the *Ṛgveda* and *Atharvaveda* relating that six of the Seven Ṛṣis are god-born twins while the remaining Ṛṣi is born alone,[4] and we discussed there the applicability of this idea to the Seven Ṛṣis in the sky, noting the pair-wise latitudinal formation of six of the seven stars with which the fifth star in order of enumeration (starting from the western end) is unaligned. In standard forms of the first main list of the Seven Ṛṣis, the fifth Ṛṣis is Atri, and since Atri is in other contexts set apart from

1. See Chapters 5 and 6.
2. *Āśvalāyana Gṛhya Sūtra* 1.7.2.
3. *Kāma-sūtra* 2.10.21-22.
4. *Ṛgveda* 1.164.15: *Atharvaveda* 9.9.10, 10.8.5.

the other Ṛṣis,[1] we may infer that in the first main list the Ṛṣis Viśvāmitra, Jamadagni, Bharadvāja, Gotama, Atri, Vasiṣṭha and Kaśyapa are to be identified respectively as the stars, α, β, γ, δ, ϵ, ζ, and η Ursa Major. This is further implied by the fact that Arundhatī is always listed next to Vasiṣṭha, or between Vasiṣṭha and Kaśyapa[2] : whence Vasiṣṭha is to be identified as the sixth star ζ Ursa Major, and Arundhatī as the small star Alcor next to it. Similarly in the case of the second main list of the Seven Ṛṣis in post-Vedic literature, we noted in Chapter 1 a passage in which Varāhamihira lists each of the Ṛṣis in turn (this time starting with the eastern end, and moving from η to α Ursa Major) together with Arundhatī next to Vasiṣṭha or ζ Ursa Major. We shall here cite also the poetic description given by Varāhamihira of the Ṛṣis in the sky :

> I shall describe, according to the opinion of Vṛddha Garga, the course of those Seven Ṛṣis by whom the region of Kuvera [namely the north] is, as it were, protected; because of whom she glitters as if with a string of pearls, as if joyfully garlanded with white lotuses—and through whose rotations the northern region seems to be constantly dancing, to the instructions of Dhruva [the Pole star] as overseer. The Seven Ṛṣis always rise in the north-east, together with the chaste wife (Arundhatī). At the eastern end is lord Marīci, next to him is Vasiṣṭha; then comes Aṅgiras, then Atri, and then Pulastya; then Pulaha, and then lord Kratu—each in order, beginning at the east. Chaste Arundhatī has there resorted to the excellent *muni* Vasiṣṭha.[3]

Thus we can see how each of the Ṛṣis in both of the main lists of the Seven Ṛṣis is in turn identified as one of the stars of Ursa Major. It is worth citing here one further simile, in addition to Varāhamihira's likenesses to a string of pearls and a garland of white lotuses. This appears in one of the plays ascribed

1. See Chapter 1 section B.
2. For example *Hiraṇyakeśin Gṛhya Sūtra* 2.8.19.2-7: see also Chapter 1 section B.
3. *Bṛhat-saṃhitā* 13.1-6.

to Bhāsa, and is spoken by the king after his jester has pointed out to him a flock of cranes flying through the sky :

> "Certainly I see it [the flock of cranes]: now stretched out in a line, now wide apart; now sinking low, now soaring high—curved like the Seven Ṛṣis in its twists and turns, like a boundary-line cutting across the sky.[1]

Many further poetic similes and descriptions of the Seven Ṛṣis in the sky are met with—which is scarcely surprising, since the constellation is perhaps the most imposing and easily-recognisable star-group in the northern hemisphere.

Turning next to the position of the constellation, we have already seen in Chapter 3 that the Seven Ṛṣis are consistently associated throughout Vedic, Epic and Purāṇic literature with the northern region. Particularly noteworthy in the present context is the designation of the Ṛṣis as the Seven Oxen, a term which—as we have seen above—appears in many Latin languages as a synonym for the North; as also a passage which relates that the Ṛṣis constitute the mid-point of the sky :

Where these Seven Ṛṣis are, there is the centre of the sky.[2]

We have already discussed the significance of the "centre" in this passage as representing the northern celestial Pole, or the point around which all other stars and constellations appear to be turning—as is implied also by Varāhamihira in the passage cited above.[3] The northern celestial Pole—which at the present day is represented by the star Polaris—was some two to three millenia ago (namely around the time when this passage was written) represented by the star Thuban or α Draconis, midway between Polaris and Ursa Major.[4] At that time, therefore, Ursa Major would without doubt have been the constellation closest to the symbolic "centre" of the sky—while in still earlier times, the northern celestial pole would have been located within the constellation itself.

---

1. *Svapnavāsavadattam* 4.2.
2. *Jaiminīya Upaniṣad Brāhmaṇa* 4.26.12.
3. See Chapter 3 section C (a).
4. See for example Macdonell & Keith, *Vedic Index*, vol. 1 p. 406-references: P. Moore, *Atlas of the Universe*, p. 216.

The northern celestial Pole, or the fixed point in the sky around which all else turns, is known in Sanskrit as *dhruva* or fixed. The myth of Dhruva's elevation to the sky provides in some respects an explanation for why the northern celestial Pole was seen to have shifted slightly away from Ursa Major; for it is said that, because of his *tapas* Viṣṇu (or in some accounts Brahmā) assigned Dhruva a place in the sky even more exalted than that of the Seven Ṛṣis :

> Dhruva was born the son of king Uttānapāda, but in his childhood he abandoned worldly concerns and devoted himself to ascetic pursuits. When he entered the forests to perform *tapas*, he met the Seven Ṛṣis and asked how he might attain a superior status; they instructed him in *tapas*, which he then performed for 3,000 years. In reward for his *tapas*, Viṣṇu gave him a place above the sun and moon, above the planets and the gods—a place comparable to his own, an unmoving and paramount region above even the Seven Ṛṣis; and Uśanas sang, "How wonderful is the *tapas* of the son of Uttānapāda, placing him in front of the Seven Ṛṣis".[1]

Thus the Seven Ṛṣis were in a sense slightly displaced by Dhruva : inasmuch as it was Dhruva who was thereafter established at the "centre" of the sky, and represented the fixed place or *dhruva* around which both they and all the other constellations revolved. Other passages correspondingly relate that Dhruva is established above the Seven Ṛṣis, and constitutes the third or highest footstep of Viṣṇu—the other two being on the earth and in the atmosphere.[2] Further passages describe the distance in *yojanas* (one *yojana* being equal to between seven and eight miles) between the earth and the various celestial realms : giving distances—for the stars and planets in Svarloka—in turn from the sun to the moon, the Nakṣatras, Budha (Mercury), Śukra (Venus), Aṅgāraka (Mars), Bṛhaspati (Jupiter), Śani (Saturn),

1. *Harivaṃśa* 2.10-13: *Agni Purāṇa* 18.5: *Liṅga Purāṇa* 1.62.3-41: *Matsya Purāṇa* 4.36-37: *Skanda Purāṇa* 4.1.19.1-124: *Viṣṇu Purāṇa* 1.11.29-56.

2. For example *Agni Purāṇa* 120.27-29: *Brahmāṇḍa Purāṇa* 1.2.24.122: *Kūrma Purāṇa* 1.39.26: *Liṅga Purāṇa* 1.56.31: *Matsya Purāṇa* 124.112, 128.74: *Padma Purāṇa* 5.3.150: *Vāyu Purāṇa* 1.53.97.

the Seven Ṛṣis, and Dhruva. In most such contexts, the Seven Ṛṣis are said to be 100,000 *yojanas* above Śani (the highest of the planets), while Dhruva is in turn said to be 100,000 *yojanas* above the Seven Ṛṣis;[1] although distances are also given of 110,000 *yojanas* from Śani to the Ṛṣis,[2] and of 600,000 or 1,300,000 *yojanas* from the Ṛṣis to Dhruva.[3] In turn above Dhruva are the four worlds Mahar, Jana, Tapas and Brahma Lokas. The regions between the sun and the Seven Ṛṣis—particularly the region known as the Nāgavīthī or Path of the Elephant—are said to be the abodes of many ascetics and sages;[4] while Viṣṇu—in the form of a *śiśumāra* or porpoise—is said to be spread out in the region around Dhruva and the Seven Ṛṣis, with Dhruva at the tail and the Seven Ṛṣis at the waist.[5]

When, at the end of each Manvantara, the three worlds are burnt to ashes and then flooded to form a single ocean, the waters are said to rise until they reach the realm of the Seven Ṛṣis—whereafter they recede, and a new Manvantara commences.[6] We may note here a certain ambiguity : for while the Seven Ṛṣis—as the stars of Ursa Major—are said to be situated in Svarloka, nonetheless the Manvantara tradition of the Purāṇas depicts them as residing in Maharloka (the world immediately above Svarloka), and as moving from there to Janaloka at the end of each Manvantara through affliction at the great heat caused by the burning of the three worlds. We should perhaps consider this alongside the further point that the Seven Ṛṣis are elsewhere also said to reside in Brahmaloka; and while different theories might be proffered in explanation—such

1. *Brahma Purāṇa* 23.9-10: *Brahmāṇḍa Purāṇa* 3.4.2.133: *Kūrma Purāṇa* 1.39.11-12: *Śiva Purāṇa* 5.19.6: *Vāyu Purāṇa* 2.39.134-135: *Viṣṇu Purāṇa* 2.7.9-10.

2. *Bhāgavata Purāṇa* 5.22.17: *Devībhāgavata Purāṇa* 8.16-17.

3. *Agni Purāṇa* 120.8-9: *Devībhāgavata Purāṇa* 8.16-17.

4. For example *Yājñavalkya Dharma Śāstra* 3.187: *Brahmāṇḍa Purāṇa* 1.2.21. 168-169: *Vāyu Purāṇa* 1.50.216-217: *Viṣṇu Purāṇa* 2.8.85-86.

5. For example *Bhāgavata Purāṇa* 5.23.4-7: *Devībhāgavata Purāṇa* 8.17.10 ff.: *Matsya Purāṇa* 127.24-29: *Viṣṇu Purāṇa* 2.11.1 ff.

6. For example *Agni Purāṇa* 349.4-13: *Brahma Purāṇa* 231.1—232.49: *Brahmāṇḍa Purāṇa* 3.4.2.32-55: *Garuḍa Purāṇa* 233.1 ff.: *Kūrma Purāṇa* 2.43.11 ff.9: *Mārkaṇḍeya Purāṇa* 46.23 ff, : *Saura Purāṇa* 33.9 ff. : *Vāyu Purāṇa* 2.39.34-58: *Viṣṇu Purāṇa* 1.3.1 ff., 6.2-3. See further in Chapter 2.

as that different groups of Seven Ṛṣis variously live in Svar, Mahar and Brahma Lokas—it is nonetheless most sensible to conclude that we are here dealing with originally separate traditions, formulated at different periods. The tradition of their residence in Svarloka—as the stars of Ursa Major—is essentially associated with the Vedic conception of only three worlds; the idea of their residence in Brahmaloka merely represents the adaptation of this idea of their being in the highest realm to the Epic and post-Epic conception of seven worlds, while the tradition of their residence in Maharloka—which is almost exclusively a Purāṇic idea—represents a further adaptation within the context of the developing Manvantara conceptions.

Finally, in considering the position of the Ṛṣis in the sky, we may notice also the position of Agastya, who is so closely associated with—and very occasionally included among—the Seven Ṛṣis. As we have seen in earlier chapters, Agastya is consistently associated with the southern region; and astronomical works leave little doubt that he is to be identified as Canopus, one of the brightest stars in the southern sky.[1]

1. See *Sūrya-siddhānta* 8.10, 9.12-15, 13.8-9: *Bṛhat-saṃhitā* 12.1-21: *Mahāsiddhānta* 10.8: *Pañcasiddhāntikā* 14.40-41; also Chapter 3 sections B and C.

8

THE SEVEN ṚṢIS IN THE BODY

A. Introduction

We have already seen that the Seven Ṛṣis are not merely those who perform *tapas* on the earth and attain the realm of heaven; they are also those who, as sons of the Creator, participate in and put into effect the works of the Creator—who themselves act as the creators of gods, men and demons and of all animate creation. It is in this context that they come to be viewed as constituting the very essence of life itself : for just as *tapas* or heat is the medium by which Brahmā brings the creation into existence—and the Ṛṣis, by transforming their whole being into glowing and fiery heat, both attain heaven and also continue the task of creation—so too *prāṇa* is conceived as being the vital essence of all living beings, the breath of life which animates creation and brings into effect the cycle of creation—and the Ṛṣis are in turn identified as *prāṇa* or as the seven *prāṇas*. The primary meaning of *prāṇa* is wind, air or breath; the concept underlying it is that of the dynamically creative breath, the primal force or movement which first set in motion the entire creative process—like the *ruach* or *ruh* of God which, moving over the waters, began the cycle of creation,[1] or the *pneuma* (wind or breath) which is the divine Spirit, the creative animating activity of God.[2] The Ṛṣis, through sacrifice and *tapas*

1. *Genesis* 1.1 ff.

2. See especially the role of the *pneuma* in Stoic, Jewish-Hellenistic and early Christian thought.

transform their being into *prāṇa* and are thereby conceived as being identical with the primal *prāṇa* which brought the universe into being. The supreme abode of *prāṇa* is visualised as being in the head; and the Ṛṣis, as *prāṇa* or the *prāṇas* are visualised as residing in the head (particularly as the "openings" or sense-organs by which the body communicates with the outside world—namely the ears, eyes, nostrils and mouth)—while the meditator or ascetic, by perceiving the Ṛṣis within his head, himself attains liberation.

B. The Ṛṣis and the Soma Sacrifice

The concept of the Seven Ṛṣis as the *prāṇas* is especially prominent in Vedic literature, and originates in the context of the *soma* sacrifice.[1] The central feature of this sacrifice was the ritual drinking of *soma*-juice—*soma* being almost certainly some kind of plant whose juice, when pressed and extracted, had a drugging effect upon the body.[2] In the *Ṛgveda*, Ṛṣi-hood itself was said to be attainable by drinking *soma*, the inspirer of hymns and the stimulator of seers; thus *soma* is said to have gained the title of Ṛṣi for Jamadagni,[3] while another hymn expresses in a more general way the wish that the *soma*-drinker might become a Ṛṣi:

> You will surely make me a Ṛṣi, since I have drunk *soma*.[4]

Even in the *Ṛgveda*, the Seven Ṛṣis are frequently seen not merely as the *pitṛs* or ancestors of men—the first-born who attained heaven through sacrifice.[5]—but also as divine figures in the sky who come to earth in order to attend the *soma* sacrifice. One hymn relates for example that the Ṛṣis—as humans (*manuṣya*) and "Our Fathers of Old", the ancestors

1. On topics related to this chapter, see J. E. Mitchiner, 'Rishi-hood and the Soma Cult'.
2. On the nature of *soma*, see especially R. G. Wasson, *Soma, Divine Mushroom of Immortality*, and J. Mulholland, 'Soma, an attempt to classify the drug and the plant'.
3. *Ṛgveda* 9.97.51.
4. Ibid., 3.43.5.
5. For example *Ṛgveda* 4.1.12-13, 4.42.8, 6.22.2: *Taittirīya Saṃhitā* 5.7.7: *Vājasaneyi Saṃhitā* 18.52: *Atharvaveda* 18.3.16.

of the race—gained success when sacrifice was first created; and that they thereafter returned—as heavenly ones (*daivya*)—with hymns, metres and rules of conduct for the sacrifice.[1] Thus the Ṛṣis are here visualised once again as attaining heaven through sacrifice, and then returning to give instruction to men—a role which we have already noted in other contexts;[2] and the status of the Ṛṣis both on the one hand as the *pitṛs* or ancestors of mankind and also on the other hand as those who attain heaven and become *devajas* (born of the gods), *daivyas* and *divasputras* (sons of heaven or sons of the gods) is an idea which is frequently met with throughout vedic literature.[3] In a similar manner, the Ṛṣis are also themselves termed *devas* or gods in some *Ṛgveda* hymns: as for example where it is related that the Seven Ṛṣis, as gods or divine figures, sat down in *tapas* to discuss the question of whether Soma (personified as a deity) should return the wife of Bṛhaspati;[4] and again where it is said that the Seven Ṛṣis or *vipras*, as gods, take delight in the ordinances or sacrifices of the gods.[5] In further hymns, these heavenly figures of the Ṛṣis are seen as coming from Svarga or heaven in order to attend the sacrifices of men, and as being both summoned and generated on earth by the sacrificer himself. Thus in one hymn the seer seeks to generate on earth the Seven Ṛṣis or *karus* (Praisers) while the *soma*-juice is being drunk[6], in another hymn, the Seven Ṛṣis or *vipras* are urged to hasten to the sacrifice;[7] and in a further hymn, they are said to have approached

1. *Ṛgveda* 10.130.6-7: *Vājasaneyi Saṃhitā* 34.49; see a discussion of this hymn in 'Rishi-hood and the Soma Cult'.

2. See Chapters 2 and 6.

3. For example *Ṛgveda* 1.164.15, 3.53.7-9, 4.2.15, 10.62.4: *Taittirīya Saṃhitā* 2.6.3.2-4, 5.2.8.4-5, 5.3.9, 5.4.2, 6.2.6, 6.3.4, 7.1.4: *Atharvaveda* 9.9.16: *Aitareya Brāhmaṇa* 1.16, 4.17, 6.34-35: *Jaiminīya Brāhmaṇa* 1.224, 2.115-117, 2.122-124, 3.187-188, 3.216: *Kuaṣītaki Brāhmaṇa* 30.6: *Pañcaviṃśa Brāhmaṇa* 16.12.1-4, 25.16.2: *Śatapatha Brāhmaṇa* 1.6.2.1-4, 3.5.1.13-23: *Taittirīya Brāhmaṇa* 3.9.21.1.

4. *Ṛgveda* 10.109.1-7.

5. Ibid., 3.7.7; see also *Taittirīya Saṃhitā* 5.7.4.3: *Atharvaveda* 19.41: *Taittirīya Āraṇyaka* 3.11.9.

6. Ibid., 4.16.3.

7. Ibid., 3.31.5.

king *soma* as he sits in the *camas*—bowls ready to be drunk.[1] The aim of the *soma*-drinker was not merely to summon the Seven Ṛṣis, but to gain mystical vision of those his ancestors:

> Using my mind [*manas*] as my eye, I perceive in vision those (Seven Ṛṣis) who formerly offered this sacrifice.[2]

A new emphasis appears in the *Yajurveda*, where the Seven Ṛṣis are not merely present beside the *soma*-drinker but are visualised as residing within his own head. One passage thus relates:

> The Seven Ṛṣis are established in the body, the Seven carefully guard their dwelling-place.[3]

Through the medium of drinking *soma*, the sacrificer himself attains the realms of the gods and achieves immortality: provided that the effects of the drink— like those of alcohol or drugs—rise upwards in his body, and do not have a bad effect by descending downwards. Thus the *soma*-drinker prays, in anachronistic terms, that he may not have a bad trip—entreating that the effects of *soma* might rise upwards to the Seven Ṛṣis, who are now clearly visualised as residing in the head:

> O *soma*, be auspicious to me: approach the Seven Ṛṣis, do not go downwards beyond my navel.

After saying this, he then exclaims in ecstasy:

> We have drunk *soma*, and become immortal; we have seen the light, and found the gods.[4]

A similar request is made in a further passage:

> O *soma*, going upwards, approach the Seven Ṛṣis : O Vācaspati [lord of speech], drunk by Indra, rise to the Seven

---

1. Ibid., 9.92.2.
2. Ibid., 10.130.6.
3. *Vājasaneyi Saṃhitā* 34.55.
4. *Taittirīya Saṃhitā* 3.2.5.3-4: see also *Vaitāna Sūtra* 19.18.

Ṛtvigs [priests]; be pleased with your station, do not descend downwards.[1]

Thus the sacrificer himself goes to heaven by drinking *soma*; and like the Ṛṣis before him, sees the light and gains immortality—hence the implication underlying the statement that "You will surely make me a Ṛṣi, since I have drunk *soma*". We may here note the symbolism of light—one of the components of fire—which we have already seen to be a means whereby the Ṛṣis attained heaven; so too it is partly through the same light-symbolism that the word *soma* in later times comes to mean "the moon". Thus while the Ṛṣis are said elsewhere to attain heaven through sacrifice, *tapas*, or drinking *soma*, the *soma*-drinker here seeks to gain both Ṛṣi-hood and heaven through *soma*; the Seven Ṛṣis, having earlier been summoned from heaven to be present at his sacrifice, are here visualised as being present within his head, and it is through the ascending of *soma* to the Seven Ṛṣis that he is able to achieve his goal.

C. The Ṛṣis in the Head

What, then, is the meaning of the Seven Ṛṣis' residing in the head of the *soma*-drinker? To answer this we must look at the symbolism of the head itself, which comes to be seen as the residence of *brahman* (the Absolute, Supreme or All)—as Brahmaloka itself—whence the entire creation is sent forth. In this context, *prāṇa*—the vital breath or essence which animates all creation, thereby representing the creative activity of the Creator himself—is also the protector and guardian of *brahman*, and is in a sense the embodiment and essence of *brahman*. For one of the basic themes underlying the mystical equation of *ātman* (the individual essence) and *brahman* is that they both share the same vital or essential nature, of which *prāṇa* is both the embodiment and the manifestation (see further in the next section). One passage in the *Atharvaveda* speaks in such terms of

1. *Pañcaviṃśa Brāhmaṇa* 1.5.5; also *Jaiminīya Śrauta Sūtra* 14.14-16.

the head of Atharvan, the primal sacrificer and fire-priest and the symbol of every individual[1] :

> Atharvan sewed together his head and heart; Pavamāna [the purifying one, *soma*], above the brain, sent forth this world from that head. That head of Atharvan is a vessel of the gods, pressed together; *prāṇa* protects that head, which is called the fortress of *brahman—brahman* has entered that gilded and invincible stronghold, the golden one shining brightly and pervaded by glory.[2]

Here *brahman* is visualised as residing in the head, while *prāṇa* acts as the guardian of *brahman* and *soma* acts as the creative and motive principle through which the entire creation comes into being. A further passage in this same work speaks of the Seven Ṛṣis in this connection, implicitly identifying them as the *prāṇa* by which *brahman* is protected :

> There is a bowl [namely the head] with its opening at the side and with its bottom upwards, in which is deposited the glory of all forms; there the Seven Ṛṣis are seated together, they have become the guardians of that great one.[3]

This idea is further elaborated in one Upaniṣadic passage. Quoting this last verse, the teacher identifies the bowl as the head and the Ṛṣis as the *prāṇas*, and points out to his pupil each of the Ṛṣis as one of the "openings" in the head :

> Then there is this verse : "There is a bowl with its opening on this side and with its bottom upwards, in which is deposited the glory of all forms; the Seven Ṛṣis are seated on its rim". This here is that head : the Ṛṣis are the *prāṇas*. These two (ears) are Gotama and Bharadvāja : this is Gotama, this is Bharadvāja. These two (eyes) are Viśvāmitra and Jamadagni: this is Viśvāmitra, this is Jamadagni. These two (nostrils)

1. On Atharvan as the fire-priest parallel to the Athaurvan, Āthravan or Magian priest in Iran, see *Khodād Yasht* 10: *Ābān Yasht* 86, 91: *DīnYasht* 6.17: *Vendīdad* 18.1; R. C. Zaehner, *The Dawn and Twilight of Zoroastrianism*, pp. 163, 169.
2. *Atharvaveda* 10.2.26-33; see also *Atharvaśiras Upaniṣad* 6.
3. Ibid., 10.8.9; see also *Nirukta* 12.38.

> are Vasiṣṭha and Kaśyapa : this is Vasiṣṭha, this is Kaśyapa. The mouth [or voice, *vāc*] is Atri : for food is eaten by the mouth, and the word "eater" [*atti*] is the same as Atri.[1]

We may note here that the Seven Ṛṣis are explicitly identified as the *prāṇas*, in the sense of the ears, eyes, nostrils and mouth; six of them are depicted as being "twinned" with one another, while the seventh is independent—an idea which we saw earlier to be present in Vedic hymns, which relate that six of the Ṛṣis are god-born twins while the remaining one is born alone (or, born from the One—*ekaja*).[2] A further hymn adds that it is through the Ṛṣi who is born alone that self-abandonment is sought—in the sense of the abandonment of the material self and the world in order to attain the realisation of *ātman* or the One :

> Recognise this, O Savitṛ : six are twins, one is born alone [or born of the One]; they desíre abandonment through that one of these who is born alone.[3]

The one who is "alone" in the above-cited Upaniṣadic passage is the Ṛṣi Atri, who is identified with the mouth or voice; and we may here keep in mind the ideas both of chanting hymns in order to attain heaven (namely gaining heaven through the voice) and also of the essential nature of both speech/breath and food as *brahman*—the latter of which is particularly characteristic of certain forms of Upaniṣadic speculation.[4] Both of these ideas are embryonically present in this *Atharvaveda* hymn.

The Seven Ṛṣis—as the *prāṇas* who guard the head—are in a sense mediators between the head and the outside world, between *brahman* and the creation. As we have seen above, the entire creation is said to be sent forth from the head of

1. *Bṛhadāraṇyaka Upaniṣad* 2.2.3-4.
2. *Ṛgveda* 1.164.15: *Atharvaveda* 9.9.16. See also Chapter 1.
3. *Atharvaveda* 10.8.5.
4. For example *Bṛhadāraṇyaka Upaniṣad* 5.12: *Praśna Upaniṣad* 1.14: *Taittirīya Upaniṣad* 2.1-2, 3.7-10.

Atharvan, impelled and set in motion by the stimulation of *soma*; and in other contexts the Ṛṣis themselves—as the *prāṇas*—are the primal force and essence through which the universe came into being. The act of creation is itself a dynamic process, involving movement and change; and as we have already seen in this and earlier chapters, the Ṛṣis are embodiments of movement and change; exerting themselves (√*ṛṣ*) in the performance of *tapas* or transformative heat; and the very term "creation" (*sṛṣṭi*) denotes pouring or sending forth (√*sṛj*), just as *soma* "sent forth" the creation. Thus the Ṛṣis as *prāṇas* are said to kindle the Creator himself (Prajāpati, lord of beings) through the heat of their *tapas*, and to thereafter resort to his head which is the embodiment of glory :

> Formerly the Ṛṣis, as the *prāṇas*, were present before all this world existed; desiring it, they exerted themselves [*ariṣan*] through austerities [*śrama*] and *tapas*—that is why they are called the Ṛṣis. When the *prāṇas* were kindled, they created seven different persons [*puruṣas*], and then made those seven different persons into a single person. They gathered upwards whatever glory [*śri*] and essence [*rasa*] had resided in those seven persons, and it became the head [*śiras*] of this single one; because the *prāṇas* resorted to it [*aśrayanta*], for that reason also it is called the head. That person became Prajāpati.[1]

The Ṛṣis as *prāṇas* thus constitute the essence of all creation, the energy which enlivens and brings into being all matter. Just as *tapas* or ascetic heat is the medium by which Brahmā/Prajāpati in further contexts creates the worlds, so too the Ṛṣis as *prāṇas* are said to constitute the essence of Agni or fire, and to gain a share in him.[2]

In addition to being identified as the *prāṇas*, the Ṛṣis are also in places identified as the *indriyas*—the vital powers in the body, which in such contexts are again said to be manifested as the seven "openings" in the head.[3] Yāska recounts

1. *Śatapatha Brāhmaṇa* 6.1.1.1-5.
2. For example *Śatapatha Brāhmaṇa* 6.5.7.11, 8.4.1.5, 8.4.3.7, 8.6.1.5, 8.7.4.18-21.
3. *Pañcaviṃśa Brāhmaṇa* 22.4.2-3.

a further tradition that the Ṛṣis are the six *indriyas*—which he does not identify — together with *vidyā* or received knowledge as the seventh; he adds that, in this form they are also identical with the seven rays of the sun.[1] As we saw in the last chapter, one Āraṇyaka passage identifies the seven *prāṇas* with the seven suns;[2] in both of these latter instances, the identification of microcosm and macrocosm is explicit—in other words, the underlying essence or energy which animates and resides in the head is the same as the essence of energy residing in and pouring out from the sun, while this same energy constitutes the essential nature of the Ṛṣis.

D. Prāṇa and the Prāṇas in the Upaniṣads

In Upaniṣadic thought—as also indeed in much preceding Brāhmaṇa speculation—the concept of *prāṇa* is of central importance to the understanding of *brahman* and *ātman*. *Brahman* is the inner essence and reality of all, the single source from which arises the multiform creation. *Prāṇa*—as vital breath, wind or essence—is frequently identified with *brahman* : sharing the essence of *brahman*, yet also the mode in which *brahman* manifests and diversifies itself. When Yājñavalkya is questioned as to the number of gods, he successively reduces their number from 3306 to just one—and this one is *prāṇa*, which is also *Brahman.*[3] *Brahman* is in places said to consist of two levels : a formed *brahman* which is the essence of the actual, and a formless *brahman* which is the subtlest essence of all and which is identified as moving, immortal breath (*prāṇa*) or wind (*vāyu*).[4] In other places, *prāṇa* is said to arise and be born from *ātman*;[5] one account relates that Prajāpati, wishing to create beings, performed *tapas*—whence arose matter (rayi) and life-energy (*prāṇa*), which multiplied creation for him.[6] *Prāṇa* is not ultimately separate from Prajāpati or *brahman*, but is the form in

1. *Nirukta* 12.37.
2. *Taittirīya Āraṇyaka* 1.7.2-6.
3. *Bṛhadāraṇyaka Upaniṣad* 3.9.1-9.
4. Ibid., 2.3.1-6.
5. *Chāndogya Upaniṣad* 7.26.1: *Praśna Upaniṣad* 3.3-11.
6. *Praśna Upaniṣad* 1.4.

which *brahman* is manifested in all beings. Just as Prajāpati, upon creating the world through *tapas*, entered into it,[1] and as the spider spins its web from its own body and draws it back into itself,[2] so too *brahman* produced *prāṇa* from itself which is yet the *ātman* of all beings, the inner essence and the life-force of all creatures.[3] *Prāṇa*—in the form of *brahman*—is often identified with the sun, the wind, and fire, these being its three principal manifestations;[4] *prāṇa* is that which shines forth in all things,[5] and it is this same life-force which underlies and animates all creation and which is accordingly manifested as both the sun in the sky and the breath in the body.[6] *Prāṇa* thus represents the flowing-out of *brahman* from itself; the whole world is said to be created from and to move in *prāṇa*,[7] which is hidden in all things as their *ātman* or innermost self.[8] To perceive this *prāṇa*—and to perceive the *ātman* as *prāṇa*—is to merge with it, to become one with it and to know *brahman*; the mortal and perishable is thereby abandoned, and both immortality and heaven are achieved,[9] since *prāṇa* is itself Life, supreme and undying.[10]

Prāṇa is said to be yoked to the body as an ox to a cart;[11] it is also likened to the hub of a wheel on which all else is fixed.[12] The *prāṇas* are the different manifestations of *prāṇa* in the body : just as *brahman* or Prajāpati produced creation from his own being, evolving the many from the One yet retaining unit among the many through his own pervading essence, so too *prāṇa* gives rise to the *prāṇas* which are differentiated from but not separate from itself.13 The

1. *Taittirīya Upaniṣad* 2.6.
2. *Muṇḍaka Upaniṣad* 1.1.7.
3. *Chāndogya Upaniṣad* 7.15.1; *Muṇḍaka Upaniṣad* 2.1.2-4.
4. For example *Bṛhadāraṇyaka Upaniṣad* 1.1.2.1 ff., 1.5.21-22: *Chāndogya Upaniṣad* 1.3.1-4.
5. *Muṇḍaka Upaniṣad* 3.1.4.
6. *Praśna Upaniṣad* 1.8, 2.4-13, 3.3 ff.
7. *Kaṭha Upaniṣad* 6.2.
8. Ibid., 3.12.
9. *Kauṣītaki Upaniṣad* 3.2: *Kaṭha Upaniṣad* 3.12, 6.2.
10. *Taittirīya Upaniṣad* 2.3.
11. *Chāndogya Upaniṣad* 8.12.3.
12. *Kauṣītaki Upaniṣad* 3.8: *Muṇḍaka Upaniṣad* 2.2.6: *Praśna Upaniṣad* 2.6, 6.6.
13. *Bṛhadāraṇyaka Upaniṣad* 1.1.2.6: *Chāndogya Upaniṣad* 1.5.21-22.

Supreme produced *prāṇa*, which is both *brahman* and also the *ātman* of all : he produced the seven *prāṇas* which move in the worlds and dwell in the secret place of the heart;[1] so too it is said that *prāṇa* was born from *ātman*, and established itself in the eyes, ears, mouth and nose.[2] In many Upaniṣadic passages, the *prāṇas* are listed as five in number : namely speech, breath, sight, hearing and mind;[3] in some passages, either seed, heart or intelligence are added as a sixth.[4] In many other passages, the five *prāṇas* are the winds or breaths in different parts of the body : this being, as we shall see in the next section, the concept which is most frequently adopted in later contexts.[5] These five are said to be the door-keepers of heaven, the bridge to immortality and the means for perceiving *ātman* :[6] for just as Svayambhū originally pierced openings outwards in the head and body, so the wise man perceives his *ātman* by looking within rather than without.[7] *Ātman* is further spoken of as the hearing of the ear, the thought of mind, the voice of speech, the breathing of breath and the sight of the eye;[8] while the supreme *prāṇa* is also identified with *brahman*, of which mind is the messenger, the eye is the watchman, and speech is the servant.[9] All of these various functions are united and merge together during deep sleep;[10] at death, all the *prāṇas* (in the sense of eye, ear, *etc.*) reunite in their essence as *prāṇa*,[11] and while the body dies, its essence as *prāṇa*—of which *ātman* is the finest essence—

1. *Muṇḍaka Upaniṣad* 2.1.2-8, 2.2.2-5.
2. *Praśna Upaniṣad* 3.3-11.
3. For example *Chāndogya Upaniṣad* 5.1.6-15: *Kauṣītaki Upaniṣad* 2.14: *Kena Upaniṣad* 1-2.
4. For example *Bṛhadāraṇyaka Upaniṣad* 4.1.1-7, 6.1.7-14: *Kauṣītaki Upaniṣad* 2.4.
5. For example *Bṛhadāraṇyaka Upaniṣad* 3.9.26: *Chāndogya Upaniṣad* 1.3.1-4, 3.13.1-7, 5.19.1—5.23.2: *Praśna Upaniṣad* 4.3-4.
6. *Chāndogya Upaniṣad* 3.13.1-7: *Muṇḍaka Upaniṣad* 2.2.5, 3.1.9.
7. *Kaṭha Upaniṣad* 4.1.
8. *Kena Upaniṣad* 1.2.
9. *Kauṣītaki Upaniṣad* 2.1.
10. For example *Kauṣītaki Upaniṣad* 4.19-20.
11. Ibid., 3.2-3.

does not die[1] but re-emerges in a different form or body.[2] *Prāṇa* is thus the life-energy which cannot die, which appears in different forms yet remains unitary; to perceive the unity and identity of *ātman*, *prāṇa* and *brahman* is to flow back to the One, as rivers flowing back to an ocean[3]—it is to become this All, to become the *ātman* or inner essence of the gods, a process which even the gods themselves cannot prevent.[4]

The Upaniṣads contain a number of diverse ideas on *prāṇa* and the *prāṇas* : for example as to the number and precise identity of the *prāṇas*. Yet the overall conception of *prāna* is, like its nature, unitary. *Prāṇa* is of the nature of both *ātman* and *brahman*, usually conceived as being produced or evolving from *brahman* as its mode of self-manifestation and self-diversity in creation; it is the real and undying essence underlying all change, the vital life-force which is superior to mortal life and death alike. *Prāṇa* is the breath in the body, just as it is the fire in the sun; and to realise the nature of *prāṇa* is to know *ātman* or the real self and *brahman* or the Self of all, and to know the unity of all three. For it is to know that he who is in fire is both yonder in the sun and here in the heart[5] : the external forms differ, yet the internal and abiding essence is one.

Just as *prāṇa* is supremely manifested in fire, the sun, and the heat of the breath, so the Ṛṣis—by transforming their being into fire or the sun through *tapas*—merge with and become *prāṇa* itself. Seen in this light, their self-heating through *tapas* does not so much lead to the realisation of *brahman* in the sense of an intellectual perception : *tapas* is a form of *brahman*, it is the means by which *brahman* is kindled, and the means by which the whole being is transformed into *brahman*. The supreme heat of *tapas* is itself *brahman* ; and when

1. *Chāndogya Upaniṣad* 6.11.1-3.
2. *Kauṣītaki Upaniṣad* 2.12-13.
3. *Praśna Upaniṣad* 6.4.
4. *Bṛhadāraṇyaka Upaniṣad* 1.4.10.
5. *Maitrī Upaniṣad* 6.17, 7.7: *Taittirīya Upaniṣad* 2.8. For further discussion of such Upaniṣadic speculation, see especially P. Deussen, *The Philosophy of the Upanishads*, and A. B. Keith, *The Religion and Philosophy to the Veda and Upanishads*.

the Ṛṣis attain this height of *tapas*, their nature is transformed from the gross and material into the subtle life-essence of *prāṇa*, which is itself the form and manifestation of *brahman*. There is therefore no discontinuity or change of level between the performance of *tapas* and the realisation of *brahman* : through *tapas* the Ṛṣis become *brahman* and grow into their own divinity.

E. The Eclipse of a Concept

The identity of the Seven Ṛṣis as the *prāṇas* does not generally appear in post-Vedic contexts. This is due in large measure to a change in symbolism of the term *prāṇa*, whereby the *prāṇas* —as we saw in the last section—are more generally considered to be five rather than seven in number. This change is evident already in the Brāhmaṇas, where for example one passage identifies the Ṛṣis Atri, Jamadagni, Viśvāmitra, Bharadvāja and Vasiṣṭha as the mouth, eye, ear, mind and breath of the body respectively.[1] In this passage, the identification of Atri as the mouth or speech is the same as that noted earlier; while the identification of Vasiṣṭha as the breath itself may be seen as an attempt to emphasise the superiority of Vasiṣṭha in relation to the other Ṛṣis—comparable to further examples noted in chapter 3. Such an interpretation is indeed made explicit in several Upaniṣadic contexts, where the five *prāṇas* (namely mouth, eye, ear, mind and breath) dispute as to which of them is superior. Prajāpati tells each to depart in turn from the body and the first four depart and return; but when breath starts to depart, it cannot leave the body without destroying it and is thus shown to be superior to the others.[2] In subsequent literature—especially throughout the Epics, Purāṇas and Tantras—the Seven Ṛṣis are rarely identified as the seven *prāṇas*. They are nonetheless connected with *prāṇa* in several contexts; and many Purāṇas relate an account of the births of Ṛṣis from the body and the various *prāṇas* of Brahmā :

---

1. *Śatapatha Brāhmaṇa* 8.1.1.6—8.1.2.6.
2. *Bṛhadāraṇyaka Upaniṣad* 6.1.7-14: *Chāndogya Upaniṣad* 5.1.6-15: *Kauṣītaki Upaniṣad* 2.14, 3.2-3.

> Then Brahmā created Rudra, who arose from his anger; Saṅkalpa [purpose] and Dharma [righteousness], the two foundations of all creation—Brahmā created Good Conduct [namely Dharma] from his agreeable nature, and Saṅkalpa was born from his will. He created Dakṣa from his *prāṇa*, and Marīci from his two eyes; and Bhṛgu, the Ṛṣi born of water, was born from his heart. Aṅgiras was born from his head, and Atri from his ear; Pulastya from his *udāna*, and Pulaha from his *vyāna*; Vasiṣṭha from his *samāna* and Kratu from his *apāna*. These are known as the twelve best sons of Brahmā; and he looked upon those, who were endowed with *sattva* [virtue] and were born from his *prāṇa* [*prāṇaja*].[1]

All of the Ṛṣis—together with Rudra, Saṅkalpa and Dharma —are here said to be from the *prāṇa* of Brahmā, and thus to be creations of his vital energy and breath. Yet the meaning given to the term *prāṇa* in this passage is quite evidently more generalised than that found in most Vedic texts. Throughout post-Vedic literature—and especially in Tantric works—the *prāṇas* are commonly said to be five in number; as in several Upaniṣadic contexts, these are *prāṇa* (the wind in the upper part of the body, especially in the lungs), *apāna* (the wind going downwards and out at the bowels and phallus), *samāna* (the wind in the abdomen and stomach), *vyāna* (the wind diffused throughout the whole body), and *udāna* (the wind rising upwards to the throat and head).[2] One Epic passage increases their number to seven by adding *avāk* (downward-going wind) and *pravaha* (upward-going wind), and thereafter mentions also

1. Different details are added in different Purāṇas: see for example *Bhāgavata Purāṇa* 3.12.21-23: *Brahmāṇḍa Purāṇa* 1.1.5.72-84, 1.2.9.20-29: *Brahmavaivarta Purāṇa* 1.8.25-28: *Kūrma Pūrāṇa* 1.7.33-37: *Liṅga Purāṇa* 1.70.178 ff.: *Śiva Purāṇa* 2.1.16.4-7: *Vāyu Purāṇa* 1.9.92-103.

2. On Vedic ideas of the *prāṇas*, see also M. Eliade, *Yoga : Immortality and Freedom*, pp. 384-385: A. H. Ewing, 'The Hindu Conception of the Functions of Breath', pp. 249-308: J. Filliozat, *La Doctrine Classique de la Medicine Indienna*, pp. 142 ff. On Tantric ideas, see J. Woodroffe, *Introduction to Tantra Shastra*, pp. 30 ff., and *Shakti und Shakta*: A. Bharati, *The Tantric Tradition*: C. Chakravarti, *Studies in the Tantras*: P. Rawson, *Tantra* and *The Art of Tantra*.

the Seven Ṛṣis—yet it makes no attempt to equate or identify the Ṛṣis with the *prāṇas* :

> A man will attain liberation [*mokṣa*] when he has come to perceive the *prāṇa*, *apāna*, *samāna*, *vyāna* and *udāna*, together with the *avāk* and *pravaha*—the seven winds, and all the others—while following a practice in seven different ways; and when he has come to perceive the Prajāpatis, the Ṛṣis, the many excellent paths, and the many Seven Ṛṣis and royal Ṛṣis, O hero.[1]

The passage thus witnesses that, even when the *prāṇas* were still considered in certain contexts during later times to be seven in number, these were no longer associated or identified with the Seven Ṛṣis in the manner of the Vedic identity.

We can consequently trace a gradual change in symbolism of the term *prāṇa*. In Vedic literature, the *prāṇas* represent in the first place the openings in the head—namely the ears, eyes, nostrils and mouth—through which the vital breath or life-force flows backwards and forwards between the head and the outside world, and through which sense-impressions are both received and sent forth; and it is primarily in this context that the Seven Ṛṣis are identified as the *prāṇas*. However, from the Brāhmaṇas onwards we encounter the ideas both of only five *prāṇas*—namely the mouth, eye, ear, mind and breath—and also of an extension of meaning to encompass breath or wind in the body as a whole, rather than exclusively in the head. Thereafter, in post-Vedic contexts, both of these latter ideas are further elaborated : the *prāṇas* are generally said to be five in number, and are taken to represent winds or airs in different parts of the body. The very basis of the identity of the Seven Ṛṣis as the *prāṇas* is consequently undermined, through the change in the number of the *prāṇas*; although the Ṛṣis are nonetheless on occasions associated with the concept of *prāṇa*, as in accounts of their birth from the *prāṇa* of Brahmā. It is interesting to note in this latter instance also a slight change in the role of the Ṛṣis :

---

1. *Mahābhārata* 12.290.26-29: *Brahma Purāṇa* 239.27; see also *Mahābhārata* 14.22.1—14.23.20 *et. al.*

for whereas in certain Brāhmaṇa acccounts it is the Ṛṣis who, as *prāṇas*, kindle and create the Creator, in such Purāṇic accounts on the other hand—as indeed in many Upaniṣadic contexts—it is the Creator who gives birth to the Ṛṣis from his own *prāṇa*. In both sets of accounts, the Ṛṣis are nonetheless seen as embodiments of creative power and energy, as the Life-force which animates the creation and sets in motion the entire creative process.

9

"THEN SHALL THEY SEE GOD"

A. Introduction

We have already examined in previous chapters various aspects of the nature and role of the Ṛṣis; in this chapter we shall survey their main roles, especially in the light of their relation on the one hand to the creation, and on the other hand to *brahman* and Brahmā. Many of the points which we shall be discussing in this chapter presuppose, refer to and are developed from themes which have already been examined in earlier chapters : reference should accordingly be made to such earlier contexts where appropriate.

B. The Turning Wheel

The Seven Ṛṣis are primarily creators and re-creators : created by Brahmā for the express purpose of continuing his own work of creation, they in turn create gods, men and demons, birds, beasts and fishes, trees and plants—indeed, the entire animate creation. This role of the Ṛṣis is especially prominent throughout the Epics and Purāṇas, and is associated with their designations as Prajāpatis and Sons of Brahmā which we shall be looking at in a minute. But it also appears in Vedic literature, and in the Vedic *saṃhitās* themselves. In the *Atharvaveda*, the Seven Ṛṣis are in several contexts referred to as *bhūtakṛts* or "makers of being", a term synonymous with *prajāpati*. In one context, they are said to have kindled Agni :

> O Agni, may you be born; Aditi is cooking *brahman*-rice here, requesting and desiring sons; may the Seven Ṛṣis, your *bhūtakṛts*, kindle you here, togther with offspring . . . . the Seven Ṛṣis, your *bhūtakṛts*, have given birth to you, Agni—may you bestow all strength on that woman.[1]

The Ṛṣis, as *bhūtakṛts*, are thus said both to belong to Agni and also to give birth to him—as is similarly said of them in other Vedic contexts.[2] In another passage, the *bhūtakṛts* are called creators of the second *sruc*, the wooden ladle used to pour ghee onto the sacrificial fire :

> This second *sruc* is the hand of Aditi; the Seven *bhūtakṛt*-Ṛṣis made this.[3] In one further passage, they are said to have sought cattle through their song, sacrifice and *tapas* :

> The *bhūtakṛt*-Ṛṣis in former times sang out for cattle on this earth—those Seven creators, through sacrificial session, sacrifice and *tapas*.[4]

Here, then, we are once again presented with an idea which we have already encountered in many other contexts : namely that the Seven Ṛṣis were formerly on earth, and performed sacrifice and *tapas*—thereby attaining not merely an exalted status but also such material or worldly gains as children and cattle. The term *bhūtakṛt* used in such contexts may be taken to refer both to their role in raising offspring and being the ancestors and founders of the race, and also to their nature and role as both sons and creators of Agni: as we have seen, both of these roles are ascribed to the Seven Ṛṣis in the *Ṛgveda*, as well as throughout subsequent literature. The collective designation of the Seven Ṛṣis as Prajāpatis does not appear in later Vedic literature and is only met with in the Epics and Purāṇas, although in several instances a Ṛṣi is individually referred to as being (a) Prajāpati. We may perhaps see here something of a difference

---

1. *Atharvaveda* 11.1.1-3.
2. See Chapter 7 section B (b).
3. *Atharvaveda* 11.1.24.
4. Ibid., 12.1.39.

in outlook between especially later-Vedic and post-Vedic literature : for in the former, the term Prajāpati symbolises and designates only a single creator-figure, who comes to be identified as Brahmā himself. We have seen that one Brāhmaṇa passage relates that the Ṛṣis brought Prajāpati into being through their exertion and *tapas*;[1] while they are also said to have been born when the seed of Prajāpati fell into the sacrificial fire.[2] In both of these cases, the emphasis falls upon the role of creative heat and movement, the Ṛṣis being in one case the authors and in the other case the products of such creative activity—while in both cases they are nonetheless clearly separated from Prajāpati, just as in later literature they are separated from yet embodiments of Brahmā. Certain Brāhmaṇa passages speak of an equivalence between a particular Ṛṣi and Prajāpati; one instructs that hymns of Jamadagni should be recited at the *aśvamedha* sacrifice in order to supply the sacrifice with its own deity, since both the *aśvamedha* and Jamadagni are Prajāpati;[3] while another instructs that in order to obtain a desire one should recite a verse of Vasiṣṭha, since Vasiṣṭha is Prajāpati and it is in Prajāpati that one attains all desires.[4] In both of these instances, however, the Ṛṣi concerned is not so much identified as being Prajāpati but rather equated as being of the same nature as Prajāpati, in the manner of countless other such Brāhmaṇa equations. Another context in which a Ṛṣi is termed a Prajāpati appears in the *Maitri Upaniṣad*, in the form of a conversation between Kratu Prajāpati and the Vālakhilyas;[5] yet this Upaniṣad is of such manifestly late date in comparison with the other principal Upaniṣads[6] that it should better be considered alongside Epic rather than Vedic literature—as indeed is implied by the appearance of Kratu himself, who is otherwise unmentioned in Vedic literature as a personi-

1. *Satapatha Brāhmaṇa* 6.1.1.1-5.
2. For example *Aitareya Brāhmaṇa* 3.34: *Jaiminīya Brāhmaṇa* 3.263: *Śatapatha Brāhmaṇa* 4.5.1.1-8.
3. *Śatapatha Brāhmaṇa* 13.2.2.14.
4. *Kauṣītaki Brāhmaṇa* 25.2, 26.15.
5. *Maitrī Upaniṣad* 2.3—4.6.
6. See for example the discussion in A. B. Keith, *A History of Sanskrit Literature*, pp. 194-196.

fied Ṛṣi rather than as the sacrificial fire (*kratu*). One other Ṛṣi who is not merely equated with but identified as Prajāpati in Vedic literature is Kaśyapa, who as the tortoise is identified in one Brāhmaṇa passage with the creative activity of Prajāpati.[1] Passages such as these emphasise the creative role and activity of the Ṛṣis, which they share with the creator; the relative lack of references to them as Prajāpatis in Vedic or ritual literature in no way minimises their creative roie in that literature, but rather reflects the distinctive theoretical—or theological—outlook of Vedic literature, wherein the term *prajāpati* denotes but a single figure, namely the creator himself.

As we saw especially in Chapter 1, the Seven Ṛṣis are termed both Prajāpatis and Mind-born Sons of Brahmā throughout the Epics and Purāṇas. Such designations are applied to them especially in the context of their birth from or creation by Brahmā, many accounts of which are along the following lines:

> Brahmā first created offspring who did not increase; these he abandoned [or in some cases destroyed]. Then he created the Seven Mind-born Sons : Marīci, Atri, Aṅgiras, Pulastya, Pulaha, Kratu and Vasiṣṭha, resembling himself; these are called the Seven Brahmās in the Purāṇa, and have attained certainty. I shall now describe all these Prajāpatis.[2]

There occur several variants upon this basic form, particularly in respect of the number of Ṛṣis born in this way; but in most accounts, the passage continues to relate the creative activity of these Ṛṣis in marrying and begetting offspring, thereby increasing and engendering the entire animate creation. The designation of Ṛṣis as Prajāpatis thus essentially emphasises their role as creators and sustainers of the three worlds (*trailokyabhāvanāḥ*, *trīn lokān dhārayanti*, *lokasya santānakarāḥ*);[3] they are lords of creation in the literal sense of being the

---

1. *Śatapatha Brāhmaṇa* 7.5.1.1-6.

2. For references and individual variants, see the passages cited in Chapter 1 sections D and E.

3. For example *Mahābhārata* 12.201.2 ff.: *Harivaṃśa* 12.13-14: *Brahmāṇḍa Purāṇa* 2.3.1.-48: *Vāyu Purāṇa* 2.4.48.

progenitors of animation through sexual propagation. It is in this context that they are also termed the *prakṛti*-elements (*sapta prakṛtayaḥ*)[1] : namely the primal constituent elements which give rise to the material world; for they are the basic forms of created existence in the same sense as they are the *prāṇas* or life-force which animates and enlivens all creation. In begetting offspring and thereby propagating the creation, they are fulfilling the task appointed them by their father Brahmā, who rejected the sons whom he first created since they did not increase creation or beget offspring, and instead created these other sons—resembling himself (*sadṛś*), equal to himself (*svayamiś-varāḥ*), and created for the express purpose of further creation (*prājāpatyena kalpitāḥ*).[2] The Ṛṣis are said to be born not by sexual propagation but from the being and mind of Brahmā (*madbhāvā mānasā jātāḥ, brahmaṇaḥ putrā mānasāḥ*)[3]—just as they are also said to be born from the *prāṇa*, the vital essence or life-force, of Brahmā.[4] *Manas* or mind in this context represents not so much the cognitive mind as it passively receives impressions from the outside world, but rather the mind in its active and willing role as the motivator and agent for activity, for which the body is the instrument. We have already seen that, in the Brāhmaṇs, *manas* or mind is listed as one of the five *prāṇas* or life-forces, and is in that context identified as the Ṛṣi Bharadvāja,[5] while it similarly appears as one of the five *prāṇas* in much Upaniṣadic speculation.[6] The nature of *manas*—like that of *prāṇa* itself—is thus essentially creative, active, and life-giving, insofar as its appearance in these contexts is concerned; and the birth of the Ṛṣis from the *manas* of Brahmā similarly denotes dynamic creativity on the part of the creator. Like the concept of *manas* in the *Yogavāsiṣṭha*, the *mānasa*-creation of sons by Brahmā represents his own self-transformation into thought-activity, by which he creates from himself objects similar to

1. *Mahābhārata* 12.322.26-28, 12.327.29.
2. For example *Mahābhārata* 12.327.61-62: *Brahmāṇḍa Purāṇa* 1.2.32.96: *Matsya Purāṇa* 145.90-91: *Vāyu Purāṇa* 1.59.88.
3. See throughout sections D and E of Chapter 1.
4. See Chapter 8 section E.
5. *Śatapatha Brāhmaṇa* 8.1.1.6—8.1.2.6: see also Chapter 8 section E.
6. See Chapter 8 section D.

and sharing the essential nature and character of himself[1] : sons who are both manifestations and embodiments of his own dynamic creative energy. In the Epic and Purāṇic accounts, Brahmā does not himself continue the creation of the three worlds after giving birth to these Mind-born Sons, but instead deputes this task to them. Several mythological explanations are offered for this : one passage for example relates that he lost his creative powers—amassed through *tapas*—on account of his lust for Sāvitrī, and so instead sent his sons to carry on the work of creation;[2] while another relates that he was unable to create the three worlds without help, and for that reason created his Mind-born Sons.[3] The dynamically creative role of these Ṛṣi-sons is again emphasised through their further designation as Brahmās (*sapta brahmāṇaḥ*). We should bear in mind that although the philosophical or mystical Absolute and the mythological creator-figure are conventionally distinguished for clarification as *brahman* and Brahmā, both are denoted by the same noun *brahman* (used as a neuter or masculine noun respectively) and are consequently only distinguishable from one another in many instances through contextual usage; yet the essential idea underlying both terms is that of dynamism and creativity.[4] The term *brahmāṇaḥ* as used of the Ṛṣis is the masculine nominative plural form of the noun *brahman*, thus denoting that the Ṛṣis are the Seven Brahmās, creator-figures whose essence is *brahman* and who share the same nature and role as Brahmā himself. The designations of the Ṛṣis as both Prajāpatis and Brahmās consequently emphasise yet again their creative function : one step removed from, yet in essence identical with, the creator himself.

In their roles as Prajāpatis, Brahmās, and Mind-born Sons of Brahmā, the Ṛṣis become the agents and instruments through which Brahmā expresses his own creative will; they are his means for increasing and expanding the creation, the agencies

1. Especially *Yogavāsiṣṭha* 3.91—3.96; discussed in S. N. Dasgupta, *A History of Indian Philosophy*, Vol. 2. pp. 228-272.
2. For example *Matsya Purāṇa* 3.30-41.
3. *Liṅga Purāṇa* 2.85.12.
4. See Chapter 8 section D, and the next section of this chapter

through which all animate life is kindled. Their task is not so much to create the material world—since this is said in nearly every instance to have been undertaken by Brahmā before creating these sons—but rather to endow it with life and vitality; and we have seen that it is similarly in this connection that they are termed the *prāṇas*, the life-energies which animate the entire creation. As such, they are not essentially separate from Brahmā, but manifestations of his own creative activity—an activity which is especially characterised by heat, denoting transformative change. They are thus like particles of pure energy which, dispersing their power in material creativity and movement, gradually come to rest in the form of matter; and when once at rest, they yet again internally recharge themselves through the production of heat, gradually retransforming themselves into that same pure energy which first impelled them to their creativity. It can be seen that this concept of Ṛṣi-hood is in many respects emanatory in character : not merely in the sense that the Ṛṣis flow from the very essence of Brahmā, but more especially in their role as carrying out his will through creative activity and as ultimately returning to their source in him. Useful parallels may consequently be drawn between these ideas and those in especially Philoan,[1] Plotinian,[2] and Kabalistic[3] speculation; although we must also note that in the case of the Ṛṣis, there is no question of them creating matter as opposed to spirit, and thus no opposition between the supreme creator and the world of matter. In a sense, the *māyā* or "illusion" of the universe denotes, as far as the Ṛṣis are concerned, that the material world has no real existence until it is suffused with the *prāṇa* of life-energy from which it evolves, and no continuing existence once that *prāṇa* departs. Yet unlike the Biblical account wherein Yahweh first creates Adam and then breathes life into him, animate existence flows from the Ṛṣis as

1. For example *De Somniis* 1.22; see also E. Brehier, *Les Idées Philosophiques*: I. Heinemann, *Philons Griechische und Jüdische Bildung*: H. A. Wolfson, *Philo*.

2. For example *Enneads* 5.1.6, 5.5.9; see also E. Brehier, *La Philosophie de Plotin*: W. Inge, *The Philosophy of Plotinus*: H. R. Schwytzer, 'Plotinus'.

3. See especially *Sefer ha-Yetzīrāh* and *Sefer ha-zo hār*; also J. Abelson, *Jewish Mysticism*: C. D. Ginsburg, *The Kabbalah*: G. G. Scholem, *Major Trends in Jewish Mysticism* and *On the Kabbalah and its Symbolism*.

both material existence (as in their giving birth to children, animals, trees and so forth) and also "spiritual"—or life-essence (as in their nature as the *prāṇas* in the body). *Prāṇa* is itself the subtlest essence and true inner reality of matter, as well as its source; hence there is no sharp distinction between existence and essence, matter and spirit, as tends to be developed in the emanatory contexts cited above. The role of the Ṛṣis is in certain respects analogous to that of the seven Archangels in Biblical and Apocryphal thought, who put into effect the commands of God;[1] and like the angels on Jacob's ladder,[2] the Ṛṣis too move from heaven to earth and back again, first propagating living beings and then returning through sacrifice or *tapas* to their original source—then yet again returning to earth in every age to renew the teaching of *dharma* and to continue the expansion of the universe.[3]

The Ṛṣis are, then, on the one hand the creators of all living being. They give birth not only to men, but also to demons and gods, birds, beasts and fishes, trees and plants, the sun (Vivasvat) and the moon (Soma), the rain (Indra), the storm (Maruts) and the fire (Agni). Parallel to this is their role as sustainers and re-creators of life : in darkness, they create or become the sun and moon; and when the earth sinks, they rescue and replace it. This last instance—which we have seen to be especially related of Kaśyapa in his role as the world-

1. For example *Tobit* 12.15: *Enoch* 20.1-8, 81.5, 87.2, 90.21: *Revelation* 8.2, 15.1, 16.1; at *Enoch* 20.1-8 the seven Archangels are listed as Uriel, Raphael, Raguel, Michael, Saraqael, Gabriel and Remiel. Note however that at *Enoch* 19.1 the seven Archangels are distinguished from the fallen angels—who are incidentally identified as stars—since the latter had intercourse with women, whereas the Seven Ṛṣis are distinguished from the sons first created and then abandoned by Brahmā since the latter sons *refused* to marry and beget offspring; this difference would again seem to arise from the distinction between matter and spirit in especially the Hellenistic-Jewish tradition, and the lack of such a sharp distinction in the Hindu tradition. Also note the possible correspondence between *Aṅgiras,* Persian *ayyapos* and Greek *ἄγγελος,* "messenger" or "angel": see A. Hillebrandt, *Vedische Mythologie,* Vol. 1 pp. 173 ff.

2. *Genesis* 28.12.

3. On this and related topics, see J. E. Mitchiner, 'The Concept of Emanation'.

tortoise[1]—reappears in a slightly different form in the Flood myth. Although the Seven Ṛṣis are not mentioned in the earliest Brāhmaṇa account of the Flood,[2] several later accounts relate that when the great flood of the worlds occurred, Manu entered his boat—like Noah and Ziusudra in the Biblical and Sumerian accounts—along with the Seven Ṛṣis and the seeds of all living creatures; they alone survived the flood, and thereafter became the propagators of a new creation.[3] The Flood-myth is in turn linked to the appearance of the Ṛṣis in the Manvantara tradition, where they not only propagate mankind—both after the flood and also in every Mahāyuga—but also create and spread knowledge by instructing men in *dharma* and the Vedas.[4] In such contexts, the Ṛṣis are teachers of *dharma* : not only through their words, but also in their actions they ensure the correct ordering and running of the worlds, the correct balance of *dharma* between good and evil, the gods and the demons. When evil threatens to overwhelm good, they destroy the evil and allow the good to flourish; and when they accomplish this by either creating demons (to chastise unrighteous gods and men) or destroying demons and enemies through their curse, the fire of their anger is directed not so much against an individual as against an offence. Here we return to the theme of the continuing involvement of the Ṛṣis in the world. The Ṛṣis are not gentle, meek and humble indivi-

1. For example *Śāṅkhāyana Śrauta Sūtra* 16.16.3-4: *Mahābhārata* 3.114.17-22 12.49.39-80, 13.139.1 ff.; see also Chapter 7 section B (c). Compare the world-tortoise in Siberian and North American Indian mythologies: Holmberg, *Finno-Ugric and Siberian Mythology*, pp. 314ff., 326ff., 342ff., 361ff.; Alexander, *North American Mythology*, pp. 42 ff., 152, 217 ff. See also the Singpho tribal myth in Elwin, *Myths of the North-East Frontier of India*, pp. 128-130.

2. *Śatapatha Brāhmaṇa* 1.8.1.1ff.; compare *Matsya Purāṇa* 1.10—2.19. For these accounts, see O'Flaherty, *Hindu Myths*, pp. 179-184.

3. For example *Mahābhārata* 3.185.1-54: *Agni Purāṇa* 2.3 ff.: *Bhāgavata Purāṇa* 8.24.1 ff.; see S. Shastri, *The Flood Legend in Sanskrit Literature.* Compare also the tribal myths wherein seven people create and repopulate the world after the flood: Elwin, *op.cit.* p. 20, *The Baiga* p. 316, and *Myths of Middle India* pp. 114-115. Also Holmberg, *op.cit.* pp. 322 ff., 361 ff., and Alexander, pp. 42 ff., 217 ff. For the Biblical account, see *Genesis* 6.1—9.27: for the Sumerian, *The Epic of Gilgamesh.*

4. On both the flood-myth and the Manvantara traditions, see Chapter 2.

duals devoted to the pursuit of unworldly aims; through their *tapas* they become detached from the unreal and the phenomenal aspects of material existence, yet merge with the real which is an integral part of—and indeed the very essence of—the phenomenal and material. Through their *tapas*—as also through sacrifice and through the singing of hymns—they become transformed into *brahman* itself, embodiments of inner power and might[1], endowed with the energy of fire and the sun. Thus while anger against individuals on a personal level (as in the rivalries of Viśvāmitra and Vasiṣṭha) represents an attachment and a passion which must be overcome, nonetheless impersonal anger against offenders of *dharma* is intrinsic to the very nature of Ṛṣis as embodiments of fire and of *brahman*. It is indeed only because they have merged with *brahman*, and realised their own essential nature as *brahman*, that they manifest the power and nature of *brahman* when necessary as the fire of righteous anger; just as it is only by withdrawing from the world—from the world of appearance and material form—that they merge with the formless and thereby become in turn totally committed to the world as its undying and vital life-force. In mythological terms, this is required of them : for while *tapas* is of its nature creative, excess *tapas* or heat is destructive unless properly channelled; and just as the gods must grant the wishes of performers of *tapas* in order to prevent the destruction of the worlds, so too the continuing *tapas* of the Ṛṣis must be directed positively in the form of further creations and external projections of the internal energy amassed through *tapas*. Thus the Ṛṣis, by transforming themselves into *brahman* through the heat of their *tapas*, in turn become the embodiments of heat and light, of motion and transformative change which is the *Prāṇa* or life-force of living beings; they become the means whereby the creator effects the work of creation, and their primary role is then to create movement and animation in the universe, to maintain and expand the harmony of the worlds.

1. On the power of sacrifice and *brahman*, see especially S. Lévi, *La Doctrine du Sacrifice dans les Brāhmaṇas*, particularly pp. 9 ff.: J. Abbott, *The Keys of Power: a Study of Indian Ritual and Belief*.

C. The Turning Centre

The Seven Ṛṣis, after performing sacrifice and *tapas* on the earth, are said to have attained Svarga or heaven and the realm of the gods. In Vedic literature, they are usually said to reside in Svargaloka, the highest of the three worlds; similarly in the Epics and Purāṇas—apart from within the Purāṇic Manvantara tradition—they are said to be residents of Brahmaloka, the highest of the seven worlds, where they attend and wait upon Brahmā. Yet they do not remain constantly in heaven or in the company of Brahmā; particularly in the Vedic context of the *soma* sacrifice, they return from heaven to be present either with or within the sacrificer, while in the Manvantara tradition they periodically return from heaven to earth in order to propagate and teach mankind, thereafter returning to their abode in the sky until the same process is repeated in the next Mahāyuga. Similarly in their role as the *prāṇas*, they are the breaths or vital life-energies which guard the abode of *brahman* in the head and are the mediators and means of communication between *brahman* and the outside world—and as life-force, they reside within all animate beings, manifestations of the creative activity of *brahman* within the creation.

The word *brahman* essentially conveys the meanings of both growth and power (√*bṛh*) ; *brahman* is thus the principle of dynamic growth and expansion, the One which of its very nature gives rise to the many. In later Vedic times, this (neuter) creative life-force becomes personified as (the masculine) Brahmā, the supreme creator; while in earlier Vedic times, the role of creator is occupied especially by such figures as Prajāpati ("the lord of beings") and Viśvakarman ("the activity/maker of the universe") as well as by various other minor figures and principles. The Ṛṣis—whether as the *prāṇas* or as sons of the creator—are usually depicted as being of the same nature as, but spatially or temporally separate from, this creative principle or creator; thus one *Ṛgveda* hymn speaks of the One (symbolising *brahman*) as being beyond the Seven Ṛṣis :

The wishes of Viśvakarman delight in pleasure there, where

> they say that beyond the Seven Ṛṣis is the One [*sapta ṛṣin para ekam āhuḥ*].[1]

Viśvakarman—the author of all activity and motion—is also called both Ṛṣi and father; he, it is who, entering into all, brings forth both earth and sky.[2] The Seven Ṛṣis, as the *prāṇas*, have a similar role in creating the living worlds; so too they share in the nature of Agni, who is also on occasions called a Ṛṣi,[3] who is said to create Ṛṣis from men,[4] and who is himself brought into existence by the Ṛṣis.[5] The term Ṛṣi in such contexts comes to denote not so much an individual or a status as rather an activity, a creative movement ($\sqrt{}$*ṛṣ*); and there arises from this a personification of Ṛṣi-hood, in the figure of Eka-Ṛṣi or the Sole Ṛṣi. Eka-Ṛṣi is referred to in a number of Vedic contexts; in the *Atharvaveda*, for example, he is identified with the cosmic cow, a prototype and microcosm of all creation;[6] and he is also said to be established—along with the first-born Ṛṣis—in the *skambha* or cosmic pillar :

> *Tapas*, divine law [ṛta], ordinances and truth are in the *skambha*; from it originates Agni, and the three worlds are contained in it, maintained by Prajāpati. *Brahman* and the thirty-three gods reside in it; in it are established the first-born Ṛṣis, the *Ṛg*, *Sāma* and *Yajur vedas*, and Eka-Ṛṣi; there both immortality and death are placed together. The earth is its foundation, the atmosphere its belly, the sky its head, Agni its mouth and the Aṅgirases its eyes; it sustains all worlds, and has entered into existence—if you know the *brahman* in man, then you know Prajāpati and the *skambha*.[7]

The pillar symbolises the link between heaven and earth, and is also the embodiment of the universe; it both contains and also indicates the path leading from earth to heaven—just

1. *Ṛgveda* 10.82.2.
2. Ibid., 10.81.1.
3. For example *Ṛgveda* 1.31.1.
4. For example *Ṛgveda* 1.31.16, 4.1.12, 10.62.5-6.
5. For references, see Chapter 7 section B (b).
6. *Atharvaveda* 8.9.26; on the cow, see also 4.11.9, 9.8.1-26.
7. Ibid., 10.7.1 ff; see also 10. 8.1 ff.

as it was in the pillar (in the form of the sacrificial *yūpa*) that the gods hid the sacrifice, by discovering which the Ṛṣis were able to go to heaven.[1] The *skambha* is in a sense a further embodiment of *brahman* and Prajāpati, and the appearance of both the Ṛṣis and Eka-Ṛṣi within it underlines the role of both as manifestations of *brahman* and as the links which bind together the divine and human realms. Eka-Ṛṣi further appears in the Upaniṣada : he is mentioned in the *vaṃśa* or list of teachers who hand down Upaniṣadic knowledge,[2] and he is also identified as *prāṇa*[3] and as the sun, the offspring of Prajāpati.[4] One relatively late passage further relates that the sun, in the form of Agni or fire, is established in the head as Eka-Ṛṣi—and explains that there are four kinds of fire in the body, of which that in the head is known as Eka-Ṛṣi.[5] As we have seen, all of these identifications—as *prāṇa*, as the sun, and as Agni—as well as the association with the head, are related also of the Seven Ṛṣis;[6] Eka-Ṛṣi in this respect merely symbolises the various characteristics and features which we have already noted in connection with the Seven Ṛṣis.

Another abstract figure who may be considered in a context parallel to Eka-Ṛṣi is Eka-Vrātya, the supreme deity and symbol of the Vrātyas. Eka-Vrātya is described, among other things, as stirring up and becoming Prajāpati;[7] as performing *tapas*;[8] as possessing seven *prāṇas* or breaths within him, which he projects outwards to produce the earth, the sky, and other parts of creation;[9] and as being the Uncreated and the origin of the gods.[10] In one passage, Eka-Ṛṣi is set on a level

1. *Taittirīya Saṃhitā* 6.3.4: *Śatapatha Brāhmaṇa* 1.6.2.1-7, 3.2.2.2-3; see also Chapter 7 section B (a).
2. *Bṛhadāraṇyaka Upaniṣad* 2.6, 4.6.
3. *Praśna Upaniṣad* 2.8-11.
4. *Bṛhadāraṇyaka Upaniṣad* 5.14.8: *Īśa Upaniṣad* 16.
5. *Prāṇāgnihotra Upaniṣad* 1, 2.
6. See especially Chapters 7 and 8.
7. *Atharvaveda*, 15.1.1 ff.
8. Ibid., 15.3.1.
9. Ibid., 15.15-18.
10. *Jaiminīya Brāhmana* 3.21.

with the Vrâtya, although not with Eka-Vrâtya;[1] and Eka-Vrâtya approaches in many respects to the concept of *brahman*, particularly in sending forth creation through his seven *prāṇas*.[2] Eka-Ṛṣi is as it were one step removed from this, being himself identified as *praṇa* and as the offspring of Prajāpati; he thus symbolises both the nature and the role of Ṛṣi-hood, a manifestation of creative activity whose nature is that of fire and movement.

The difference between the Ṛṣis and *brahman* is not so much one of nature as one of role. The nature of both is essentially movement (√*ṛṣ*), creation (√*sṛj*) and increase (√*bṛh*); but while *brahman* originates such movement and growth—particularly through internal self-transformation and heat—the Ṛṣis represent the first manifestation of that dynamically creative growth; they in their turn then cause increase and growth, bringing the multiplicity of animate beings into existence through their exertion and *tapas*. For the Ṛṣis, there can in a sense be no still point, no state of rest; they are constantly —like Brahmā himself—impelled to motion and change, ceaselessly involved in creating. In performing *tapas*, they are like matter which transforms itself by heat into pure energy—whereafter that energy is again retransformed into matter; so too, again and again, the Ṛṣis attain the world of heaven—only to return again to earth, to propagate and teach mankind; so their role continues, through endless Mahāyugas, Manvantaras and Kalpas.

As we have had good cause to note, many divergent and sometimes contradictory ideas appear within the Ṛṣi traditions. The Epic and Purāṇic traditions, for example, show at times marked traces of Sāṅkhya, Vaiṣṇava and Śaiva sectarian influence, which accordingly influence the form in which the Ṛṣi traditions are presented. Similarly, some texts—such as the *Devībhāgavata Purāṇa*—in places show marked anti-ascetic bias,

---

1. *Praśna Upaniṣad* 2.11.

2. On the Vrâtyas and their cult, see especially J. Charpentier, "Bemerkungen über die Vrâtyas': R. C. Choudhary, *The Vrâtyas in Ancient India*: J. Hauer, *Der Vrâtya*, and *Die Anfänge der Yogapraxis*: J. Heesterman, 'The Vrâtya and the Sacrifice'.

which is again reflected in their presentation of the Ṛṣi-traditions. Yet none of these is sufficient to obscure the main theme underlying the role of the Ṛṣis, which emphasises over and again, in many diverse ways, that there is no real state of stillness, no still centre even at the heart of the turning wheel. The creative energy which animates and impels the Ṛṣis is itself the very energy and life-force of the creator and of *brahman*; it is a force which is never at rest, but which of its very nature moves dynamically ever onwards, ceaselessly creating and re-creating, increasing and expanding. The Ṛṣis, as the sons of the creator and as the manifestations of his life-force, are—like the creator—never truly in a state of rest; they are constantly undergoing and effecting transformation—whether externally through their creative activities in the world, or internally through their performance of *tapas*, attainment of heaven and re-absorption into *brahman*. When one cycle ends—as when they merge with *brahman* and attain heaven—so too a new cycle begins, whereby they animate existence, return to earth and renew their external creative activity. In this respect, their roles as both ascetics and begetters of copious offspring are not opposed but complementary : it is because the Ṛṣis perform *tapas* that they generate the power to create offspring, just as it is because they are re-absorbed through *tapas* into the dynamically creative energy of *brahman* that they themselves become embodiments of that energy, diffusing and manifesting it in the form of further creations.

When the Ṛṣis turn their backs on the world in order to devote themselves to ascetic practices, theirs is not a denial but ultimately a reaffirmation of the world; it is a denial of the purely material world, yet an affirmation of the vital spirit and life-force which animates and sustains it. Through their *tapas*, the Ṛṣis cease all bodily movement but inwardly kindle and heat themselves until they ultimately transform their whole being into the nature of *prāṇa*, the subtle breath and essence of life, and thereby merge with and are reabsorbed into *brahman*.[1]

1. Zaehner has perhaps not done full justice to the ascetic tradition, in terming it as springing from "that most polluted of all sources, the Satanic sin of pride, the desire to be 'like gods' " (*Our Savage God*, p. 235) In the

Vedic literature in places tends to regard the realisation of *brahman* and the attainment of immortality and heaven as a final goal of the Ṛṣis; yet by the Epics and Purāṇas a clear change of emphasis is apparent. The Ṛṣis follow the paths of the Śaiva, the Vaiṣṇava and the Vedāntin in achieving the goal of absorption in the one supreme reality; yet for the Ṛṣis, this is not the end or the final goal. In most accounts of why Brahmā abandons or destroys his first-born sons and instead creates his Mind-born Sons to act for him, it is because they refuse to increase or propagate, and instead remain satisfied without moving from the abode of Brahmā; in one account, Brahmā laments to Nārada that they should regard this as their goal, preferring to remain ascetic devotees of Viṣṇu and becoming thereby indifferent to the world and disobedient to his commands.[1] For the Ṛṣis, on the other hand, this can never be their final goal; their self-transformation and reabsorption into *brahman* brings with it a realisation that the very nature of *brahman* is dynamic, creative, and ever impelling to motion and change. *Brahman* is not a static concept or entity, but—like *prāṇa* itself—a dynamically creative force. *Brahman* of its very nature gives rise to the entire cycle of creation, entering into it as its innermost and subtlest essence;[2] this realisation is, for the Ṛṣis, not merely the end or goal of their endeavours but also the start of a new task or cycle in a transformed mode of being. Their inner nature being transformed into the very essence and nature of *brahman*, they thereafter return once more to the world : to

Ṛṣi traditions, external forms of asceticism are a means to increase internal "heat" for affecting transformation into and merging with *brahman*; this internal transformation whereby self-hood is destroyed is indeed aimed at making man 'like the gods" and transforming him into the nature of the divine—yet to decry this is ultimately to condemn not only the ascetic tradition, but also all mystical traditions which seek to achieve any degree of merging with—rather than passive or experiential knowledge of—the divine. However, a full discussion of this topic lies beyond the scope of the present book.

1. *Brahmavaivarta Purāṇa* 1.8.1 ff., 1.24.1 ff. The former of these is in part translated in O'Flaherty, *Hindu Myths*, pp. 48-53.

2. See for example *Bṛhadāraṇyaka Upaniṣad* 2.3.1-6: *Īśā Upaniṣad* 4-5: *Maitrī Upaniṣad* 6.17, 7.7; see further in Chapter 8 section D. Note also the analyses in G. Dumézil, *Flamen-Brahman*: J. Gonda, *Notes on Brahman*: L. Renou, 'Sur la notion du *brahman*'.

animate and increase it through further creation and re-creation, to establish *dharma* and ensure the correct balance of good and evil, and to instruct men in *dharma* and the Vedas. The vision of God, in the Ṛṣi traditions, is ultimately inseparable from the vision of the world : for *brahman* is the creative principle or power which gives rise to and sustains the worlds, and the Ṛṣis—as Brahmās and embodiments of *brahman*—are themselves committed by their own nature to an ever-ongoing cycle of creation and re-creation which is fuelled and generated by their *tapas.* The Ṛṣi traditions thus illustrate the supreme creativity ascribed to the ascetic, inasmuch as it is through ascetic practices and inner self-transformation that the Ṛṣis come to merge with brahman, to share the dynamically creative nature of *brahman*, and thence to be impelled by that very nature towards further creation and re-creation. The Ṛṣis' attainment of the centre of the turning wheel brings with it the acknowledgement that this centre is itself not the negation but the affirmation of motion; indeed, the centre *is* motion, and it is this very motion of the centre which provides the impetus for and is itself embodied in the turning of the wheel.

CONCLUSION TO PART TWO

Each of the traditions which we have examined in this part of the book is largely complementary to the others, and each illustrates in a different way the precise nature and role of the Ṛṣis in Indian thought. The Ṛṣis are primarily depicted as performers of *tapas* or asceticism : the forms of their *tapas* include such cultic observances as the performance of sacrifice, but centre more especially upon the performance of *yoga* and similar ascetic practices which are aimed at increasing the inner heat and symbolic mystical energy of the performer. We have especially noted the prominent role of fire—and light—symbolism in the Ṛṣi traditions, which is evident above all in the Ṛṣis' performance of *tapas*; thus it is through their *tapas* that the Ṛṣis take the place of Agni/Fire and the sun, and attain transference to the sky as the stars of Ursa Major or the Great Bear. It is similarly through *tapas* that the Ṛṣis transform their own inner or essential natures into the nature of *brahman* itself : through rising above individuality and egotism (*ahaṅkāra*), they merge with the vital flow of life-energy symbolised by *brahman*, and as such they are visualised as both the *prāṇas* or vital breaths in the body and thence as *prāṇa* or the breath of life which animates all creation. It is in this way that they come to be seen as supreme creators, as brahmās and Prajāpatis; and as sons of the creator, their own task becomes in turn to create gods, men and demons together with the entire animate creation as also to establish *dharma* and to sustain the worlds. This in turn therefore leads back to the Ṛṣis' further roles on earth in marrying and begetting offspring, in interacting with the political order, and eventually in once again performing *tapas* in order to merge once more with *brahman* and complete a further circle within their ever-continuing cycle.

The Ṛṣis' ascetic *tapas* is essentially anti-sexual and anti-social in its performance; yet it is also the means whereby the Ṛṣis become supremely sexual and committed to society as the progenitors and teachers of all beings. It is, indeed, only because the Ṛṣis withdraw to ascetic pursuits that they amass their creative power, merging with *brahman* and thereby in turn becoming Brahmās and creators. The Ṛṣis are thus above all those who are ever involved in movement ($\sqrt{}$*ṛṣ*) : firstly the inner movement of self-transformation through *tapas*, and secondly the external movement of causing change, growth and increase in creation. The Ṛṣi traditions revolve around the complementary cycles of asceticism and creation; when one such cycle ends, the next begins, and the Ṛṣis are thus constantly building up and discharging their inner creative energy which is itself the energy and nature of *brahman*.

In the Ṛṣi traditions, the universe is in constant flux, an arena of dynamic activity; there is no state of rest, since the very nature of the Absolute (*brahman*) and the Divine (Brahmā) with which they merge is that of outward-flowing energy, movement and self-expansion ($\sqrt{}$*bṛh*) which of its very nature constantly creates and re-creates. Thus the Ṛṣis' task does not stop at merely merging with and flowing into *brahman*: transformed into its nature and essence, they in turn become Brahmās and the progenitors of all animate creation, and become the means whereby *brahman* is manifested in further creation. This, then, becomes the goal of the ascetic and mystic within the Ṛṣi-traditions : to merge with *brahman* or the Absolute, and thence to become identified with the creative self-expansion of *brahman* within the creation.

GLOSSARY

The words and names listed here are the main technical terms and proper names which appear throughout the book, particularly where they are not explained in the contexts in which they appear. The names of individuals and of groups are not listed here : many of these may be found in Chapter 6 section B (c), and reference may also be made to such general works on Hindu mythology as J. Dowson, *A Classical Dictionary of Hindu Mythology*; A. B. Keith, *Indian Mythology*; A. A. Macdonell, *Vedic Mythology*; E. Moor, *The Hindu Pantheon*; and W. J. Wilkins, *Hindu Mythology*.

adharma Contrary to *dharma* : unrighteousness, that which offends against the proper order.

Āraṇyaka A forest treatise : a class of literature and part of the Veda, incorporating mystical speculations on the nature of sacrifice.

āśrama 1. A hermitage or retreat : the abode of a Ṛṣi.
2. A stage or period in a Brahmin's life, of which there are four : *brahmacarya* or religious studentship, *gārhasthya* or house-dwelling, *vānaprastha* or forest-dwelling, and *sannyāsa* or renunciation of all material attachment.

aśvamedha The horse-sacrifice : performed by a king, especially in order to expand his territories.

ātman The principle of life, the individual soul, self or essence.

avatāra A descent : especially of Viṣṇu and other gods, a descent and incarnation on earth.

bhakti Homage, worship or loving devotion, especially towards a deity.

Bhūr The earth : the lowest of the Lokas.

Bhuvar The atmosphere : the second of the Lokas.

Brahmā (Written *brahman* in Sanskrit, masculine) One versed in sacred knowledge; more especially, the personification of *brahman*, the god of creation.

brahmacārin One who practises the āśrama of *brahmacarya* : or, one who is immersed in *brahman*.

brahman (neuter) Growth or expansion; the one self-existent impersonal Spirit, Soul or Absolute, the essence and source from which all created things emanate or with which they are identified and to which they return.

Brāhmaṇa That which embodies, possesses or is derived from *brahman* : a class of literature and part of the Veda, dealing especially with explanations of the sacrifice and speculations on its nature.

Brahmaloka The realm of Brahmā or *brahman*: the seventh and highest of the Lokas.

brahma-Ṛṣi A Ṛṣi who holds the status of a Brahmin, or a Ṛṣi who has attained knowledge of or merged with *brahman*.

brahmavādin One who speaks of *brahman*, or whose speech embodies *brahman*; or, an expounder of the Veda.

Brahmin (Written *brāhmaṇa* in Sanskrit) One who has knowledge of *brahman*; a member of the highest *varṇa*, a priest.

cakra A circle, wheel or disk : applied especially to the celestial circles or spheres, and to the centres of power in the body.

camas A bowl or other vessel, especially used at sacrifices for drinking *soma*.

dakṣiṇā A present, gift or offering, especially to Brahmins at the completion of a ceremony.

deva-Ṛṣi A Ṛṣi who holds the status of a god : a godly or divine Ṛṣi.

dharma The proper state of affairs, the correct performance of one's duties; righteous conduct, virtue.

dhruva That which is fixed or firm : personified as Dhruva, the Pole star.

Dvāpara The third of the four Yugas.

Epic A class of literature, consisting of the *Rāmāyaṇa*, the *Mahābhārata*, and sometimes also the *Harivaṃśa*.

gaṇa A group or collection : the descendants of a Ṛṣi.

gotra A family, race or lineage : especially that tracing genealogical descent from one of the Ṛṣis.

gṛhastha One who practises the *āśrama* of *gārhasthya*, marrying and becoming a householder.

guṇa A quality or attribute : especially the three qualities which are the constituents of all created beings, namely *sattva*, *rajas* and *tamas*.

guru A father or elder : more especially, a spiritual teacher or guide.

hotṛ A sacrificial priest, one who recites the *Ṛgveda* during a sacrifice.

Janaloka The realm of virtuous men, the fifth of the seven Lokas.

Jñāna Knowledge derived from thought or meditation rather than from study.

Kali The fourth and most evil of the Yugas, the present age.

Kalpa A division of time, equivalent (in the Purāṇas) to 14 Manvantaras or 1,000 Mahāyugas; a day of Brahmā's lifetime.

kāmadhenu A wish-granting cow, a cow which yields all desires to its owner.

kāṇḍa A section or part; a division, volume or book of a work.

karma A deed or action; especially associated with the idea that every action brings its own inevitable effect, binding one to the rule of time.

Kṛta The first and most righteous of the four Yugas, also called Satya or the Age of Truth.

Kṣatriya A member of the second of the four *varṇas*: a warrior.

liṅga The phallus or penis, the male organ of generation.

Loka A world or region; a division of the universe : usually either three or seven in number, set one above the other; and in the Purāṇas sometimes fourteen, including seven lower or nether worlds.

Mahāyuga A division of time, representing the succession of the four Yugas (literally a "great Yuga") : also, called a Caturyuga ("four-Yuga").

Maharloka The realm of light or sacrifice, the fourth of the seven Lokas.

maṇḍala A circle, group or collection : especially a division or book of a work.

mantra A sacred prayer or text, a mystical clause or phrase meditated upon and recited in praise of a deity; also a magical incantation.

Manvantara A division of time within a Kalpa, the period which is presided over by a Manu (literally the "interval" or "period" of a Manu) ; in the Purāṇas, there are usually 14 such Manvantaras within a Kalpa.

māyā Deceit or illusion; false or unreal appearance; especially the idea that the universe has no permanent reality apart from *brahman.*

mokṣa Release or liberation : especially from *karma* and *māyā*, which constitutes the realisation of *brahman.*

muni A sage or ascetic.

Nakṣatra A lunar mansion, one of the 27 or 28 stars and constellations passed over by the moon.

nirvāṇa Blowing out or extinction : especially of the false notion of self-hood (*ātman*) as a permanent and unchanging reality.

om The most sacred of all *mantras*, whose sound embodies *brahman* : also written as *aum.*

parvan A part, division or book of a work.

pitṛ A father or parent; a forefather or ancestor.

Prajāpati A lord of procreation and of created beings : especially in the Vedas, a name or designation of Brahmā.

prakṛti Natural form or state; the material from which anything is made; the nature or form of the material world.

prāṇa Breath, wind or air; power or energy; vitality or life.

prāṇāyāma The practice of restraining or suspending the breath.

pravara A line of ancestors; also, a particular ancestor who contributes to the status of a *gotra*.

Purohita A hereditary family-priest who conducts all ceremonial rites for family.

Purāṇa A class of literature, concerned especially with legendary history (literally "Tradition" or "Past Event"). These are often divided into 18 major Purāṇas (Mahā-Purāṇas) and 18 minor Purāṇas (Upa-Purāṇas).

rajas The quality of passion, the second of the three *guṇas*.

rājasūya A sacrifice performed by a king at his consecration, especially to emphasise his superiority and sovereignty over other princes.

ṛk A hymn of praise or worship : especially those incorporated in the *Ṛgveda*.

saṃhitā A collection or compilation, especially of verses or texts.

sannyāsin One who practises the *āśrama* of *sannyāsa*, renouncing all attachment to the temporal concerns of the world.

śāstra A rule or precept; a treatise or collection of teachings on a particular subject.

sattva The quality or purity or truth, the highest of the three *guṇas*; also existence, power or vitality, natural character.

siddha One who has accomplished his goals, a perfected being; one who has attained *siddhi*.

siddhi An accomplishment or attainment; success or perfection; also, superhuman or magical power.

śloka A stanza or verse of two *padas* or lines.

smṛti Law or tradition handed down by human authors.

soma The drugging juice of the *soma*-plant, the nectar of immortality : personified as Soma, the moon.

śrāddha A funeral rite or ceremony, performed either for a departed individual or for the *pitṛs*.

śrama Ascetic effort or self-exertion.

śruti Sacred or revealed knowledge; the Veda.

Śūdra A member of the fourth or lowest *varṇa* : a servant.

Sūtra — A class of literature, containing short precepts and aphorisms derived primarily from the Veda : hence termed a Vedāṅga. Literally, a thread : many non-Vedāṅga works of a similar structure are also termed *sūtras*.

Svar — The sky : the third of the Lokas; particularly in Vedic literature, heaven or the abode of the gods; also referred to as Svarga.

tamas — The quality of darkness, the lowest of the three *guṇas*.

Tapaloka — The realm of heat or *tapas* : the sixth of the Lokas.

tapas — Warmth, heat or fire : especially the inner heat generated through various religious or ascetic practices; also, austerity or asceticism itself.

tejas — Glare or brilliance : fiery energy; the external manifestation of inner *tapas*.

tīrtha — A sacred pool or tank; the bank of a sacred river; also, the area surrounding such pools or rivers.

Tretā — The second of the four Yugas.

udgītha — The chant of hymns, especially of the *Sāmaveda*; also, a designation of the syllable *om*.

Upaniṣad — A class of literature and part of the Veda, concerned especially with mystical teachings on the nature of *brahman*; also termed Vedānta, or "the consummation of the Veda".

ūrdhvaretas — Having the seed drawn upwards : abstaining from sexual intercourse, living in celibacy.

vāc — Word, sound or speech; the voice or mouth; personified as Vāc or Sarasvatī, the goddess of speech and learning.

Vaiśya — A member of the third of the four *varṇas* : a commoner, one who engages in trade or agriculture.

vaṃśa — A collection or assemblage : a family, race or lineage.

varṇa — Literally, a colour : a class, tribe; especially the four principal classes or castes, namely Brahmins, Kṣatriyas, Vaiśyas and Śūdras.

Veda — A class of literature (literally "Knowledge"), the most sacred scriptures of Hinduism : comprising the four *saṃhitās* (*Ṛgveda*, *Sāmaveda*, *Yajurveda* and

Atharvaveda), together with the further classes deriving from these *saṃhitās* (Brāhmaṇas, Āraṇyakas and Upaniṣads). The Veda is regarded as a *śruti* or revealed work. The plural term "Vedas" is also sometimes used, to refer (in correct terms) to the collection of all of these works : it is also used by some writers to refer only to the four *saṃhitās*.

Vedāṅga A class of literature auxiliary and supplementary to the Veda (literally a "limb of the Veda"), consisting of six branches : Śikṣā or pronunciation, Chandas or prosody, Vyākaraṇa or grammar, Nirukta or etymology, Jyotiṣa or Astronomy, and Kalpa or ritual (including Śrauta Sūtras, Gṛhya Sūtras and Dharma Sūtras). These are all regarded as *smṛti* works.

Vedic Pertaining to or derived from the Veda : the Vedic tradition, and Vedic literature, includes both the Veda and the Vedāṅga.

vidyā Knowledge : especially received or learnt knowledge, as opposed to *jñāna*.

vipra An inspired seer : also, in later literature, a Brahmin.

virāj Beauty, splendour; a Vedic metre.

yoga Conjunction or union : especially referring to the union of the individual *ātman* with the Divine or Absolute; also. the meditation by which such union is achieved.

yogin One who performs *yoga*.

yoni The vulva, the female organ of generation.

Yuga A division of time, an age or era; especially the four Yugas Kṛta, Tretā, Dvāpara and Kali, which together constitute a Mahāyuga.

yūpa A sacrificial post or pillar, especially that to which a sacrificial victim is tied.

ABBREVIATIONS

AA	*American Antropologist*
ADMG	Abhandlungen der Deutschen Morgenländischen Gesellschaft
AIKT	All-India Kashiraj Trust
AITM	Ancient Indian Tradition and Mythology
AKAWB	Abhandlungen der Königlichen Akademie der Wissenschaft zu Berlin
AO	*Acta Orientalia*
AOSP	American Oriental Society Publication
AR	*Asiatic Review*
ASS	Ānandāśrama Sanskrit Series
Bib.Ind.	Bibliotheca Indica
BIAVRI	*Bulletin of the International Association of the Vrindavan Research Institute*
BORI	Bhandarkar Oriental Research Institute
BSOAS	*Bulletin of the School of Oriental and African Studies*
BSPS	Bombay Sanskrit and Prakrit Series
BSS	Bombay Sanskrit Series
BTLVNI	*Bijdragen tot de Taal-, Land- en Volkenkunde van Nederlandsch-Indië*
CII	Corpus Inscriptionum Indicarum
CIS	*Contributions to Indian Sociology*
CSCRS	Calcutta Sanskrit College Research Series
Ep.Ind.	*Epigraphia Indica*
ERE	Encyclopaedia of Religion and Ethics (ed. J. Hastings, *q.v.*)
EVP	Études Védiques et Pāṇiniennes
FGS	Forbes Gujarati Sabha
HOS	Harvard Oriental Series

Ind. Stud.	*Indische Studien* (ed. A. Weber, *q.v.*)
IIJ	*Indo-Iranian Journal*
JA	*Journal Asiatique*
JAF	*Journal of American Folklore*
JAIH	*Journal of Ancient Indian History*
JAOS	*Journal of the American Oriental Society*
JAS	*Journal of the Asiatic Society*
JBBRAS	*Journal of the Bombay Branch of the Royal Asiatic Society*
JRAS	*Journal of the Royal Asiatic Society*
JRAS-NCB	*Journal of the Royal Asiatic Society, North China Branch*
JSA	*Journal de la Société des Américanistes*
JSFO	*Journal de la Société Finno-Ougrienne*
KSS	Kāśī Sanskrit Series
LCL	Loeb Classical Library
MAR	Mythology of All Races
MASI	Memoirs of the Archaeological Survey of India
NKGWG	*Nachrichten von der Königlichen Gesellschaft der Wissenschaften zu Gottingen*
n.s.	New Series
OST	Original Sanskrit Texts (ed. J. Muir, *q.v.*)
PIFI	Publications de l'Institut Français d'Indologie
PTS	Pāli Text Society
RAS otf	Royal Asiatic Society Oriental Translation Fund
RCA	Realencyclopäedie der Classischen Altertumswissenschaft
SBE	Sacred Books of the East
SBH	Sacred Books of the Hindus
SIFGAos	Smithsonian Institute, Freer Gallery of Art Oriental Studies
ŚP	Śata Piṭaka Series
SVS	Sarasvatī Vihāra Series
TITLVK	*Tijdschrift voor Indische Taal-, Land- en Volkenkunde*
TP	*T'oung Pao*
TSS	Trivandrum Sanskrit Series
VBJP	*Viśva-Bhārati Journal of Philosophy*
VIS	Vishveshvaranand Indological Series
WZKM	*Wiener Zeitsckrift zur Kunde des Morgenlandes*
ZDMD	*Zeitschrift der Deutschen Morgenländischen Gesellschaft*

BIBLIOGRAPHY

1. TEXTS AND TRANSLATIONS

The works listed here are the textual editions which have been cited in the notes throughout the book, together with their translations into European languages wherever these exist. The works are listed under five headings :

A. Vedic Texts (including both the Veda and the Vedāṅgas) ;

B. Epic and Purāṇic Texts;

C. Further Sanskrit, Hindi and Prakrit Texts;

D. Tamil Texts;

E· Extra-Indian Texts.

A. VEDIC TEXTS

Aitareya Āraṇyaka. Ed. R.L. Mitra. Bib. Ind. Calcutta, 1876.

——— Ed. & Trans. A.B. Keith. Oxford, 1909 : rep. 1969.

Aitareya Brāhmaṇa. Ed., with the commentary of Sāyaṇa, S. Sāmaśramī. Bib. Ind. 4 vols. Calcutta, 1894-1906.

——— Trans. A.B. Keith. HOS 25. Cambridge (Mass.), 1920 : rep. Delhi, 1971.

Aitareya Upaniṣad. See Upaniṣads.

Āpastamba Dharma Sūtra. Ed. G. Buhler. BSPS 44 & 50. Poona, 1932.

——— Trans. G. Bühler. SBE. 2 Oxford, 1870 : rep. Delhi, 1969.

Āpastamba Śrauta Sūtra. Ed. R. Garbe. Bib. Ind. 3 vols. Calcutta, 1881-1903.

——— Trans. (German) W. Caland. Amsterdam, 1921-28 : rep. Wiesbaden, 1969.

Āśvalāyana Gṛhya Sūtra. Ed. & Trans. A.F. Stenzler. ADMG. Leipzig, 1864-78.

——— Trans. H. Oldenberg. SBE 29. Oxford, 1886 : rep. Delhi, 1969.

Āśvalāyana Śrauta Sūtra. Ed. R. Vidyaratna. Bib. Ind. Calcutta, 1874.

Atharvaśiras Upaniṣad. See Upaniṣads.

Atharvaveda. Ed. R. Roth & W.D. Whitney. 2nd ed. revised M. Lindenau. Berlin, 1924.

——— Trans. W.D. Whitney. HOS 7-8. Cambridge (Mass.), 1905 : rep. Delhi, 1971.

Baudhāyana Dharma Sūtra. Ed. A. Chinnaswami Shastri. Banaras, 1934.

——— Trans. G. Bühler. SBE 14. Oxford, 1882 : rep. Delhi, 1969.

Baudhāyana Śrauta Sūtra. Ed. W. Caland. Bib. Ind. Calcutta, 1904-24.

Bṛhadāraṇyaka Upaniṣad. See Upaniṣads.

Chāndogya Upaniṣad. See Upaniṣads.

Gopatha Brāhmaṇa. Ed. R.L. Mitra. Bib. Ind. Calcutta, 1872 : rep. Delhi, 1972.

Hiraṇyakeśin Gṛhya Sūtra. Ed. J. Kirste. Vienna, 1889.

——— Trans. H. Oldenberg. SBE 30. Oxford, 1892 : rep. Delhi, 1969.

Hiraṇyakeśin Śrauta Sūtra. Ed. K.B. Āgāṣe. ASS 53. Poona, 1907-32.

Īśa Upaniṣad. See Upaniṣads.

Jaiminiya Brāhmaṇa. Ed. R. Vīra. SVS 31. Nagpur, 1934.

——— Trans. (German, part) W. Caland. Amsterdam, 1919.

Jaiminiya Śrauta Sūtra. Ed. & Trans. (Dutch) D. Gaastra. Leiden, 1906.

Jaiminiya Upaniṣad Brāhmaṇa. Ed. & Trans. H. Oertel. *JAOS* 16, 1896, pp. 79-260.

Kaṭha Upaniṣad. See Upaniṣads.

Kāṭhaka Saṃhitā. Ed. L. von Schröder. 4 vols. Leipzing, 1909-22 : rep. Wiesbaden, 1970-72.

Kauṣitaki Āraṇyaka. See *Śāṅkhāyana Āraṇyaka*.

Kauṣitaki Brāhmaṇa. Ed. E.R.S. Sarma. Wiesbaden, 1968.

——— Trans. A.B. Keith. HOS 25. Cambridge (Mass.), 1920 : rep. Delhi, 1971.

Kauṣitaki Upaniṣad. See Upaniṣads.

Kena Upaniṣad. See Upaniṣads.

Maitrāyaṇi Saṃhitā. Ed. L. von Schröder. 4 vols. Leipzig, 1881-86 : rep. Wiesbaden, 1970-72.

Maitri Upaniṣad. See Upaniṣads.

Mānava Śrauta Sūtra. Ed. & Trans. J.M. van Gelder. Śp 27. Leiden, 1921 : rep. Delhi, 1961-63.

Muṇḍaka Upaniṣad. See Upaniṣads.

Nirukta of Yāska. Ed. & Trans. L. Sarup (with the *Nighaṇṭu*). 2 vols. Oxford, 1921-27.

Pañcaviṃśa Brāhmaṇa. Ed., with the commentary of Sāyaṇa, A. Vedāntavāgīśa. Bib. Ind. 2 vols. Calcutta, 1870-74.

——— Trans. W· Caland. Bib. Ind. Calcutta, 1931.

Prāṇāgnihotra Upaniṣad. See Upaniṣads.

Praśna Upaniṣad. See Upaniṣads.

Ṛgveda. Ed., with the commentary of Sāyaṇa, M. Muller. 4 vols. London, 1890-92.

——— Trans. (German) K.F. Geldner. HOS 33-36. Cambridge (Mass.), 1951-57.

——— Trans. (French) L. Renou. EVP. Paris, 1955-69.

——— Trans. H.H. Wilson. 5 vols. London, 1886 : rep. Delhi, 1977.

Ṣaḍviṃśa Brāhmaṇa. Ed. K. Klemm. Guterslow, 1894.

——— Trans. W.B. Bolleé. Utrecht, 1956.

Sāmaveda. Ed., with the commentary of Sāyaṇa, S. Sāmaśramī. Bib. Ind. 5 vols. Calcutta, 1874-78.

——— Trans. R.T.H. Griffiths, Benares, 1896 : rep. 1963.

Śāṅkhāyana Āraṇyaka. Ed. T. Pāṭhaka. ASS 90. Poona, 1922.

——— Trans. A.B. Keith. RAS otf 18. London, 1908.

Śāṅkhāyana Gṛhya Sūtra. Ed. S.R. Seghal. Delhi, 1960.

——— Trans. H. Oldenberg. SBE 29. Oxford, 1886 : rep. Delhi, 1969.

Śāṅkhāyana Śrauta Sūtra. Ed. A. Hillebrandt. Bib. Ind. 4 vols. Calcutta, 1889-99.

——— Trans. W. Caland & L. Chandra. SVS 32. Nagpur, 1953.

Śatapatha Brāhmaṇa. Ed., with the commentary of Sāyaṇa, S. Sāmaśramī. Bib. Ind. 7 vols. Calcutta, 1896-1906. (part)

—— Ed., with the commentary of Sāyaṇa, A. Weber. Bib. Ind. Calcutta, 1903.

—— Trans. J. Eggeling. SBE 12, 26, 41, 43, 44. Oxford, 1882-1900 : rep. Delhi, 1969.

Satyāṣāḍha Śrauta Sūtra. See *Hiraṇyakeśin Śrauta Sūtra.*

Taittirīya Āraṇyaka. Ed., with the commentary of Sāyaṇa, R.L. Mitra. Bib. Ind. Calcutta, 1872.

Taittirīya Brāhmaṇa. Ed., with the commentary of Sāyaṇa, R.L. Mitra. Bib. Ind. 3 vols. Calcutta, 1859.

Taittirīya Saṃhitā. Ed., with the commentary of Mādhava, E. Roer and G.B. Cowell (vols. 1-2), M. Nyāyaratna (vols. 3-5), and S. Sāmaśramī (vol. 6). Bib. Ind. Calcutta, 1860-99.

—— Trans. A.B. Keith. HOS 18-19. Cambridge (Mass.), 1914 : rep. Delhi, 1967.

Taittirīya Upaniṣad. See Upaniṣads.

Talavakāra Brāhmaṇa. See *Jaiminiya Brāhmaṇa.*

Tāṇḍya-mahā Brāhmaṇa. See *Pañcaviṃśa Brāhmaṇa.*

Upaniṣads. Ed. V.P. Limaye & R.D. Valdekar, *Eighteen Principal Upaniṣads.* Poona, 1958.

—— Ed. *One Hundred and Eight Upanishads.* Bombay, 1913.

—— Trans. R. Hume, *The Thirteen Principal Upanishads.* London, 1877 : rep. Madras, 1968.

—— Trans. (German) P. Deussen, *Sechzig Upaniṣad's des Veda.* Leipzig, 1921.

Vaikhānasa Śrauta Sūtra. Ed. W. Caland. Bib. Ind. Calcutta, 1941.

Vaikhānasa Sūtra. With *Pravarapraśna.* India Office ms. Keith 4684 : Aufrecht 17, folios 183-192.

Vaitana Sūtra. Ed. R. Garbe. London, 1878.

—— Trans. W. Caland. Amsterdam, 1910.

Vājasaneyi Saṃhitā. Ed., with the commentary of Mahīdhara, A. Weber. Berlin, 1849.

—— *Pravarapariśiṣṭha,* in A. Weber, *Die Handschriften und Verzeichnisse der Königlichen Bibliothek zu Berlin.* vol. 1 no 251 (Weber 13,8). Berlin, 1853.

——— Trans. (part) in A. Weber, *Ind. Stud.* 2, and in J. Muir, OST 4.

——— Trans. R.T.H. Griffiths. Benares, 1927.

Vāsiṣṭha Dharma Sūtra. Ed. A. Fuhrer. Bombay, 1883.

——— Trans. G. Bühler. SBE 14. Oxford, 1882 : rep. Delhi, 1969.

Vedāṅga-jyotiṣa. Ed., with the commentary of Somākara, M.S. Dvivedin. Banaras, 1908.

Yajurveda. See *Kāṭhaka*, *Maitrāyaṇi*, *Taittiriya* and *Vājasaneyi Saṃhitāṣ.*

B. EPIC AND PURĀṆIC TEXTS

Agni Purāṇa. Ed. B. Upādhyāya. KSS 174. Banaras, 1966.

——— Trans. M. N. Dutt. 2 vols. Calcutta, 1903-4 : rep. Banaras, 1967.

Bhāgavata Purāṇa. Ed. & Trans. C.L. Goswami. 2 vols. Gorakhpur, 1971.

——— Trans. J.L. Shastri. AITM 7-11. Delhi, 1976.

Bhaviṣya Purāṇa. Ed. K. Śrīkṛṣṇadāsa. Bombay, 1904 : rep. 1959.

Brahma Purāṇa. Ed. H. N. Apte. ASS 28. Poona, 1895.

Brahmāṇḍa Purāṇa. Ed. J.L. Shastri. Delhi, 1973.

Brahmavaivarta Purāṇa. Ed. V. G. Apte. ASS 102. 2 vols. Poona, 1935.

——— Trans. R.N. Sen. SBH 24. 2 vols. Allahabad, 1912-22 : rep. New York, 1973.

Bṛhaddharma Purāṇa. Ed. Hara Prasād Śāstrī. Bib. Ind. Calcutta, 1887-97.

Bṛhannāradiya Purāṇa. Ed. Hṛṣīkeśa Śāstrī. Bib. Ind. Calcutta, 1891.

Devibhāgavata Purāṇa. Ed. M. Abhimanyu. Banaras, 1955.

——— Trans. Swami Vijñānānanda. SBH 26. 3 parts. Allahabad, 1921-23 : rep. New York, 1973.

Garuḍa Purāṇa. Ed. R. Bhattacharya. KSS 165. Banaras, 1964.

——— Trans. J.L. Shastri. AITM 12-13. Delhi, 1977-78.

Harivaṃśa. Ed. P.C. Vaidya. BORI. 2 vols. Poona, 1969-71.

——— Trans. (French) S.A. Langlois. London, 1834-35.

——— Trans. M.N. Dutt. Calcutta, 1897.

Kālikā Purāṇa. Ed. K. Śrīkṛṣṇadāsa. Bombay, 1907.

Kūrma Purāṇa. Ed. & Trans. A.S. Gupta *et.al.* AIKT. Banaras, 1972.

Liṅga Purāṇa. Ed. G.B. Nātu. Bombay, 1924.

——— Trans. J.L. Shastri. AITM 5-6. Delhi, 1973.

Mahābhāgavata Purāṇa. Ed. M.I. Desai. Bombay, 1913.

Mahābhārata. Ed. B.S. Sukthankar *et.al.* BORI. Poona, 1933-59.

——— Trans. J.A.B. van Buitenen (in progress). Chicago, 1974—.

——— Trans. P.C. Roy. Calcutta, 1884-96.

Mahārāṣṭa Purāṇa. Trans., from a ms. in the Bengali Dept. of Calcutta University, E.C. Dimock & P.C. Gupta. Honolulu, 1965.

Mārkaṇḍeya Purāṇa. Ed. F.E. Pargiter. Bib. Ind. Calcutta, 1862.

——— Trans. F.E. Pargiter. Bib. Ind. 2 vols. Calcutta, 1884-1904 : rep. Delhi, 1969.

Matsya Purāṇa. Ed. H.N. Apte. ASS 54. Poona, 1907.

——— Trans. S. Vidyārṇava. SBH 17. Allahabad, 1916-17 : rep. New York, 1973.

Nārada Purāṇa. Ed. K. Śrīkṛṣṇadāsa. Bombay, 1925.

Narasiṃha Purāṇa. Ed. Uddhvācārya. Bombay, 1911.

Padma Purāṇa. Ed. M. Ch. Apte. ASS 131. 4 vols. Poona, 1893-94.

Rāmāyaṇa. Ed. G.H. Bhatt *et. al.* Baroda, 1960-75.

——— Trans. Hari Prasad Shastri. 3 vols. London, 1953-59 : rep. 1962-70.

Sāmba Purāṇa. Ed. K. Śrīkṛṣṇadāsa. Bombay, 1899.

Saura Purāṇa. Ed. V.G. Apte. ASS 18. Poona, 1924.

——— Trans. (part) W. Jahn, *Das Saurapurāṇam*. Strassburg, 1908.

Śiva Purāṇa. Ed. K. Śrīkṛṣṇadāsa. Bombay, 1929.

——— Trans. J.L. Shastri. AITM 1-4. Delhi, 1970.

Skanda Purāṇa. Ed. K. Śrīkṛṣṇadāsa. Bombay, 1910.

Vāmana Purāṇa. Ed. & Trans. A.S. Gupta *et.al.* AIKT. Banaras, 1968.

Varāha Purāṇa. Ed. Hṛṣīkeśa Śāstrī. Bib. Ind. 2 vols. Calcutta, 1893.

Vāyu Purāṇa. Ed. R.L. Mitra. Bib. Ind. 2 vols. Calcutta, 1880-88.

Viṣṇu Purāṇa. Ed. J, Vidyasagara. Calcutta, 1882.

——— Trans. H.H. Wilson, London, 1840 : rep. Calcutta, 1972.

Viṣṇudharmottara Purāṇa. Ed. K. Śrīkṛṣṇadāsa. Bombay, 1912.

Yuga Purāṇa. Ed. & Trans. J.E. Mitchiner. Bib.Ind. Calcutta, 1986.

C. FURTHER SANSKRIT, HINDI AND PRAKRIT TEXTS

Abhijñānaśākuntalam of Kālidāsa. Ed. M.R. Kale. Bombay, 1896 : rep. 1957.

——— Trans. C.R. Devadhar, *Works of Kālidāsa*, vol. 1. Delhi, 1966 : rep. 1972.

Bṛhaddevatā of Śaunaka. Ed. & Trans. A.A. Macdonell. HOS 5-6. Cambridge (Mass.), 1904.

Bṛhajjātaka of Varāhamihira. Ed. & Trans. V. Subrahmaṇya Sāstrī. Mysore. 1929.

Bṛhatkathāmañjari of Kṣemendra. Ed. Sivadatta & K. P. Parab. Bombay, 1931.

Bṛhatkathāślokasaṅgraha of Budhasvāmin. Ed. & Trans. F. Lacotte. 2 vols. Paris, 1908.

Bṛhat-saṃhitā of Varāhamihira. Ed. H. Kern. Bib. Ind. Calcutta 1865.

——— Trans. H. Kern. *JRAS* n.s. 4-7, 1970-75.

Brāhmasphuṭa-siddhānta of Brahmagupta. Ed. M.S. Dvivedin. Benares, 1902.

Gotrapravaramañjari of Puruṣottma Pandit. Ed. P. C. Rao, *Gotrapravaranibandhakadambaṇ*. Mysore, 1900.

——— Trans. J. Brough, *Early Brahmanical System of Gotra and Pravara*. Cambridge, 1953.

Harṣacarita of Bāṇa. Ed. P.V. Kane. Bombay, 1918 : rep. Delhi, 1965.

——— Trans. E.B. Cowell & F.W. Thomas. London, 1897 : rep. 1929.

Jivābhigama Sūtra. Ed. Ahmedabad, 1883.

Kādambari of Baṇa. Ed. P. Peterson. BSS 24. Bombay, 1900.

——— Trans. C.M. Ridding. London, 1896.

Kāma-sūtra of Vātsyāyana. Ed. Gosvāmī Dāmodar Śāstrī. KSS 29. Benares, 1929.

——— Trans. R. Burton. London, 1883 : rep. 1969.

Kathāsaritsāgara of Somadeva. Ed. D. Prasad & K.P. Parab.

Bombay, 1930.

——— Trans. R.H. Tawney (ed. & rev. N.M. Penzer), *The Ocean of Story*. 10 vols. London, 1925-28 : rep. Delhi, 1968.

Kavyādarśa of Daṇḍin. Ed. & Trans. S.K., Belvalkar. Poona, 1924.

Kumārasambhava of Kālidāsa. Ed. & Trans. M. R. Kale. Bombay, 1923: rep. Delhi, 1967.

Mahā-siddhānta of Āryabhaṭa. Ed. M. S. Dvivedin. Benares, 1910.

——— Ed. & Trans. (part) S.R. Sarma, *The Pūrvagaṇita of Āryabhaṭa's (II) Mahāsiddhānta*. Marburg, 1966.

Majjhima Nikāya. Ed. V. Trenckner (vol. 1) & Lord Chalmers (vols. 2-3). PTS. London, 1888-99 : rep. 1949-51.

——— Trans. I.B. Horner. PTS. 3 vols. London, 1954-59.

Mānava Dharma Śāstra. Ed. G. Jhā. Bib. Ind. 3 vols. Calcutta, 1832-39.

——— Trans. G. Bühler, *The Laws of Manu*. SBE 25. Oxford, 1886 : rep. Delhi, 1969.

Mṛcchakaṭika of Śūdraka. Ed. J. Vidyasagara. Calcutta, 1891.

——— Trans. J.A.B. van Buitenen, *Two Plays of Ancient India* ("The Little Clay Cart"). New York, 1968.

Muhūrtamārtaṇḍa. Ed. Kapileśvara Śāstrī. KSS 145. Banaras, 1947.

Nārada Dharma Śāstra. Ed. J. Jolly. Bib. Ind. Calcutta, 1881.

——— Trans. J. Jolly. SBE 33. Oxford, 1889 : rep. Delhi, 1969.

Pāñcasiddhāntikā of Varāhamihira. Ed. & Trans. G. Thibaut & M.S. Dvivedin. Benares, 1889 : rep. 1968.

Prabandhacintāmaṇi of Merutuṅga. Ed. Durgāśaṅkara Kevalrāma Śāstrī. FGS 14. Bombay. 1932.

——— Trans. C.H. Tawney. Bib. Ind. Calcutta, 1901.

Rājataraṅgiṇi of Kalhaṇa. Ed. V. Bandhu. VIS 5-6. Hoshiarpur, 1963-65.

——— Trans. M.A, Stein, *Kalhaṇa's Chronicle of the Kings of Kashmir*. 2 vols. London, 1900.

Rāmacaritamānasa of Tulsīdās. Ed. C.L. Goswami. Gorakhpur, 1968.

——— Trans. W.D.P. Hill, *The Holy Lake of the Acts of Rāma.* London, 1952 : rep. Bombay, 1971.

Sattasai of Hāla. Ed. & Trans. R. Basak, *The Prakrit Gāthā-Saptaśati.* Bib. Ind. Calcutta, 1971.

Sūrya-siddhānta. Ed. F. Hall. Bib. Ind. Calcutta, 1859.

——— Trans. E. Burgess. *JAOS* 6, 1860 pp. 141-498.

Svapnavāsavadattam of Bhāsa. Ed. T. Ganapati Sastri, *Thirteen Plays of Bhāsa.* TSS. 15. Trivandrum, 1912.

——— Trans. A.C. Woolner & L. Sarup, *Thirteen Trivandrum Plays attributed to Bhāsa.* London, 1930-31.

Vāsavadattā of Subandhu. Ed. A.V.W. Jackson & Trans. L.H. Gray. New York, 1913.

Vikramacarita or *Siṃhāsanadvātriṃśaka.* Ed. & Trans. F. Edgerton. HOS 26-27. Cambridge (Mass.), 1926.

Viṣṇu Dharma Śāstra. Ed. J. Jolly. Bib. Ind. Calcutta, 1881.

——— Trans. J. Jolly, *The Institutes of Viṣṇu.* SBE 7. Oxford, 1880 : rep. Delhi, 1969.

Yājñavalkya Dharma Śāstra. Ed. & Trans. J. F. Stenzler. Berlin & London, 1849.

Yoga-sūtras of Patañjali. Ed., with the commentary of Vyāsa, & Trans. B. Baba. Delhi, 1976.

——— Trans. E.H. Woods. HOS 17. Cambridge (Mass.), 1914 : rep. Delhi, 1966.

Yogavāsiṣṭha (*-rāmāyaṇa*). Ed. V.B. Sastri Panasikara. 2 vols. Bombay, 1918.

——— Trans. D.N. Bose. 4 vols. Calcutta, 1962.

D. TAMIL TEXTS

Cucintirastalapurāṇam of Muttamilkkavirāyar. Ed. Ti.M.C. Pillai. Tirunelveli, 1894.

Irāmāvatāram of Kampan. Ed. Madras, 1953-55.

Kāñcipurāṇam of Civañānayoki. Ed. Kāñcipuram, 1933.

——— Summarised in R. Dessigane, P.Z. Pattabiramin & J. Filliozat, *Les Légendes Civaites de Kāñcipuram.* PIFI 27. Pondichery, 1964.

Kandapurāṇam of Kacciyappacivācāriyer. Ed. Madras, 1907.

——— Summarised in R. Dessigane & P.Z. Pattabiramin, *La Légende de Skanda selon le Kandapurāṇam tamoul et l'iconographie.* PIFI 31. Pondichery, 1967.

Kāveripurāṇam of Tiruccirrampalumunivar. Ed. P. Cuppaiyatecikar. Madras, 1871.

Paripāṭal. Ed. and Trans. F. Gros. PIFI 35. Pondichery, 1967.

Tirukkuṛṛālātalapurāṇam of Tirukūṭaräcappan Kavirācamurttikal. Ed. Maturai, 1910.

Tirumūrttimalaipurāṇam of Aruṇācala Kavuṇṭar. Ed. Pa. Venkaṭācala Mutaliyār. Madras, 1936.

Tiruppatistalapurāṇam of I. Munucāmināyuṭu. Ed. Cittur, 1928.

Tiruvaiyārrupurāṇam of Nānakūttar. Ed. Mu.Rā. Aruṇācalakkavirāyar and A. Muttuttāṇṭavaraya Pillai. Madras, 1930.

Tiruvilaiyāṭarpurāṇam of Parancontimunivar. Ed. Madras, 1965.

—— Summarised in R. Dessigane, P.Z. Pattabiramin and J. Filliozat, *La Legende des Jeux de Civa a Madurai.* PIFI 19. Pondichery, 1960.

Tulākkāverimānmiyam of Ma.Ti. Panukavi. Ed. Madras, 1917.

E. EXTRA-INDIAN TEXTS

Ābān Yasht. See Yashts.

Agastyaparva. Trans. (Dutch) J. Gonda. 'S-Gravenhage, no date: taken from *BTLVNI* 90. 92 and 94, 1933-36.

Bibliotheke of Apollodorus. Ed. and Trans. J.G. Frazer. LCL. 2 vols. London and New York, 1921.

Compendium of Solinus. In R.C. Majumdar, *Classical Accounts of India,* and in J.W. McCrindle, *Ancient India as Described by Megasthenes and Arrian.*

De Somniis of Philo. In *Works,* Ed. and Trans. F.H. Colson, G.H. Whitaker and R. Marcus. LCL. 12 vols. London and Cambridge (Mass.), 1929-62.

Din Yasht. See Yashts.

Enneads of Plotinus. Ed. P. Henry and H.R. Schwytzer. Paris, 1951- (in progress).

—— Ed. and Trans. (Erénch) E. Bréhier. 7 vols. Paris, 1924-38.

—— Trans. S. MacKenna and B.S. Page. 3rd ed. London, 1962.

Enoch. Ethiopic text ("*I Enoch*"). Trans. R.H. Charles, *The Book of Enoch.* 2nd ed. Oxford, 1912 : rep. London,

1921. Also in ibid., *The Apocrypha and Pseudepigrapha of the Old Testament.* 2 vols. Oxford, 1913.

Genesis. Ed. in *Biblia Hebraica,* ed. R. Kittel. 7th ed. Stuttgart, 1951.

——— Trans. in *The Jerusalem Bible,* ed. A. Jones. London, 1966.

Gilgamesh. Ed. and Trans. R. Campbell Thompson, *The Epic of Gilgamesh.* Oxford, 1930.

Iliad of Homer. Ed. and Trans A.T. Murray. LCL. 2 vols. London and New York, 1924-25.

India of Albīrūnī. Trans. E. Sachau. 2 vols. London, 1888 : rep. Delhi, 1964.

Indica of Arrian. Ed. and Trans. E.I. Robson. LCL. 2 vols. London and New York, 1929.

Khodad Yasht. See Yashts.

Metamorphoses of Ovid. Ed. and Trans. E.J. Miller. LCL. 2 vols. London and New York, 1916-29.

Naturalis Historia of Pliny. Ed. and Trans. H. Rackham *et.al.* LCL. 10 vols. London and Cambridge (Mass.), 1939-62.

Odyssey of Homer. Ed. and Trans. A.T. Murray. LCL. 2 vols. London and New York, 1919.

Poetica Astronomica of Hyginus. Ed. B. Bente. 1875.

——— Trans. M. Grant, *The Myths of Hyginus.* Kansas, 1960.

Revelation. Ed. British and Foreign Bible Society. London, 1937.

——— Trans. in *The Jerusalem Bible,* ed. A. Jones. London, 1966.

Sefer ha-Yetzirāh. Trans. (interp.) K. Stenring, *The Book of Formation.* London, 1923.

Sefer ha-Zohār of Moses ben Shemtob de Leon. Trans. (part) H. Sperling, M. Simon and P.P Levertoff. 5 vols. London, 1931-34.

Sirozah. Ed. K.F. Geldner, *Avesta : The Sacred Books of the Parsis,* vol. 2. Stuttgart, 1896.

——— Trans. J. Darmesteter. SBE 23. Oxford, 1833 : rep. Delhi, 1969.

Si-yu-ki of Hiuen Tsiang. Trans. S. Beal, *Buddhist Records of the Western World.* London 1884 : rep. Delhi 1969.

Tir Yasht. See Yashts.

Tobit. Ed. in *The Old Testament in Greek according to the Septuagint,* ed. H.B. Swete. 3 vols. Cambridge, 1887-1912.

——— Trans. in *The Jerusalem Bible*, ed. A. Jones. London, 1966

Vendidad. Ed. K. F. Geldner, *Avesta : The Sacred Books of the Parsis*, vol. 3. Stuttgart, 1896.

——— Trans. J. Darmesteter. SBE 4. Oxford, 1880 : rep. Delhi, 1969.

Yashts. Ed. K.F. Geldner, *Avesta : The Sacred Books of the Parsis*, vol. 2 Stuttgart, 1896.

——— Trans. J. Darmesteter. SBE 23. Oxford, 1883 : rep. Delhi, 1969.

2. SECONDARY SOURCES

Note : This part of the Bibliography, like the last, refers only to those works which have been cited during the course of the book.

Abbott, J. *The Keys of Power : A Study of Indian Ritual and Belief.* London, 1932.

Abegg, Emil. *Der Messiasglaube in Indien und Iran.* Berlin, 1925.

Abelson, Joshua. *Jewish Mysticism.* London, 1913.

Alexander, Hartley Burr. *North American Mythology.* MAR 10. Boston, 1916 : rep. 1964.

Ali, S.M. *The Geography of the Purāṇas.* Delhi, 1966.

Allen, R.H. *Star Names, their Lore and Meaning.* New York, 1899 : rep. 1963.

Bailey, Sir Harold W. 'Gāndhārī'. *BSOAS* 11, 1949, pp. 764-797.

——— 'Indo-Iranica III'. *BSOAS* 13, 1951, pp. 389-409.

Barbeau, Marius. 'Bear Mother'. *JAF* 49, 1946, pp. 1-12.

Basham, A.L. *The Wonder That Was India.* London, 1954 : rep. 1967.

Beal, Samuel. *Buddhist Records of the Western World.* 2 vols. London, 1884 : rep. Delhi, 1969.

Bedi, Sohinder Singh. *Folklore of the Punjab.* Delhi, 1971.

Benveniste, Emile. 'The Study of Indo-European Vocabulary'. Lecture delivered at the University of London, 1949.

Bhandarkar, Ramkrishna Gopal. *The Early History of the Deccan.* Poona, 1884 : 2nd. edition rep. as *Collected Works* vol. 3, 1927.

Bharati, Agehananda. *The Tantric Tradition.* London, 1965.

Bhargava, P.L. *India in the Vedic Age.* Lucknow, 1956 : rep. 1971.

Biardeau, Madeleine. 'La Decapitation de Reṇukā dans le Mythe de Paraśurāma'. In J.C. Heesterman, G.H. Scholeker & V.I. Subramaniam (ed.), *Fratidānam : Indian, Iranian & Indo-European Studies presented to Franciscer Bernados Jacobus Kuiper*, pp. 563-572. The Hague, 1968.

——— 'The Story of Arjuna Kārtavīrya without Reconstruction.' *Purāṇa* 12.2, 1970, pp. 286-303.

Billard, Roger. *L'Astronomie Indienne.* Paris, 1971.

Blair, Chauncey. *Heat in the Rig Veda and Atharva Veda.* AOSP 45. Cambridge (Mass.), 1961.

Bouché-Leclerq, A. *L'Astrologie Grecque.* Paris, 1899.

Bréhier, Emile. *Les Idées Philosophiques et Religieuses de Philon d'Alexandrie.* 2nd ed. rev. Paris. 1925.

——— *La Philosophie de Plotin.* Paris, 1952. Trans. J. Thomas, *The Philosophy of Plotinus.* Chicago, 1958.

Brough, John. *Early Brahmanical System of Gotra and Pravara.* Cambridge, 1953.

——— 'The Early History of the Gotras'. *JRAS*, 1946, pp. 32-45.

Brown, W. Norman. *The Story of Kālaka.* SIFGAos 1. Washington, 1933.

Bühler, Georg. *A Detailed Report of a Tour in search of Sanskrit Manuscripts. JBBRAS* extra number, 1887.

Chakraborti, Haripada. *Asceticism in Ancient India.* Calcutta, 1973.

Chakravarti, Chintaharan. *The Tantras : Studies in their Religion and Literature.* Calcutta, 1963.

Charpentier, Jarl. 'Bemerkungen über die Vrātyas'. *WZKM* 25, 1911, pp. 359-388.

Chatley, Herbert. 'Ancient Chinese Astronomy'. *AR* 34, 1938, pp. 140-146.

Choudhary, Radhakrishna. *The Vrātyas in Ancient India.* Banaras, 1964.

Church, Cornelia Dimmitt. 'The Myth of the Four Yugas in the Sanskrit Purāṇas—a Dimensional Study'. *Purāṇa* 16. 1, 1974, pp. 5-25.

——— 'The Purāṇic Myth of the Four Yugas'. *Purāṇa* 13.2, 1971, pp. 151-159.

Colebrooke, Henry Thomas. *Miscellaneous Essays.* 3 vols. London, 1873.

Coomaraswamy, Ananda K. *Spiritual Authority and Temporal Power in the Indian Theory of Government*. New Haven, 1942.

Cunningham, Sir Alexander. *A Book of Indian Eras*. Calcutta, 1883 : rep. Benares, 1970.

Dasgupta, Surendranath. *Hindu Mysticism*. Chicago & London, 1927 : rep. Delhi, 1976.

——— *A History of Indian Philosophy*. 5 vols. Cambridge, 1922-55 : rep. Delhi, 1975.

Day, Lal Behari. *Folk-Tales of Bengal*. London, 1888 : rep. 2nd ed. 1912.

Deussen, Paul. *The Philosophy of the Upanishads*. Edinburgh, 1905: rep. New York, 1966.

Dowson, John. *A Classical Dictionary of Hindu Mythology*. London, 1913 : rep. Delhi, 1973.

Dubois, Jean Antoine. *Hindu Manners, Customs and Ceremonies*. London, 1816 (French) : 3rd ed. trans. Henry K. Beauchamp, rep. Oxford, 1972.

Dumézil, Georges. *Flamen-Brahman*. Paris, 1935.

Dumont, Louis. *Homo Hierarchicus*. Paris, 1968 : rep. London, 1970.

Dyrenkova, N.P. 'Bear Worship among Turkish Tribes of Siberia'. In *Proceedings of the 23rd International Congress of Americanists* (1928), pp. 411-44 New York, 1930.

Eliade, Mircea. *Shamanism : Archaic Techniques of Ecstasy*. 2nd ed. Princeton, 1964 : rep. 1974.

——— *Yoga : Immortality and Freedom*. 2nd ed. Princeton, 1969 : rep. London, 1969.

Elmore, Wilber Theodore. *Dravidian Gods in Modern Hinduism : A Study of the Local and Village Deities of Southern India*. Lincoln (Nebraska), 1915.

Elwin, Verrier. *The Baiga*. London, 1939.

——— *Myths of Middle India*. Madras, 1949.

——— *Myths af the North-East Frontier of India*. Shillong, 1958.

——— *Tribal Myths of Orissa*. Calcutta, 1954.

Ewing, Arthur H. 'The Hindu Conception of the Functions of Breath'. *JAOS* 22, 1901, pp. 249-308.

Farquhar, John Nichol. *An Outline of the Religious Literature of India*. Oxford, 1920 : rep. Delhi 1967.

Filliozat, Jean. *La Doctrine Classique de la Mêdicine Indienne*. Paris, 1949.

Führer-Haimendorf, Christoph von. *The Raj Gonds of Adilabad : A Peasant Culture of the Deccan. I. Myth and Ritual.* (Vol. 3. of *The Aboriginal Tribes of Hyderabad*). London, 1948.

Gai, G.S., and Sankaranarayanan, S. 'A Note on the Date of Hisse-Borala Inscription of the time of the Vakataka Devasena'. *Ep. Ind.* 37, 1967, pp. 5-8.

Geden, A.S. 'Asceticism (Hindu)'. ERE 1, 1908, pp. 87-96.

Ginsburg, Christian D. *The Kabbalah : Its Doctrine, Development and Literature*. London, 1920.

Gokhale, Shobhana. 'The Hisse-Borala Inscription of Devasena, Śaka 380'. *Ep. Ind.* 37. 1967, pp. 1-4.

Goldman, Robert P. *Myth and Metamyth : The Bhārgava Cycle of the Mahābhārata*. New York, 1976.

Gombrich, Richard F. 'Ancient Indian Cosmology'. In Carmen Blacker and Michael Loewe (ed.), *Ancient Cosmologies*, pp. 110-142. London, 1975.

Gonda, Jan. *Notes on Brahman*. Utrecht, 1959.

——— 'The Old Javanese Agastyaparva'. *Purāṇa* 4.1, 1962, pp. 158-175.

——— *Die Religionen Indiens*. 1. *Veda. und Alterer Hinduismus*, 2. *Der Jüngerer Hinduismus*. Stuttgart, 1960-63.

Grant, Michael. *Myths of the Greeks and Romans*. New York, 1962.

Graves, Robert. *The Greek Myths*. 2 vols. Hormondsworth, 1955 : rep. 1971.

Hallowell, A. Irving. 'Bear Ceremonialism in the Northern Hemisphere'. *AA* n.s. 28, 1926, pp. 1-175.

Hastings, James (ed.). *Encyclopaedia of Religion and Ethics*. 13 vols. Edinburgh, 1908-26.

Hauer, Jakob Wilhelm. *Die Anfänge der Yogapraxis*. Stuttgart, 1922.

——— *Der Vrātya : Untersuchungen über die nichtbrahmanische Religion Altindiens*. Stuttgart, 1927.

Hayley, Audrey, 'Aspects of Hindu Asceticism'. In Ian Lewis (ed.), *Symbols and Sentiments*. Tavistock, 1976.

Hazra, Rajendra Chandra. *Studies in the Purāṇic Records on Hindu Rites and Customs.* Dacca, 1948.

——— *Studies in the Upapurāṇas.* 1 *Saura and Vaiṣṇava Upapurāṇas,* 2. *Śākta and Non-Sectarian Upapurāṇas.* CSCRS 11 & 22. Calcutta, 1958-63.

Heesterman, Jan C. 'Power and Authority in Indian Civilisation'. Paper presented at the University of London, 1973.

——— 'The Vrātya and the Sacrifice'. *IIJ* 6, 1963, pp. 1-37.

Heinemann, Isaac. *Philons griechistche und jüdische Bildung.* Breslau, 1932.

Hentze, Carl. 'Le Culte de l'ours et du tigre et le t'ao-t'ie'. *Zalmoxoris* 1, 1938 pp. 50-68.

Hillebrandt, Alfred. *Vedische Mythologie.* 2 vols. Breslau, 1891-92 : rep. 1927-29.

Holmberg (Harva), Uno. *Finno-Ugric and Siberian Mythology.* MAR 4. Boston, 1924 : rep. 1964.

Inge, William. *The Philosophy of Plotinus.* 2 vols. London, 1929.

Iyengar, P.T.S. *A History of the Tamils to* 600 *A.D.* Madras, 1929 :

Jacobi, Hermann. 'Das Kālakācārya-Kathānaka'. *ZDMG* 34, 1880, pp. 247-318.

Kane, P.V. *History of the Dharmaśāstra.* 9 vols. Poona, 1930-62.

Kaye, G.R. *Hindu Astronomy.* MASI 18. Calcutta, 1924.

Keith, Arthur Berriedale. *A History of Sanskrit Literature.* Oxford, 1920 : rep. Delhi, 1973.

——— *Indian Mythology.* MAR 6. Boston, 1917 : rep. 1964.

——— *The Religion and Philosophy of the Veda and Upanishads.* HOS 31-32. Cambridge (mass.), 1925 : rep. Delhi, 1970.

Kinnier Wilson, J.V. *Indo-Sumerian.* Oxford, 1974.

Kirfel, Willibald. *Die Kosmographie der Inder.* Bonn & Leipzig, 1920 : rep. Hildesheim, 1967.

——— *Das Purāṇa Pañcalakṣaṇa.* Bonn, 1927.

——— *Das Purāṇa vom Weltgebäude.* Bonn, 1954.

Knipe, David. *In the Image of Fire : Vedic Experiences of Heat.* Delhi, 1975.

Knorozov, Yuri V. *et.al. Proto-Indica.* 2 vols. Moscow, 1972.

Kolte, V.B. In Gokhale, *loc.cit.*, & in *Dr. Mirashi Felicitation Volume*, pp. 372ff.

Kugler, F.X. *Sternkunde und Sterndienst in Babel.* Munster, 1907.

Law, Bimal Charan. *Historical Geography of Ancient India.* Paris, 1964 : rep. Delhi, 1976.

Lehtisalo, T. 'Der Tod und die Wiedergerburt des Künftigen'. Schamanen, *JSFO*, 48.3, 1937, pp.1-34.

Lévi, Sylvain. 'Kaniṣka et Śātavāhana, deux figures symboliques de l'Inde auler siecle'. *JA* 228, 1936, pp. 61-121.

——— *La Doctrine du Sacrifice dans les Brāhmaṇas.* Paris, 1898 : rep. 1966.

Loeb, Edwin Meyer, 'Shaman and Seer'. *AA* n.s. 31.1, 1929, pp. 60-84.

Macdonell, Arthur Anthony. *Vedic Mythology.* Strassburg, 1879 : rep. Delhi, 1971.

Macdonell, A.A., and Keith, A.B. *A Vedic Index of Names and Subjects.* 2 vols. London, 1912 : rep. Delhi, 1967.

Mackay, Ernest J.H. *Further Excavations at Mohenjo Daro.* 2 vols. Delhi, 1938 : rep. 1976.

Majumdar, Ramesh Chandra. *Classical Accounts of India.* Calcutta 1960.

Majumdar, R.C., and Pusalker, A.D. (ed). *The History and Culture of the Indian People.* 9 vols. (esp. 1. *The Vedic Age*, 2. *The Age of Imperial Unity*, 3. *The Classical Age*, 4. *The Age of Imperial Kanauj*). Bombay, 1950-57 : rep. 1971.

Marshall, Sir John. *Mohenjo Daro and the Indus Civilisation.* 3 vols. London, 1931 : rep. Delhi, 1973.

McCrindle, J.W. *Ancient India as described by Megasthenes and Arrian.* London, 1877 : rep. Calcutta, 1960.

Mironov, N.D., and Shirokogoroff, Sergei M. 'Śramaṇa-Shaman : Etymology of the Word "Shaman", *JRAS-NCB* 55, 1924, pp. 105-130.

Mitchiner, John Edward. 'The Concept of Emanation in Purāṇic Creation Accounts'. *VBJP* 10.1, 1973, pp. 56-61.

——— 'The Evolution of the Manvantara Theory, as illustrated by the Saptarṣi Manvantara Traditions'. *Purāṇa* 20. 1, 1978, pp. 7-37.

——— 'Legends concerning Vikrama and the origin of the Vikrama Era'. In M. Mitchiner, *op. cit.* 9, 1976, pp. 806-807.

———'The Paris Manuscript of the Yuga Purāṇa'. *BIAVRI* 4, 1978, pp. 18-21.

——— 'The Purānic Lists of Andhra Kings'. In M. Mitchiner, *op. cit.* 9, 1976, pp. 857-859.

——— 'Rishi-hood and the Soma Cult : the interiorisation of Rishi-symbolism in Vedic literature'. In *Proceedings of the 29th All-India Oriental Conference* (1978). Poona, in press.

——— 'The Śaka Era of A.D. 78'. In M. Mitchiner, *op. cit.* 9, 1976, pp. 816-817.

——— 'The Saptarṣi Yuga : elucidation of a cyclical era'. *JAIH* 10, 1978, pp. 52-95.

——— *Studies in the Indus Valley Inscriptions.* Delhi, 1978.

——— 'The System of Dating in the Hisse-Borala Inscription of Devasena'. *JAS* 20, 1978, in press.

———'The Yuga Purāṇa'. In M. Mitchiner, *op. cit.* 9, 1976, Appendix 6, pp. 918-924.

——— *The Yuga-Purāṇa : critically edited, with an English translation and a detailed introduction.* Calcutta, in press.

Mitchiner, Michael. *Indo-Greek and Indo-Scythian Coinage.* 9 vols. London, 1975-76.

Moor, Edward. *The Hindu Pantheon.* London, 1810 : rep. Delhi, 1968.

Moore, Patrick. *An Atlas of the Universe.* London, 1970.

Muir, John. *Original Sanskrit Texts on the origin and history of the people of India, their religion and institutions.* 5 vols. 2nd ed. London, 1872 : rep. Delhi, 1972.

Mulholland, Jean. 'Soma : an attempt to classify the Drug and the Plant'. *JAS* 18, 1976, pp. 47-55.

Murty, K. Satchidananda. *Nagarjuna.* Delhi, 1971 : 2nd ed. 1978.

Narr, Karl J. 'Bärenzeremoniell und Schamanismus in der Alteren Steinzeit Europas'. *Saeculum* 10.3, 1959, pp. 233-272.

Nawab, S.M. *The Collection of Kālaka Story* (*sic*), 2 vols. Ahmedabad, 1949-58.

Neugebauer, Otto, 'Tamil Astronomy'. *Osiris* 10, 1952, pp. 252-276.

O' Flaherty, Wendy Doniger. *Asceticism and Eroticism in the Mythology of Śiva*. London, 1973 : rep. Delhi, 1976.

——— *Hindu Myths : a sourcebook translated from the Sanskrit*. Harmondsworth, 1975.

——— *The Origins of Evil in Hindu Mythology*. Berkeley, Los Angeles & London, 1976 : rep. Delhi, 1977.

Oldenberg, Hermann. 'Nakṣatra und Sieou'. *NKGWG*, 1909, pp. 544-572.

Oman, John Campbell. *The Mystics, Ascetics and Saints of India*. London, 1903.

Oppert, Gustav. *On the Original Inhabitants of Bharatvarsha or India*. London, 1893.

Pargiter, Frederick Eden. *Ancient Indian Historical Tradition*. London, 1922 : rep. Delhi, 1972.

——— *The Purāṇa Text of the Dynasties of the Kali Age*. Oxford, 1913 : rep. Banaras, 1962.

Parpola, Asko, *et.al*. *The Decipherment of the Proto-Dravidian Inscriptions of the Indus Civilisation*. Copenhagen, 1968. (Plus subsequent works)

Peek, W. *Constellations*. Edinburgh, 1934.

Pocock, David. 'The Anthropology of Time-Reckoning'. *CIS* 7, 1964, pp. 18-29.

Poerbatjaraka, R.M.Ng. *Agastya in den Archipel*. Leiden University thesis, 1926.

Rahmann, Rudolf. 'Shamanistic and Related Phenomena in Northern and Middle India'. *Anthropos* 54, 1959, pp. 681-760.

Rahurkar, V.G. *The Seers of the Rigveda*, Poona, 1964.

Rawson, Philip. *The Art of Tantra*. London, 1973.

——— *Tantra*. London, 1971.

Raychaudhuri, Hemchandra. *A Political History of Ancient India*. Calcutta, 1927 : 7th ed. rep. 1972.

Reiner, Erica. 'The Etiological Myth of the Seven Sages'. *Orientalia* 30, 1961, pp. 1-11.

Renou, Louis. 'Sur la Notion du *brahman*'. *JA* 237, 1949, pp. 7-46.

Renou, L., and Filliozat, J. *L'Inde Classique : Manuel des Études Indiennes*. 2 vols. Paris, 1947-53.

Roy, S.B. *Ancient India : a Chronological Study*. Delhi, 1975.

Ruben, Walter. 'Schamanismus in alten Indien'. *AO* 17, 1939, pp. 164-205.

Sastri, K.A. Nilakantha. 'Agastya,. *TITLVK Bataviaasch Genootschap* 76, 1936, pp. 471ff.

——— *A History of South India*. Bombay. 1955 : 4th ed. rep. 1976.

——— The Mauryas and the Satavahanas. London, 1957.

——— *Sources of Indian History, with special reference to South India*. London, 1964.

Saussure, Léopold de. 'Les Origines de l'Astronomie Chinoise'. *TP* (series 2) 10, 1909, pp. 121-182 & 255-305. Rep. as *Les Origines de l'Astronomie Chinoise*. Paris, 1930,

Scholem, Gershom G. *Major Trends in Jewish Mysticism*. New York, 1946.

——— *On the Kabbalah and its Symbolism*. London, 1965.

Schwytzer, H.R. 'Plotinus'. RCA 21, 1951, pp. 471-592.

Sethna, K.P. 'Megasthenes and Indian Chronology as based upon the Purāṇas'. *Purāṇa* 8-10, 1966-68.

Shastri, Suryakanta. *The Flood Legend in Sanskrit Literature*. Delhi, 1950.

Shulman, David Dean. *Tamil Temple Myths : Sacrifice and Divine Marriage in the South Indian Śaiva Tradition*. Princeton, 1980.

Sircar, Dinesh Chandra. *Ancient Mālwā and the Vikramāditya Tradition*. Delhi, 1969.

——— (ed.) *The Bharata War and Purāṇic Genealogies*. Calcutta, 1969.

——— *Select Inscriptions bearing on Indian History and Civilisation*, 1. Calcutta, 1942 : rep. 1969.

——— *Studies in the Geography of Ancient and Medieval India*. Delhi, 1960.

Thalbitzer, William. 'The Heathen Priests of East Greenland (Angakut)'. In *Verhandlungen des* 16 *Internationalen Amerikanisten-Kongresses* 2 (1908), pp. 447-464. Vienna & Leipzig, 1910.

——— 'Les Magiciens esquimaux, leurs Conception du Monde, de l'Âme et de la Vie, *JAS* n.s. 22, 1930, pp. 73-106.

Thieme, Paul. 'Agastya und Lopāmudrā.' *ZDMG* 113, 1963, pp. 69-79.

Tilak, Bal Gangadhar. *The Arctic Home in the Vedas.* Poona, 1903. rep. 1971.

——— Orion, or Researches into the Antiquity of the Vedas. Poona, 1893 : rep. 1972.

Tod, James. *Annals and Antiquities of Rajasthan.* 2 vols. London, 1829-32 : rev. ed rep. New Delhi, 1971.

Wasson, R. Gordon. *Soma: Divine Mushroom of Immortality.* New York, 1968.

Weber, Albrecht. *Die Handschriften und Verzeichnisse der Königlichen Bibliothek zu Berlin,* 1. Berlin, 1853.

——— (ed.) *Indische Studien.* 18 vols. Berlin & Leipzig, 1850-98.

——— *Die Nachrichten von den Nakṣatra.* AKAWB. Berlin, 1862.

Whitehead, Henry. *The Village Gods of South India.* 2nd ed. London & Calcutta, 1921.

Whitney, William Dwight. 'Jacobi and Tilak on the Age of the Veda'. *JAOS* 16, 1896, pp. lxxii-xciv.

Wilkins, W.J. *Hindu Mythology, Vedic and Purāṇic.* London, 1882 : rep. Delhi, 1973.

Winternitz, Moriz. *A History of Indian Literature.* 2 vols. Leipzig, 1908 : 2nd ed. rep. Calcutta, 1963.

Wolfson, Harry A. *Philo : Foundations of Religious Philosophy in Judaism, Christianity and Islam.* 2 vols. 3rd ed. rev. Cambridge (Mass.), 1962.

Woodroffe, Sir John George (alias Arthur Avalon). *Introduction to Tantra Shastra.* 2nd ed. Madras, 1926: rep. 1969.

——— *Shakti and Shakta.* 3rd ed. Madras, 1929 : rep. 1969.

Yazdani, G. *The Early History of the Deccan.* 2 vols. London, 1960.

Zaehner, Robert Charles. *The Dawn and Twilight of Zoroastrianism.* London. 1961.

——— *Our Savage God.* London, 1974.

Zimmer, Heinrich. *Myths and Symbols in Indian Art and Civilisation.* Princeton, 1946 : rep, 1972.

Zvelebil, Kamil V. *The Smile of Murugan.* Leiden, 1973.

INDEX

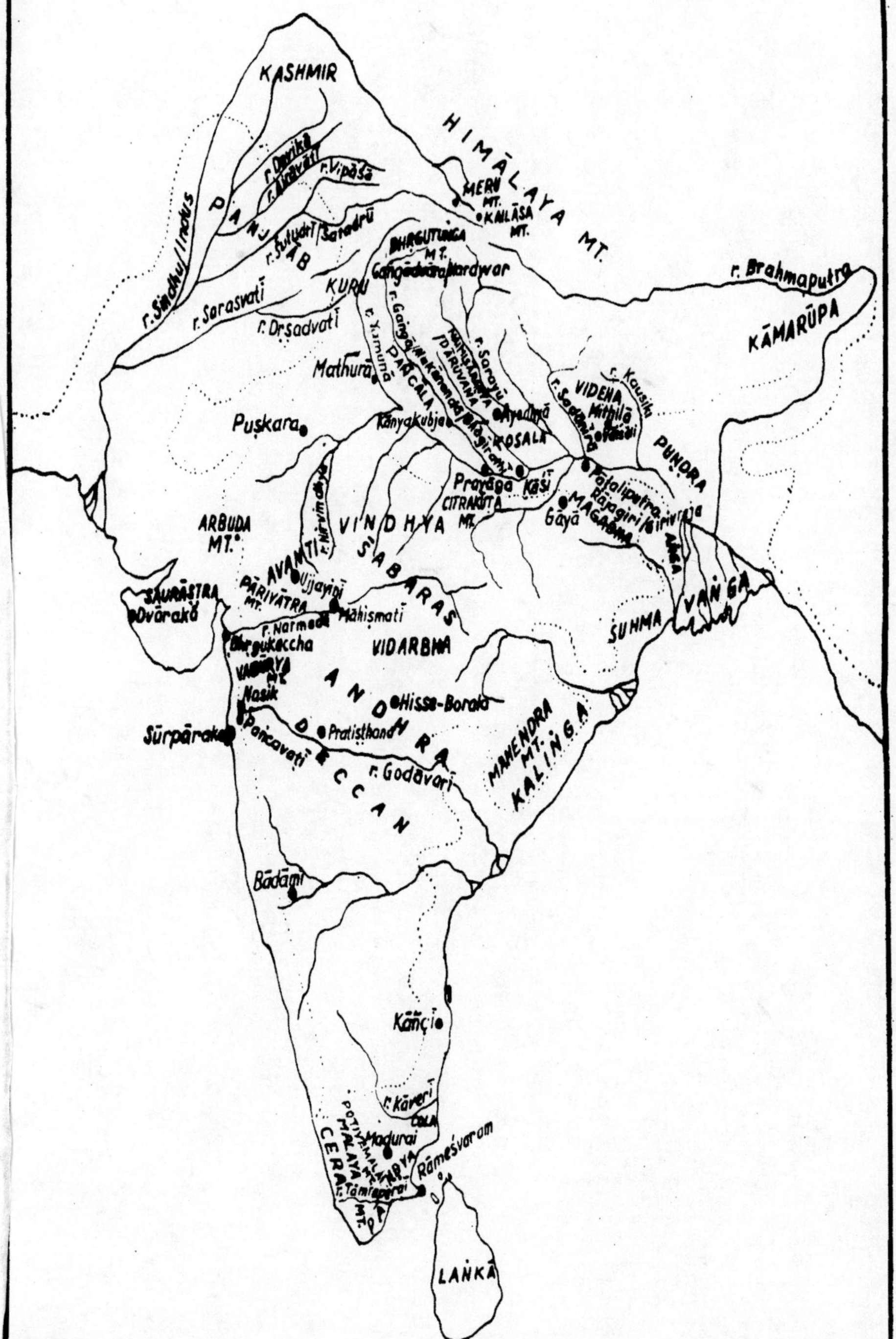

Map: Principal Localities associated with the Ṛṣis